WIN-WIN SURVIVAL HANDBOOK

All-Hazards Safety and

Future Space Colonization

WIN-WIN SURVIVAL HANDBOOK

All-Hazards Safety and Future Space Colonization

Marshall Masters

Your Own World Books

Nevada, USA

DomeCommunity.org
Yowbooks.com

COPYRIGHT

Win-Win Survival Handbook: All-Hazards Safety and Future Space Colonization

No part of this book may be reproduced or transmitted in any form or by any means, graphic, electronic, or mechanical, including photocopying, recording, taping, or by any information storage retrieval system, without the written permission of the publisher.

Copyright © 2021 by Knowledge Mountain Church of Perpetual Genesis, NV, USA All rights reserved.

Your Own World Books
An Imprint of Knowledge Mountain Church of Perpetual Genesis, NV, USA
Author: Marshall Masters

Trade Paperback
First Edition — January 2021
ISBN-13: 978-1-59772-172-1
www.domecommunity.org
www.yowbooks.com

Notice: Every effort has been made to make this book as complete and as accurate as possible, and no warranty or fitness is implied. All of the information provided in this book is provided on an "as is" basis. The authors and the publisher shall not be liable or responsible to any person or entity with respect to any loss or damages arising from the information contained herein.

Fair Use: This book contains copyrighted material and is made available for educational purposes, to advance the understanding of preparedness research and related survival issues, etc. This constitutes a "fair use" of any such copyrighted material as provided for in Title 17 U.S.C. section 107 of the US Copyright Law. In accordance with Title 17 U.S.C. Section 107, the material in this book is made available for non-profit research and educational purposes.

Trademarks: All terms mentioned in this book that are known to be trademarks or service marking have been capitalized. Knowledge Mountain Church of Perpetual Genesis cannot attest to the accuracy of this information and the use of any term in this book should not be regarded as affecting the validity of any trademark or service mark.

Book Images: Stock images from Dreamstime.com (various artists), photos and illustrations by Marshall Masters, Monolithic.org images with permission of David South and other fair use images.

About This Handbook

Everything we're taught about surviving the "end-of-life-as-we-know-it" is wrong, according to *Win-Win Survival Handbook* author, Marshall Masters, and here is why:

The conventional Plan A is about building to fail and playing the odds. When the odds do not pan out, Plan B is about huddling in a box in the ground, eating dead food, and wondering what comes next.

With a Win-Win, you build for continuity of life so that, while others are hitting walls, you're going over speed bumps. Your Plan B is the noble and life-affirming mission to prepare your progeny to colonize distant worlds.

This book guides you through the development process with detailed instructions for designing, building, and shielding communities for self-sufficiency, survival, and colonization.

For those interested in starting a Win-Win, Marshall's first advice is, build your community around veterans and first responders. Not only for their skills but, more importantly, for their love of God and comradery.

In a country blessed with Win-Wins, there will always be hope for the future, no matter what comes our way.

About the Author

Marshall Masters is a retired Silicon Valley systems engineer, and since 1999 he has authored several books on survival and space threats. In 2015, he attended an Ed Dames remote viewing class and viewed himself and others surviving a future catastrophe together.

Inspired to build what he viewed, he started crisscrossing the USA in search of suitable survival regions and solutions. Marshall intensively studied the 21st-century technologies necessary to shelter and feed communities and shares a comprehensive solution for the common man in this work.

Food is a crucial concern. Through divine guidance, Marshall developed an all-season, continuous harvesting aquaponics system for survival and colonization. Dubbed "EcoTech," it is a complete, grow-to-diet system that can survive human-made and natural disasters with little or no downtime.

A Win-Win is not about the end of this civilization, but rather, a clean slate for the beginning of the next with blue skies, sweet water, and happy pioneer families.

Presently, the two most likely funding sources for a Win-Win are philanthropists or cannabis and hemp entrepreneurs.

Philanthropists

Win-Wins are worthy "prime the pump" projects because they are at the forefront of humanity's need to colonize the stars. They also offer an ideal way to "prime the future" with nursery colonies organized to foster inter-galactic trading communities.

Farming and ranching are conventional concepts, but what is uncommon about a Win-Win is its organization. In the simplest terms, a Win-Win church is a lawful gathering of citizens to serve the will of God, whereas religion is an explanation.

The Constitution is clear: a church does not need to explain itself with a religion. For this reason, Win-Wins operate in the same manner as military chaplain corps, where faith is treated as a personal right of heritage and must be respected by all.

Making a difference is good, but making a good future in the process is even better. In a country blessed with Win-Wins, there will always be hope for the future; no matter what comes our way.

Cannabis and Hempcrete Entrepreneurs

Permitting and taxes are ever-pressing concerns for hemp and cannabis entrepreneurs and landowners alike. For these industries, a Win-Win survival community is also a constitutional church based on Judeo-Christian principals. Organized on a United States Chaplain Corps model, it farms and teaches farming.

Win-Win communities are the ideal way to showcase the many benefits of hemp. They will grow and process it for the same reasons that American colonists did but with an eye to space colonization.

On future new Earths, the need to produce clothing, paper, rope, fodder, medicinals, and other hemp products will be even more critical. This is why cultivating hemp is a necessary first step for a Win-Win, and it offers a sound financial route to community independence.

Table of Contents

Dedication

I dedicate this book to all Win-Win survival communities and especially to you good men and women of the future. While I can only speculate as to how the coming great migration of our species shall unfold, this much is certain; it will be magnificent. How do I know this?

During the day, I now bear witness to our species building the bold foundations of your future, and with every fiber of my being, I know that you are inevitable. Likewise, at night I dream of you departing on kilometer-long colony ships for distant new Earths as history repeats itself once again.

America was founded by immigrants, and most crossed the Atlantic Ocean in large steam ships. They traveled in steerage class, and although the accommodations were spartan, they were nonetheless comfortable and the food was good. For ship owners, steerage revenues covered the operating costs of their ships. Upper class passenger revenues went purely to profit.

In your future, new waves of intrepid souls with the price of steerage in their pockets and dreams of a new beginning in their souls will venture to the stars. Steerage then will be about broadcasting loved ones to the stars like intergalactic tumbleweeds.

However, this is not a Win-Win destiny, because these communities serve an entirely different role. For Win-Win communities it will be about extending their families into space, and they will do so with great care and love.

When mile-long colony ships launch for distant new Earths, once again, steerage will pay the way for their ship owners but the loved ones of Win-Win communities shall not be there. They will be in first class and in the cargo hold, their kit will contain the best money can buy, well-packed and ready to go.

Upon landfall, it is boots in the mud for everyone, steerage and first class alike, but with one big difference. Win-Win colonists will land knowing their loved ones are already sending them a steady stream of future cargo shipments to ensure their success.

To you intrepid souls of the future, all my hopes and love. May the wind always be at your backs and the sun upon your face.

Acknowledgments

This book represents a culmination of over five years of intensive research and authoring. This book and this project would not have been possible without the wonderful members of the Win-Win editorial team.

First, I wish to acknowledge the Mars Beta technical leadership:

- Duane Brayton, KMC Steward/Co-Author
- Joseph Lewis, KMC Vice-Steward/Lead Editor
- Michael Goldman MBA, Project Management
- Dee Captuo FAICP, Acquisition and Permitting
- Connie Mack Lill, Sheriff (Ret.) Security
- Judy Barnes M.A.Ed. Metadata Editor
- Brenda Norris, Team Coordinator

Whenever people compliment me on finding great people, I always answer. "I didn't find anyone. God sent them to me."

These divine encounters have brought wisdom, love, and passion to the creation of this book, and the value of their contributions are beyond measure.

Above all, my sincerest thanks to all of you who have supported my work through the years.

Introduction

The story of how this book came to be begins when I was sixteen years old. At the time, I was driving through a parking lot on a Sunday in Phoenix, Arizona. Hardly a soul was there and as I slowly drove over the speed bumps, I wondered out loud what would my life be like?

I got an answer and I heard it as clear as day. I heard from Spirit that I would have a difficult life with many twists and turns, and at that time of life, I would write a spiritual book. It turned out to be the quintessential spoiler because it played out exactly that way. I wondered about this for the better part of my life.

After 2013, my writing shifted toward more spiritual discussion; each time I authored a new book, I would wonder: Was this the book that God whispered to me? However, nothing clicked; so when I began writing this book, I chose not to think about it.

That changed halfway through the authoring of this book. I realized that Win-Win Survival Communities is the book that I believe God called me to write when I was sixteen. I want to tell the story of how this all evolved and to acknowledge some very special contributors along the way.

The Win-Win Vision

As a retired Silicon Valley systems analyst and technical writer, what they say is true. A lot of amazing ideas really do start out as simplistic sketches on cocktail napkins. In a manner of speaking, this is exactly how the Win-Win concept came into being.

In 2015 my friend, Gloria Tumlinson, told me about an Ed Dames remote viewing class being held in Reno, NV on April 18th and 19th and invited me to come. I told her I wanted to do it, but it was beyond my financial reach at the time. Gloria came back a few weeks later and said that she had found an anonymous donor to pay my class fee, and of course I accepted. To that donor: I remain deeply grateful for your kind patronage.

A quick explanation of remote viewing is that this is a psychic information gathering technique that was developed by the CIA and the KGB during the Cold War. US intelligence preferred remote viewers like Ed Dames over psychics while Russian clandestine services preferred the opposite.

Both methods use the right side of the brain. However, the edge that remote viewing has is safety. Remote viewing avoids the greatest concern of channeling, impostor entities. This is why learning how to talk to God is very easy. Learning how to protect yourself from impostors takes time; so those interested in this should start with remote viewing.

MAJOR ED DAMES PRESENTS
SURVIVING THE KILL SHOT

On Sunday, April 19, 2015, the second day of the class, I remote viewed a Win-Win survival community during the last exercise of the class. The way Ed Dames does it, you get a cryptic code number and the instruction to remote view it. It could be a photograph in Ed's briefcase or anything else he dreams up. You never knew; so you just did it. When it was done, Ed would tell you what it was that you were tasked to remote view.

What Ed tasked us to remote view in that last exercise was where we would be during a major cataclysm, one he refers to as the "Kill Shot." Ed was describing a solar sprite or cosmic lighting. A bolt of lightning literally bursts forth from the surface of the sun and strikes a planet or other large body.

According to Ed, after a large planet or object passes between the orbits of Earth and Venus, it will trigger a solar sprite that strikes Earth. In such a case, it will be bad for all of Earth, but this is especially true for those on the side of the planet that faces the sun when it hits.

What happens should a kill shot solar sprite strike the Earth? One possible example is the Valles Marineris which is on Mars. Much larger than the Grand Canyon, it is the largest canyon system in the solar system, and water erosion fails to explain the size and complexity of this system. Instead, a solar sprite does.

What I remote viewed was a structure within a structure that was underground on a hillside with a slope of approximately 30 percent. I saw myself inside a shelter structure with a spouse or significant other and there were many others around us. We could hear awful sounds like Earth trumpeting outside of the shelter and feel a slight tremble beneath our feet. Everyone knew that something terrible was happening outside, and they were all grateful for being there. The idea for Win-Win was born on that day and in that remote viewing class.

For those who follow Ed Dames, he created a video based on this training event, and it features a cameo of the two of us, where he began intently talking directly to me. I appreciate the cameo very much.

Dome Community Construction

In "Chapter 02 – Enabling Technology," I explain the unique way destiny intertwined my life with that of concrete dome inventor David B. South. In that chapter, I acknowledge his engineering contribution to humanity, but here I make a special acknowledgment.

Companies are often frugal in the amount of information they openly share of their technologies and methods and prefer a less-is-more approach. David had the vision and the wisdom to develop a vast online repository at www.monolithic.org.

Because this repository has grown over the years, it is deep but not well connected. However, it was all there. As a former Silicon Valley system analyst, I could reconstruct David's construction processes and methods, just as I used to do for my clients such as AT&T, Lockheed Martin, Hewlett Packard, Oracle and Sun Microsystems.

What David South did was out of a sense of caring and service. What I sought to do was to compile, document, and curate the technical processes of constructing dome homes. The procedures documented in this book are the next best thing to taking a $2,000 class.

When I finished writing the chapters regarding Dome Community Construction, my attention turned to the production of food.

EcoTech Farming and Ranching

The process of writing a technical book such as this is much like making a baby elephant. It requires lots of trumpeting and heavy thumping, but eventually, something big falls out. That pretty much sums up the first half of the book.

It was not until it came time to author the chapters in the EcoTech Farming and Ranching part of the book that things changed. I had nobody's shoulders to stand on as before. Now I have to talk about growing food.

Given that I'm a retired systems analyst who couldn't grow weeds if he tried, this was a daunting prospect. After months of research and contemplation, I was frustrated. I knew what I needed to do but couldn't find anyone doing it.

One pleasant afternoon, on a shady table next to a fast-moving creek, I was sitting across from an old friend. As we munched, I explained what was needed, an all-hazards way to produce fresh food in an extreme environment.

He made the interesting observation that NASA is going to use aquaponics on Mars to feed the astronauts. He could only see a difference of about fifteen to twenty percent between the technical concerns for growing food on Earth during a cataclysm compared with growing food on Mars.

What a fabulous epiphany that was. The direct result was that I finally had a launch point for the topic and this is described in "Chapter 14 – Feeding 1,000 Martians." My first response was yippee! My second response was a continuous replay of, "I'm a retired systems analyst who couldn't grow weeds if he tried."

At that point, I had only two choices. Write a skimpy chapter that will look like a magic hat with no magic in it, or bump this upstairs to the magic man himself, God.

It was time to channel the answer. It was time for God.

For me, I'm on a mission and turn to God for help much in the same way the junior member of a firm looks for insights and tips on how to deal with a problem. In terms of God's personality, two words sum it up: pleasant persistence. I always get what I need when I need it.

Because God sees the world about you through your physical senses, I will often create images or text about a problem I need to resolve. I'll have them up on my computer screen beforehand and use speech to text to record the dialog.

This time, there was no need for images or text. I had a simple question in mind when I reached out to God to begin the channeling session. We need a continuous supply of fresh food to survive a tribulation and go to the stars. What do I do?

I received two very short answers. The first was the three rules for selecting plant and animal species: authenticity, diversity and resilience. The second was that I would have to change the way people think. You're probably wondering how a retired Silicon Valley systems analyst, who couldn't grow weeds if he tried, could create a whole new way to feed people. And not just here on earth, but also in space and then on future worlds and with a whole new paradigm for growing food, called EcoTech.

Candle-to-Candle

God gave me the launch point. Species selection. It makes you feel like Noah, watching animals arrive two-by-two. Changing people's minds was a dark tunnel for me. I knew there was an opening on the other side, and that getting there meant a clueless journey in darkness to get there.

I knew that, and yet I was not concerned. What happened next was a fusion of skills I had learned as a systems analyst, as a remote viewer, and as a channeler as God lit the darkness for me with answers.

It was a step-by-step process, where I would come to a problem or a question in the dark and reach out for help. Then, further down the tunnel a candle would light, and I would walk to it. There on the wall in the feeble light was the answer, which I immediately used.

After that I would reach out with the next problem or question. As before, a candle would light; I would walk to it; and there would be the answer. Eventually, I came to the end of the tunnel and found myself in another time far away and in a home even farther.

All this did not work because I always found an answer in the candlelight. That was what happened.

Why it worked was that I always believed it would, and what you believe will be the test of it.

– Marshall Masters

Part I – Win-Win Strategic Planning

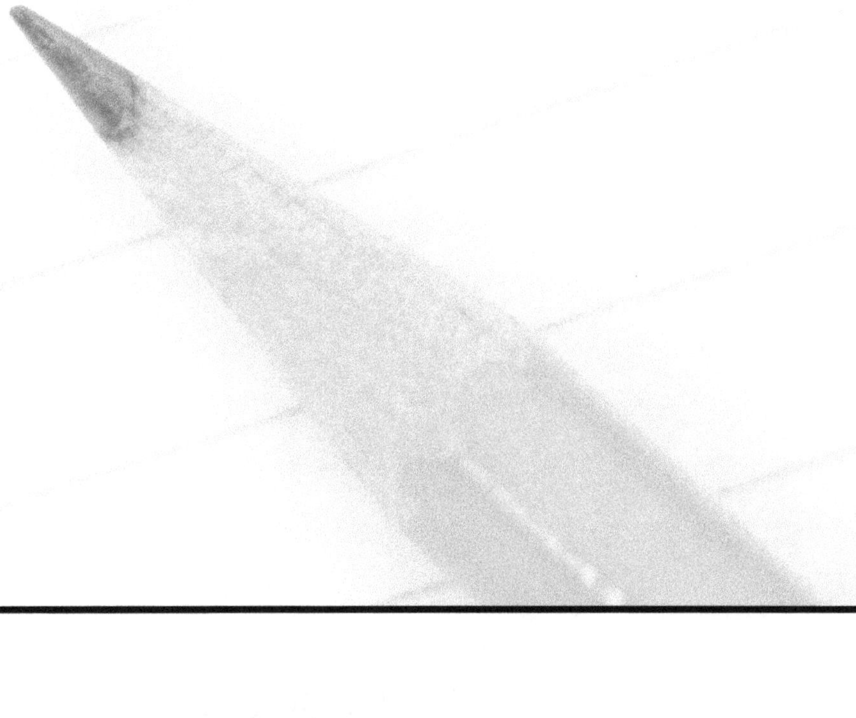

1

Surviving With Our Heritage

This is a business plan for the common man. The race is on to survive with communities for the difficult times ahead and to colonize space. It takes you step-by-step through the process from inception to escrow.

When you have finished reading this book, you will know how to found and build a permanent Win-Win survival community capable of feeding ten times its own numbers, here on this planet during the worst of times and on distant planets. This is about being in it for the species.

In 2017 renowned physicist Stephen Hawking (1942 – 2018) warned us that we must colonize space or perish. Do government and industry get it? Yes, and for reasons that are unique to the 21st century:

- The holy grail of astronomy is the search for Earth-like exoplanets in our galaxy.
- We now have a new branch of the military. The United States Space Force.
- The race is on to Mars.

It is obvious that the powerful ultra-wealthy elite are acting on their privileged intelligence, because it explains their "spare no expense" sense of urgency to seek their own survival options. But what about the non-elites? Where is their sense of urgency? Things are changing.

More each day are finding the courage to ask themselves the dreaded question of awareness:

What exactly am I looking at?

Awareness is typically triggered by concerns over the troubling man-made and natural disasters that push the headlines from grim to grimmer.

Everyone knows any attempt to answer that question will change their world. After that it will be a bumpy ride with a mixed cargo of awareness, mockery, ridicule, and denial. Yet, more are taking that ride and this begs the question, who becomes aware and how?

There are those who become aware through cognitive perception. They come to it through a rational process of observation and deduction.

The rest come into awareness via profound spiritual experiences. They are driven by prophetic dreams, visions and premonitions, often beginning in childhood.

In terms of the overall population, those in awareness of the profound planetary changes are a small, lonely minority. Since I began writing on the topics of space threats and earth changes in 1999, I've witnessed the isolation of awareness countless times. Here is what I see.

Imagine a vast dark cavern, lit by a symphony of candles. This is how I perceive all those in awareness, and the unfortunate truth is that the candles are so far apart, they can only see themselves. This is why I've always been driven to help the newly aware to know they are not alone, and they have magnificent brothers and sisters in awareness all across the globe.

For those who are adventurous and ready to go on this knowledge journey, let's get down to the business of surviving with our heritage.

Who Decides?

The unaware will be largely indifferent to how a few governments and ultra-wealthy elites decide who goes to space and how. Nor will they deeply consider the consequences of entrusting to human cultures the beliefs that have evolved worldwide for countless generations to their safekeeping. This is expedient, but what are the consequences?

Powerful ultra-wealthy elites could decide upon an all-in-one solution for population control, and humanity goes to space with beliefs that they control. No matter what walk of life or faith you are from, this is an existential issue of common concern.

What if elites choose only one faith belief system to go forth into space? The victor will write the history, and future generations will be carefully taught about why your heritage was rightfully abandoned on the launch pad.

The point here, is that we need to expand our definition of survival beyond the confines of physical survival on the surface of the planet. We need to think of ourselves as future space colonists, who must first survive a catastrophic event on Earth.

We must work together and overcome adversity to do this so that we may thrive and venture to the stars with the promise of a good life. This is why a Win-Win survival community is not just about surviving what comes. It is about overcoming limiting societal programming, becoming free, and staying free with your heritage and values intact. Otherwise, you're a slave.

Win-Win Survival Strategy

If powerful ultra-wealthy elites can force us to abandon our heritage for the sake of survival, what comes next is the yoke of slavery and for countless generations to come. This is why we must take this challenge head-on with a whole new strategy. Why?

It is not just about survival alone.

People never stop to think about what they'll do after things settle down, and they finally come out of their bunkers back to the surface. They never stop to fully consider what life will be like for them. They will surface as strangers in a strange land and to what?

Will they band together like people do after natural disasters? Or, will their world already be devolved into hunters and the hunted?

Most likely, it will be a bit of both and that is the point of this book: to prepare for cooperation, not confrontation, with a "safety through numbers" approach to survival for a strong defense.

So what is this really about?

A Win-Win survival community (Win-Win) is a self-sufficient survival community church. Its mission is to manage resources, raise children, and to be a shining light of hope for all. Initially, its membership will be relatively small, but the eventual goal is to establish a 400+ acre ranch property capable of sustaining 100 to 150 members.

Organizationally, a survival church is different from traditional faiths.

It is a church. Not a religion.

A church is a gathering of people to serve the will of God, that being that humanity survives, thrives, and evolves closer to God. Religion is an explanation, and by law, a church is not required to have one.

In a survival church, religion is a matter of one's personal heritage. Hence, a survival church operates like the Chaplain Corps of the US Military. There is no official religion for the organization; rather, the religion of the individual is honored as a sacred right of heritage.

Another difference is that traditional faiths are affective and express emotion and love through fellowship.

A survival church is effective because it is about producing the following six life-quality benefits:

- **All-hazards Construction:** Habitats, designed within limits, to protect us from the worst nature and man can throw at us.
- **Continuity:** Food production and life continue in an orderly manner without disruption during and after extreme events
- **Quality of Life:** A spiritual lifestyle choice that respects the inalienable right of personal and family heritage.
- **Service to Others:** For economic viability, you grow ten times as much food as needed to feed the community. Following a cataclysm, food production shifts to feeding survivors through local non-profit food banks.
- **Good Neighbors:** Foster mutual protection through a good neighbor program and local alliances.
- **Robust Communications:** Use of effective two-way radio communications to share knowledge with other survivors and communities near and far.

Here is the good news. Everything needed to achieve this is available now, off-the-shelf, and with a wide range of best of class offerings. With that in mind, let's take a quick look ahead.

A Look Ahead

Survival is about learning what works and what hurts; with the goal that you learn enough about what works before what hurts harms you.

For this reason, the Win-Win strategy is merit-based. You always look for best business practices, sound science and technology with open standards and open source models, and best of class products.

This book uses a building block approach to guide community founders and leaders along each step in their management decision path. They are organized into the following four parts:

1. Win-Win Strategic Planning
2. Dome Community Construction
3. EcoTech Food Production
4. Human Resources and Alliances

This business plan is for every man. It walks you through the process of founding a survival church from initial concept to escrow closing. When you have finished reading it, you will know how to organize and launch your own Win-Win survival church.

Part I – Win-Win Strategic Planning

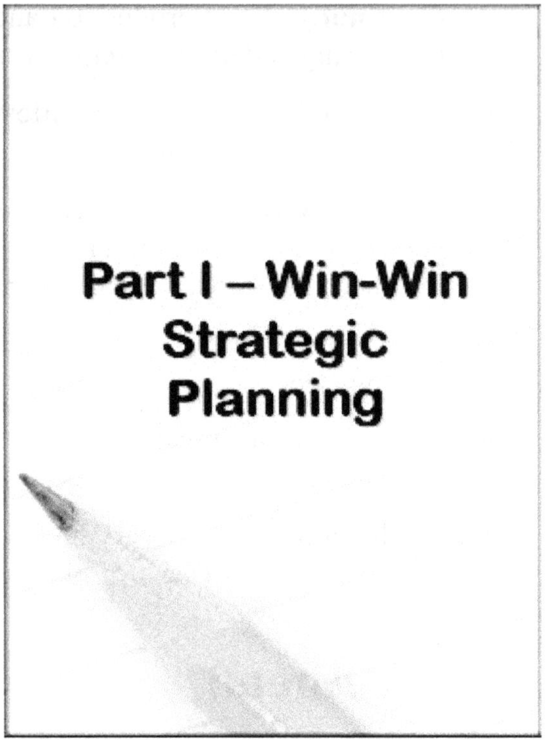
Part I – Win-Win
Strategic
Planning

A Win-Win survival community church sparks into life the moment a dreamer says, “I’m doing this.” What comes next are fundamental choices about how to organize with others.

Chapters

- Enabling Technology
- Forming Your Survival Church
- Community Bylaws
- Building Membership
- Plan B Basic Concepts

The survival church model in this book is a basic version. Use it as a reference to create a church of like-minded members with one simple message: Intolerance is not tolerated. Other than that, be bold, be beautiful, be you, and find common ground. For example, this book is published by the Knowledge Mountain Church of Perpetual Genesis.

We are a constitutional Win-Win survival church. Our mission is to serve the will of God by forming small communities to survive extreme disasters and to colonize space for the survival of our species. When this church goes to the stars, the US Constitution goes with it.

On the other hand, let’s say a tribe wants to start a Native American survival church; they could base it on the sacred right of the vision quest. The point is, there are no restrictions.

Part II – Dome Community Construction

In terms of all-hazards safety, the strongest structure is a concrete dome. As for radiation shielding, exotic materials are unnecessary. Simple works best.

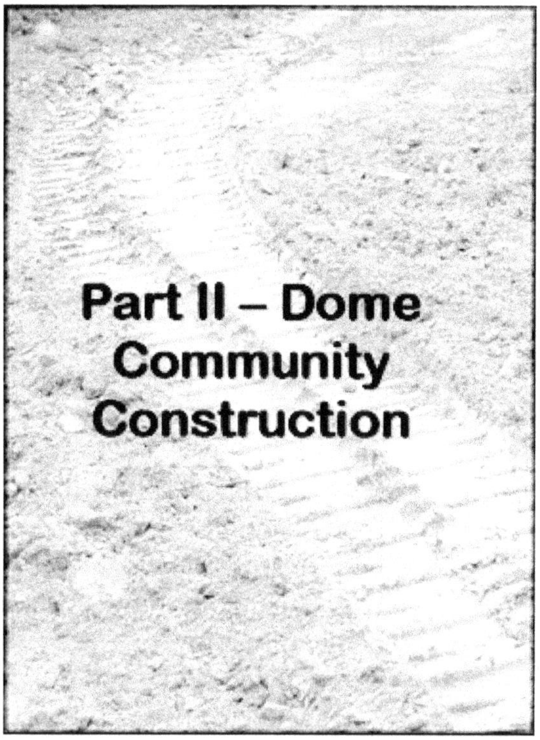
Part II – Dome
Community
Construction

Chapters

- Radiation Shielding Strategy
- Dome Design
- Dome Materials
- Design Team and Infrastructure
- EcoShells I & II
- DBS Domes and Overcover
- Overcover

These chapters provide information for the process of land development for infrastructure and survival structures.

Step-by-step process explanations that are easy enough for novices to follow are also written to professionals, including the details they need to successfully execute the process.

Part III – EcoTech Food Production

EcoTech is a term invented by the author to describe an all-natural ecology hosted within a technosphere, and this part of the book uses the science fiction film, *The Martian* (2015) to introduce the Win-Win strategy for feeding survivors and future colonists.

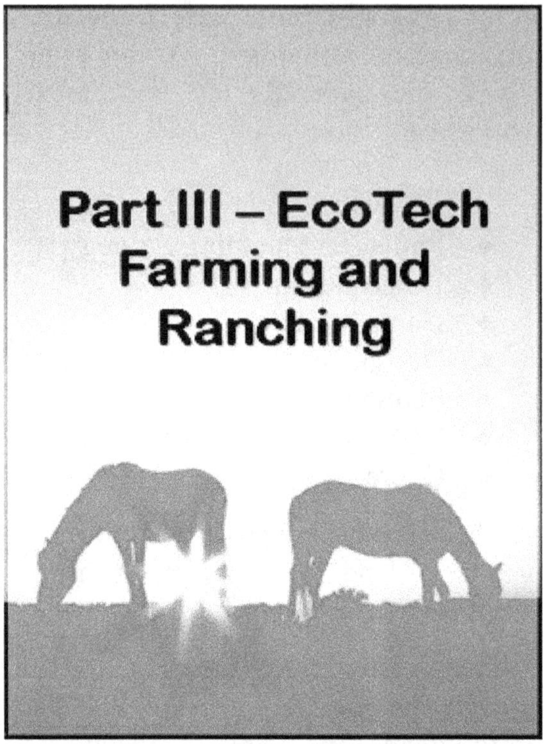
Part III – EcoTech
Farming and
Ranching

It begins with an ambitious goal: to colonize mars and grow enough fresh food for 1,000 people each day.

Chapters

- Feeding 1,000 Martians
- EcoTech Farming and Ranching
- EcoTech Planning
- EcoTech Engineering
- EcoTech Aquaponics
- EcoTech Cropping
- EcoTech Supersystem
- Inner Sanctum

Commercial farming is about growing to market. For survival on Earth and space colonization, Win-Win survival churches will need to grow complete diets. The two diets we will discuss are for survival on Earth and in space. The primary food production method is below-ground all-hazards aquaponics.

NASA plans to use aquaponics on Mars to feed explorers, and so will Win-Win churches, and their dishes will taste like Mom cooked them.

Part IV – Human Resources and Alliances

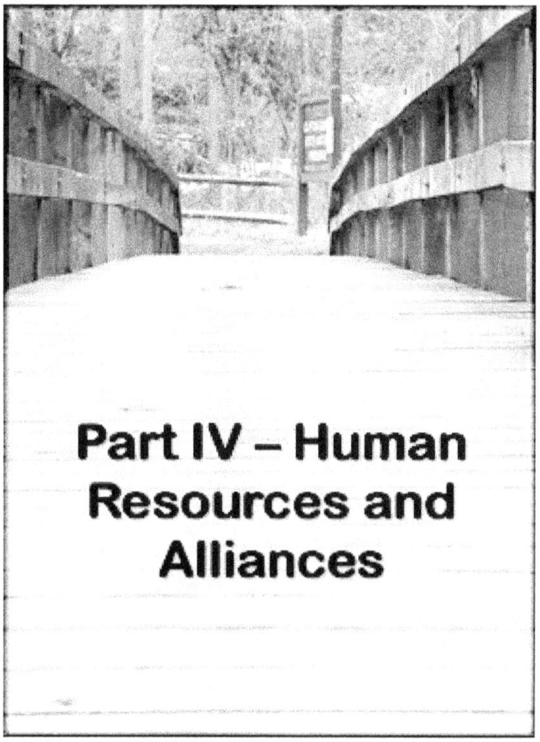
Part IV – Human
Resources and
Alliances

If you are going to survive hard times, you'll need to build a comradery of survival within your membership, and veterans are your edge. They and your first-responders will lead by example because their mission will be to turn civilians into colonists.

Chapters

- Life Umami
- Food Club and Folk School
- Strategic Alliances
- Spread the Word

At least one-third of the community should be a home guard, comprised of veterans and first-responders with practical skills. The other two-thirds are civilians who are carefully recruited and provide wide ranging sets of skills to cover health, homesteading, building and electrical trades, etc. for community self-reliance.

Your home guard will be your noble guardians and they will play an essential role in helping your community to develop survival comradery within the membership. They will also help to establish alliances with local sheriffs and other mutual-defense partners.

In the final chapter, "Spread the Word," the focus is on communications and how your home guard will play a vital role in protecting your communities with a robust signals intelligence system and how teaching members to use it they build comradery.

Win-Win Funding

A Win-Win survival community represents a multi-million dollar convergence of social values, sustainable technology, and compassionate capitalism in search of a common pathway to success.

Creating that pathway begins with a bold vision. A huge vision, such as the one that first launched the race to put a man on the moon.

"We choose to go to the Moon! We choose to go to the Moon in this decade and do the other things, not because they are easy, but because they are hard."

September 12, 1962
John F. Kennedy Moon Speech
Rice Stadium in Houston, Texas

> "We choose to go to the moon in this decade and do the other things, not because they are easy, but because they are hard, because that goal will serve to organize and measure the best of our energies and skills, because that challenge is one that we are willing to accept, one we are unwilling to postpone, and one which we intend to win, and the others, too"

That's the plan, folks. It worked then and it works now. That means our task is simple. To plan the work and work the plan and the first step is to choose a funding model.

Funding Models

The two Win-Win survival community funding strategies featured in this book are incremental self-funding and turnkey funding.

- **Incremental Self-funding:** This bootstrap strategy is ideal for dreamers seeking to found a church with a series of small-capitalization investments from founders and other sources. These investments are used to acquire the initial hobby farm and to create a retreat for membership development with approximately 7+ acres of land. Then membership fees from recruiting will be used to purchase a self-sustaining church ranch with 400+ acres. The subsequent build-out will then occur in several stages with available funding sources and overlaying sources of revenue from operations.

- **Turnkey Funding:** A complete church is fully financed with multiple retreats for membership development, a full-scale permanent farm, and a permanent ranch. With turnkey funding, membership development, facility acquisition, and construction will launch simultaneously on parallel tracks. The goal is, that once the facilities are ready for use, a complete, mission-ready membership will take residence and begin operations.

It is a given that Win-Win communities must generate revenue to meet obligations and to grow the church. For this reason, the Win-Win business plan also includes leasing all or part of an aquaponics facility to commercial clients. In states that permit cannabis grows, it is the number one cash crop.

Premium Cannabis Ready (PCR)

Win-Win survival community food production is based on below-ground, all-hazards aquaponics. Above-ground ranching and farming operations are made as survivable as possible.

The technology model for below-ground aquaponics is premium cannabis production. This all-organic medicinal-grade product is intended for cancer patients who have become averse to chemicals. It sells for more per pound than truffles and is difficult to grow because of its potency and purity. As that stuff smoked back in college, ignorance is bliss.

With premium cannabis ready (PCR) facilities, you can grow with a precise microclimate control system. Grow whatever you wish, because you can recreate any commercial growing environment in the world. And the crops, that you grow, treat them all like valued guests and it will be just another day in paradise.

Whether you grow cannabis or not, building to the PCR standard will give you real revenue power thanks to its all-hazards continuous harvesting capability. Come hell or high water, your Win-Win survival ranch produces delicious, fresh food each day.

Funding Alliances

Funding a Win-Win is about being in it for the species. With this endeavor, there are two funding alliance groups: Angels and Pioneers.

- **Angels:** Whether you are addressed as a lender, funder, grantor, benefactor, or donor, your financial support will make a galactic difference, by helping enable a multi-generational effort to secure the survival of our species. This makes you an angel.
- **Pioneers**: When it comes to off-world colonization, everyone will talk the talk, but it takes a true pioneering spirit to walk the walk. This not only means the pursuit of unknown territory it also includes opening new areas of thought, research, and development as well.

Win-Win is an idea whose time has come for angels and pioneer leaders alike, and there are different considerations for both. What drives the process will be the use of money. In terms of Win-Win survival communities, money is used for one of three reasons:

- **Money to Make Money:** We know it as conventional financing and venture capital. It is about return on investment (R.O.I.), and you'll need to show lenders how they'll get their money back and how soon. While these are not ideal funding sources for launching a pioneering movement, once it has been established, these sources will become far more useful.
- **Money to Make a Difference:** Win-Win survival communities are inevitable, so the question is not if, but when. The problem with later instead of sooner is the wasted time, lives, and money reinventing the same wheels. However, with philanthropic support, an opportunity exists to create a system of open standards and open sources for all survival communities, so that humanity can do it right the first time and for a lot less.
- **Money to Do Both:** In recent years, we've seen an upwelling of what some could call a compassionate capitalism. This is where the common man has equal access to direct and new Internet funding venues such as crowdfunding, cryptocurrency and commu-

nity-based tokens. In the near term, here is where Win-Win survival communities will find the greatest number of funding opportunities and methods.

The Win-Win concept is based on several enabling technologies. The two that directly make this possible today are off-grid power technologies and Internet funding.

All of this needs to be funded; so we must ask an obvious question. How will pioneers and angels work together?

This author will use a unique combination of experience and skills that were gained during the years that led up to December 21, 2012 and the Mayan Calendar prophecy.

Due Diligence

In the lead up to December 21, 2012, television networks played on public concerns with a lie. The premise that life as we knew it would end on December 21, 2012. After the subsequent non-event, the public chalked it up to a cruel hoax.

It was a hoax because all true prophecy comes in two parts. The harbinger and the event. The harbinger is non-threatening. It is an observable sign that you are on the timeline of a prophetic event and an indication to take action.

Beginning January 1, 2013, the harbinger signs for the Mayan Calendar prophecy began to materialize. Since then there has been a steady yearly uptick in the number of earthquakes of all magnitudes and observed fireballs. Virtually every consecutive year has set a new record, and there are other concerns.

Throughout the lead-up to 2012, I was active with media appearances. In 2007 I began receiving inquiries for survival location consulting. The requests came from wealthy people who were building bunkers. Most cost between one to two million dollars.

What was the difference between a one million dollar bunker and a two million dollar bunker? Not much, because a two million dollar bunker had its construction crews flown in from hundreds of miles away. They were then driven to the site at night in a blacked-out van, and they remained onsite until the job was finished and then returned home the same way they had come.

I served this clientele and they would reach out to me shortly after going into escrow on a property. As part of their due diligence, I was typically given a road junction or map coordinate within 20 to 30 miles of the bunker site.

These consulting revenues helped to fund my work, but I also did it because I really liked these people. They were impressive and wonderful to work with. What I respected most about them was that they did their homework and knew the right questions to ask.

Here is how it typically worked.

I would interview them and use Internet tools to evaluate and grade their bunker site locations. I used a survivability scale of zero to 10, where zero equals you die badly. Any site that is 7.0 or higher is survivable, and ten is as good as it gets. There are no tens in America.

After a detailed interview, I would give them my assessment, and here was the amazing part. It was always somewhere between an 8.5 and a 9.5. They always appreciated that, but what they really wanted to hear was, "You nailed it. Go close escrow."

The only thing I ever regretted was I never had a business plan to offer them, such as a Win-Win survival community. It was an opportunity lost, but then again, it is only in recent years that breakthrough advances in off-grid power and other technologies have made this possible. So, let's cut to the chase.

On a rational level, we know the Earth is changing. A reliable solution for producing large quantities of fresh food in adverse conditions is going to be the next big thing. Those who can perform reliably in such times will be supported in many ways.

Yes, now is the time for Win-Win survival communities, and whether you are an angel or a pioneer, you have a plan in hand; the purpose of which is to be of service.

Now let's set that thought aside for a moment, as we explore another vital aspect on a personal level, because a time of magic lays before us all.

Time of Magic

May 5, 1961 was the most amazing day in the universe for 2nd graders such as myself. It was the day that Astronaut Alan Shepard took the first sub-orbital flight in Freedom 7.

We watched all this on grainy B&W televisions. I remembered thinking that this rocket looked like NASA had stacked a bunch of water heaters, one-atop-the other, and then topped it off with a capsule which was everyone's point of interest.

Walter Cronkite was the rock star of space exploration for me. His stately on-camera persona was what made a time of magic possible for me. During those long, interminable launch holds, he filled the air with magic.

Cronkite would hold in one hand a Revel plastic model of the Freedom 7 capsule and in the other, a small beach ball. This was when he recited the magic incantation of space travel as he hefted the capsule and ball before him. "Of course, these objects are not to scale."

For 2nd graders, those were heady days, and that was the launch code for imagination. You were no longer looking at a B&W low-resolution stack of water heaters sitting on a rather unimposing launch pad. You were there, in the theater of the mind, and it was IMAX real.

Survival and colonization are necessary; so a powerful convergence of human and technology capital is underway, and what is coming will be a time of magic.

Dear Reader, wouldn't your inner self love to experience something magic like this? And even if it is to happen on another's watch, when you hold an unsigned check in your hands, imagine that next generation of 2nd graders. A little magic is a good thing.

But there are things that are not so magical. Sacrifices, both in terms of sweat equity and treasure, and for this angels and pioneers need a common rally point.

Rally Point

In a military sense, a rallying point is a designated fall back location, where soldiers can re-assemble and reorganize as necessary. But another rally point is for when things go wrong, everyone goes to Grandma's house.

A "me-and-mine" self-serving strategy, of surviving for the sake of survival, can only offer an expedient and uncertain journey to a dark and unforeseen future.

In contrast to that, a service to others strategy is less about holding onto things and more about holding on to each other. How can angels and pioneers do that? With a rally point.

The rally point for angels and pioneers is found in the title of this chapter. "Surviving With Our Heritage." A Win-Win community is about being in it for the species.

Why? Because if we let our heritage die, the truth of our lives dies with it.

Dylan Thomas said it best. "Do not go gentle into that good night."

Calling all Angels

We all have different motivations for what we do, but in the end, it is the desired outcome that matters. This is why those with the wherewithal and willingness to support this grand journey are an invaluable resource for humanity. I can only hope that each of you understands fully how precious you are to the future of our species.

With this in mind, I will now speak directly to my survival location clientele, with whom I consulted during the lead-up to 2012. I'm going to give you an insight for evaluating Win-Win survival community proposals.

Bankable Pioneers

The book is a very powerful tool. It unveils a business that is designed to help people to organize and build survival churches.

Angels, let's assume that this plan becomes widely used, and you start seeing more email traffic about it in your inbox each day. What you're looking for are pioneers you can trust to go the distance.

Folks with the right stuff, who will demonstrate something I call the three C's: Character, Commitment, and Courage. In terms of character and courage, you Angels have the metrics for that well-covered, so let's focus on commitment.

Before you unseal the proposal, the first thing you want to know is whether you are talking to a pioneer or a consumer. This is critical, because:

- Pioneers reach for the stars.
- Consumers reach for low hanging fruit.

When it comes to wanting to live and colonize, who doesn't? The question is what are they prepared to do?

How will you know you are dealing with pioneers? The first step is to stick a post-it note to the bezel of your computer's screen with the following:

Survival is not a place, person, thing, or time. Survival is a state of mind.

The reason why consumers are a bad risk is that they see the topic of survival in terms of places, people, things, and times.

How does this translate? They'll bring you a deal with their fingers crossed behind their backs. Their reasoning is if things become inconvenient, they can always bail. They avoid things that are difficult or uninteresting and use their time to pursue more entertaining aspects, such as social media click-bait videos. For example, if they are already interested in guns, then guns will become their primary survival tool.

Either way, consumers lack the pioneering discipline and they tend to favor what entertains them, as opposed to what is necessary.

Survival is a state of mind with pioneers. This is the preferable mindset, one of commitment and knowledge gathering. They have the discipline to do the things that are difficult and uninteresting. There is a simple test for evaluating the strength of their commitment.

Walk-the-Walk

The leaders of a Win-Win survival community will be the principals in the deal, and those most responsible for a successful return. You'll know them by their primary tool, and you will have a quick way to winnow the wheat from the chaff.

Everyone wants to live, and everyone talks-the-talk.

Pioneers walk-the-walk, which is why you need to see signs of pioneer commitment.

The fastest way is to begin with their principal tool. For example, stethoscopes are about doctors, saddles are about ranchers, and hammers are about carpenters.

Two-way radios are the primary tool for Win-Win survival community leaders. A robust system for command, control, and signals intelligence are necessary, and I can use our own current church as a reference here.

As a constitutional Win-Win survival church, the designated primary tool for each leader is an FCC General Class HAM license. Each steward in our church holds a current general license and has a call sign, because as leaders, we must set the bar for commitment.

This may sound harsh, but remember what President John F. Kennedy said. "We choose to go to the moon in this decade and do the other things, not because they are easy, but because they are hard."

The people you want for funding must embody that!

Accept no substitutes and you'll do just fine.

2

Enabling Technology

A Win-Win survival community must be engineered to provide all-hazards protection for earthquakes, tornadoes, fires, volcanic debris and ash, meteorite showers, solar storms, and more. Some threats can be countered, and for others the effects can be mitigated.

One needs to keep in mind the difference between prepping and all-hazards strategies.

Prepping strategies are principally based on untested Cold War doctrines about how to survive a civilization-ending event with temporary sheltering and stockpiles.

The assumption is that after you survive the event, you'll be smart enough to sort things out on your own. This is convenient and expedient thinking without a plan for what happens afterward.

Conversely, with all-hazards strategies, the goal is to create a permanent, highly-survivable lifestyle. When a major event happens, the community can survive the event with minimum damage and afterward have the ability to restore normal operations quickly. Having effective two-way communications with other Win-Win survival communities is also included in this.

Therefore, an all-hazards strategy does not, like prepping, focus on the end of this civilization. Instead, it is about creating a clean slate for the beginning of the next.

For this reason, there are only two kinds of technologies to be considered. Those which are useful and those which are not. Obviously, if a technology is not useful, pass it by. Your attention should be focused on what does work.

When finding useful technology, you need to look for best-of-class solutions, no matter how old they are. A Win-Win survival community will combine today's leading-edge technologies with those that are tried and proven, even if they are thousands of years old, to create optimal solutions.

This being said; the most important useful technology one can use is called an "enabling technology."

Enabling Technologies

Enabling technologies are profound because they will foster a diverse range of derivative technologies. For example the microprocessors that were developed to land astronauts on the moon were an enabling technology that produced a radical change in our technology and culture.

I knew from the beginning that for a Win-Win survival community to build the most robust possible above-ground structures, I needed to find was an enabling technology that offered a systematic approach to building large concrete structures that are 100x stronger than a conventional wood-frame home and yet cost much less to make.

Furthermore, this enabling technology would propagate widely. Therefore, it must be something church members can do on their own, learn within days, and master after building a few of these structures. In other words, enabling technologies must propagate virally to be successful.

The key enabling technology Win-Win communities needed to propagate virally would be concrete domes which are as tough as hell. Why? Because when Mother Nature rages, it does not behave like a Pollyannaish PowerPoint presentation; instead, it's brutal and deadly.

This much is certain and I learned this first-hand most poignantly on Tuesday, October 17, 1989 at 5:04 PM local time.

Like Waves on the Ocean

When the 1989 San Francisco Loma Prieta earthquake happened, I was nearly five miles south of the stadium and the World Series. I worked in a business park that had been built on a landfill, and we had experienced numerous small earthquakes during the previous two weeks. I remember people saying that these smaller events often heralded a much larger near-future earthquake event.

On Tuesday at 5:03 PM local time, I was sitting in my car in my client's parking lot in South San Francisco, CA. The lot was empty except for my car. The office staffers had left earlier that afternoon because they were on flex commute schedules.

The parking lot was surrounded on three sides by commercial buildings. It was approximately 22 yards wide and 45 yards deep with marked spaces on both sides. The asphalt had been refinished earlier that year, and the white stripes were still somewhat bold.

I had just started my car's engine when, at 5:04 PM local time, I felt the ground tremble and roar as though I were a few feet away from a speeding freight train.

Coming on the heels of that were the horizontal earthquake waves and they were violent. They hit broadside, causing my car to rock side-to-side. The rocking motion was so severe that I feared my car would roll over; so I turned off the ignition.

There I was buckled in with the ignition off. What more could I do?

I looked over at two small trees next to an entrance at the back of the parking lot. They were swaying back and forth like windshield wipers and in perfect unison like something out of a Walt Disney movie. However, what really caught my attention was the asphalt in the lot.

I saw a series of horizontal earthquake waves rippling across the asphalt like ocean waves. Because the white striping added scale, I could see the height of each wave at about ten to twelve inches. Needless to say, seeing asphalt rolling like that was an unforgettable eye-witness introduction to the power of Mother Nature, and in a few days would come my second experience.

North Beach Ogre

That following weekend after the earthquake, I parked at a friend's apartment and walked the several blocks into the North Beach area. Known as "Little Italy" in San Francisco, the North Beach area was built on a landfill created in the late 19th century.

The business's parking lot I was at in South San Francisco was also built on landfill, but it was much younger than the North Beach landfill.

Unfortunately, time and pressure took their vengeance on the North Beach landfill, and the area suffered extreme damage due to liquefaction.

As I walked through the debris-strewn streets of what had been a quaint and beautiful neighborhood, was eerily quiet.

First responders had things in hand and residents were being allowed back. When I studied the damaged buildings, what I saw was unforgettable.

Most North Beach structures were two-story wood-frame homes with a garage on the first floor which though commonplace, is an inherently flawed design. As I stood in the middle of the street, I looked around, and as I did an odd thought came to mind.

It looked as though some horrible North Beach ogre had swung a mighty energy sword through the first story of every structure on the block. This mighty sword had sliced through the first floors of these buildings and knocked them apart so that the upper story collapsed upon the remains of the first.

The ogre's sword was actually the sway that caused the same horizontal earthquake waves I had witnessed rippling across the asphalt in South San Francisco.

The Epicenter

The epicenter of the Loma Prieta earthquake was located in the Nisene Marks State Park outside Aptos, California. If you draw a large 'V' on a map, the bottom is the quake's epicenter. The top left of the 'V' is in South San Francisco, and the top right of the "V" is in the East Bay area where David B. South was when the earthquake struck. Dave and I were both approximately 50 miles away from the epicenter when the quake struck.

In May 2001 I had the opportunity to join a small group of folks for a hike into Nisene Marks State Park. At the time it was still a red tag area, but we hiked in to the exact spot for the epicenter.

To get to the epicenter, we inched our way across a ledge created by the uplift and used exposed roots to steady ourselves. The epicenter itself was so broken that we could only work our way up to the outer edge of it.

Standing on the epicenter, I saw the land around it had been thrown around like rag dolls, and huge sections had been torn and uplifted by the vertical forces of the earthquake.

Between this hike to the epicenter and my previous earthquake experiences, I was able to witness firsthand the immense power of both horizontal and vertical earthquake waves.

- October 17, 1989 – I experienced and witnessed the asphalt rolling with the horizontal waves in South San Francisco.
- October 21, 1989 – I saw how the sway from the horizontal waves sheared the first floors of the homes and businesses in the San Francisco North Beach area.
- May 2001 – I personally saw how the earthquake tore the land asunder with massive uplifts and collapses at the epicenter in Nisene Marks State Park.

Was all this coincidence? No, because everything happens for a reason.

I believe that was the case here. I had those experiences, which I now believe to be divine appointments, because I would have a job to do write this book though, at the time I did not know that.

In a similar vein, I also recognize a divine appointment that connected me so many years later with a brilliant visionary; a man who would become one of my personal heroes, David B. South. He invented the perfect enabling technology for Win-Win survival communities, concrete domes.

My cosmic link with David began on Tuesday, October 17, 1989, at 5:04 PM local time.

Concrete Domes and Loma Prieta

When the Loma Prieta earthquake struck, inventor and builder, David B. South, was in a concrete dome he had built for an apple grower in the East Bay area. The main domes for apple storage and processing were 140' and 180'.

When the earthquake struck, David was standing in a 30' foot dome that was used as a control center for the processing operation. Luckily, he was able to brace himself. Workers in the larger domes were thrown to the ground by the earthquake.

Shortly after things had settled down, David inspected all three concrete domes for his client and found no structural damage to any of them. Why? Because concrete domes are simply the strongest man-made structures and can handily survive the worst earthquakes, tornadoes, and tsunamis, nature can throw at us.

Does this mean that concrete domes are the enabling technology I was looking for to build Win-Win dome communities? No, because while concrete domes are a useful technology that has been in use for thousands of years, they are not the easiest structures to build.

Therefore, understanding these issues will help one truly appreciate the genius of inventor and builder, David B. South.

The Need for an Enabling Technology

Concrete domes are tough and long-lasting. A superb example of such durability is the Pantheon in Rome which dates back to 126 AD.

The front of the Pantheon is a wide portico with an entrance into the main structure called a rotunda. The term rotunda describes a large and high circular hall or room in a building, which is typically capped by a dome.

It is also interesting to note that The Pantheon inspired the United States Capitol Rotunda. Both structures feature an oculus which is an opening at the top center of the dome, and provides natural lighting for the interior.

The bottom line here is that concrete domes are the most durable types of man-made structures which makes them ideal for Win-Win survival communities. However, the concern is the labor and time involved in their construction.

The Romans could organize armies of slaves to construct their domes; so labor was never a problem for them. But for a Win-Win survival community, slavery is obviously a non-starter.

This is why an enabling technology is so necessary, and the ideal strategy must reduce overall costs while speeding the construction of all-hazards and permanent structures. The goal is the ability to raise an all-hazards concrete dome residence in just a few weekends. With this in mind, let's see how our ancestors have made domes for thousands of years.

Bricks, Dirt or Wood

Building a small dome can be relatively easy and fast. Such is the case with Inuit/Eskimo Igloos, which are seasonal shelters made from snow. The critical thing to remember is that an igloo is a temporary shelter. Consequently, igloos offer inhabitants excellent protection from the elements.

Conversely, building a large and permanent dome has always been a labor and time intensive process.

Large domes are constructed in a number of ways depending on the type of construction method. They can be constructed, like Igloos and the Pantheon, using bricks. Or, a form can be used. A form is a shaping device which is used to build the desired structure.

Dirt Forms

Dirt can be used effectively, and an excellent example of this type of dome construction is found in the Arcosanti experimental town. It was founded in 1970 and located in central Arizona 70 miles north of Phoenix, the state capital.

I was able to visit Arcosanti in 1975 while attending Arizona State University. The initial structures had been completed, and I was mesmerized by their use of dome structures.

The Arcosanti dome construction method was brilliantly simple and worked well for building domes of any size, and it is well suited to very large structures.

You begin by building a mound of dirt in the shape you want. Then rebar (short for reinforcing bar) is brought in.

The first step is to poke rebar hangers (a.k.a "pigs" – short lengths of rebar) into the dirt. They are used to attach the reinforcing rebar that is needed to strengthen the structure.

Once that is completed, successive layers of concrete are poured around the form until finished. After the concrete cures, you remove the dirt, cut off the rebar pigs, and plaster and paint. Voila, you now have a strong, beautiful structure that will last for a hundred years.

Today, the same dome structures I saw at Arcosanti in 1975 are still as strong and beautiful as the day I saw them. That said; the Arcosanti dirt form dome construction method requires immense amounts of time and elbow grease.

Wood Forms

A faster way to build domes than with earth forms is to use wood forms. These are quite effective for building small to moderate-sized concrete dome structures. Optimal size for a small structure suitable for one or two occupants is roughly 20' in diameter.

Wood forms are constructed, assembled, disassembled, and then re-used. Therefore, the ability to build one and then re-use it many times is a real advantage.

To begin, the wood form is assembled over the foundation. The structure material is then applied over the form. After the concrete cures, the forms (which are now inside the structure) are disassembled and removed through the dome's entrance. As long as they are not damaged, they can be used repeatedly.

The takeaway here is whether you are using bricks, or dirt, or wood to build your domes, there has never been a useful method for building large domes such as those required by a Win-Win survival community.

David B. South changed that! His large dome construction method dramatically lowers construction costs, labor demands, and the time to completion so that large concrete domes are well within practical reach. Did David do it for money? No, though he did build a profitable, world-renown construction company.

Rather, David did it for God after receiving a divine calling. So, for the sake of your own survival and that of your friends and loved ones, you need to know this story.

Marshall and Dave

Divine connections are difficult to see because we lead serial lives. Yet, God sees all, and what may appear to be disconnected, a slice of time in which an event occurs, is just a waypoint in a vast span of years that reaches far beyond our immediate line of sight.

This is how we are divinely guided to a future we cannot see, but God does. Therefore, it is not about the destination. It's about getting there one small step at a time. This is how I began to research this book in 2013.

I had no idea of where things would go back then, but my research quickly led me back to my 1975 visit to the Arcosanti.

The concrete domes I saw at Arcosanti in 1975 were built using huge dirt forms, and this made a profound impression on me. Decades later, this experience would lead me to a divine appointment with David B. South in early 2015.

After studying David's website at www.monolithic.org, I reached out to David with an invitation to appear on my Cut to the Chase with Marshall Masters podcast. He graciously accepted and we recorded his interview which aired on September 27, 2015. It was titled, *Rapid Construction Survival Communities — Monolithic Domes Inventor, David B. South.*

The nice thing about doing a popular radio show or podcast is it gives you amazing access to subject matter experts like David. Offer them a good show that helps to promote their books or products, and you've got their undivided attention.

Our interview was awesome, and David was very enthusiastic about using his dome construction method to build survival communities. He stated his enthusiasm for this project several times during conversations before and after our interview.

I was so impressed with his method that in July 2016, I devoted an entire chapter to using concrete domes for survival in my book, *Surviving the Planet X Tribulation: A Faith-Based Leadership Guide.* David contributed considerable time to my research for that chapter, and several concepts from that book will also appear in this one.

One of the things that endeared me to David's DBS concrete dome method was what I also learned in 2016. It was during a classroom training course for certified Community Emergency Response Team (CERT) volunteers with the Washoe County Sheriff's office in Reno, NV.

FEMA and Concrete Domes

At the time Dave and I were doing the podcast interview; I was a certified Community Emergency Response Team (CERT) volunteer and a certified Amateur Radio Emergency Service (ARES) volunteer. I was therefore able to avail myself with hundreds of hours of classroom and online FEMA emergency courses as part of my research for this book.

FEMA never refused me any training course I signed up for, and the instruction was awesome. Yes, this Federal agency does get a lot of mixed coverage, but the rank and file first responders and volunteers I trained with are the very people you want to have as neighbors.

Of all the FEMA courses that I completed, the one that had the most direct bearing on this book was an all-day intensive training on March 7, 2016 for ATC-20, Post Earthquake Safety Evaluation of Buildings, and FEMA P-154, Rapid Visual Screening for Potential Seismic Hazards.

The purpose of the training was to prepare certified volunteers to assist the Sheriff's office in evaluating structures following a catastrophic earthquake. As a part of a special response team, we would evaluate damaged structures to determine if people could reenter them to retrieve possessions. If a structure was determined to be unsafe, it would be red-tagged.

I have one hint for those who have never been in an earthquake. If you survive and you are physically able, shut off the gas as fast as you can; be extremely careful when attempting to retrieve possessions (if allowed), and of course, never stand under a chimney.

During the afternoon break, I approached the instructor with a few questions. He was a very successful seismic engineer from California, and he specialized in earthquake retrofits and new construction.

My first question to him was about concrete domes. According to the FEMA field forms we were using, there were 22 types of structures. Some of them I had never heard of, but one type was noticeably absent, concrete domes.. I wanted to know why; so I asked.

The instructor chuckled and we discussed it at length. The upshot was this. Imagine that you have three laboratory earthquake simulation shake tables that are used for structure testing.

- On the first table is a model of a residential wood-frame house.
- On the second table is a light steel building.
- On the third is a concrete dome.

When you turn all three shake tables on, the subsequent failures will occur in the following order:

- The residential wood-frame home model on the first shake table succumbs to sway and fails.
- The light steel building model on the second shake table succumbs to sway and fails.
- The third shake table under the concrete dome model fails. 10,000 years in the future, alien archaeologists will discover the remains of the concrete dome model sitting in a pile of useless shake table rubble.

The reason why FEMA does not include a concrete dome category on post-earthquake structure evaluation forms is because when properly constructed, they do not fail. In fact, not only can concrete domes handily survive large earthquakes, they can also survive direct hits by F5 class tornadoes. This is why FEMA subsidizes the construction of large concrete dome sports arenas and cafeterias in public schools throughout America's Tornado Alley.

Tornadoes and Earthquakes

The principal geographic area for Tornado Alley or the tornado belt, as it is called by storm chasers, extends from northern Texas, through Oklahoma, Kansas, Nebraska, Missouri, Iowa, South Dakota, and North Dakota.

FEMA subsidized sports arenas / shelters are typically 300' and larger in diameter. When an alert sounds, students and residents know to get to the dome shelter fast; as in, feet don't fail me now. After the tornado passes, there will be minor damage to doors and windows but not to the structure itself, and everyone inside will be safe.

Afterwards, I asked my instructor why the FEMA field forms we were using did not include concrete domes as a structure type. I also wanted to know how well subterranean domes would handle an earthquake. What he told me is vital for you to understand; please commit this to memory.

The shape of any structure built underground is irrelevant to seismic resistance. It can be a dome, a silo, a single-story honeycomb structure, or whatever you wish. The key is that regardless of the type structure used; it must be in full contact with the earth on all sides. This allows the horizontal earthquake waves to pass through and around the structure. As far as the vertical earthquake waves are concerned, man-made structures are constructed to be load-bearing.

However, my FEMA instructor made the point, that if there is any open-air space between the structure and the earth surrounding it, the structure will be just as vulnerable to sway as if it were built above the ground.

What he told me that day was the final confirmation of what I'd already sensed for some time. The enabling technology for Win-Win survival communities that I was looking for was not concrete domes per se. It was how to build them.

The method Monolithic Domes Inventor, David B. South, created uses inflated vinyl air-forms instead of bricks, or dirt or wood forms. A single concrete dome can be as large as a city block and raised using a single airform. The elegance of this is you can use airforms to build anything. Domes, silos, honeycomb boxes, and anything else you can imagine.

Open Source Naming

The company David founded is Monolithic Constructors, hence the term "Monolithic dome" which is based on a business name. David's primary website can be found at www.monolithic.org.

Unlike most commercial web sites, David's offers an amazing and vast source of freely available information about domes and how to build them. What is notable is how he shares his own process of discovery and development warts and all. This is what an open source website looks like.

The term "open-source" refers to something people can modify and share because its design is publicly accessible.

In keeping with this open-source tradition, the term DBS dome, for David B. South dome, will be used instead of the term "Monolithic dome" which implies a proprietary solution. (There are precedents for this naming convention.)

Open-source technologies are named typically for their inventors. For example, the "Linux operating system" is a contraction using the inventor's name, Linus Torvalds, and the Unix-like open-source operating system he created.

DBS Concrete Domes

Thanks to David's loving largess, DBS dome technology is now the essential enabling technology for creating viable survival communities. This open-source knowledge must be shared along with other essential survival skills and here is the full story.

Meeting with David in 2019

By early 2019, I'd completed much of my research for this book, but before I could present concrete domes built using the DBS dome method as an enabling technology, I needed to get boots on the ground and visit David's construction in Italy, Texas, south of Dallas.

David South and Marshall Masters (2019) Italy, TX

I flew to Dallas and joined up with research team volunteers, Dan Dean (design engineer) and his wife Sheila Dean (ranching consultant). The next day we drove to Italy, Texas where we personally met with David and members of his engineering team.

It was a delightful meeting where our teams worked together to address construction-related issues with an emphasis particularly on aquaponics. David also gave us a tour of his personal dome home which was quite impressive.

Dave pointed out several features. Something that he insists be included in every survival dome is a centrally located fire hose that can reach every room in the home, and I could not agree more.

That visit with David left no doubt in my mind that the DBS method for building concrete domes was absolutely the best way to build all-hazard survival domes for families.

David has built over the years a successful and prestigious international dome-building business, but as a visionary, his primary motivation was not the money. Rather, David did it for God after he received a divine calling. But, like any good businessman, he filed a patent.

Intellectual Property

Our team was reviewing the data for the authoring phase in early August 2019, when they raised an issue regarding usage of DBS domes. Namely, David's intellectual property rights.

Through our research, we learned that other companies were using the DBS concrete dome method, and they were manufacturing both airforms and complete domes. There are companies overseas that even make and sell complete airforms.

Nonetheless, David holds a patent issued in 1979 (US4155967) for his DBS concrete dome construction method. We needed to inquire about airform licensing for survival communities that choose to build their own domes or use another construction company.

To resolve this issue, I gave David a call on August 13, 2019. I asked him about this, and he told me that because he wants people to build domes, he has never enforced his dome patent. He did emphasize the fact that he does actively enforce the patent on his hangar door.

David also confirmed that other companies use his method to build domes; one of which is owned by his brother, and this was fine with him.

David confirmed our research that there were companies overseas that would make airforms to specification. He also added that his company, Monolithic, offers training, equipment, construction, and consulting.

I remember him saying brightly, "Give us a try." It's a good idea.

David's Calling

The fact that David has never enforced or ever intended to enforce his patent, awarded in 1979, essentially makes his method an open-source solution. At least that's how I see it since I worked in the computer industry for 24 years.

I was stunned by David's largess and just had to ask, "Why?" Here is what he told me.

After he had finished building his first concrete dome using his airform method, he stepped inside and stood in the center of the dome. Never in a million years, could I have expected to hear what David said next.

He began in a quiet voice and told me that God had spoken to him that day in a clear voice. The calling he received was, and I quote, "You must build these all over the world."

The reason I remember that word-for-word was the loving presence that attended it. It was electric because of what I felt and how David said it.

When David said, "You must build these all over the world," it was as though he'd heard those words earlier that same day. This is the way of true callings.

True callings are like polished diamonds that shine forever. I know that David relived that experience with each sharing. He could see himself every time in his mind, standing in that brand new dome, a half a lifetime ago, and hearing the calling for the first time.

I would like to believe that in the future, when church members raise a new DBS method concrete dome, the finishing touch will be to affix a brass plaque above the door which reads:

David B. South's Calling
You Must Build These All Over the World

The critical takeaway here is that the true enabling technologies must be open-source and this is David's gift to humanity.

3

Forming Your Survival Church

In the previous chapter, you learned about the DBS concrete dome method and why it is an essential enabling technology for Win-Win survival communities. We will now address the need for incorporating your community as a survival church.

Why incorporate as a church instead of a community, denomination, fellowship, house of prayer, public worship, religious order, or temple? The answer is, the designation that is consistently referenced in Federal and States laws is "Church."

A Survival Church Defined

In the Bible the word translated "church" is the Greek term ekklesia. Ekklesia means any gathering of people, and the Bible never uses the term or the concept of "ekklesia/church" to refer to a building. Therefore, for the purpose of survival, a church is a spiritual gathering of people for a common cause. In the case of a religion, is is an explanation of faith.

The mission of a Win-Win church is to manage resources, raise children, and to be a shining light of hope for all. It is a gathering of like-minded people with a sense of mission to serve God's will for humanity with morality, science, and common sense.

To achieve this, you must build and foster an environment of acceptance and mutual respect. Community members must never proselytize any religious belief within the community.

It will be helpful to incorporate a simple definition of proselytization when forming your church. Use these three simple rules that will help to avoid disputes.

- **No Judgment:** Historically, religious wars begin with judgments and end with death. Therefore, members may not pronounce judgments upon others with regards to their spirituality.
- **No Unrelated Answers:** When answering questions about matters of heritage, answers must be short and to the point. Using a query to introduce unrelated answers is not allowed.
- **No Call to Action:** Never finish an answer with a call to action by telling the questioners what they must do next, as in adopting a faith or studying a religious text.

Whatever rules you do implement, remember that to thrive, a Win-Win survival church must be a place of safety from religious intolerance and prosecution. All members must show tolerance and respect for whatever faith or religion another member holds dear because this is their universal right of individual heritage.

Why must members faithfully respect and honor this right for all? Because neither the Constitution of the United States nor any of our nation's many bodies of law designate an "official" or "approved" religion. A core belief of America is that each of us has the right to walk humbly with our God as we see fit.

Therefore, let's examine the aspects of forming your congregation as a "church" under American law and what that means.

Free Church or State Church

Founding your survival church will require that founders form multiple non-profit church corporations. Here is where you need a lawyer to help you with your incorporation. Ideally, a lawyer well versed in tax and real estate matters.

To help with your selection of a suitable lawyer and also to evaluate your options, there are important incorporation issues you may wish to discuss with your lawyer before proceeding with incorporation.

The first decision you need to make is the most fundamental choice you will ever make.

Will you operate as a Free Church or as a State Church?

The difference is this: a Free Church does not solicit donations; a State Church does.

501(c)(3) State Church

Churches were added to the 501(c)(3) section of the IRS tax code (IRC) in 1954, thereby ending the historical ability of churches to influence our nation and its government. Consequently, when a church files for 501(c)(3), it enters a partnership with the government.

Acquiring 501(c)(3) status results in the church voluntarily waiving its freedom of speech in order to assure solicited donors that their contributions are tax-deductible. Furthermore, at the state level, additional requirements may be necessary in order to solicit contributions.

Therefore, can a non-501(c)(3) church receive tax-deductible, unsolicited donations is the obvious question? The answer is Yes, and this is addressed in IRS Publication 526.

IRS Publication 526 (2019), Cat. No. 15050A
Charitable Contributions, For use in preparing 2019 Returns
Page 2, Organizations That Qualify To Receive Deductible Contributions

> "You can deduct your contributions only if you make them to a qualified organization. Most organizations, other than churches and governments, must apply to the IRS to become a qualified organization."

The takeaway is that churches are not required to apply to the IRS to become a qualified 501(c)(3) organizations. Therefore, if your survival church does not solicit donations, applying for 501(c)(3) status is not necessary.

This is also addressed in IRS Publication 557, which explains 501(c)(3) guidelines in more depth. It is important to note how the IRS evaluates churches that apply for 501(c)(3) status:

Publication 557 (Rev. January 2019), Cat. No. 46573C
Tax-Exempt Status for Your Organization
Religious Organizations

> "To determine whether an organization meets the religious purposes test of section 501(c)(3), the IRS maintains two basic guidelines.
>
> That the particular religious beliefs of the organization are truly and sincerely held.
>
> That the practices and rituals associated with the organization's religious belief or creed aren't illegal or contrary to clearly defined public policy."

While it is unnecessary for your church to apply for 501(c)(3) status because it is not soliciting donations, these IRS guidelines should be cardinal rules for any self-declared Church, regardless of its tax status, particularly with regard to unsolicited donations.

508(c)(1)(A) Free Church

A properly founded survival church will operate as a free church because it does not solicit donations, which is not to say that your church cannot receive tax-deductible *unsolicited* donations. You can, because when the need for recognition of exemption is removed, what essentially remains is the Constitutional separation of church and state.

Publication 557 (Rev. January 2019), Cat. No. 46573C
Tax-Exempt Status for Your Organization
Religious Organizations

> "**Churches**: Although a church, its integrated auxiliaries, or a convention or association of churches isn't required to file Form 1023 to be exempt from federal income tax or to receive tax-deductible contributions, the organization may find it advantageous to obtain recognition of exemption."

Further down in this IRS Publication 557, there is a critical insight into your right to join with others in service to God's will.

Publication 557 (Rev. January 2019), Cat. No. 46573C
Tax-Exempt Status for Your Organization
Religious Organizations

> "Because beliefs and practices vary widely, there is no single definition of the word church for tax purposes."

Therefore, if your church does apply for 501(c)(3) status, where does that leave in you in the tax code? You are a 508(c)(1)(A) Free Church.

Title 26. INTERNAL REVENUE CODE
Section 508. Special rules with respect to section 501(c)(3) organizations

> **(a) New organizations must notify Secretary that they are applying for recognition of section 501(c)(3) status** Except as provided in subsection (c), an organization organized after October 9, 1969, shall not be treated as an organization described in section 501(c)(3)—
>
> **(c) Exceptions**
>
> **(1) Mandatory exceptions:** Subsections (a) and (b) shall not apply to—
>
> **(A) Churches**, their integrated auxiliaries, and conventions or associations of churches, or associations of churches...

The takeaway here is, when selecting an attorney to assist you with the incorporation of your church, if he or she insists that you must apply for 501(c)(3) status, say thank you, and then find a lawyer who understands how to help you create a 508(c)(1)(A) Free Church.

Once you find that lawyer, you'll also need to discuss the need to create multiple corporations for your survival church, not all at once though, but over time.

Corporate Organization

As a church, your first incorporation will be the creation of a holding corporation for your church's property, and you have two basic options, a non-profit corporation or a corporation sole.

It is very difficult to obtain a corporation sole these days, though a good attorney may be able to find an existing corporation sole that can be acquired. This is why most churches incorporate as non-profits.

However, when you do a search for corporation soles with a secretary of state office, you'll find that they are held by large religious organizations such as Catholic and Mormon churches.

There are two principal differences between a corporation sole and a non-profit corporation. A corporation sole is a legal entity with a single ("sole") natural person. This allows for a designated successor to assume the identical powers and possessions of a predecessor.

If you cannot acquire a corporation sole and form a non-profit corporation, you still need to operate as a corporation sole.

Corporation Sole

With a corporation sole, your organization may have and hold, but it may not transact business. However, it can be funded through membership fees, unsolicited donations, rents, royalties, and interest income. This is known as passive income.

No other corporate structure is better than a corporate sole for holding church property and guaranteeing the continuous operation of the church. However, if you open a website offering products for sale to the public, that is transacting business. Do this through a corporation sole, and you will jeopardize it. This is why you will need to form auxiliaries in the form of non-profit entities that can transact business.

For example, you name your organization, The Lifeboat Church as a corporation sole, to hold property purchased for the Church. Whether you form it as a sole or as a conventional non-profit, you need to operate this holding entity as a corporate sole.

After forming the property holding entity (corporation sole or non-profit), you will create Church auxiliary corporations, wholly owned by the holding entity.

These auxiliaries will be the corporate entities that you use to transact business, open credit card and merchant bank accounts, and to collect and pay sales taxes.

Corporate Location

When meeting with your lawyer to plan your incorporation strategy, you may find it useful to form the holding corporation for the Church in a state different than the one in which your property is located.

For example, many major corporations do business worldwide, but their holding companies are located in favorable states like Delaware and Nevada. Therefore, your Church holding corporation is simply a "foreign" corporation that owns the property, but it is not transacting business in the state.

However, it is advisable that the auxiliary corporation you form to transact business be incorporated in the same state as the property it serves. This eliminates the need to register a corporation formed out of state as doing business in-state as a foreign corporation.

Remember, you will be building your Church in stages, and the first stage is to build a retreat and research station. Ideally, the retreat is located in the same state where the majority of your initial members reside.

The advantage for Church members who reside in a metroplex (large metropolitan area with several cities and their suburbs) is they can use the Church retreat address as a permanent address. Why? Because of the potential for road blocks and checkpoints.

When things go sideways and the government begins to set up checkpoints, whoever is behind the wheel, when you arrive at a roadblock, needs to hand the sentry a driver license and say, "I'm returning home with my family to the address on my license."

It will not guarantee that you get through the checkpoint, but it will significantly reduce your chances of being told to return to a metroplex.

Naming Your Community

When naming a holding corporation or its auxiliaries, here are a few suggestions to keep in mind when naming them:

- **Never Name Your Physical Location:** If your church is located in Anytown, USA, do not include that in the name of your holding corporation. In other words, it is preferable to simply name your holding corporation as Lifeboat Church, instead of The Lifeboat Church of Anytown, USA.
- **Never Name a Religious Figure:** Let's assume that you are a Christian, and you want to name your church, The Lifeboat Church of Jesus Christ. That's got a nice ring to it, but remember, you're founding a survival church because you see how life, as we know it, could go sideways after a major disaster.

Should that happen, dramatic political changes will occur, and whoever assumes control may be hostile to specific faiths. Could this happen here in America? The answer takes us back to the second cardinal rule in IRS Publication 557.

Publication 557 (Rev. January 2019), Cat. No. 46573C
Tax-Exempt Status for Your Organization
Religious Organizations

> "That the practices and rituals associated with the organization's religious belief or creed aren't illegal or contrary to clearly defined public policy."

In other words, if things go sideways and our government begins arbitrarily persecuting faiths as Communist China has done, your Church's name could put you and your membership at the top of a rendition target list.

While we assume this couldn't happen, if political efforts to deconstruct the underpinnings of our constitutional republic prevail, the victors will be vengeful and brutal.

Branding Your Community

You need to brand yourself wisely, because the main revenue stream for all Win-Win survival communities will be food production, and this will be the first church auxiliary you incorporate. While the first property for the church will be a retreat, the second property will be a sizable ranch.

Therefore, you want to create a branded name for your food production sales auxiliary. For example, your holding corporation is Lifeboat Church, and your auxiliary corporation is the brand name, Lifeboat Ranch.

Finding the Right Lawyer

Given the attractive incorporation packages available online, is a lawyer required? No, there are plenty of do-it-yourself options offering generic templates for your articles of incorporation.

That said; a competent and honest lawyer will be instrumental in founding your Church in a way that avoids potential future difficulties by building additional safeguards into your articles of incorporation.

Once your entity is created, the attorney will typically become your registered agent, and remember, no one sends love letters via USPS certified mail.

When you select a lawyer, the first criterion is chemistry. Does it feel right? Then, size up the situation, and if the chemistry is good, then a competent, reputable local lawyer is a good choice.

However, a competent, reputable local lawyer with a personal interest is an even better choice.

Here is where some preparation, before you meet with a prospective lawyer, can give you a unique evaluation tool.

When you have a calling to found a Win-Win survival community and begin to take action on that calling, you will not be alone. There are others who will find this appealing, and the more often you explain what you're doing in five minutes or less, the better.

The process of observing people's response to your five-minute pitch will help you begin to see classifiable responses. When you've reached that point, you're ready to go lawyer shopping. Do your due diligence.

Set the meet for lunch or just afterward and do your thing. By that time, you should be able to tell if the pair of eyes facing you from across the table can see your vision. If it connects, you'll know. If the only interest is monetary, you'll know that too. So, try again.

When you find a lawyer who resonates with your vision and develops a personal interest in the success of your Church, this is a relationship worth cultivating because great care must be taken when you create your community bylaws.

4

Community Bylaws

When forming a church, creating the bylaws that will govern your community is a critical task. It must be handled with diligence and much thought; you want to avoid the unnecessary risks should a cataclysm cause an unfortunate turn of political fortunes for the nation.

America was founded on the precepts of religious tolerance and freedom. It was not an easy path for our nation, but today, every American has the right to worship God in their own way, and they must respect the right of others to do the same.

It is a core belief for Americans, so it is hard for us to imagine life without it. But it is possible, and the ensuing suppression would be the result of political aims.

Should dark forces seize power, they will bully the suffering masses to achieve their aim to change the world to suit themselves. They will target their perceived political and religious foes for abuse.

As founder of a survival church, you must accept this risk. It has its roots in history and it cannot be denied.

Therefore, you should organize your church to be as politically innocuous as possible. You want to avoid needlessly provoking harm or mischief should a radical change of national leadership results in intolerance and persecution, whether at the local, regional or supra-regional level.

Remember, a survival church is people coming together to serve the will of God for humanity with morality, science, and common sense without dogmatic religious overlays.

Survival is not about standing up for your particular denomination of faith. It's about still standing after the tribulation has passed. Therefore, when organizing your church, the number one goal is to develop a Plan B approach that sidesteps the unnecessary political risks to your community.

Operational Phases

After creating your articles of incorporation, you need to organize the bylaws of your church. Working with a lawyer who has a personal interest gives you a big advantage when organizing the operational phases addressed in your bylaws.

- **Phase 1 – Pre-tribulation Bylaws:** Mission and leaders
- **Phase 2 – Transition Event:** An end of life as we know it event that triggers Phase 3
- **Phase 3 – Tribulation Bylaws:** Community justice after a complete breakdown of law and order

Why is it necessary to address these three operational phases in your bylaws? Survival-related bylaws must anticipate dramatic shifts in the operation of the community during and following a major catastrophic event.

Furthermore, in the absence of a published religious doctrine, your bylaws must provide church members with a broad set of rules that can adapt to substantial changes in circumstances.

Phase 1 – Pre-tribulation Bylaws

When drafting your articles of incorporation and community bylaws, always remember that perception is reality, especially in survival situations where time is short and emotions are high. Therefore, two things to be careful with are the church's mission and leadership titles.

Church Mission

When defining a survival community, a mission statement must appear in your articles of incorporation and your bylaws. It must include and make one very important distinction, "You are not a religion."

Although this may sound counter-intuitive to some, a church is not a religion, and neither is a religion a church. While the two terms are inherently different from each other, they are often overlapped in popular usage. Yet, they are very different terms.

The etymology of the word "church" dates back to the ancient Greek term, "ekklesia" which describes a gathering of people. With a survival church, the gathering is to serve the will of God.

On the other hand, a religion is not a gathering. It is a belief system that is held in common with others. It provides an explanation of creation by a power or powers that govern it, and where we (humanity) fit into the grand scheme of things.

Such beliefs are codified through systems of doctrine and practice. So, when incorporating your church, you never name it using a location or a religious figure.

Why is this necessary? Assume you're well into the tribulation and outsiders appear seeking to assert control.

You have gathered with others for a simple mission: to serve the will of God for humanity with morality, science, and common sense without religious overlays. If outsiders are non-threatening, they can be engaged and offered the community's hospitality. Otherwise, they must be handled according to security protocols.

Dear Reader, survival is about having a Plan B to survive a tribulation.

A tribulation is an experience that tests one's endurance, patience, or faith.

Therefore, your church's mission is to survive and thrive as a clean slate for the beginning of the next civilization once the tribulation has passed.

This is the Creator's will, that our species survives, thrives and evolves spiritually.

Church Leadership Titles

Another important thing you can do to shield your church is to use innocuous leadership titles.

Commonly recognized religious leadership titles such as priest, rabbi, minister, and so forth are time-honored and revered. Conversely, titling your leadership positions with for-profit designations will be awkward and create unnecessary questions. You need titles that convey the roles just right.

One possible approach is to use titles that are not associated with for-profit entities or churches. For example:

- **Chief Steward:** Survival church leader
- **Steward:** Member of the church leadership
- **Coordinator:** Special events and projects
- **Advocate:** Community health and saftey

Leadership titles like these will help your church appear as politically innocuous as possible.

For other leadership positions in your community, adopting the Incident Command System (ICS) is an approach you'll find very useful.

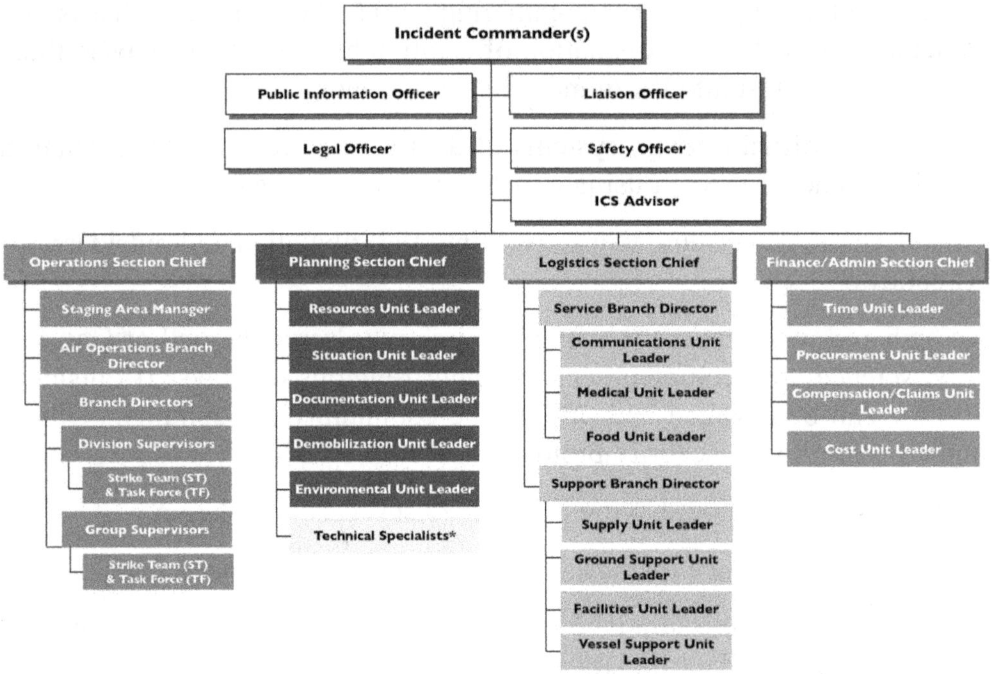

ICS is an established national doctrine that police, fire and rescue use to ensure a standardized approach to the command, control and coordination of their emergency response efforts.

First responders rely on ICS to organize rapidly-growing management structures that are also scalable when a large incident situation requires the assets of multiple departments and agencies to handle it.

The ICS begins with the first responder to arrive on the scene, and then evolves and expands as needed to ensure a consistent chain of command. We'll discuss ICS as part of your strategic alliances efforts later in this book.

Phase 2 – Transition Event

Of the three phases, the second phase is the tricky one. This is where the community must adapt to the changing circumstances, which result from a breakdown of supply chains and of law and order, due to a catastrophic transition event.

Of necessity this should be a smooth transition of the community's governance from a pre-tribulation way of life to a tribulation way of living. The range of events that trigger the time for transition should be well-defined and well-practiced. Everyone must be on the same page when the time comes to evacuate to safety.

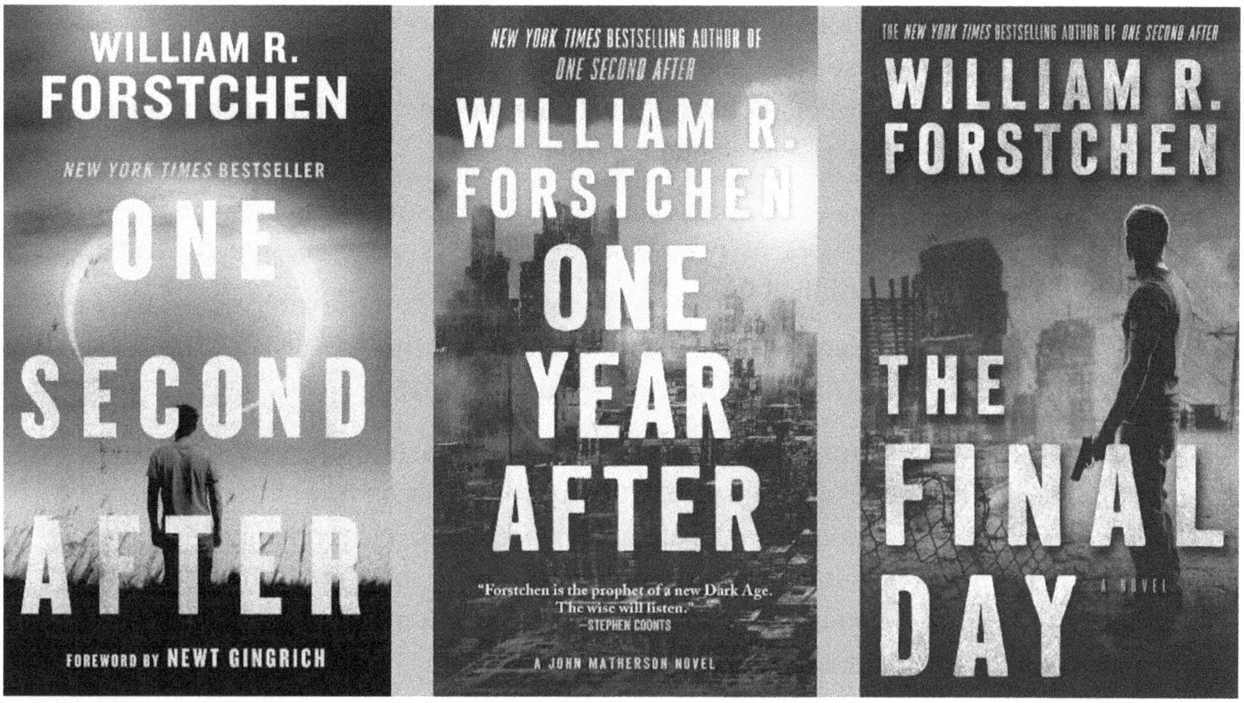

An excellent example is *One Second After* (2011) by William R. Forstchen. It was the first installment of a best-selling trilogy about surviving an Electromagnetic Pulse (EMP) attack on the United States by rogue nuclear powers.

Forstchen's bestseller was widely read by policymakers throughout the nation's capital because it was based on a study conducted by the EMP Commission. The commission was first created by Congress in 2001 and then later reestablished in 2006. Consequently, it presents a very believable doomsday scenario that is based on two medium ballistic missiles with EMP warheads that are deployed against America.

What made One Second After so powerful was that it led to the early determination by the Commission that an electromagnetic pulse event could kill nine out of ten Americans.

This pronouncement was shocking and for many years most could not accept the magnitude of it. In a subsequent report that the Commission issued in 2017, an explanation was provided that could help Americans to wrap their heads around the risk.

Assessing the Threat from Electromagnetic Pulse (EMP) – July 2017

> "A long-term outage owing to EMP could disable most critical supply chains, leaving the U.S. population living in conditions similar to centuries past, before the advent of electric power. In the 1800s, the U.S. population was less than 60 million, and those people had many skills and assets necessary for survival without today's infrastructure. An extended blackout today could result in the

> death of a large portion of the American population through the effects of societal collapse, disease, and starvation. While national planning and preparation for such events could help mitigate the damage, few such actions are currently underway or even being contemplated."

Even when most people read the words "an extended blackout," they assume it refers to a period of days or perhaps a week or two. However, this is not consistent with the actual threat as outlined by the Department of Energy.

Large Power Transformers and the U.S. Electric Grid – January 2015

> "Large power transformers are essential critical infrastructure to the electric grid, and are huge, weighing up to 820,000 pounds. If large power transformers are destroyed by a geomagnetic disturbance (GMD), electromagnetic pulse (EMP), cyber-attack, sabotage, severe weather, floods, or simply old age, parts or all of the electric grid could be down in a region for 6 months to 2 years. This is because the USA imports 85% of them."

Sadly, there is little or no mention of this threat by the mainstream media. Yet, if you want to point a finger at the one disaster that would cause the greatest loss of life, this is it.

Nearly all doomsday scenarios in numerous Hollywood films, includes a catastrophic collapse of the Nation's power grid.

Therefore, the most universally credible tribulation event, for triggering a transition of the community into survival operations, is a catastrophic nationwide failure of the power grid.

There is no hard sell here and that is a huge advantage. Therefore, your bylaws should have the most credible trigger event which is likely to occur, to signal the transition into a world where state law and order has collapsed.

By citing a failure of the nation's power grid as that signal event, you give your leadership broad discretionary power to initiate a transition based on that or any other cause with a similar wide impact. This is critical because your community will begin to transition into the realities of a tribulation world at that time.

Phase 3 – Tribulation Bylaws

The bylaws for the third phase are the most difficult to create because you must anticipate how people will react. Remember what the EMP commission said, "In the 1800s, the U.S. population was less than 60 million, and those people had many skills and assets necessary for survival without today's infrastructure."

This prediction by the EMP commission will resonate much more with people in rural areas than those living within a metropolitan area. This is important to understand because part of your membership recruiting efforts will be in metroplex areas.

This raises a pivotal point in creating your bylaws due to how most city dwellers think of preparedness.

What typically comes to mind first is a bug out bag. A school backpack is filled with survival items like field rations, water filters, prescription medications, a change of underwear, and so forth; there's enough to last a few days until "normal life" is restored.

Therefore, city dwellers tend to assume that:

- When disaster strikes, it will be near or where you live and work.
- Help for all of the survivors will pour in to the affected areas.
- Relief efforts will sustain survivors as repairs and reconstruction begins.
- Public utility infrastructures will fail, but be restored within a few days.
- "Normal" life is expected to resume within days or a few weeks at most.

These assumptions constitute the majority of the urban masses' expectations and preparation efforts. However, the reality of a tribulation will far exceed these expectations. There are three barriers to long-term preparedness planning: cost, effort, and denial.

How does this manifest? Let's use the issue of cost as an example.

During Hurricane Katrina in 2005, there were several reports of unfortunate residents in New Orleans who drowned in the attics of their homes. Why? During Hurricane Katrina, the difference between drowning in the attic of your New Orleans home and being rescued was having an axe in the attic.

Those who had an axe in their attic were able to use it to punch a hole through the roof of their home, climb out, and wave for help. Those who didn't drowned in their attics.

This is where the cost of preparedness was the deciding factor and not a large amount but by the smallest amounts.

Although this thinking is shortsighted, this is how city dwellers are programmed to think about preparedness. I call it, "prepare to fail public programming."

As a community leader, you need to be ever-mindful of this programming, even when people agree with the need to prepare. Their thinking will still be deeply influenced by the " prepare to fail mindset."

This is a problem for many who have been in awareness awhile. They have seen the need to prepare, but due to the mockery they have suffered at the hands of family members and friends, awareness for them has been a living misery.

This may explain why too many people in awareness compensate by their focus on Internet media and websites reporting Earth changes. They hope to find a smoking gun that will shift their friends and family from mockery to acceptance.

Nothing shatters a window of opportunity better than a smoking gun, and when it comes to survival preparation, the takeaway is everyone will talk the talk. Even though most are still influenced by prepare to fail public programming, and they are totally unaware of its role in their thinking.

As a consequence, only a small minority will have the commitment and presence of mind to walk the walk. These are the people that you want. The ones you can depend on not only to talk the talk, they walk the walk.

We will discuss this more, but for now let's develop a deeper understanding of how prepare to fail public programming can boomerang, and cause terrible divides within your community as it endures the hardships of a tribulation.

How would it do it? Here's a case study to show how.

Survival Screening Scenario

While doing research in 2016, I started two study groups. One was to address the needs of a community and the other was for the technology. The technology group was highly effective and the efforts generated many of the essential concepts presented in this book.

However, the other group, that was focused on building community, revealed a glaring example of how prepare to fail public programming can still divide a community long after the beginning of the tribulation.

For the purpose of our study, we used an imaginary survival scenario to help us evaluate prospective new members for our community study group. This scenario takes place in the future, in the midst of a tribulation following a complete breakdown of law and order. Here is the security scenario we presented to our survival study groups.

Security Screening Scenario

Rather than summarize the process, it is vital to understand the security from the candidate's perspective and how that is shaded by present-day sensibilities. It is important to note that this scenario is based on the kind of security issues that faced American pioneers as they crossed the country. Win-Win survival communities will face similar scenarios in the future.

> *SCENARIO: As the leader of a survival community with 100 members, security is always your number one concern; because beyond the safety of your walls there can be renegades who want to steal what you have, rape and abuse your women and children, and then work all those who have no value as slaves.*

They have observers watching every movement every day in your community, ever vigilant for a moment of opportunity.

In the midst of all this, one of the senior members of your community becomes angry and irrational. He claims that he is not appreciated for all that he has done for the community and that he is denied his rightful role as a leader. Therefore, he is going to leave and start his own community somewhere else and prove that he has better ideas.

You and others in your community go to great lengths to reconcile his differences. He nonetheless attempts to leave unannounced with a small cart when a sentry intercepts him.

He is arrested by the officer in command of the guard and four members of the community are switched from housing and food production tasks to guarding the prisoner. It becomes obvious that there is no path to success with this man.

The situation reaches an untenable stalemate and a resolution is needed. As the leader of the community, what will you do?

This scenario was presented to over 25 candidates in our study group, and their responses were equally divided in two response categories: Defender and Free Choice. Here are their respective views of the matter.

- **Defender:** Half of the candidates quickly answered that he had to be terminated.
- **Free Choice:** The other half of the candidates would often struggle with the scenario and ask what-if questions; though in the end, they all would say that the man was free to leave the community without any restrictions.

After receiving this first answer, we would then ask a follow-up question, "Why did you answer this way?" These answers were also revealing and consistent:

- **Defender:** All of the defenders were former or active military, or paramilitary first responders, and they had the same reasoning. This man possessed critical intelligence about the community, and in the hands of the enemy, that information would result in the community being overrun due to its compromised security. Consequently, the man needed to be terminated to protect the community.
- **Free Choice:** The other half of the candidates viewed the scenario through their current sensibilities. They insisted that the man has the right to choose and that he needs to be free to go wherever he pleases. Or, at least imprison him for however long it takes until he comes to his senses and settles down.

Who got it right? The Defenders got it right. Imprisoning the man for any length of time would be a burden on the community, and there would always be the risk of escape.

They gave the correct answer for the study, termination with extreme prejudice. Therefore, we would tell them, "Congratulations. You passed. Welcome aboard."

But what about the Free Choice candidates?

With those cases, we would politely thank them for the answer and continue the questioning with, "Is it likely that this man will get not get far before he is captured?"

"That could happen," they all agreed.

Then we would ask, "How long do you think this man could endure having the skin on his feet burned away with a blowtorch before telling his captors everything he knows?"

"Not long I imagine," they all answered.

At this point we would get to the crux of these free choice discussions with the following question, "Let's assume that he reveals all of this information either because he is spiteful or because he is tortured. Either way, your community is attacked and many of the members die violent deaths. As you look at the dead and dying bodies, is letting that man go free still the right decision?"

To our amazement, each one said the same thing. "It's his right to choose. You still have to let him go free."

This is the immense and intractable power of prepare to fail public programming. It gives its disciples the ability to disassociate personal freedom with community safety. Here is the bottom line when it comes to comparing the two study groups.

- **Defender:** The safety of the community is the transcendent need. A defender must be proficient with firearms and a strong supporter of the 2nd amendment.
- **Free Choice:** The right of the individual to choose outweighs the safety of the community. Those who advocate free choice typically do not know how to safely handle a firearm and have no interest in doing so, even if the community is attacked.

The takeaway is that you will need people from both sides of the scenario to ensure a useful diversity of skills and funding for the community. So, how do you deal with it?

You can use a screening scenario or, address this in your community bylaws by requiring that every adult on a church property, must demonstrate a basic proficiency with firearms.

This requirement can be met by complying with one or more of the mandatory firearm safety options in your bylaws. For example:

- **Firearm Proof of Purchase:** A valid gun purchase shows that the individual is able to pass a background check and physically possesses a firearm. This is the most basic option and it is sufficient. However, the other three options are more desirable.
- **Firearm Proficiency:** The applicant has an honorable discharge from a combat arms military unit, or is a former or current first responder with weapons proficiency and the ability to pass a background check.
- **Recognized Firearm Safety Program:** There are a lot of firearm safety programs available. One of the best is the family-based Project Appleseed (appleseedinfo.org) program. They offer training and proficiency certification, and community members should consider joining the program as range safety and training volunteers.
- **Concealed Carry Permit:** This is the gold standard for firearm safety and different states have different policies for concealed carry firearms. Some states make it difficult to obtain a permit, while others treat it as a straightforward process and require an authorized completion of training certificate. After submitting your carry permit application, you will be photographed, fingerprinted, and subjected to a very thorough background check before the permit is issued.

When people adamantly ignore the logical need to provide for the safety of the community during the initial screening, they may eventually change their thinking, especially to protect themselves or someone they love. Ergo, blood ties are thicker than sensibilities when it matters to you.

Therefore, what you are about to read next may be disturbing to you, and it could make your attorney's skin crawl, but do this you must.

In the tribulation phase of your bylaws, you need to state in clear and unequivocal terms that following the total breakdown of law and order, the leadership of the community will be the sole governing body, and that they must have the ultimate authority to apply at their discretion capital punishment for major offenses such as murder, sedition, treason, child molestation, and any offenses of similar magnitude. In such cases, the leader must never be the one to perform an execution.

Aside from reason, is there another reason for a bylaw like this?

Yes, and this came about towards the completion of our study group's enrollment process.

One particular study member, a retiree, was an adamant Free Choice supporter. I asked her, "This man will be easily captured by predators, and he will reveal your community's secrets. Are you good with this?"

Her answer, "It's his right to choose. You still have to let him go free."

Then I asked. "If your enemies use this information to attack your community, the loss of life will be substantial. Are you good with this?"

She answered, "It's his right to choose. You still have to let him go free."

Then I asked. "A woman who just lost her husband and child blames you because you defend this man's right to leave and turns the whole community against you. Are you good with this?"

She answered, "It's his right to choose. You still have to let him go free."

At this point, the process was in an obvious stalemate so a new question was necessary.

I asked her, "You are opposed to terminating this man because he has a right to choose; now many people in the community have died as a result; and the survivors hate you and blame you for it. Is there one thing that would have changed your mind?"

She answered, "Yes, if it were in the community's bylaws that you had the right to terminate him for the safety of the community, that would be different."

"OK," I answered, "We've just updated the bylaws with that very authority. Now what do you say?"

Without giving it a moment's thought or concern, she immediately replied, "Kill him."

Wow, that was a revealing and useful bit of information.

The takeaway here is that when crafting your community bylaws, the third stage of operation in a tribulation must address what happens after the rule of law and order has collapsed. This is why your community bylaws must confer upon the leadership the power of life and death in the absence of law and order during a tribulation.

When prospective new members evaluate your church, you must make sure that they have access to your bylaws. When they submit their initial application to the church for membership, located right above the signature line, it must read, "I have completely read and understand the bylaws of the community and faithfully pledge to honor the bylaws without reservation."

5

Building the Membership

In "Chapter 1 – Surviving with Our Heritage," we presented two funding strategies, incremental self-funding and turnkey funding. Both strategies require the use of one or more church retreats to build the membership of a church farm and church ranch.

- **Incremental Self-funding:** A bootstrap strategy for dreamers seeking to fund a church through a series of small-capitalization tranches (portions) from founders and other sources. The first acquisition will be a hobby farm which will function as a retreat and be used to build the membership.
- **Turnkey Funding:** A single funding source is used to build one or more retreats for membership development and then a full-scale permanent church ranch with 150 members in residence.

With both of these efforts, once the facilities are ready for use, a complete mission-ready membership will then take up residence and begin operations.

When building your church membership with either strategy, the same core concepts apply, optimal community size and the advantage of human capital.

With turnkey funding, those who are funding the community will already have a population of survivors in mind. How you evaluate these potential survivors will be a process largely driven by whoever is providing the turnkey funding.

Therefore, this chapter will focus on how to build your church with an incremental self-funding strategy.

Optimal Community Size

Is there a "best" or "right'" number of people for a successful survival church? Yes, and it is called the Dunbar Number, in honor of British anthropologist and evolutionary psychologist Robin Ian MacDonald Dunbar.

There is Strength in Numbers – Idiom

The optimal size for a survival community as defined by the Dunbar Number System is a minimum of 100 members to a maximum of 250 members. The most cited Dunbar Number is 150, and this is the target for a survival church. There are five very good reasons:

1. **Safety in Numbers:** Let's compare a small band of preppers with expensive assault rifles against a survival community of adequate size, with fifty WW II-era surplus rifles. How does this play out? With preppers, attackers are not threatened by an expensive assault rifle in the hands of a sleeping sentry. That's when they'll attack. On the other hand, the larger-sized group is far more likely to have a rotating shift of well-rested guards. The larger community with fifty old surplus bolt action military rifles is an alert wall of death. If you are a predator, the smart move is to go for the soft target. The preppers.

2. **Stable Relationships:** Dunbar's number represents a cognitive limit to the number of members a community can sustain with stable social relationships. With an optimal community population of 150 members, each will know and be able to relate to the

other members. Therefore, use the Dunbar Number as a guide for building a viable community. Add more than this and you'll begin to have strangers among you.

3. **Relaxed Rules and Norms:** Once your community outpaces the Dunbar Number, it will become large enough to support strangers among you. In this case in order to maintain community cohesion, your bylaws will require more restrictive rules, laws, and enforced norms. If not, you risk creating problematic divides within the church membership.

4. **Continuity of Progeny:** A tribulation can last a decade or more, and if your community membership is reduced to fifty-year-old and ten-year-old survivors, your community will likely fail under harsh conditions. Therefore, to be viable, a community must be endowed with a natural continuity of progeny where each generation is well-represented. Remember, the mission of a Win-Win survival church is to manage resources, raise children, and to be a shining light of hope for all.

5. **Pay It Outwards:** When building a church ranch with 400+ usable acres for 100-150 members, additional opportunities for additional population growth must be available. A viable Win-Win community needs to create an outer ring of smaller satellite communities that surround the core church ranch with multiple construction campgrounds. Selected families can then construct their own shelters using prepositioned construction equipment and supplies. Also, administrative and family hygiene facilities are needed at each construction site. Do this, and you will be surrounded by grateful people with whom you can build solid security alliances.

Should you recruit all 150 members from the beginning? Yes, if you are using a turnkey funding strategy. With an incremental self-funding strategy, begin with a smaller more manageable group and slowly increase it to a point where you have sufficient funds to purchase a large ranch property.

Human Capital and Recruiting

Human capital is a term created by Gary Becker (1930-2014) Nobel Laureate in Economics from the University of Chicago. It speaks to the value of a worker's experience and skills, which granted is a non-quantifiable asset.

While accountants have ways of adding non-quantifiable assets such as customer loyalty and brand reputation to a company's balance sheet, human capital remains one of those non-quantifiable asset things that requires a bit of creative for-profit accounting. However, for a survival church, human capital is something all can see and treasure with every decision.

A viable survival church will be a magnificent talent magnet. People will be drawn to it from every walk of life and with a virtually endless pool of knowledge, experience, and insight. When praying, celebrating, and mourning together, who really thinks of this? Yet, this diversity will play an essential role when planning for and surviving a major disaster.

During emergencies, governments are obligated to serve those who apply for aid and assistance. On the other hand, a survival church must operate as a self-sustaining, gated community with a merit-based vetting process for its new members.

A member vetting process must help you in your recruitment of prospective members while eliminating potential troublemakers, interlopers and disingenuous curiosity seekers.

These rogue actors may be motivated to inject their own issues into the church body. They may also be there to self-promote or to disrupt and sabotage somehow the functioning of the church for other undisclosed motives.

There are several ways to vet prospective members, and two that we address are online screening and personal referral.

Online Screening

Assuming you will initiate this effort through the Internet; let's compare that with using personal referrals. As a general rule, troublemakers and interlopers prefer to work anonymously and to use fabricated online identities.

If you make it easy for a rogue to join, they will, and after that, here is what you can expect as your ranks swell with new members in an uncontrolled manner.

- **Self-Promotion:** Self-promoters typically ingratiate themselves for self-promotion opportunities. One thing to look for is a pattern of congratulatory postings that compliment other members without adding substance such as, "Great post. Thanks for the information." This is how they gain the goodwill of others; so they can pitch to them whatever they're selling.

- **Lurking:** If they are looking for useful information for free, they'll peruse your web site and use what they want. Typically, you'll see their logins through the administration features of your forum or web site, but you will not see them posting. Or, they will only participate enough for the benefit of the doubt, and no more.

- **Identify Theft:** If your online system shares personal contact information with members, they will harvest and steal the identities of other members. They will be especially interested in email addresses.

- **Covert Issues:** When recruiting new members, you're looking for people who resonate with the mission of your church for genuine reasons and have a sincere desire to work with others for the benefit of all. Here is where a rogue will join and not disclose their covert issues. Then, they'll use the church to promote unrelated political, religious, or social issues. These can be the most difficult to evaluate, so be mindful.

Never forget; survival is a very emotional process, and it can turn sane, rational, and unprepared people into pathological liars when things go sideways. This is when they will look you in the face with absolute sincerity and say anything to achieve their goals. You must anticipate and prepare for this.

Now, if you're wondering if all this front end work is necessary, why not wait and see how things develop before going through the time and effort to implement a proactive strategy?

Here is why.

There are two basic approaches to adding members online, proactive screening or post-enrollment moderation. With proactive screening, you invest time and effort upfront which mitigates or virtually eliminates disruptive troublemakers and interlopers, and without ever giving them an account.

If you allow for easy enrollment with a weak screening system, rogues will gain access and infiltrate the church's forums, and you'll have to deal with them then through post-enrollment moderation.

Post-enrollment Moderation

If you are the one making the decision and you are the kind of person who does not tolerate fools lightly, moderation is simple. Delete the troublemaker's account. However, if other members of your church are tasked with moderation, you will put them in a position of awkward fairness.

When you have members who are aggressive with others and behave badly, volunteer moderators are typically hesitant to delete an account unless there is a smoking gun. Rather, in the spirit of free speech, they will attempt to find common ground with the troublemaker and negotiate a resolution that makes everyone happy.

Most volunteer moderators will want to do this, and the brick wall they hit will be the egos of the rogues. These characters will use any entreaty for fairness as an opportunity to pursue their aims with myopic focus. This results in your volunteer moderator being hamstrung and unable to deal with these disruptive behaviors.

Now is when this hot potato gets dumped on your lap, and then congratulations, the moderator has chosen to play the role of good cop, and you now are the bad cop.

As a bad cop who does not suffer fools lightly, you terminate the rogue's account. Wait for it; for then comes the fun. The rogue can go from being a Dr. Jekyll to a Mr. Hyde. You'll be inundated with malicious social media attacks. Worse yet, your moderator has become so discouraged that you get a message from them, "I'm stepping down as a moderator because I'm obviously not good at this."

Therefore, by waiting to see what develops in a case like this, you could end up with a "twofer" and lose a moderator and a member.

If post-enrollment moderation is how you wish to proceed, then know the risks. But, there is a way to mitigate those online risks.

The one thing rogues avoid like the plague is an online vetting process that begins with a financial transaction. The amount which can be small is not the issue; it is the fact that they must disclose personal information to complete the transaction.

Once a transaction is completed, send a confirmation of payment along with an enrollment questionnaire and a few simple questions.

- **Home Residence:** Use Google Earth to visually verify the address. If you get an address for an empty lot or a business storefront, be extremely cautious.
- **Interest in Preparing:** Look for a sincere answer to why they are interested in your church. Serious people will give you a serious answer. On the other hand, something like "I'm kinda interested," usually translates to feckless window shopping behavior.
- **Your Core Belief System:** The last thing you need is folks joining who are into the dark arts or other such belief systems. Ask them about their present faith and to whom they pray.
- **Code of Conduct:** Below this question should be your online terms of service (TOS) for your forum with specific guidelines for behavior. Make sure they answer in writing that they will obey the rules.

When drafting your TOS, here is where you may want to add something like "we reserve the right to refuse membership for reasons of negative affiliations with beliefs or nations currently engaged in violent political acts, dishonesty with other faiths or in any way advocates or supports the subjugation of women and children."

After candidates purchase a membership and satisfactorily complete the questionnaire, you issue them a basic membership with limited access to your online forum.

The next step for them is to complete a second, one-on-one vetting interview with a senior member of your community. Assuming that they pass muster, you then give them full member access to your online forum.

Once a new member has been given full access, monitor them for a few months. You want to know the frequency and number of their logins and posts. As a rule, it is good to see at least one login a week. Rogue members will also post, but their intentions will often become obvious with their 13th post to the church forum.

At this point, you may wonder if this online vetting may seem a bit much, and if so, is there another way to vet prospective candidates? Yes, through personal referrals.

Personal Referrals

If you're a dreamer and use an incremental self-funding strategy, you are likely to do what every multi-level marketing company tells you is the best way to recruit. You start with your own circle of friends and family.

For example, if your goal is to raise $50K to start the church and to acquire and finance a hobby farm for your retreat, you can join with nine other friends, associates, and family members; each of whom becomes a founder by paying a membership fee of $5K.

It is important that your articles of incorporation include detailed rights and responsibilities for the founders, and included among them is the right of permanent residency in any church property. This will codify their position in the church as founders and as leaders.

After you incorporate and secure your first property, you will begin to recruit new church members. As an example, you have negotiated for 400+ acres of land at a cost of $400K.

With your retreat as a tool for recruitment, you need to find an additional 80 new members at $5K each, and you will have enough to buy the land for cash outright. Given that your target is for 100-150 members, at this point you have 10 founders and 80 members and open slots for another 60 members.

So, how do you make the magic happen?

Print plain business cards. Black ink on white card stock with the following:

Win-Win

(xxx) xxx-xxxx

That's it. Win-Win and a telephone number.

If you want to add an email address to the card, never use a private or primary email address. Rather, use email forwarding. For example, the URL for your church web site is lifeboatchurch.org. Your hosting plan will enable you to give each member a unique address such as first-name@lifeboatchurch.org, which then forwards emails to their permanent accounts.

While you're waiting for the business cards to be printed, this will be a good time to work on your pitches, and that begins with what you're looking for in a prospective founder or member.

Sizing Up Prospective Members

It has been estimated that there are as many as 150 different stories of a Great Deluge, in the folklore, teachings and ancient writings of different peoples from across the world. One of them is the Biblical account of Noah and the Flood.

As the story goes, after the animals entered the ark, God closed the door behind them, and the only survivors of the flood were Noah and those with him in the boat. When the rains came and the waters rose, those who had mocked Noah over the years were now pounding on the hull of the ark with their fists and desperately pleading for their lives. Yet, the door never opened.

Now let's imagine that we're in the ark and observing Noah. What we see is a man in misery. He hears the wails and pleas but cannot help by opening the door.

With this in mind, let's expand the story with a more technical, leadership-oriented point of view.

Noah was the builder, commander, and master of a special purpose vessel. God was the owner and Noah's mission was to restore terrestrial life to the planet following a catastrophic deluge event. Everyone on board with Noah was equally dedicated to this mission and had prepared for it over a course of many years.

Conversely, the hull-knockers floundering in the floodwaters and pleading for their lives had only mocked Noah, because they chose not to understand his mission.

What would have happened if Noah had ignored God and opened the door to let them in?

The first day would have been a celebration of Noah's wisdom and kindness. By the end of the second day though, someone among the unprepared will inevitably say, "I do not know what I'm doing, but I know one thing for sure; I've got to be the boss."

At that point, things go political and a newly appointed captain of the ark convenes a show trial; after which Noah and his family are thrown overboard for counter-revolutionary treason.

That night the ark's stores are raided for a huge victory celebration; during which the ark catches fire and sinks. The result is this; the mission fails and terrestrial life is not restored to the planet's surface following the deluge, as God intended.

When working on your Win-Win pitches, imagine yourself as the master, commander, and builder of a special purpose community. One created not for the end of this civilization, but rather, to serve as a clean slate for the beginning of the next.

Please keep this in mind as you recruit prospective new members to your survival church, but what are you looking for?

Skills can be acquired but integrity, commitment, and a common sense of purpose is another thing, and there is only one question you need to ask about anyone you approach.

After you finish speaking with a prospective new member, ask yourself, "Could this person be a useful member of my community." If all you get is dead air, there's your answer. Keep the business card in your pocket, move on, and keep working on your Win-Win pitches.

Remember, your sense of mission, dedication, and sacrifice must always be worthy of a Noah.

Win-Win Pitches

One could say that we live, in a sense, in a world of prospective hull-knockers. You can expect to encounter rejection as you hone your strategies. But once you put a fine edge on them, you'll learn quickly to spot the "tells" of the walkaway, so you do not waste your time.

This is why you cannot perfect your 5-minute pitch in a vacuum. Start talking with people, and never forget that this is a process.

Over time, you will develop effective Win-Win pitches, and here are some ideas to help you get started.

- **Be Yourself:** People love authenticity, so be authentic about yourself and what your church is all about.
- **Be Professional:** Never forget, you're dealing with a topic that involves life or death. First impressions count.
- **Be a Good Listener:** People have their own ideas, concerns, and desires. How you listen will say more about your wisdom than anything else. If you want their full attention, make sure they believe that you've heard and understood them. Never interrupt, listen attentively and ask confirming questions like, "Is this what you mean?"
- **Main Action Points First:** People tend to build a case that leads to an outcome, saving the main action points for the end. This is counterproductive because people lose interest as an argument is presented from the bottom up. Rather, start at the top, and tell them what you're about to tell them, tell them; then tell them what you told them.
- **Ask for Action:** In the world of professional sales, ten percent of the sales force will close ninety percent of the business. There are many reasons for this, but the number one reason is the top ten percent always ask prospective customers for their business which is something most under performers fail to do. When you feel that there is genuine interest and a possible fit, do not say "sleep on it" because they will just go to sleep. Rather, ask for action, as in, "If you want to know more, here is the next step."

Then, when you believe that you have suitable candidates that have a genuine interest - sign the back of the referral card, hand it to them and ask for action. Here is an example:

"We only accept new members by referral, and I'm very impressed with you. If you're interested in learning more, please call the number on this card."

How will you know this personal referral strategy is working for you? When people call using your referral card, they'll already be leaning towards the concept before they pick up the phone.

Then, when a candidate is ready for a real serious conversation, they will come to the conversation with a range of questions and assumptions, many of which will be tainted by prepare to fail public programming. You'll have to mitigate or overcome this failure programming.

Failure Programming

Prepare to fail public programming encourages people to believe that life as we know it will continue indefinitely. Yet, if history has taught us one thing, it's that Mother Earth is not onboard with that plan. This fact is often overlooked as most folks tend to behave as though history started the day they were born.

However, this will be different for those who've come into awareness as a result of prophetic dreams, visions, and premonitions. They will understand this, but they'll still succumb to prepare to fail public programming through the abuse and mockery of friends and family in denial. This will result in their procrastination; even though they see the need.

When a candidate says, "It's all bullsh*t, nothing is going to happen, and I don't want to hear about it," the programming is indelible. Thank them but never waste time on a committed hull-knocker.

Those in awareness who are trapped in procrastination can break through that failure programming. However, rational verbal dialogues will still be difficult.

An alternative to verbal dialogue is what I call tactile emphasis, where you connect awareness in a physical manner to a major technology that defines daily living. In this case, you could use a candidate's own smartphone to break through the programming.

Tactile Emphasis

While there are many doomsday scenarios to consider, they will inevitably lead to the same result, and this is not conspiracy nonsense. It is a warning based on solid science and funded with tax dollars.

During "an extended blackout," as the Congressionally funded Commission calls it, a natural or man-made Electromagnetic pulse (EMP) event will cause the nation's power grid to fail catastrophically.

In order to help the prospective candidate visualize an extended blackout, employing tactile emphasis is an effective strategy to free them from procrastination so you can have a rational, and effective dialogue.

Extended Blackout Presentation

In our scenario you're having coffee with a prospective candidate. Instead of inundating them with facts and arguments, you take a more low-key approach. You begin by clearing the table and asking the candidate to place his or her smartphone on the table between you.

Once they do this, you explain that in a major catastrophe, essential service providers will have contingency plans in place for backup power for blackouts that last a few hours or perhaps a few days or so. However, very few of these have the ability to continue operations during an extended blackout that last for weeks or months.

Yet, most people do not think about something like an extended blackout when we use our smartphones each day. So let's use the candidate's smartphone with the following seven tactile emphasis steps to demonstrate what will happen when an extended blackout occurs.

Step 1: Place your hands on the table, palms up on each side of the smartphone.

Pitch: "Welcome to day one of an extended blackout. Your home is dark, but your smartphone still works, as usual. Hospitals will work, as usual. Water will pour from your taps, as usual. Your toilets will flush, as usual. This is because essential services have backup power systems. Typically, diesel-powered generators with sufficient fuel to operate for three or more days."

Step 2: Flip your hands palms down on the table on each side of the smartphone.

Pitch: "On day two of an extended blackout, smartphone services will begin to throttle down due to automated programming. Voice and texting services continue, but data services, like social media sites, will be terminated. This conserves the remaining fuel on hand for the emergency generator."

Step 3: Place your hand so it covers a third of the smartphone.

Pitch: "On day three, cellular voice services will continue, but texting and data services are terminated to conserve fuel for the tower's emergency generator."

Step 4: Place your right hand so it covers another third of the smartphone.

Pitch: "On day four of an extended blackout, whatever fuel that remains for the tower's emergency generator will reach a critical point, and the only cellular service remaining will be 911 emergency services, and there is no guarantee that someone will answer. All other cellular services will have been terminated by this point."

Step 5: Move your hands towards each other until they cover the entire smartphone.

Pitch: "It is now day five of an extended blackout, and there is no cellular service because the fuel for the tower's emergency generator has run out. The only people able to talk to others over any distances, at this point, are using two-way radios."

Step 6: Push the smartphone back towards its owner and center your hands on the table.

> **Pitch:** "The tribulation has begun and it will be a long time before your smartphone works again as it does today, but it will still be useful as a camera. However, the supply chains for food and basic necessities will begin to break down threatening the very survival of yourself, your family and everyone around you.

Let that last statement hang in the air. This is because the awareness will need to percolate for a while. So, do you push your arguments? No, and neither should you expect to hear the candidate excitedly exclaim, "Oh my, I never thought about that. Now I get it!"

Rather, let the prospective candidate take the next step, in which case they'll either bolt or ask a question. Either way, they'll never see their smartphone in the same way again.

If they still bolt. Let them go. But if they ask a question, you have cut through the fog of prepare to fail public programming. This is the time for an authentic, compassionate, and caring conversation.

What do you talk about then? Plan B and a pathway to success.

6

Plan B Basic Concepts

We've completed the primary necessities. Now it's time to kick the tires, light the fire, and make this dream fly. To launch that effort, you need a Plan B to help to build a pathway to success that will create community consensus and commitment.

Your Plan A is where you live and work presently. Your Plan B is an alternative lifestyle where you will live and work in a permanent all-hazards community that is designed to enable families to survive and thrive during a tribulation.

Before you build a church ranch with 400+ usable acres and 100 - 150 people, you need to build your pathway to success that will foster community commitment and consensus.

Therefore, this chapter will begin with a discussion of the motivational issues when building a community and how to use your church retreat and research station to qualify suitable design team candidates. Then we will construct your first concrete dome structure using the DBS concrete dome method.

For now, let's begin building commitment and consensus for our community.

Small Moves

We introduced the concept of using tactile emphasis as part of an extended blackout presentation, and our example used a smartphone. It demonstrated how a cellular system fails in a series of stages over a course of days.

Imagine this is day one of a blackout, and although everyone expects the power to be restored, you gather your family together and gleefully announce, "Hey everyone, let's drive for four or five hours to our 8-foot wide by 30-foot long steel tube in the ground and lock ourselves in for a few days? Doesn't that sound swell? So, what do you think family? Who is with me?"

This is where the family begins glaring at you. Obviously, this is a hard sell, so let's change the tune.

On day one of the blackout, your ten-year-old daughter starts dancing and chanting, "retreat bug out, retreat bug out, retreat bug out." Why is she suddenly dancing and chanting with such enthusiasm?

Because she is hoping for any excuse to bug out to your Place B, a Win-Win dome community retreat. It has all the wonderful lifestyle benefits of an Intentional Community or Ecovillage and she likes it there. It is green and beautiful, and there are dogs and cats, rabbits, goats, fish and gardens, lots of cool things to do, and kind and friendly people that she feels safe with. What's not to like?

The take away? When formulating your Plan B, the pathway to success begins with you thinking more like a tour operator pitching an exciting travel destination, rather than a prepper pitching an 8 foot wide by 30-foot long steel tube in the ground.

Here are the fundamental differences between Win-Win and prepper strategies.

- **Prepper Strategy:** Prepper strategies are about a difference of kind. Your Plan A is the familiar way your life works today. Your Plan B begins with a terrifying departure from that familiar and comfortable world to a dark and damp, spartan shelter, and under the worst of conditions.
- **Win-Win Strategy:** The pathway to success is about a difference of degree – not kind. Instead of jumping from Plan A to a stark and minimalist Plan B setting, a Win-Win community offers a smoother transition to Plan B. In other words, while others are hitting walls, Win-Wins are going over speed bumps.

When you find a survival destination that is worth the trip, the battle is half won. To win the other half, you need a starting destination that is a few hours outside the city. This is your next step after you have incorporated your church and completed the bylaws.

Retreat Reconnaissance

Once the paperwork is done, you and your fellow founders will begin looking for prospective members and suitable properties for your church retreat. When doing the reconnaissance, the criteria for a church retreat is much different than those for a church ranch.

With a church retreat, you're helping people take the small steps that lead up to the move to a permanent church ranch and a whole new way of living.

Whether you are using the turnkey funding or incremental self-funding strategies, you should still build a retreat first. The actual location of your church's ranch, whether you already have one or still have to acquire one, remains on a need-to-know basis until prospective candidates are offered and accept membership in the church. But for now, let's address the essential reconnaissance criteria for a church retreat:

- **Property:** 4+ usable acres in an attractive, scenic, and quiet setting with an existing farmhouse, barn, and other useful outbuildings. The ideal property will be situated in an unincorporated area of a county and have electric service, a working water well, a well-maintained septic system, and reliable internet service.
- **Boundary:** You want a retreat property that is surrounded by private properties. This will give you the option to expand your retreat through the acquisition of the adjacent properties should they become available. Also, you need a property with frontage on a county-maintained road with two ways into and out of the property and no easements or covenants.
- **Shape:** A square property provides a lot of options for layout and the addition of new structures. Whereas, properties that are narrow and long are difficult to maximize. Also, no matter where you are on the property, you never want to see a clear line of sight to hilltop homes as these will often be absentee owner rentals or vacation homes. During a tribulation, they'll become squatter magnets, and this could turn into a real problem if they are predatory or aggressive.
- **Terrain:** Look for rolling hills, tall trees, soft earth, and lots of water. Springs and creeks that flow year-round are also desirable as well as an unobstructed view to the south and southwest for solar power.
- **Physical Location:** It should be a two to three-hour drive from the nearest metropolitan area and no less than 100 miles downwind or 50 miles upwind of any nuclear facility. Your location should also be at least 150 miles away from any large body of water or a major fault line.
- **Elevation:** While you will principally rely on indoor farming systems for food production during a tribulation; the ability to plant and grow in raised bed plots and fields will be a plus. Therefore, the ideal location for a church retreat will be in the foothills of a major mountain range at an elevation of 2,000' to 4,000'. Remember, elevations above 5,000' require high-altitude farming methods with shorter growing seasons.

1. **Permitting:** As a general rule, permitting a professionally engineered project will be easier in a conservative red state than in progressive/liberal blue states. California is the worst state in the USA for permitting, and sadly, it is also the one most at risk.

> Yet, ask contractors about building in California, and just watch their eyes roll up as they moan, “Oh no. Not California!” The reason is excessive bureaucracy. But, as growing food insecurity fuels public concerns, that may improve.

Later, we’ll delve more deeply into other reconnaissance strategy criteria for both church retreats and ranches. For now, we have enough to discuss the three basic Win-Win dome configurations, with a focus on the configuration that you’ll want to use for your retreat.

Basic Win-Win Dome Configurations

When constructing domes on church properties, there are four basic Win-Win all-hazard dome configurations used depending on their purpose:

- **Above-ground Dome:** A concrete dome or dome cluster built above ground on flat earth using the DBS method offers excellent protection from earthquakes, tornadoes, and cyclones.
- **Covered Above-ground Dome:** A covered above-ground dome or dome cluster is constructed above ground on flat earth and covered over with layers of clay, certified clean dirt, and basalt aggregate rock or tailings. In addition to the protection from earthquakes, tornadoes, and cyclones, these structures are also hardened against solar storms, EMP weapons, and meteorite showers.
- **Partially Below-Ground Dome:** This is the covered above-ground option with a twist. If your site is well above the water table and you’ve double-checked this yourself, you can generally excavate to one-half the height of the tallest dome.
- **Below-ground Dome:** The most survivable configuration, a below-ground dome or dome cluster, is constructed on a terrace cut into the side of a hill or mountain. It is then overcovered with a minimum of twelve feet of clay, certified clean dirt, and basalt aggregate rock or tailings. A below-ground dome offers significantly more protection for the same threats as a covered-ground dome, plus the ability to add additional protection from nuclear, biological, and chemical threats as well.

When planning the layout of your church retreat, a community center and other structures such as hothouses, chicken coops, compost piles, raised bed gardens, and a barn for work animals also need to be included.

Working this out in advance can be tricky for beginners because there is no set dimension for an acre of land. Consequently, the two sides of a 1-acre rectangular lot can be any length as long as multiplying one by the other gives 43,560’. Therefore, it can very difficult to visualize a parcel of land’s use with mathematics.

A simpler way to visualize how it’s going to work for you, when doing reconnaissance on a property, is to visualize how many football fields can be laid out on the usable raw land.

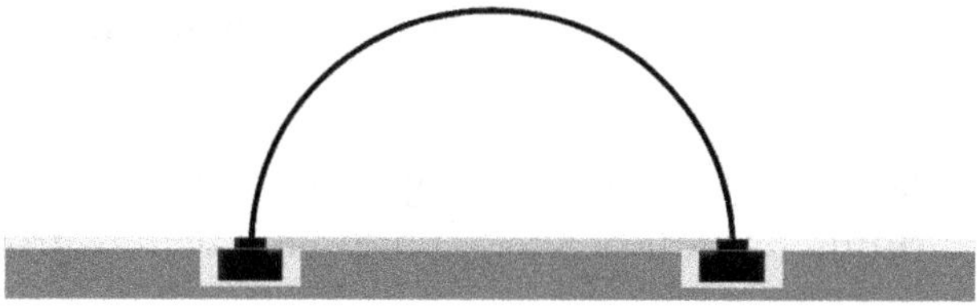

Above-ground Dome

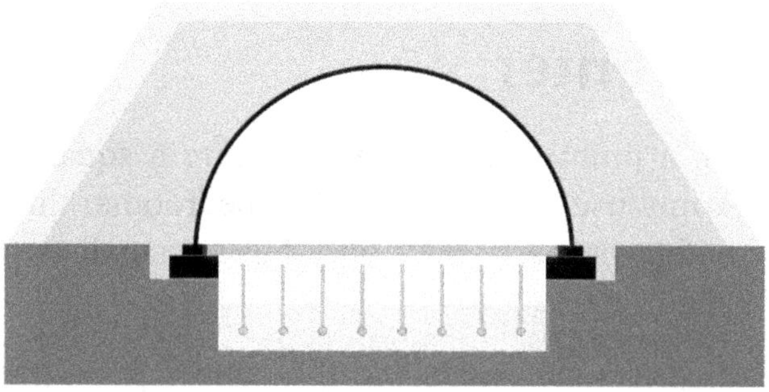

Covered Above-ground Dome

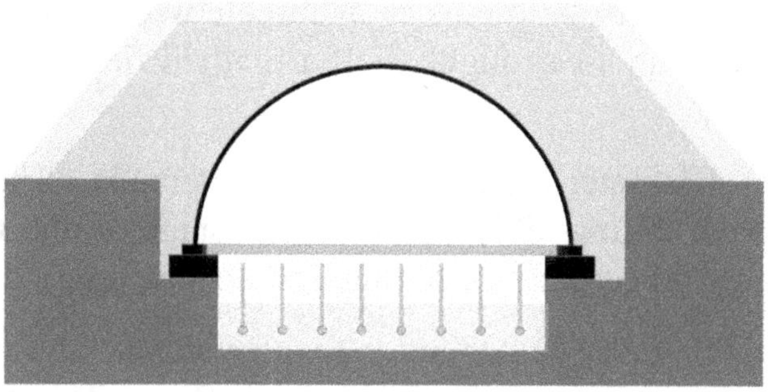

Partially Below-Ground Dome

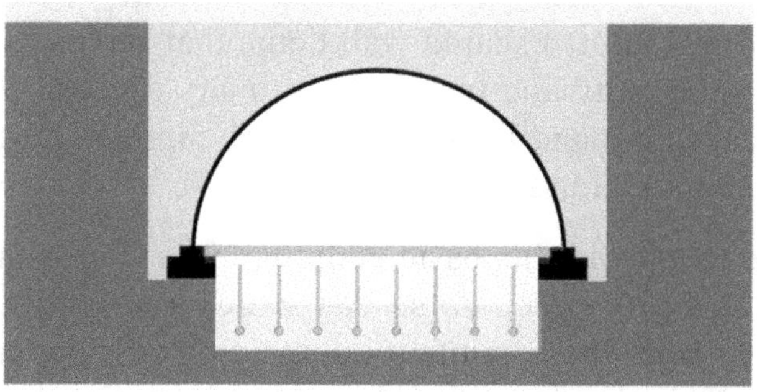

Below-ground Dome

A football field is approximately 1.3 acres in size. Using that as your rule of thumb, you want a property that is able to contain, at a minimum, three football fields in the layout of the available raw land.

Ideally, you want an existing farmhouse, barn and outbuildings, plus three or more usable acres of raw land. Two+ acres are for farming and one+ acre to build a covered-ground dome cluster community center.

Once you've acquired a suitable property, your next project will be raising funds and engineering the designs for building an all-hazard community center on the retreat.

All-Hazard Community Center

When purchasing a hobby farm or ranch, a plum of a deal will feature a squarish property with ample raw acreage, an attractive farmhouse with four or five bedrooms, three or more bathrooms, and a barn. That said, a suitable property may only have a small two-bedroom home with a single bathroom and a tool shed.

Either way, if the property is well-suited to your needs and the county permitting process is straightforward, you'll want to use a reputable, state-licensed engineer to help design your community center and to sign off on the final design.

A basic community center configuration will be a cluster of three covered, above-ground all-hazard DBS concrete domes situated on an area roughly half a football field in size. Your permitting must address the following:

- **Community Dome:** 2-story, 60' Diameter (2,827 sq. ft.) with veranda. The community dome will have a full kitchen, dining tables, and a small stage on the first floor. The second floor is used for class and conference rooms, and also storage.
- **Residential Dome:** 2-story, 60' Diameter (2,827 sq. ft.) with veranda. As mentioned in Chapter 6, smaller private sleeping quarters are on the first floor. Two partitioned dormitories with bunk beds for young adults and children are on the second floor, along with additional areas for storage.
- **Service Dome:** 44' Diameter (1,521 sq. ft.) shared wall dome that serves as a shared-wall passageway between the community and residential primary domes. It will also serve as a safe room, mechanical room, and laundry area with commercial-grade machines. (Dexter is a useful benchmark brand.)

Later, you'll see how easy it can be to expand this basic configuration. For example, you could add a separate 30' kitchen and food processing dome that shares a wall with the community dome. By removing the kitchen from the community dome, you will increase its occupant capacity. Safety is also increased since you can build an emergency fire door to separate the community and kitchen domes and contain grease fires or other emergencies.

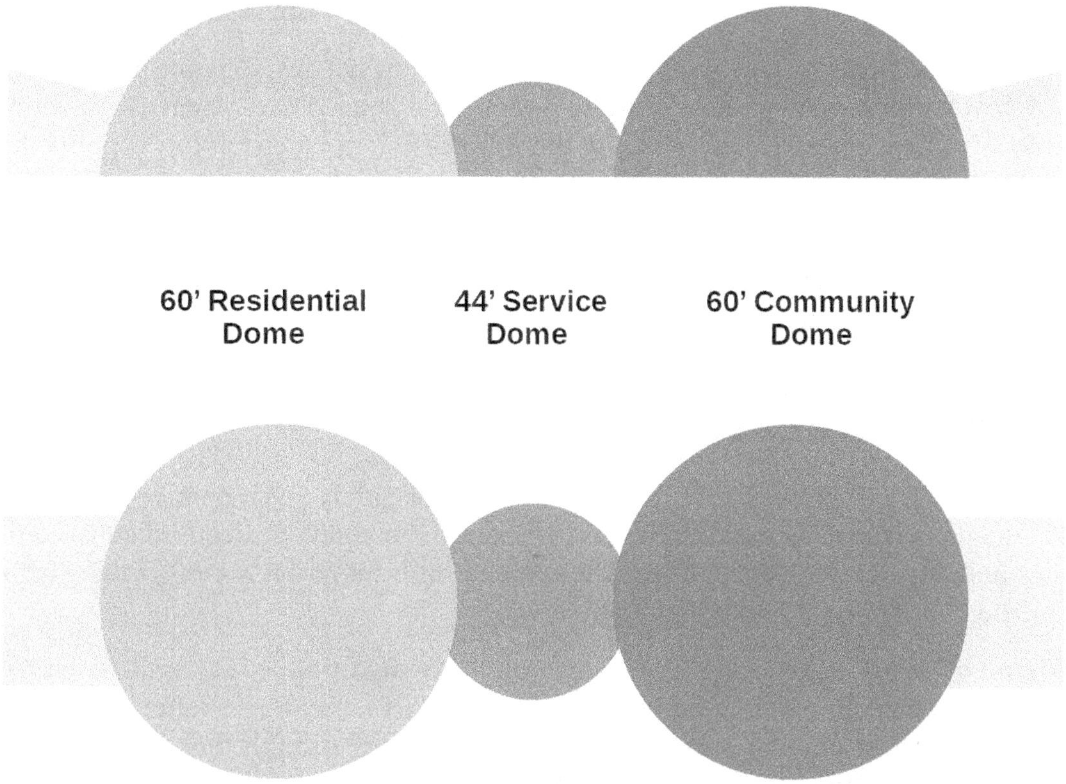
60' Residential Dome
44' Service Dome
60' Community Dome

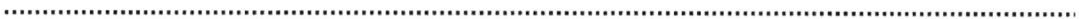

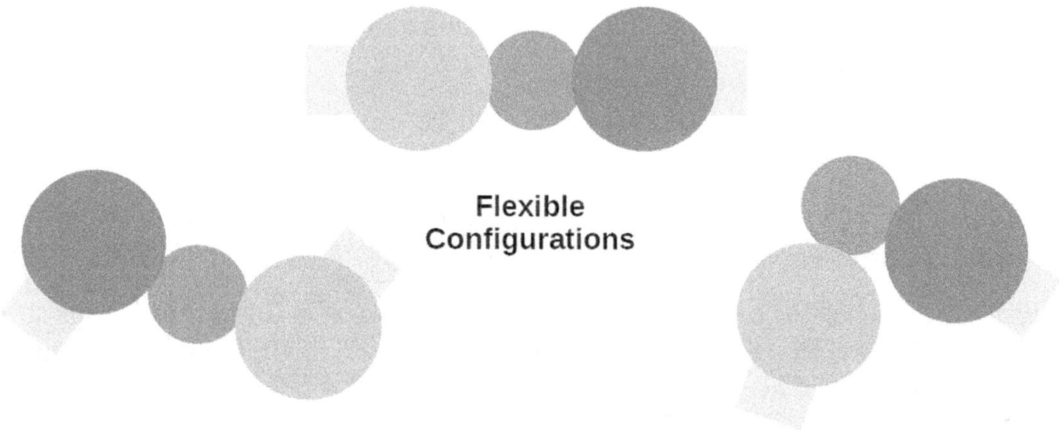
Flexible Configurations

Separate kitchen and food processing domes will enable your community to prepare large amounts of packaged survival foods for internal use. You will use foods grown and raised on your retreat and also work with local farmers, ranchers, and co-operatives.

Whatever your final design, your engineer must also plan for separate water wells, geothermal HVAC, septic systems for all of the domes, and solar power panels with battery storage. Your off-grid power system needs to provide sufficient electricity to support the maximum occupant capacity designated for all structures on the property if the nation's power grid collapses.

Yes, there is more to this than you may have first thought. Consequently, as you begin to organize your Plan B, you may wonder if you will find yourself mired in the classic dilemma of trading comfort for safety. If so, be careful!

Comfort vs. Safety

Do-it-yourself (DIY) "prepper" designs typically favor safety over comfort. Another common DIY mistake is that they are often built without the insights of licensed construction professionals and engineers. Hence, fatal flaws can be built into a DIY bunker that will eventually push the entire project into a nightmare crisis.

This kind of self-defeating DIY thinking partially stems from decades of untried Cold War strategies where bunkers were to be used as hardened but temporary shelters. They were designed to provide just enough protection to keep you alive through the worst of the tribulation. Afterwards, the operating assumption was that you would be clever enough to figure out what to do after climbing out of your bunker. For these reasons, DIY bunkers were often built on limited budgets and tended to be austere when it came to creature comforts.

Win-Win communities, on the other hand, are professionally engineered for safety, quality, and comfort. Things are not done on the cheap. Rather, you find the money and the people to do it right the first time.

The interior of a Win-Win residential dome will be more expensive to build because the goal is not to huddle in a spartan concrete bunker.

Rather, the goal is to create a permanent and comfortable all-hazard homes with family-friendly amenities that nourish mind, body and soul.

To illustrate the need for professionally engineered Win-Win domes, let's look at the one fatal DIY shelter's flaw that causes many of these "prepper" shelters or bunkers to be abandoned long before they are ever needed. It's outgassing.

Deadly Outgassing

Wood products are used extensively when building shelter interiors, and while researching for this book, I encountered several situations where DIY survival shelters had to be repaired at great cost or were abandoned altogether due to formaldehyde outgassing.

The problem was that these DIY builders had used grade C or D construction plywood when constructing shelter interiors. This fatal mistake happens for three reasons:

- **Failure Pricing:** Lower quality C or D grade construction plywood is widely available in large box stores. It is less expensive than A or B grade plywood products, which are not as widely available.
- **Death by Outgassing:** Formaldehyde outgassing from grade C or D construction plywood can last for month or years. The result is that you either bite the bullet and start over, or wear an industrial-grade gas mask, that covers your entire face, 24/7 whenever you are inside the shelter.
- **Misrepresentation:** Be careful of outgassing misrepresentation; as some manufacturers can fudge on the specifications. Always use wood products made in the USA.

The takeaway is if your church opts for a do-it-yourself (DIY) on the cheap and learn as you go strategy, you can rest assured; you are courting disaster; unless you are very diligent in your material sourcing.

On the other hand, if you engineer your domes using highest-quality wood products, the difference in livability will be substantial in the long run. But, is it worth the money?

In order to survive a tribulation lasting a decade or longer, people will need a hope for the future to make it there. Here is where livability is not an upgrade or an add-on option. It is a human necessity because it will inevitably determine how many of your church's members do survive.

Consider this. If you live in a damp, confined concrete box in the ground, how long do you think it will be before members lay their heads down to sleep and pray, "Dear God, I'm so weary of this life; please, take me in my sleep?" If God hears them, they may get their wish, but if not, they will wake to another day of misery.

Does this mean that livability refers to artwork on the walls and piping continuous elevator muzak through the dome? Only in Hollywood. A good night's sleep is what livability is all about in this context.

Another example is the sound of creaking wood when people walk upstairs and across a second-story floor. Multiply that creaking by 10 to 20 people in the community doing that one or more times a night, and you have a debilitating sound issue.

Here is where a little difference can add up to everyone having a blissful night's sleep during a tribulation.

Instead of cutting corners on the interior build out, you opt for more expensive livability materials such as I-joists for floors and laminated veneer lumber (LVL) for the stairs.

The use of these more expensive construction materials will eliminate the sound of creaking wood as people travel to and from the first-floor bathrooms.

Better yet, build with I-joists, LVL and other top-quality wood products and build bathrooms on the second floor as well. This is what livability looks like.

Remember, when building a survival community, survival is not about unprofessional, DIY bang-for-the-buck bean-counting. It is people coming together to serve God's will for humanity, with morality, science, and common sense.

A useful safety and comfort guideline is to engineer your survival community domes and other structures for what I call the DC-3 tough rule.

DC-3 Tough Rule

During the 1920s, the first generation commercial aircraft of the day employed a box-style fuselage design, which helped to keep aircraft construction costs down.

The aircraft industry, in those days, did not fully understand the susceptibility of first-generation airliner designs to metal fatigue over time. Consequently, as these aircraft aged, their box-style fuselages could fail due to the cumulative metal fatigue and with fatal results.

These first-generation airliner accidents whipped up public concerns over the safety of commercial passenger aviation, and the need to regain public trust in the safety of commercial aviation became an imperative.

This resulted in next-generation all-metal aluminum aircraft beginning with the Boeing 247, which was introduced in 1933.

Boeing 247

The Boeing 247 was the first twin-engine passenger airplane capable of flying on one engine, and it pioneered many state-of-the-art technologies that are still in use today.

However, the biggest difference was that the Boeing 247 abandoned the first generation's boxy designs, for a more cylindrical second-generation semi monocoque fuselage design such as those we see today, which is superior in terms of preventing accidents due to metal fatigue.

Metal fatigue accidents still occur with modern aircraft, but it is almost always with old aircraft that have had thousands of landing and takeoff cycles and have not been properly maintained.

The second-generation technology of the Boeing 247 changed everything for commercial aviation, and for a brief period, this elegant-looking aircraft ruled the skies. That was until a Boeing competitor, the Douglas Aircraft Company, introduced its second-generation airliner, the DC-2, in 1934 which was an instant success.

DC-3

To accommodate a special airline request for a long-distance aircraft with sleeper bunks, a wider version of the DC-2 was dubbed the DC-3 and introduced in 1936.

This sleeper version was not a commercial success with the traveling public, so Douglas replaced the sleeper bunks with seats, and voila, the DC-3 became the most safe and reliable popular airliner of its day to operate. It was also the most economical to operate of all the second-generation commercial designs on a per passenger seat basis.

Nonetheless, when the Douglas engineers designed the DC-3, the science of dealing with metal fatigue was still in its early days, and the unknowns were daunting. Therefore, Douglas engineers knew that they only had one chance to get it right the first time with the flying public – and they did!

Of all the design specifications for the DC-3, safety was the overarching design factor. This is why Douglas used a simple design rule for the DC-3, if there is any uncertainty about the stresses, then overbuild.

This was a brilliant strategy and in 1941 the military ordered a new version of the DC-3, called the C-47 Skytrain. Because the DC-3 was already overbuilt, no additional airframe reinforcement was needed for the military version. The only real differences between them were functional, such as a wide cargo door, a hoist attachment, and a strengthened floor for carrying cargo.

Many flight crews and passengers perished when their C-47 aircraft crashed or were shot down by enemy anti-aircraft fire, but the C-47 was still a war-winning technology. It played a heavy role in the success of the Allied war effort during WWII.

Because they were so overbuilt, many of these aircraft are still in commercial operation today. A living testament to the wisdom of building DC-3 tough.

The lesson is that when building survival community structures, the DC-3 tough rule applies; when you're in doubt about stresses, you overbuild.

With this lesson in mind, let's identify the single greatest disaster threat to your community, solar storms (aka space weather), and why you need to create an effective coronal mass ejection (CME) and electromagnetic pulse (EMP) radiation shield for your church retreat's community center.

Radiation Shielding

In Hollywood disaster movies, EMP events, which can result from either natural or man-made causes, happen in different ways depending on the source, but the result is always the same. Everyone's digital electronics are fried, turning highways into vast parking lots for countless abandoned cars and trucks with EMP fried ignition modules.

With a massive Earth-directed coronal mass ejection (CME), death will come knocking, and it will not be pretty. So, let's understand what happens when one of these events strikes your domes.

- **Above-ground Domes:** Above-ground concrete domes offer superb protection from earthquakes, tornadoes, hurricanes, and cyclones. However, there is not a lot of EMP protection for your electronics. For example, should a major EMP weapon air burst occur, the radiation will pass harmlessly through the human body, but unprotected electronics in above-ground structures can be rendered useless.
- **Covered Above-ground Dome:** The principal reasons for building an above-ground dome with overcover, is to harden it against solar storms, EMP weapons, and meteorite showers. The Win-Win community center discussed in this chapter has two levels of EMP and impact protection: hardened residence and community domes and an extreme event service dome which serves as a passageway, mechanical room, and bunker shelter.

- **Below-ground Dome:** The most survivable way to build a dome or any other structure, is below ground. It can be built with the same level of EMP shielding as a covered above-ground dome or several times that. Additionally, a below-ground dome offers the ability to build in more effective nuclear, biological, and chemical safeguards.

When thinking about survival structures, it is easy to focus on high technology features, but with a Win-Win strategy, the core elements of your all-hazards strategy should be as low tech as possible.

The Magic of Basalt

The most precious core element of your Win-Win survival community retreat and ranch is basalt aggregate (or tailings) and basalt rock dust.

- **Before the Tribulation:** You will use basalt rock dust to remineralize and improve the soil and gardens of your church retreat and eventually, your ranch as well.
- **During the Tribulation:** Because basalt is paramagnetic, basalt aggregate (or tailings) will help protect you from EMPs and CMEs.
- **After the Tribulation:** Any number of land-destructive, disaster scenarios will be at play during a tribulation and once things settle down, you may be surrounded by a world of dead dirt. Here is where you'll use basalt rock dust to help amend and remineralize soil. Remember, a Win-Win survival community is not about the end of this civilization. It is being a clean slate for the beginning of the next.

While these benefits of basalt are powerful, the most important is that basalt will play a significant role in helping to prevent structural failures due to the extreme stresses caused by earthquakes and meteorite impacts.

If you're a city dweller and wondering if country living Win-Win style is all about rocks, dirt, water, and poop, you're starting to get the hang of it; so let's take a quick look at rocks because you're going to be using a lot of them.

Rocks and Survival

There are three types of rocks: Igneous, sedimentary and metamorphic, and you'll use all three to one degree or another for your community.

Now let's see how these three rock types will be used when building your Win-Win survival community.

Igneous Rock

The name comes from the Latin word 'ignis' for fire, and this is most appropriate because igneous rock is formed through the cooling and solidification of magma or lava.

Basalt is an igneous rock. Born of fire, it is Earth's most abundant bedrock, and it will play an essential role in the long-term viability of your community.

When you gaze upon a common tabletop globe, the blue areas represent bodies of water, all of which are underlain by basalt.

Unfortunately, basalt is less common on land, so always check for working basalt quarries near your properties. What you'll want to inquire about, is the availability of basalt aggregate, basalt tailings and basalt rock dust.

Aggregate is a mixed crushed rock product of specific size similar to gravel, and your engineer may have a specific construction-related requirement for it. If not, a basalt radiation shield with tailings has two major benefits. The first is that tailings and aggregate are equally effective. The second is that tailings are significantly less expensive than aggregate.

When building with basalt, you will begin dome overcover with layers of clay and certified clean fill dirt. Atop this, you will lay down a two-foot thick layer of basalt aggregate and cover it with topsoil.

This layered approach will be your primary CME and EMP radiation shield, and we'll go into more detail in the next chapter.

When doing the reconnaissance for a church ranch, you will need to find a property with suitable geology for above-ground and below-ground domes.

Sedimentary Rocks

Limestone, shale, and sandstone are types of sedimentary rock. These rocks are formed through deposits of small particles over time, which become cemented and then accumulate on ocean floors and other bodies of water as mineral or organic particles.

With above-ground domes and covered above-ground domes, the key advantages are that you can build wherever the land is suitable, without excavating into a water table.

With below-ground domes, look for what real estate agents refer to as "vertical property" due to the vertical nature of knolls, hills, or mountains. Your ideal property will have some vertical land along with soft earth and sedimentary rock.

Lime is a sedimentary rock, and it will be an essential construction material when building your Win-Win survival community. For example, you'll use lime to make hempcrete, a mixture of hemp hurds and lime that is used for construction and insulation.

While you'll use hempcrete to help insulate, soundproof, and fireproof your dome interior, its main advantage is humidity control. This is important because biological life forms (such as we mere mortals) generate a lot of heat and humidity. We'll discuss this more later.

When checking to see if there are working basalt quarries near your properties, you should also check to see if there is a limestone deposit or quarry located nearby.

Lime kilns are used to heat the limestone and extract the lime. The lime can then be used to make mortar, Portland cement, and concrete. After the tribulation passes, it will be time to rebuild, and this will be an opportune time to build and operate a lime kiln.

Metamorphic Rocks

These rocks are created by transforming existing rock types through a process of heat and pressure called metamorphism. It means "change in form" and a good example is marble. Marble is in essence limestone that has been geologically cooked to perfection.

There are three basic types of Metamorphic rocks: slate, marble, and schist. In a Win-Win community, you'll use them for construction and decorative purposes, sculpture (if you have the time) and paving applications.

When building out your dome interiors, metamorphic rock such as marble can be used for countertops, sinks, and floors. However, while marble is admired for its elegance, there are survival concerns over maintenance, staining, and strength.

To give the interior of your domes the warm and inviting look of natural stone, consider using marble-looking granite instead of marble. Marble-looking granite is a more practical option for your Win-Win survival communities because it is less expensive, more durable and more versatile than marble. However, it is more difficult to work with than marble.

How durable is granite? If you're building a below-ground dome and need to excavate through granite, here is the rule: B.Y.O.D. (as in Bring Your Own Dynamite.)

Nonetheless, of all the rocks mentioned above, none will play a more pivotal role in the survival of your membership than basalt, because you will use it when creating an effective radiation-shielding strategy.

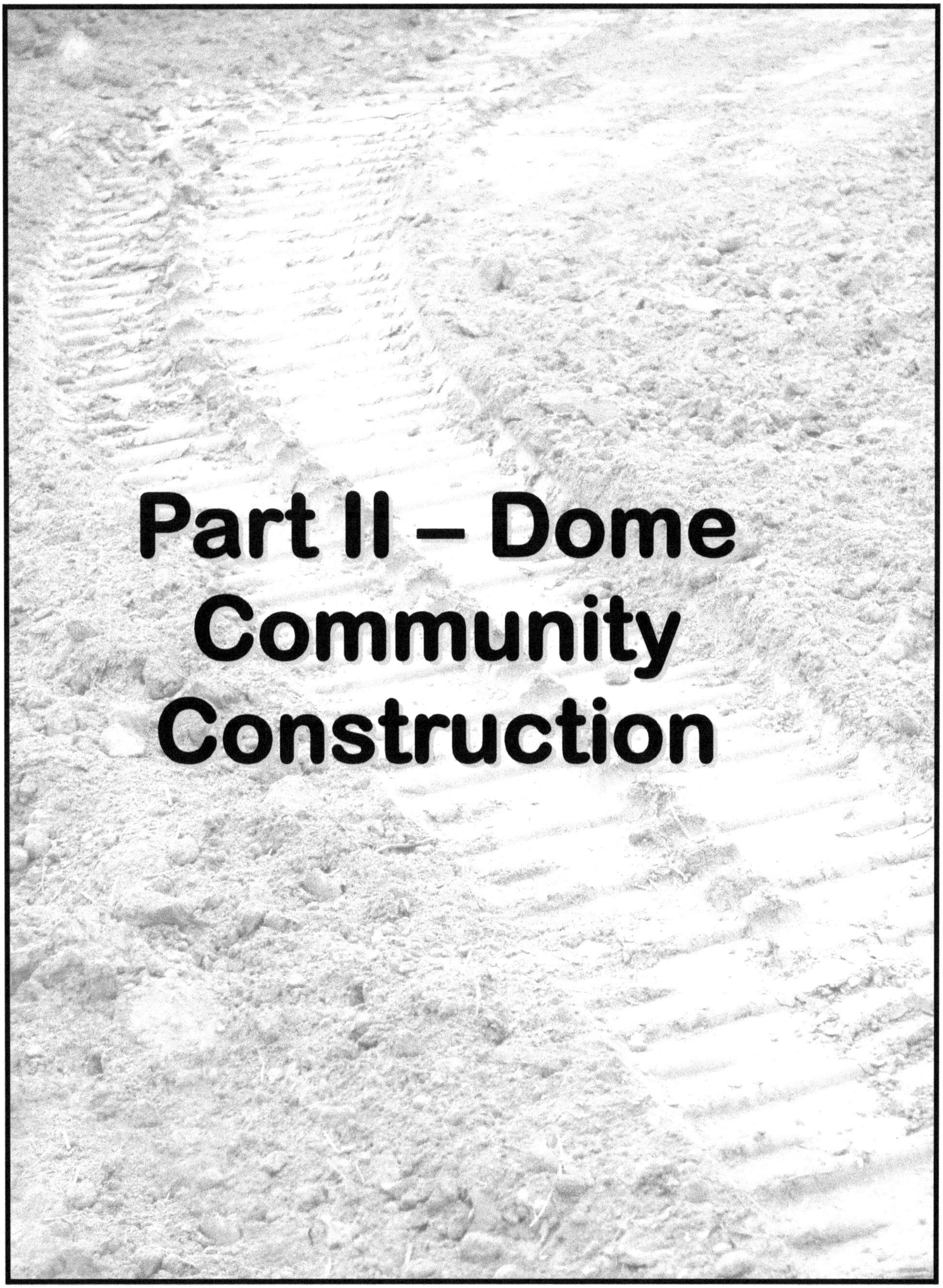

Part II – Dome Community Construction

7

Radiation Shielding Strategy

When it comes to the issue of radiation shielding, the DIRFT rule applies, (Do it right the first time). There is no second chance. Fail here and there will be death.

This is why you need a multi-layered radiation shielding strategy that addresses both natural and man-made radiation threats. However, the science of radiation shielding is evolving, and many explanations offered by experts can be highly complex for those in the mainstream.

Nonetheless, a basic working knowledge of radiation threats and shielding is essential to developing and implementing an effective, affordable and practical multi-layered radiation shielding strategy.

Now, let's consider how an effective, affordable and practical multi-layered strategy can address the areas of: Radiation sources, radiation threats and radiation shielding.

Radiation Sources

The primary radiation source that tops our list is solar storms. They typically begin as a solar flare which is then followed by a coronal mass ejection (CME).

Solar Flare

A solar flare is a sudden flash of solar brightness that results from a large eruption of energy coming off the Sun.

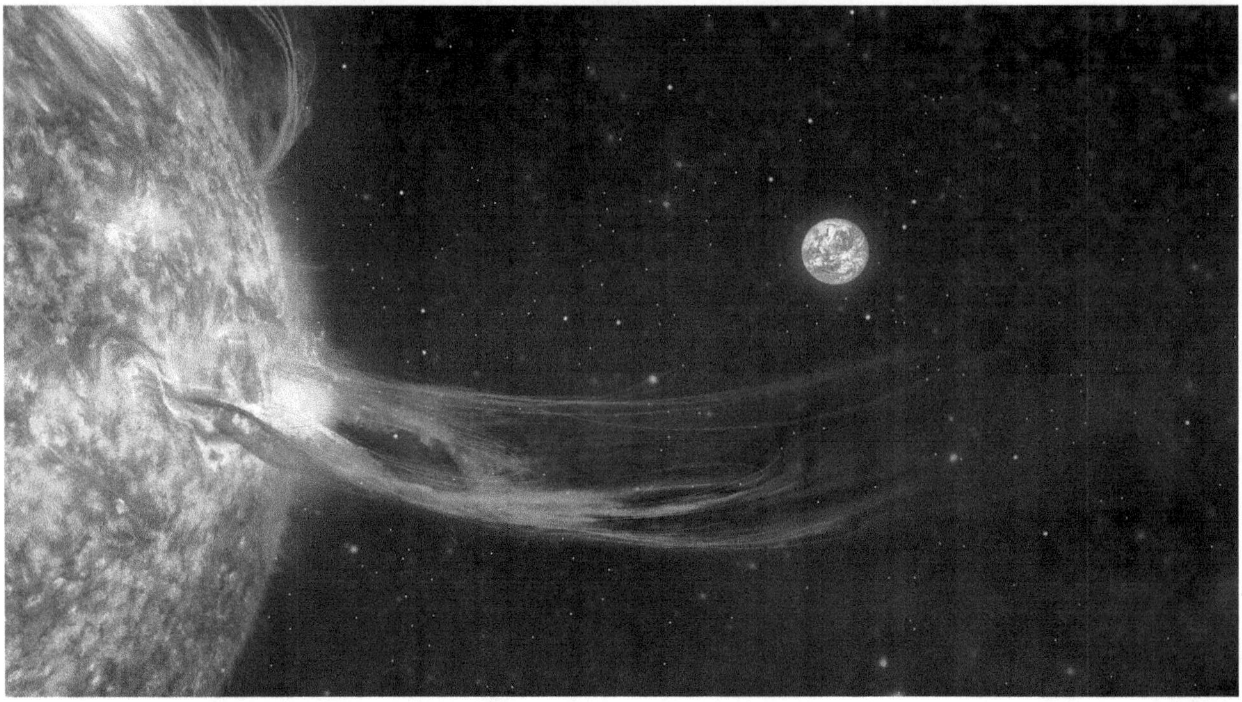

The general characteristics of solar flares are that they can:

- Last as little as a few minutes, or as long as a few hours.
- Travel at the speed of light and reach Earth in approximately eight minutes.
- Contain heat, magnetic, and ionizing radiation forms of energy.
- Cause electromagnetic disturbances that damage communication satellites and interrupt radio communications on Earth.

Of particular note, the ionizing radiation of a solar flare includes x-rays and gamma rays. For this reason solar flares are classified by their strengths. The A, B, C, and M classifications describe storms with low to high energy. The X and Y classifications are reserved for severe or extreme solar storms.

A severe solar flare can cause electromagnetic disturbances which have negative effects on the power grid, radio communications, and in extreme cases even biological life forms. Therefore, knowing why the Y category came to be in the early 21st century is important.

Solar Storm Classification

During the 20th century, solar flares were classified as A, B, C, M, and X. The X category was used to classify the most violent solar storms which were ranked from X1 to X20.

Then, on April 2, 2001, the largest solar flare in recorded history occurred. Fortunately for us, it was not Earth-directed. Had it been, we would have been thrown back to another pre-industrial age.

Estimates placed the storm somewhere between X22 and X40. The strength of this storm far exceeded the X classification and scientists had to create a Y-class mega flare classification for the April 2, 2001 solar storm. Thankfully, it was not Earth-directed.

To see what might have happened had it been, let's travel back in time to the solar storm of 1859, which is also known as the Carrington Event.

The Solar Storm of 1859

Scientists predict that solar storms like the 1859 Carrington Event will reach the Earth about once every century. By some estimates, this storm was the most powerful in the last 500 years, and it generated an Earth-directed solar flare with two subsequent major coronal mass ejection (CME) events.

In 1859, telegraph systems were in their infancy, and this solar storm caused systems all across Europe and North America to fail. Telegraph pylons threw sparks, causing a large number of forest fires, and some telegraph operators were shocked.

This early analog telegraph equipment was very simple compared with the digital technology we use today. Yet, the storm was so powerful, even these primitive communication systems were heavily affected.

For example, during the 1859 event, it only took 11 hours after the initial solar flare for the first CME to strike Earth. The plasma from a typical Earth-directed CME, on the other hand, can take a few days to reach us.

If there is a repeat of the 1859 solar storm today, power grids will fail, and most of the world will go dark for years. Even worse, nine out of ten Americans could perish according to the Congressionally funded think tank, the Electromagnetic Pulse (EMP) Commission.

Coronal Mass Ejection (CME)

A CME is the result of a violent eruption in an area of the Sun's lower atmosphere called the corona. It is often preceded by a solar flare.

CMEs produce significant releases of plasma (a giant cloud of heated, electrified gas) into the solar wind and magnetic fields. Consequently, an Earth-directed coronal mass ejection (CME) poses a terrible survival threat to life because of what it sends our way.

The long periods of quiescence between catastrophic s**olar storms are referred to as "normal" times, and in such conditions, a** CME is principally seen as a threat to satellites, spacecraft, astronauts and communications. However, this begs the question, how will we know that solar activity has taken a turn for the worse?

Let's use a solar storm tribulation scenario to see one possible outcome.

Solar Storm Scenario

When powerful CME's begin interacting with the magnetic field that surrounds the Earth, what will it look like to observers on the ground? To illustrate, let's use a realistic scenario to show what happens should our Sun enter a period of deadly activity.

- **It Begins:** The effects of solar storms begin by causing disturbances called geomagnetic storms, which can cause powerful auroras. Caused by electromagnetism, these auroras will look like the Northern Lights (aurora borealis), but they will begin to extend from the northern latitudes into the middle latitudes. Similar effects will also be observed in the Southern Hemisphere.
- **Last Window of Opportunity Opens:** Initially, there will be a few events with a mixed public concern. This is one of those opportune times to attract church membership and to acquire property. You still have affordable options available to you at this time, and an increasing pool of potential member candidates will be growing.
- **Last Window of Opportunity Closes:** The uptick in solar storm activity continues to build, and now people are witnessing recurring powerful auroras over cities like Seattle, Chicago, and New York. This is when we'll see a growing public concern that we've crossed a worst-case threshold. People will wonder if things do not turn for the better, what lies beyond?
- **Regional Solar Destruction:** After the last window of opportunity has closed, a continued uptick in solar storm activity will result in **solar storms** that are powerful enough to penetrate Earth's magnetic shield. They will randomly occur; resulting in some regions experiencing violent weather and radiation storms while others are wholly unaffected. For those unfortunately caught in the open when a powerful CME hits, the consequences could be tragic.

Hollywood likes to base catastrophic movie plots on science fact in order to create believable scenarios. Such was the case in the science fiction film, *Knowing* (2009).

In the movie, a widowed MIT astrophysics professor, John Koestler, played by Nicolas Cage, links a mysterious list of numbers from a time capsule to a solar storm that is due to vaporize the surface of the Earth.

Here is a useful fact from *Knowing* (2009). After MIT astrophysics professor John Koestler discovers that a huge solar storm is about to devastate the Earth, he says that the only way to survive it is to be two miles below ground. This fictional claim was based on science fact.

For a Win-Win community founder, this poses a thorny question. How do you build a survival fortress two miles underground? You cannot unless you use OPM (other people's money). According to government whistleblower, Phil Schneider, only a government has the power to siphon the wealth of the masses for the construction of a series of deep underground military bases (D.U.M.B.s) for a privileged few.

In the movie, the character played by Nicolas Cage says that with a solar storm of this magnitude, the only safe place is two miles down.

According to Schneider, there is a worldwide network of D.U.M.B.s that are built two miles underground and exist already, and they are supposedly interconnected with high-speed transport systems. Whether this is real or a myth, there is no point in trying to compete with it.

If it comes up in conversation, a quick way to keep conjecture from dominating the discussion is to ask, "I do not have a Golden Wonka ticket to a D.U.M.B. Do you?" That will help put things in a more constructive and useful light.

Geomagnetic Storm

A geomagnetic storm or magnetic storm is a temporary disturbance of the Earth's magnetosphere, and it can last for hours or days. There are two basic causes:

- **CME Solar Wind:** A strong surge of solar wind from a CME disturbs the outer part of the Earth's magnetic field, which undergoes a complex oscillation and creates a worldwide magnetic disturbance.
- **Magnetic Connection:** On occasion, the Sun's magnetic field links directly with Earth magnetic field. Then, charged particles, which travel along magnetic-field lines, can pierce Earth's magnetosphere.

Geomagnetic Storms can severely impact critical infrastructure. They can result in widespread power failures, pipeline corrosion, the shutdown of cable systems, and disrupt or impair satellite communication and navigation systems. A concern for humans is that medical devices such as pacemakers and hearing aids will fail.

EMP and NEMP

An electromagnetic pulse (EMP) is a short burst of electromagnetic energy. Also known as a transient electromagnetic disturbance, a naturally occurring EMP can be caused by lightning or a solar storm. An EMP caused by a nuclear explosion in the atmosphere is called a nuclear electromagnetic pulse (NEMP).

EMP and NEMP events are a profound threat to technology and can cause widespread damage to power lines, telecommunications, and electronic equipment. These short bursts of electromagnetic energy are the kiss of death for unprotected transformers, solid-state receivers and printed circuits.

Thankfully, neither an EMP or NEMP is harmful to humans, but it will cause surgically implanted electronic devices, such as pacemakers, to fail. Hearing aids may also fail. However, the area of most serious concern will be the vast numbers of electronic medical devices used to treat patients in modern hospitals and clinics.

UV Radiation

Ultraviolet (UV) radiation occurs in the electromagnetic spectrum above visible light and below X-rays, and there are three types:

- **UVA:** Photons with a wavelength between 315 and 400 nm, UVA rays can penetrate the middle layer of your skin, called the dermis.
- **UVB:** Photons with a wavelength between 280 and 315 nm. UVB rays have shorter wavelengths than UVA and reach the outer layer of your skin called the epidermis.
- **UVC:** Photons with a wavelength between 100 and 280 nm.

At normal levels, up to 99% of all UVA and some UVB rays are absorbed by the Earth's ozone layer. The 1% of rays that do reach you actually help to promote the production of vitamin D in the body.

UVA and UVB are helpful in dealing with human health issues where the body is under attack by bacteria and viruses, and Doctors have used UV therapy to treat the conditions of psoriasis, eczema, and jaundice.

Under normal conditions, UVA plus a small amount of UVB reaches our bodies. Of particular note with UVB, radiation exposure can happen even on a cloudy day, and the critical time for exposure is between 10 AM to 4 PM local time.

The problem with UVA and UVB is that at high, abnormal levels, too much of a good thing can turn into a very bad thing. However, of the three, UVC is the real killer.

UVC Danger

UVC is the most energetic form of ultraviolet light and is able to create ionizing radiation which damages living cells. Of particular concern is the DNA in our bodies which resonates at a frequency of 270 nm. Consequently, UVC exposure can destroy our DNA through its intense and destructive vibration.

UVC is also deadly to plant life because it inhibits photosynthesis and destroys life in the soil. The result will be crop failures and famine.

According to official websites, all UVC is blocked by Earth's magnetosphere and the ozone layer. Also known as the Ozonosphere, this thin layer of our lower stratosphere surrounds the planet at the height of about 20 km to 30 km and acts as a protective shield by absorbing harmful radiation.

Despite the assurances from scientists that there is no real danger from UVC during present times, new scientific reports reveal that UVC is making its way to within a few hundred feet of the Earth's surface. Here is where ozone depletion is a real public concern and has been for some time.

Initial public awareness about ozone depletion and the ozone hole fueled public concerns in the 1970s, and Americans got a very disturbing look at a dark future in the movie Soylent Green (1973) starring Charlton Heston and Edward G. Robinson.

This resulted in people at the time chanting, "Soylent Green is people," and it appears that was a wake-up call for world leaders. The people were heard and what ensued was the most successful international environmental effort to save our planet from ozone depletion when The Montreal Protocol was adopted in Montreal, Canada on Sept. 16, 1987.

Thanks to a strong governmental response, ozone levels were stabilized by the mid-1990s, and by 2000, signs of recovery were observed. However, at the present rate, the ozone layer will not return to pre-1980 levels until 2075 or later; so let's not be Pollyannaish about it. We're still living under a diminished ozone layer.

Is there a connection between **solar storms** and all forms of UV? Yes, there is, and again we return to the 1859 Carrington Event. This solar flare released 6.5 times more energy than the solar flare that occurred in 1989, which caused a major power blackout in Quebec, Canada leaving 50 million Canadians without electricity.

If another solar storm the size of the 1859 Carrington event occurred today, it would damage Earth's already weakened ozone layer, and this is a real concern. Why? Scientists who study chemical deposits in Greenland ice cores have correlated that solar flare with ozone depletion.

The ice core data from just after the 1859 solar storm indicates that it caused global atmospheric ozone levels to drop by 5%. To put this in perspective, the "Soylent Green is people" chlorofluorocarbons (CFCs) and other chemicals have depleted the ozone layer by approximately 3% in recent years.

Now imagine a time when we are being pummeled by multiple Earth-directed super **solar storms** – one after the other. Things could get brutal. Therefore, your strategy must prepare you for a period of extreme **solar storms**, and ozone depletion must be anticipated along with the harmful effects of UVA, UVB and UVC.

Radiation Threats

Nasty is the only word that describes X-Rays, UV Radiation, Gamma Rays, EMP and Magnetic storms that are spewed by solar storms.

X-Rays

The term actually applies to a man-made radiation, but it is used in science to describe any radiation that occurs within this same bandwidth. X-rays are one form of ionizing radiation, This form of radiation can be destructive to biological organisms and cause DNA damage and mutations.

- **Solar Flare Event:** Class A to Y
- **Time to Earth:** 8.3 minutes
- **Event Duration:** 1 to 3 hours
- **CME Event:** Severe
- **Primary Concern:** Carcinogenic, especially the thyroid and reproductive organs.
- **Secondary Concern:** Long term exposure can cause cataracts and bone cancer.
- **Electronics:** Normally, no effect, but lethal levels will cause electronics to fail.

UV Radiation

Of the three, UVA, UVB and UVC, UVC is the most dangerous high-energy variant of ultraviolet light. Prolonged exposure can result in acute and chronic health effects on the skin, eyes, and immune system.

- **Solar Flare Event:** Class A to Y
- **Time to Earth:** 8 to 15 minutes
- **Event Duration:** 1 to 3 hours
- **CME Event:** No
- **Primary Concern:** High doses can cause first-, second- and third-degree burns.
- **Secondary Concern:** Low doses can cause blindness and skin cancer.
- **Electronics:** Exposure reduces lifespan and degrades functionality.

Gamma Rays

Generated during a solar storm, gamma rays are a lethal combination of a short wavelength and a high-energy content. Like X-rays on steroids, gamma radiation causes serious damage when absorbed by living cells. For humans, gamma rays are the kiss of death.

- **Solar Flare Event:** Class A to Y
- **Time to Earth:** 8 to 15 minutes
- **Event Duration:** 1 to 3 hours
- **CME Event:** No
- **Primary Concern:** All X-ray concerns. Gamma rays are far more deadly.
- **Secondary Concern:** Can impair hearing aids and surgically implanted devices.
- **Electronics:** Normally, no effect, but lethal levels will cause electronics to fail.

EMP or NEMP

An EMP or NEMP is a short, fierce pulse of electromagnetic energy that occurs across multiple bandwidths. The shorter the pulse, the more severe it becomes. While devastating to electronic devices, it passes harmlessly through living cells.

- **Solar Flare Event:** Class X and Y only
- **Time to Earth:** 8 to 15 minutes
- **Event Duration:** <1 minute
- **CME Event:** No
- **Primary Concern:** Failure of medical electronics in hospitals and clinics.
- **Secondary Concern:** Can impair hearing aids and surgically implanted devices.
- **Electronics:** For unprotected electronics, it is the kiss of death.

Magnetic Storm

Storms are caused when charged particles from a CME impact upon the outer part of the Earth's magnetic field and create a worldwide magnetic disturbance.

- **CME Event:** Yes
- **CME Time to Earth:** 17.5 to 48 hours
- **CME Event Duration:** 24 to 48 hours
- **Solar Flare Event:** No
- **Primary Concern:** Medical electronics in hospitals and clinics are impaired.
- **Secondary Concern:** Can impair hearing aids and surgically implanted devices.
- **Electronics:** All communications will be diminished or disabled.

When you take a step back to get the big picture, these radiation concerns can be overwhelming. Where do you begin? What do you do? Is there a way to be confident that you're doing the right thing? You'll need a simple and consistent strategy.

Radiation Shielding Strategy

With medical and commercial radiation shielding applications, the need is usually intermittent. However, a Win-Win survival community needs an effective radiation shielding strategy for 24/7 protection, based upon the following criteria:

- **Targeted Threat:** Your community will face a multitude of threats, and most will be automatically addressed with a radiation shielding strategy. In this case, Earth-directed, Y-class flares with one or more CME's that result in damage to the ozone layer and magnetosphere intrusions.
- **Threat Duration:** An EMP or NEMP event will occur in less than a minute, and the radiation will pass harmlessly through living cells. However, the one-two punch of a severe, Earth-directed solar flare with a coronal mass ejection will take days to unfold.
- **Threat Direction:** An EMP that is caused by lightning or a man-made NEMP weapon. does not strike us from the side like wind-driven rain. Rather, the radiation and plasma generated by **solar storms** always come straight down at us from the sun. This is helpful to keep in mind.

For these reasons, the target threat to your community will be from solar storms powerful enough to penetrate Earth's magnetic shield. With this as your focus, you can develop an effective radiation shielding strategy that is based on an 8-18 solar storm plan.

8-18 Solar Storm Plan

When formulating a solar storm plan, simplicity is imperative. It is also important for community members to understand that preparing for all possible threats is something only governments can do, and then, with limited success. In other words, be realistic.

A good tool for radiation shielding is what I call the "8-18 Solar Storm Plan." This plan is based on an Earth-directed solar storm beginning with a severe X-class or Y-class solar flare which is then followed by one or more CMEs.

Eight minutes after the solar storm erupts, gamma radiation from that solar flare will begin to penetrate your body like nuclear shotgun pellets, and this deadly shower can last up to three hours. Assuming the subsequent CME is also severe, it could strike Earth within a day.

Keep in mind, during the 1859 event, it only took 11 hours after the initial solar flare for the first CME to strike Earth. However, a more practical event to base this plan on is the April 2, 2001 solar storm.

Thankfully for us, the solar storm of April 2, 2001 was not Earth-directed. It was the largest solar flare ever recorded. It was the first Y-class mega flare. Estimates placed this storm somewhere between X22 and X40, which exceeding the maximum X20 classification.

The plasma from that CME traveled at a speed of 7.2 million kilometers per hour, and had the storm been Earth-directed, the plasma would have arrived a little over 20 hours after the initial solar flare. Therefore, a reasonable assumption is to expect that a severe CME could strike the Earth's magnetic fields following the solar flare in as little as 18 hours.

For these reasons, an 8-18 solar storm plan requires that you address two separate threat phases, the solar flare, and the CME.

- **Solar Flare Phase:** Most at risk during a solar flare will be the community members who are working above ground and out in the open. Once the solar storm begins, they must immediately seek cover. Therefore, your plan must provide for suitable above-ground shelters, where members can quickly shelter themselves for at least three hours. Once that initial period is over, the community shifts to the CME threat phase.
- **CME Phase:** In addition to the X-rays from a severe CME, the magnetic storm it creates can last between 24 to 48 hours. Because a CME will follow several hours after a solar flare, the community will have time to implement shielding strategies that include specialized concrete domes with extra shielding. These domes should also have a minimum 5 to 7 day supply of necessary equipment and supplies.

Plants are also at risk during a solar storm and must be protected as well in order for you to continue harvesting with indoor farming. During a solar flare, everyone needs to get to cover ASAP, and after that passes, whatever can be done to protect above-ground gardening beds should be done, but damage and crop loss can be expected.

However, your community's principal means of food production will be with below-ground aquaponics farming, which is not dependent on sunlight.

With your primary source of fresh foods coming from your aquaponics farming operations, above-ground farming will be less a function of crop planning and more about using available opportunities to raise above-ground crops during a tribulation.

Timing is everything here because there will be long periods of relative quiescence between catastrophic events. Think of it as a plant-and-pray strategy for dealing with luck and fate.

When you create an effective strategy for your community, there are three essential terms you should remember: shielding material, half-value layer (HVL), and safety structures.

Shielding Material

Much of the information you'll find on the Internet about radiation shielding materials deals with commercial and medical applications. Of particular concern is the shielding material and where it is used.

For example, a hospital technician will stand behind a lead radiation barrier before taking an X-ray. Or, when you get a dental x-ray, if the equipment is old, the assistant may drape a lead-filled vest over you. What these two applications require is dense shielding material.

The most effective dense materials for blocking radiation are gold, uranium, tungsten, and lead. Covering your domes with these materials is very expensive and frankly unnecessary.

There is a range of inexpensive and readily available materials which can give you an equally effective shield, where thickness and weight are not the driving issues like they are in commercial and medical applications.

The shielding materials you'll primarily use to protect your community will be iron or steel, basalt, concrete and dirt, and the most critical aspect of using these materials will be their half-value layer (HVL).

Half-Value Layer (HVL)

The thickness of any given material where 50% of the energy has been attenuated is known as the half-value layer (HVL).

In other words, assuming that 100% of the radiation reaches the top surface of the shielding, only 50% of that will pass through the bottom of the shield. This is why the thickness of the material is as important as the material itself. This thickness is defined as the half-value layer (HVL).

The focus of this book is the HVL levels for iron or steel, basalt, concrete, and dirt. These values vary with each type of material and are based on the shielding thickness for gamma rays during a severe solar storm. The goal is to provide sufficient protection against gamma rays which are the kiss of death for biological lifeforms.

This brings us a new problem. What is sufficient?

EMP and NEMP Protection

When working with contractors, you'll likely hear them cite a common rule of thumb for protecting your electronics from EMP and NEMP, that five feet of compacted dirt will do the job.

Yet, in the data presented above, only 23.1 inches is necessary to block 99% of the radiation. Therefore, even if gamma radiation is the kiss of death for humans, some may argue why overbuild when a few feet of dirt will do?

It is because each type of radiation presents different risks based on its source, strength, and the length of exposure. There is no one-size-fits-all criteria.

This brings us back to the rule of thumb for EMP and NEMP shielding, and why contractors recommend five feet of compacted dirt instead of two for shielding. They are being practical and doubling down on safety, much like playing Blackjack. Why?

They know that two feet of dirt is fine for 99%, but not if that final 1% turns out to be the mother of all EMP events. That may be an acceptable risk for an actuary, but for a contractor, doubling down is the safe way to go.

A different doubling assumption is used with a Win-Win survival community, a backgammon doubling cube. When you want to up the bet, you throw the doubling cube to see what comes up, and the value can be anywhere between 2X and 32X.

For survival purposes, we'll go with the assumption that you've got a Backgammon doubling cube, and it always comes up 16X or 32X. How does this work with EMP and NEMP radiation protection using compacted dirt?

- **Covered Above-ground Dome:** With above-ground domes, you begin with the material's HVL and multiply by 16X. Therefore, when you multiply the basic HVL of dirt at 3.3 inches (84 mm) by 16 you get 52.8 inches or 4.4 feet (1.34 m) of dirt.
- **Below-ground Dome:** With below-ground domes, you will be protecting your community's most valuable assets. You begin with the material's HVL and multiply by 32X. Therefore, when you multiply the basic HVL of dirt at 3.3 inches by 32X, you get 105.6 inches or 8.8 feet (2.68 m) of dirt.

Are these 16X and 32X calculations overkill? No. Remember the DC-3 tough rule, when in doubt about the stresses, overbuild.

As mentioned above, the CME from 1859 Carrington Event only took 11 hours to reach Earth, and following the 1859 solar storm, ice core data showed that global atmospheric ozone levels dropped by 5%.

Since that 19th century storm, scientists have also discovered another very disturbing aspect of CME events. Their polarity.

If the polarity of a severe CME is opposite to that of the Earth (southward from the Sun vs. Earth's northward) it can disrupt our planet's magnetic field defenses, intrude into our outer atmosphere, and then reach well into the atmosphere with extremely deadly consequences.

Since this could be the case, let's look at the different radiation shielding materials you will use to protect your community.

Iron, Steel, Basalt

One thing you will have a difficult time researching on the Internet is the HVL of basalt aggregates, tailings, rebar, mesh, and fiber. On the other hand, material that is good enough to hide stealth aircraft from radar will work just fine for you.

What gives basalt such an impressive HVL is its paramagnetic qualities which, according to some geologists, has an HVL similar to iron and steel.

- HVL 50%: 0.7 inches (18 mm)
- HVL 75%: 1.4 inches (36 mm)

- HVL 99%: 4.9 inches (126 mm)
- HVL 16X: 0.93 feet (0.28 m)
- HVL 32X: 1.86 feet (0.57 m)

When possible, you should use basalt for shielding and strength, in every structure you build.

Concrete

The industry has come a long way with amendments, waterproofing, and other ways to enhance the natural durability and protection of concrete.

For example, a type of concrete called "shotcrete" (also known as gunite or sprayed concrete) is sprayed on. With the DBS concrete dome construction method, the recommended shotcrete mixture is 75% Portland cement and 25% fly ash.

- HVL 50%: 2.2 inches (56 mm)
- HVL 75%: 4.4 inches(112 mm)
- HVL 99%: 15.4 inches (392 mm)
- HVL 16X: 2.93 feet (0.89 m)
- HVL 32X: 5.9 feet (1.80 m)

Dirt

Three types of dirt you will consider when planning your community will be topsoil, fill dirt, and septic fill dirt. Septic fill is designed specifically for filling in and around septic tanks and is only suitable for this purpose.

However, the other types of dirt you can use for your covered above-ground and below-ground domes will be fill dirt or topsoil. Your project's engineering and permitting process are the determining factor. Therefore, before selecting fill dirt of any kind, be sure that you know what you can use and where you can buy it.

This would also be a good time to establish a strong working relationship with a local agronomist before you buy any dirt.

Agronomy is the science and technology of producing and using plants for food, fuel, fiber, and land reclamation. Based on your short-term and long-term goals, your agronomist can help you map out a live soil strategy for your retreat or ranch. I call this "Post-tribulation soil banking." We'll discuss this in greater detail later, but for now, here is what you need to know about these two types of dirt.

- **Screened, Certified Clean Fill Dirt:** Less costly than topsoil, fill dirt is suitable for radiation shielding and filling voids but not suitable for gardening. Dirt is not live soil but can be amended at a future date to serve as topsoil.

- **Screened, Certified Topsoil:** Topsoil is much more expensive than fill dirt, but gives you a two-for-one benefit. It is suitable for radiation shielding and for gardening.

Why screened and certified dirt or topsoil? Regular fill dirt often has debris in it like rocks, roots and large clay clumps. Though it costs more, certified screened fill dirt is free of most debris. This is critical because, over time, this debris can cause abrasion issues with the sealants used to waterproof the exterior of your domes.

Topsoil is free of most debris, richer and has more nutrients than fill dirt, but its content is not legally defined or guaranteed. The ideal topsoil should be a screened combination of sand, clay, and organic material with a pH level acceptable to healthy plant growth.

While some plants require slightly acidic soil and others require slightly alkaline for the best results, this is where your agronomist's input will be invaluable. (Ph is adjustable by correctly amending the soil.) However, when buying screened topsoil, always ask for a breakdown of its composition and never buy non-certified fill dirt or topsoil, sight unseen.

Safety Structures

For your church retreat, you will use a mix of above-ground and covered above-ground domes. Your ranch will have the addition of below-ground domes. All three will serve different roles in protecting your community members.

- **Above Ground:** With the DBS concrete dome construction method, you can build above-ground domes without insulation, called "ecoshells." We will discuss them in more depth later, but for now, your community will use them to build overhead shelters in strategic locations. This way members working above ground are always near an overhead shelter from solar radiation, hail, ash, and ejecta.
- **Covered above-ground:** The goal of your 8-18 solar storm plan is to protect these domes during regional solar storm destruction events.
- **Below-ground:** Here is where you can construct for maximum protection for your community's most precious assets from solar and man-made threats.

In the next chapter, you'll see how to design and build these three types of domes with this 8-18 Solar Storm Plan in mind. In the meantime, one last note of interest before we close this chapter.

The Concerns with 5G

Using medical and commercial applications to develop a suitable radiation strategy for your community can be difficult at best. However, there is a new wave of innovation coming from a fledgling industry that offers new and inventive radiation shielding solutions for Win-Win survival communities. It is the fledgling, anti-5G industry, and its offerings of innovative ways to deal with 5G's electrosmog.

The global communications industry is implementing 5G cellular service. Those who embrace it see a future with super-snappy HD movie downloads because 5G has a huge capacity for fast data. Also, metered Wi-Fi accounts will become a thing of the past.

Conversely, those who oppose 5G are stepping forward to sound the alarm. Their core concern is that 5G uses millimeter wavelengths which do not pass well through buildings and can be absorbed by plants and rain.

When clusters of small 5G cell sites begin blanketing neighborhoods all across the nation, we will see on social media and elsewhere, the numerous concerns about the health effects of 5G radiation.

As other Wi-Fi technologies such as smart meters begin to combine with 5G, this will create a dense soup of electrosmog radiation, and public concerns will rise in response.

What will drive this concern is that 5G electrosmog will have profound negative effects on skin, eyes, heart, immune system, cell growth rates, and bacteria resistance. It also has a negative effect on plant health and disrupts natural ecosystems.

For example, beekeepers report that the bees from hives within five miles (line of sight) of a 5G tower are exhibiting aggravated behaviors. Does this have a basis in science? Yes.

5G millimeter frequency weapons have been under development for years by defense agencies in the USA, Russian, China, and elsewhere for crowd control applications. The US army variant is called the Active Denial Systems. If you are standing in front of one of these crowd dispersal guns when it hits you, you will feel like your body is on fire.

These are the reasons the 5G industry is creating the radiation on the one hand, and an emerging anti-5G industry is rising up in response to it on the other. The result is new and innovative ideas for electrosmog radiation shielding, and interestingly enough, they have found that basalt offers inexpensive and effective shielding solutions.

Granted, the anti-5G electrosmog industry is still in its infancy, but new startups are already working on or creating inexpensive and effective shielding products. Imagine, for example, using a basalt wallpaper in your baby's bedroom to create a radiation-free environment for your child.

Therefore, keep track of the anti-5G electrosmog industry, and where you can support them, because the innovation they bring will be of direct benefit to your community.

8

Dome Design

Safety is everyone's responsibility in a survival community; so, everyone works. Everyone learns. Everyone teaches. Everyone fights. This is why ensuring the livability of your community requires a design effort that enjoys the participation and input of everyone.

Likewise, this is why fathers teach their sons how to raise a dome, and mothers teach their daughters how to make airforms. The obvious benefit is self-reliance, but then, what about that old saying, "Too many cooks spoil the broth?" Why make dome design a family effort?

Because next to radiation shielding, livability is the second most critical Win-Win design goal. Over time, it could be the only reason your community thrives while others fail. Therefore, ferreting out dangerous false assumptions is the first step to success.

False Assumptions

Go to a major sporting event and what do you see in older stadiums? Men go easily in and out of the men's room. Women on the other hand must queue up in long lines to use the women's room. Why is this so?

The men who designed these older stadiums did so largely without the input of women. It only seemed logical, at that time, to provide equal numbers of toilets for women as for the men because more men attended sporting events than women. However, this false assumption, born of good intentions, in fact becomes an inconvenient reality for the ladies.

When false assumptions like this creep into the design of a Win-Win survival community, the result will be the inconvenience, awkward workarounds, and regrets that will diminish the quality of life for all. Even worse in a survival situation, false assumptions can become deadly assumptions.

A Deadly Assumption

One deadly assumption I see with smaller below-ground DIY shelters deals with shelter access. These shelters are typically several feet underground, and access to the below-ground shelter is often through a corrugated steel pipe (CSP), which is typically four feet wide.

The false assumption here is that everyone will be as agile as the fit adult who designed the access arrangement. Is this what a deadly assumption looks like? Let's see.

Access to below-ground DIY shelters is often two sections of CSP with an elbow. The main entrance CSP stands vertically from the access hatch above ground to an elbow connection below ground. In most of these DIY installations, people will need to step down into the shelter on a simple rung ladder with small handrails mounted to the vertical CSP.

At the bottom of the rung ladder, they will need to re-orient themselves in the elbow, before going the rest of the way into the shelter via a horizontal CSP.

During a dangerous event, the family will be evacuating to a shelter and in the midst of this pandemonium, they'll need to navigate through the access CSP's and the following choke points:

- **Time Loss No. 1:** Twisting and contorting on the surface to enter the opening of the vertical CSP without handholds will be difficult and time-consuming for those with limited mobility.
- **Time Loss No. 2:** Simple rung ladders are unsuitable for those with limited mobility issues. Hence, loved ones may need to be lowered with a safety line as they do their best to negotiate the rung ladder while descending the vertical CSP.
- **Time Loss No. 3:** Twisting and contorting in the narrow confines of the elbow that joins the vertical and horizontal CSP's will be awkward and time-consuming for the mobility-impaired.
- **Time Loss No. 4:** Getting from the elbow to the shelter hatch will be a simple matter for healthy adults, but in the small confines of an elbow, mobility challenged seniors will need to get on their hands and knees and crawl to the shelter.
- **Time Loss No. 5:** A four-foot wide horizontal CSP will mean having to walk in a crouched position from the elbow to the shelter hatch. Due to the false assumption that everyone can walk in a crouch like a healthy adult, the horizontal CSP has no floor or handholds. Consequently, for those with limited mobility, the crawl from the elbow to the shelter's hatch will an uncomfortable and time-consuming journey over curved, ribbed steel.

When things are going sideways, and everyone is in fear for their lives, how do you mitigate the time lost waiting for those with limited mobility to enter the shelter? Worse yet, what if you only have a few minutes to get everyone into the shelter?

In this case, a loving mobility-challenged grandparent may choose to die on the surface so their healthy family members capable of scurrying into the shelter will make it to safety in time.

This would be a perfect solution to a false assumption turned deadly, but what if grandmother believes she can maneuver around the entrance hatch and wriggle a footing on the ladder below? What happens if her wriggle turns into a fall?

Deadly Assumption Scenario

Imagine that the vertical CSP leading down into your shelter is no different than a standing drain pipe under your sink. Where do clogs happen in your sink? Where there is an obstruction in the drainpipe, the same holds true here.

Should a senior become unsteady and lose his or her footing while moving their way into a vertical CSP, they'll fall straight down to the elbow below, and not much distance is needed for a bone-shattering landing below. The fact is, seniors fall and break hips in this way, every day in America. Trying to do something they think they can do.

The result, in this case, is that you now have an incapacitated senior in terrible pain that has now become an impassable obstruction that blocks a crucial choke point in your access scheme. Your loved one is now a life-threatening clog for everyone above.

Consequently, one or more healthy and agile adults will need to climb down the vertical CSP, squeeze past grandma, and do their best to drag her along the horizontal CSP into the shelter in order to clear a path for the rest. Of course, every metal rib in the CSP will be pounding on grandma's broken hip so that effort will likely take more time than expected.

Once everyone is inside the shelter, what happens next?

The prognosis for seniors with broken hips can be very poor, and everyone in the small confines of the DIY below-ground shelter hears and sees grandma's suffering. This is the type of survival situation that will fuel emotional nightmares in a world gone mad. Worse yet, what if this lasts weeks instead of days? What will you do about grandma's pain-wracked and incessant pleas to put her out of her misery?

What will the adults, who are blessed with good health, and mobility, who built this death trap, do now? In other words, who will take care of grandma; because life is for the living? Not good.

Those old enough to remember the movies from the 1970s and before computer graphics, time travel was represented with a wiggly-wiggly special effect. It wasn't realistic, but just enough for the audience to follow along.

With this in mind Dear Readers, instead of taking care of grandma because she broke her hip in the access CSP, we're going to do the wiggly-wiggly time travel special effect.

Wiggly-wiggly. Wiggly-wiggly. Wiggly-wiggly.

Now, everyone has given their input on the design, and the result is a final design that provides everyone with the confidence to know that they can climb down into a shelter as quickly and as safely as possible. In other words, you brought everyone together and you designed it right the first time (DIRFT).

A DIRFT Solution

In the case of the DIY bunker builder example above, was using a four-foot CSP the problem? No. It was how you install it, and here is the key to a DIRFT access solution that works for everyone in the community.

Instead of installing the main CSP vertically with a simple rung ladder to save money, spend a little more and install it at a 75-degree angle, with an angled ladder. Instead of rungs, the ladder features closely spaced steps with anti-skid rubber tread. The goal is to have an angled ladder that is as safe and ergonomic as an expensive, commercial-grade step ladder.

For added measure, you install two sets of handrails. They can even be the polished, oval-shaped metal handrails which are designed for a comfortable smooth grip.

The first set of oval handrails are attached to the sides of the ladder. These will be the inner handrails, and they will be ideal for small adults and children.

The second set of oval handrails will be the outer handrails. In this case, a polished, oval metal handrail is mounted on each side of the vertical CSP. They will be used by those with mobility issues, where special access is necessary.

You can also add handrails to the above-ground entrance hatch similar to those on a swimming pool. They make it much easier for everyone to have a solid footing on the steps without the need for unsupported gyrations.

Are these expensive concessions to fragile seniors with balance issues? No, because when accessibility is designed into your shelters, everyone benefits, including healthy teens and adults. Smooth handrails can provide a faster and safer way to slide down into the shelter.

Now, let's take a shorter wiggly-wiggly travel through time, back to the time loss list above, and see what happens to our five-point list.

- **Time Gain No. 1:** By adding above-ground handrails at the entrance similar to those used with swimming pools, the process of entering the vertical CSP will be well-supported, smooth, and quicker for all.
- **Time Gain No. 2:** The need to lower loved ones with mobility issues on a safety line is virtually eliminated. Using the second set of handrails in the vertical CSP means that grandma will be steady on her feet and able to descend quickly and safely.
- **Time Gain No. 3:** Adding convenient handholds in the elbow that joins the vertical and horizontal CSPs, will make it much easier for those for limited mobility to transition from the vertical to the horizontal.
- **Time Gain No. 4:** A simple way to enhance accessibility with a four-foot-wide horizontal CSP is with a floating floor, that is easy on old hands and knees.
- **Time Gain No. 5:** Crawling from the elbow to the shelter hatch on flooring for those with limited mobility will be faster and more merciful. It will now be easier and safer for those with limited mobility to pass through the CSP.

The takeaway here is that when everyone is involved in the planning, no one is going to fall through the cracks due to an unfortunate false assumption. But does this planning include the children as well? Absolutely!

Remember, as a survival church, the goals of the community are to manage resources, raise children, and to be a shining light of hope for all.

Children are not unvoiced chattels. They are the crown jewels of your community, and you must protect them in every way possible, and the best way will be to send them out to play.

Go Play

When building a permanent, family-based lifestyle for your community, the physical needs of all generations must be provided for, and two words that best define this strategy are "go play."

What does go play mean?

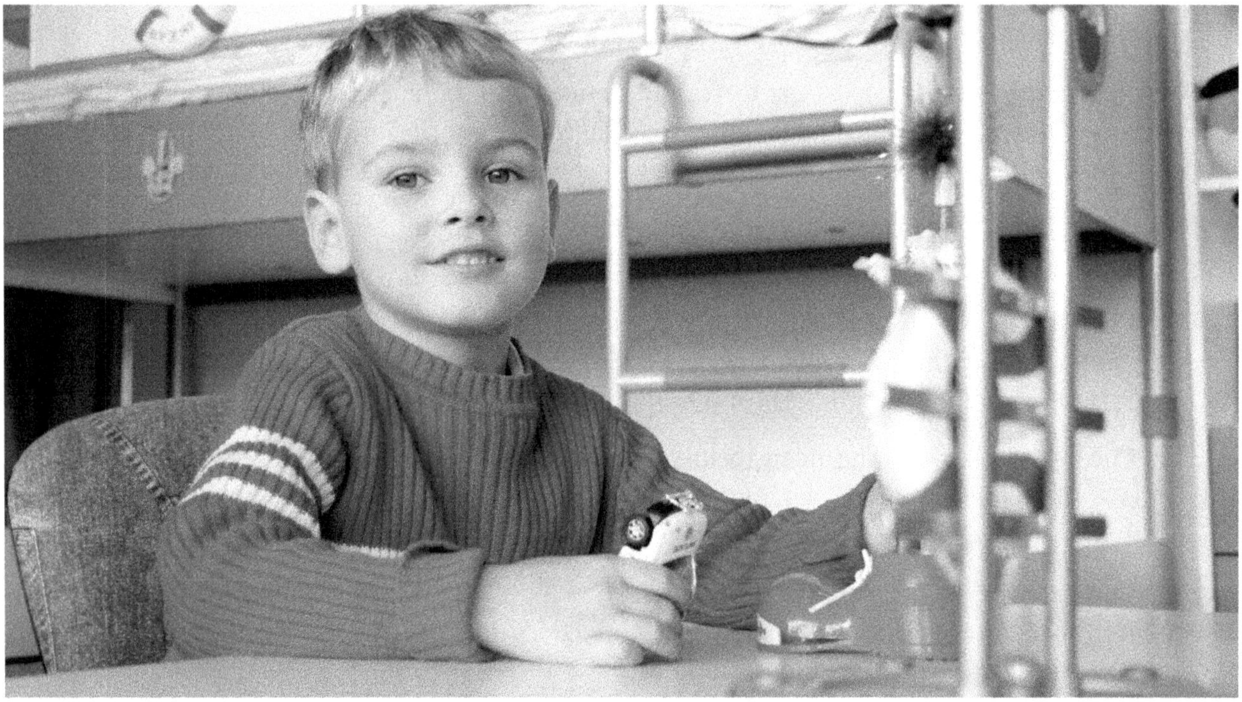

Every youngling in a survival community, as soon as they are old enough to learn, is taught that when an elder instructs them to "go play," they must immediately stop what they are doing and proceed to the nearest playroom as quickly as possible. Once there, they are to wait for an adult to arrive.

How does this work?

Community playrooms are built into the most heavily shielded structures available, whether they are above-ground, above-ground with cover, and below-ground. Each playroom must be attractive, inviting, and well-stocked with playthings for a range of ages.

How do you know the children will like them and want to play there?

Because during the design phase, they were included in the planning, and now every playroom in the community is a miniature Disneyland. Given that these playrooms will be strategically located in above and below-ground domes, what's not to like?

After everyone contributes their thoughts and ideas; now comes the first planning step. Determining the type of dome to be used, where it will be located, and its intended use.

Dear Reader, get out your pencil sharpener, because now you're ready to design a dome.

Dome Types

There are two basic concrete domes. DBS concrete domes with insulation and "EcoShells," a term coined by inventor, David B. South.

We will discuss them in depth later on, but for now, here are the simple differences.

Traditional DBS concrete domes can theoretically be an acre in size and are well insulated and expensive to build. EcoShells are an inexpensive, thin-shelled, concrete dome counterpart that is limited in size.

Regardless of the dome type, when a youngling is told to "go play," they will know to go to the nearest DBS concrete dome or EcoShell with a playroom.

Here are the essential criteria:

- **Residential Applications:** EcoShells were designed to offer an affordable way to build low-cost, above-ground residences for families in the developing world. They are designed for hot climate zones and are David South's gift to humanity. They are the ultimate poor man's home.
- **Outbuilding Applications:** In cooler climates, EcoShells offer excellent above-ground outbuilding applications that include, gazebos, workshops, garages, and storage sheds. In cooler climates, EcoShells can be insulated by adding vermiculite, polystyrene beads, or perlite into the concrete mix. The insulation in a DBS concrete dome will be significantly better than that in an EcoShell, but some insulation is always better than none.
- **Shotcrete Application:** With a conventional DBS concrete dome, the insulation and shotcrete can only be sprayed on the inside of the airform. With an EcoShell, the shotcrete can be sprayed on either the inside or the outside of the airform.
- **Dome Size:** A conventional DBS concrete dome can be built to extremely large sizes, up to an acre or more of land. However, the diameter for an EcoShell is limited to 30 feet or less.
- **EcoShell Shape:** Unlike DBS concrete domes, EcoShells often have a tall shape that looks somewhat like a small silo to allow for the maximum amount of living space in a dome with a smaller diameter. This plus the thinner shell comes at the expense of the EcoShell's strength.
- **Reusability:** Removing the airforms on DBS domes is not advised as they serve as an essential all-hazards water barrier. However, a major advantage with EcoShells is reusability. Because an EcoShell airform cannot exceed 30 feet in diameter, it can be reused 100 times when handled carefully.
- **Learning Curve:** Reusability was one concern that David South addressed. The other is learning curve. It can take two weeks of classroom training to learn how to design and build a large, complex DBS concrete dome. This is one reason why David invented EcoShells. He put a lot of love into this wonderful blessing for the poor, and his aim was to help them with EcoShells. These domes are thinner, quicker, and easier to build, and you can teach a team to construct them by raising the first few.

Up to now, we have focused on DBS concrete domes instead of the EcoShells, and there are specific differences how they are built. We'll address these difference later.

You may be wondering now, how you will use EcoShells in your community beyond the need for gazebos, outbuilding and the like? Remember, in a post-catastrophic world, the community's goals are to manage resources, raise children, and to be a shining light of hope for all.

EcoShells will play a pivotal role in creating that beacon of hope, and they will give you a small taste of what is coming. Let's see how EcoShells will serve a vital role in the success of your Win-Win survival community ranch.

EcoShells and Outer Rings

When you build a church ranch for 100 to 150 members, you will principally be using DBS domes and some Ecoshells for the core community area.

Outside the core area, your community can employ a pay-it-outward strategy for mutual defense by fostering an outer ring of smaller communities around your core.

When survivors begin to ask for refuge, you will select suitable candidates and organize them in groups with their own outer ring construction camps.

Prior to a tribulation event, the community can easily stockpile all the necessary supplies and tools for building EcoShells survival homes in the outer ring. It will also prepare to feed and support outer ring survivors until they get on their feet and teach them to build their own EcoShells.

The outer ring will repay your kindness through mutual defense and by continuing the build-it-outward strategy. Once the first outer ring is established, it will pay-it-outwards by helping the second outer ring establish itself. The second outer ring survivors will then pay-it-outward with support for the third ring, and so forth.

The result is that your Win-Win survival community will be surrounded eventually by concentric rings of allies for mutual defense and survival. Now here comes the good part.

Let's say you want to build 100 EcoShells. All you'll need is one reusable EcoShell airform and the necessary construction tools and materials. Better yet, stockpile multiple EcoShell airforms so the outer rings can be built far more quickly.

Once you have decided which type of dome to use, a DBS concrete dome or an EcoShell for any given applications, the next step is the design geometry. Both types of domes can have many different shapes.

Dome Shape

One of the greatest virtues of the DBS concrete dome construction system is that you can create airforms in virtually any shape. Consequently, airforms can be made for square structures just as easily as domes. In fact, you may find a need for that very thing, but the dome shapes you'll likely use when building a Win-Win survival community are:

- **Classic:** The semi-hemisphere shape is the classic DBS concrete dome and resembles an upside-down Tupperware mixing bowl. This is a tried-and-true strong shape for DBS concrete domes. Build these with confidence.

- **Oval:** Oval domes offer approximately 90% of the vertical load capacity of a classic dome. Instead of being perfectly round, they are oval and resemble one half of an American football but with more rounded ends. With this shape the length of the structure will be longer than its width.
- **Helmet:** I created the term "helmet" to describe a vertical prolate ellipsoid (long axis vertical) dome shape because it resembles a Viking helmet without the horns. Helmets are ideal for above-ground applications such as barns and below ground storage applications.
- **Mushroom:** This is a simple way to describe a horizontal prolate ellipsoid (long axis horizontal) dome shape. This dome shape offers a reliable, no-leak solution for water cisterns and fuel bunkers. They resemble the umbrella-shaped cap of the White Button Mushroom with its distinctive, wrap under edge. With this dome shape, the bottom edge rolls inward just above the pad. This forces the weight of the fluid inside the dome down against the foundation.

Each of these four dome shapes has an optional feature in common, a vertical stem wall.

Stem Walls

Traditional above ground frame structures, such as wood frame residences or garages, use stem walls to give them a solid footing. These vertical concrete footings rise above ground level and are used to set the walls of a building on its foundation.

With an above-ground uncovered DBS concrete domes, stem walls also add additional height for a more spacious multi-story interior.

Stem walls are ideal for EcoShells and DBS domes built above ground and without cover. However, stems walls must never be used with a covered DBS dome due to the risk of stem wall cave-in, resulting in a catastrophic structural failure.

Stem Wall Options

The DBS dome construction method offers two options for constructing a stem wall with above ground uncovered domes of any type.

The first is to build the stem-wall into the airform. The structure would be built as a unit with a stem wall below and a dome above. This is the least expensive way to add additional interior space to an above-ground dome. Keep this option in mind.

The second and more expensive way to build a stem wall works for structures of all sizes and is constructed in two stages.

After the vertical stem wall is poured and the concrete sets up, the dome is constructed atop it. The advantage of this construction method is that it makes it much easier to add extensions to the structure and for the placement of doors and windows.

The obvious concern with stem walls is cave-ins. This is a concern wherever the Earth may push horizontally against any vertical wall.

But what about DBS domes built below ground? This question brings us to a critical design concept, the radius of curvature.

Radius of Curvature

The radius of curvature describes the amount of curve from the base of the dome to its top. When choosing the right geometric shape for a DBS dome or an EcoShell, you will use the radius of curvature to determine the diameter of the dome, its height, and its vertical load-bearing strength.

In terms of a dome's interior space versus its vertical load-bearing strength, the differences are:

- **Steeper Curve:** The sharper or greater the curve will increase the vertical load-bearing strength of a dome. The trade-off is the amount of usable interior space is less due to a steeper curve.
- **Flatter Curve:** A less steep or flatter curve will increase the amount of usable interior space. The trade-off is a lessening of the dome's vertical load-bearing strength.

When designing your domes, you may have a need for a dome with a flatter curve but without sacrificing vertical load-bearing strength. In this case, is there a workaround?

Yes, and remember the DC-3 rule, when in doubt about the stresses, overbuild. Hence, you make the dome's wall thicker. We'll discuss this in more depth later. For now, let's focus on a simple way to express the radius of curvature; call it the dome profile.

Dome Profile

Regardless of the dome shape you use, its profile will be a simple way to express its radius of curvature.

- **1:2 Profile:** A dome that is 150' wide and 75' tall. The classic hemisphere, this is the ideal benchmark profile. It represents a value of 100% for a dome's vertical load-bearing strength.
- **1:3 Profile:** A dome that is 150' wide and 50' tall. It will be approximately 95% as strong as a dome with a 1:2 profile. This profile is popular because it offers a balance between dome height and vertical load-bearing strength.
- **1:4 Profile:** A dome that is 150' wide and 37.5' tall will be approximately 90% as strong as a dome with a 1:2 profile. This ratio offers a more conventional appearance and is the most popular profile for large above-ground domes with a diameter of 200' or more such as churches and sports arenas.

- **1:5 Profile:** A dome that is 150’ wide and 30’ tall will be approximately 85% as strong as a dome with a 1:2 profile. This profile is the second most popular for large domes with a diameter of 200’ or more.
- **1:6 Profile:** A dome that is 150’ wide and 25’ tall will be approximately 75% as strong as a dome with a 1:2 profile. Never use a 1:6 profile for domes with overcover.

Why is a 1:6 profile unsuitable for above-ground covered or below-ground applications? It is because of the weight of the radiation shielding in the overcover.

A dome with a 1:2 profile can easily manage up to 30’ feet or more of earth and aggregate overcover for radiation shielding. With a 1:4 or 1:5 profile, the load-bearing capability of the structure will require marginally less cover.

Is this a concern with your radiation shielding strategy? No, because the earth and aggregate overcover recommended in this book will never exceed 14’ feet. Therefore, you may wonder why not use flatter domes for more interior space. The answer is impact events.

Impact Events

The previous chapter’s focus is the need for a radiation shielding strategy when designing your domes. When building an all-hazards dome it must protect the inhabitants from a wide range of threats. At the top of the list are impact events.

When we think of impact events, meteorites or bombs come to mind, but a more likely scenario could be hyper-velocity winds or an F5 tornado that can drop heavy farm equipment on top of your dome. It will leave a mark to say the least.

But here is where a DBS dome shines. The dome shape actually lends to the inherent vertical load-bearing capability of the dome itself. As vertical forces press down upon the dome, it strengthens in response. This is where we find the magic of concrete domes.

When vertical impact forces such as those described above push down on a dome shape, its shape will distribute the force across the entire structure. Therefore, for maximum impact protection applications, a 1:2 profile dome is recommended.

What does a DBS dome offer in terms of impact event safety?

Impact Case Study

On September 27, 2015, I interviewed David B. South on my podcast, Cut to the Chase with Marshall Masters. We discussed, in that interview, the impact strength of domes by using a real-life case study of a dome built by David in Saudi Arabia in 1989.

David had built thirty domes in Iraq for grain storage and one that originally was to be a mosque but never became operational. It was a classic DBS dome with a 1:2 profile, and it was repurposed by our military as a practice target for low-altitude bombing exercises.

Pilots soon discovered that bombing the dome was not easy; so they started a pool thinking that someone would quickly win. The first pilot to penetrate the dome with a guided bomb or rocket would win the pool.

That pool turned into a living misery for the pilots because it took over a year before one of them actually won. What happened was that one lucky pilot's bomb struck the top of the dome on a small, unreinforced spot.

The bomb pierced the dome and crashed down into the structures center before detonating. The explosion blew the doors off and completely destroyed the interior contents. Yet, the only damage to the dome itself was the point of entry hole that the bomb created.

As David recounted, the debris from the interior was hauled off to a landfill and the bomb's hole was easily repaired. This restored the dome to its former strength, making it ready once again for target practice, but with new rules. After a year of frustration and unrequited bravado, the pilots decided against starting a second pool.

Here is the kicker for Win-Win communities. The typical thickness of the concrete for a classic dome with a 1:3 profile, such as the one described in the case study, is just four inches, and that's not including insulation.

To put four inches of concrete in perspective, it is more than enough for an above-ground tornado shelter or bombing target. However, when building domes for a Win-Win survival community, even more strength is needed.

When you build a true all-hazards dome, the wall thickness needs to be between six to twelve inches depending on the application. The two primary reasons are for enhanced impact resistance and for earth movement events.

Earth Movement Events

We live on a moving lithosphere; where the thin outer skin of our planet is in constant motion. Granted, the movement is geologically slow, but there are moments of sharp, catastrophic movements that are due to extreme earth movement events.

Therefore, the key concepts with earth movement events are opposition and deflection.

- **Opposition:** When moving earth opposes a box-shaped structure with vertical walls, they eventually fail due to the pressures of geological process. Ask anyone with a residential basement about leaks, cracks, buckling, bowing, sinking, flooding, smells, and mold.
- **Deflection:** When moving earth opposes a concrete dome, deflection comes into play much like the bulbous bow of a large ship. As the ship is propelled forward, the bow efficiently moves the ship through the water with the least amount of resistance.

When constructed below-ground and in full contact with the Earth around it, a DBS dome behaves in much the same way, but at a more geological pace.

The classic dome with the 1:2 profile described in the impact case study offers the optimal shape for deflecting earth movement. As the earth movement pushed against the side of the dome, what happens is the dome shape redirects the movement upward and around the dome instead of resisting it.

Therefore, the key to protecting your above-ground covered and below-ground domes from earth movement forces is deflection, most especially in the case of large earthquakes.

Deflection and Earthquakes

One way to think about deflection and earthquakes is the first lesson younglings learn when studying martial arts. A combatant of smaller stature can defeat a larger opponent by leveraging his or her greater mass. The same holds true here with movement and force.

In "Chapter 2 – Enabling Technology," I recounted my observation of horizontal earthquake waves during the 1989 San Francisco Loma Prieta earthquake. That day my car was the only one in a small parking lot nearly five miles south of the World Series stadium.

The earthquake hit my car broadside, and I witnessed a series of horizontal earthquake waves rolling across the parking lot. The rolling asphalt resembled ocean waves of about ten to twelve inches in height. What caused it?

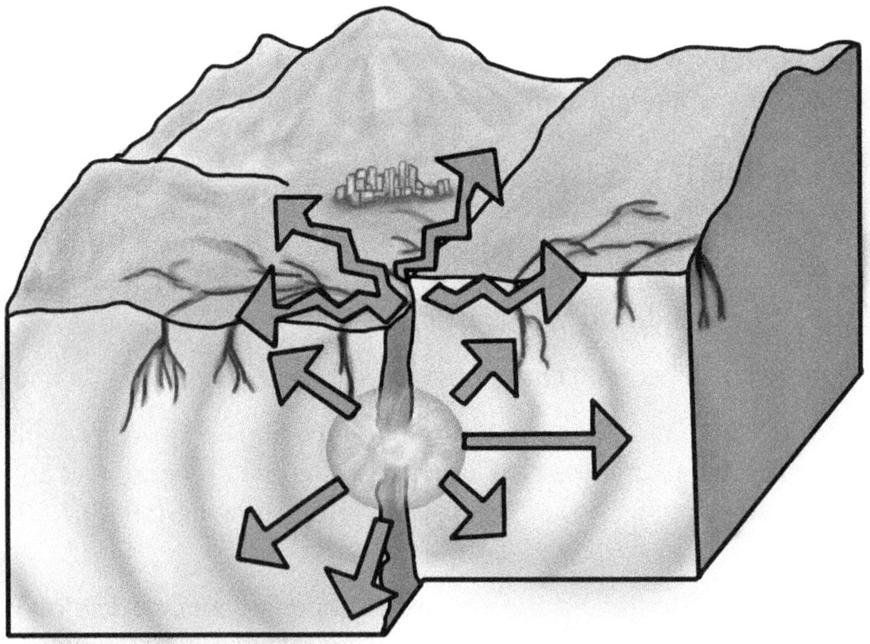

When earthquakes occur, they move the ground in three directions, vertically (up and down) and horizontally in both directions (x-axis and y-axis).

As far as the vertical shaking, modern structures are designed to be load-bearing and can handily manage the vertical shaking forces. What they often cannot handle is the sway caused by horizontal shaking.

With horizontal ground shaking, the top of a structure moves in the opposite direction from the bottom. This creates the deadly sway that causes structures to fail. However, with DBS domes, the shape of the dome eliminates the threat of destructive sway.

Remember, that when you build covered above-ground domes or below-ground domes, there must be no open air space between the structure and the ground surrounding it. While the dome's structure will survive, expect minor damage to the interior fixtures and furniture.

Does this mean that box structures are unsuitable for Win-Win survival communities? Not at all. They can have their uses as well, and they too can be very strong.

Below-Ground Box Structures

Hardened Structures of Virginia Beach, VA builds government-grade bunkers and hardened shelters. One design they offer is a single-level, honeycomb concrete structure that literally looks like a honeycomb from a beehive that has been placed flat side on the ground.

It works great for bees, and it can work well for you in certain situations and is well worth the time needed to study the various designs offered by Hardened Structures.

This design offers a balance between opposition and deflection, due to its extremely thick walls and a hexagonal honeycomb pattern.

Also, another benefit of this honeycomb design is that it requires significantly less earth-work when cutting terraces into hillsides and less fill dirt to cover the structure.

Nonetheless, there is a downside. While it will keep you safe, you'll be living in a box in the ground, and it will feel like that each day. That may be OK for a temporary bunker, but it's a bleak living environment for a permanent residence. However, with a concrete dome, the feeling is entirely different.

The Dome Experience

In terms of livability, the perceived experience of community members that live in your dome will be a paramount design issue. It will have a direct consequence on the long-term viability of your community; it is that important.

If you have never visited a DBS dome, you may wonder how it feels to be inside one.

With this in mind, let's imagine we're inside a roomy residential concrete dome with a 1:2 profile, a diameter of 60 feet, and a ceiling height of 30 feet. This much space makes for a very spacious two-story interior.

When compared to a single-level honeycomb concrete structure, the first thing, that you notice, is how much interior space appears to be wasted by the dome shape.

But is it really wasted?

Not if you want to create a warm and inviting place to live above-ground with cover or below-ground. The first time you stand in the center of a concrete dome, it's cavernous environment will feel natural and familiar in a stone age sense sort of way.

Why? From about 35,000 BC to about 10,000 BC, our ancestors existed for some twenty-five thousand years as hunter-gatherers and cave dwellers.

Consequently, when you stand in the center of a concrete dome for the first time, you will experience an ancient sense of home. This is when memory engrams buried deep within the human psyche for countless generations whisper, "Make a fire bunkie; this is a nice, safe cave."

Perhaps you have already had a similar experience when touring a cavern.

If you have, think back to what you experienced. As you entered the cave complex you walked through narrow passages filled with twists and turns.

Eventually, you enter an immense cavern, and as usual for such venues, they are wonderfully lit and feature amazing things to study. Now, think back to how you felt standing in that cavern.

You know that you are underground and in some cases way underground. Yet, you do not feel closed in. Rather, like our cave-dwelling ancestors, you feel a sense of safety and comfort. (Which sure beats huddling in an open field as predators drag you off one at a time.)

If you plan on spending years of tribulation huddled in a clammy concrete box to save money, good luck with that. Also, when a huge earthquake hits, you may find yourself looking up at the ceiling and wondering what it will feel like to wear it.

On the other hand, you can work with other members of your community and design and build DBS domes that everyone can live in comfortably and thrive.

9

Dome Materials

The purpose of this chapter is to help you make informed decisions about essential dome construction materials; so that you can competently and confidentially direct a team of professionals and church members in the design and construction of a wide variety of concrete structures.

You need to view this moment in time as a precious window of opportunity, and here is why. The Win-Win survival community concept presented in this book would not have been viable twenty or perhaps even ten years ago for that matter.

What makes the Win-Win concept possible today is a fortuitous convergence of tried-and-true ancient technologies and modern state-of-the-art technologies. It is not just any modern technologies either. It is specifically those that have evolved to a practical and affordable level of usefulness. This is especially true with off-grid, renewable power.

The good news is that the enabling technologies and tools you need are now available, and before things go sideways, you have the opportunity to build a fully integrated community with all the necessary technologies.

Do not be lulled into a convenient, formula-driven, static view of the technologies that you use in your community. Flow with evolving products and ideas and be ever-mindful of entirely new ideas and technologies as they become available.

Yes, there is the risk of failure with new ideas and products, but then, this is what survival is all about.

At an existential level, survival is about learning what works and what hurts with one goal, to learn enough about what works before what hurts kills you.

Does this give you concerns about being limited in your options? No need to worry. There is a growing universe of people interested in living with the land with modern off-grid solutions.

Whatever you need to research, whether it is making concrete, amending soil, or filtering water, there is a cornucopia freely available of how-to videos and articles on various websites and social media. People, like yourselves, finding solutions and sharing what they've learned about what works and what hurts with others of like-mind.

Concrete Structure Types

It is important to understand what you'll be writing the check for after someone hands you an invoice. And of course, what you pay will depend on what you're building.

When building domes and utility structures, shotcrete offers the fastest and most efficient way to place concrete. This is not exotic technology, and in a manner of speaking, a custom in-ground concrete swimming pool is much like an upside-down, DBS concrete dome.

The principal components for building concrete domes are:

- **Airform:** With in-ground pools, the hole in the ground is the form. With a DBS concrete dome, an inflatable airform serves the same purpose in reverse.
- **Reinforcement:** Before spraying the shotcrete, the reinforcement material is positioned first. The shotcrete is then sprayed onto it and the form, for overall structural strength. All DBS domes and EcoShells require reinforcement.
- **Shotcrete:** A concrete mix that has been designed for spraying is known as shotcrete. It is fed into a pump and sprayed directly onto the form and rebar.
- **Concrete:** You'll use conventional concrete to pour your dome foundation and floor (pad) and for other functions such as driveways, walkways, steps, and so forth.

As a Win-Win community leader, your focus should be on the materials and techniques for these four principal components. In terms of budgeting, here is where there is a constant temptation to cut corners. For those temped, here is the trade-off.

Being frugal works, but not at the expense of lives because there can be dire consequences. One day people may be digging their loved ones out of the rubble of a failed structure and glaring at you with hate. In that case, do not be surprised if there are those in your community, who conspire to lead an open rebellion against your failed leadership, which could be a bad outcome for you and for the community.

Of course, there are many other considerations and lots of granular details, but for now, what makes the four primary components mentioned above important are the materials used. With this in mind, let's begin with the most important technology of all, the airform.

Airforms

The DBS airform is a sealed inflatable bladder. In the early days, Butyl, a type of synthetic rubber, was used to make airforms. This material worked well but was expensive. Today, airforms are usually made with polyvinyl chloride (PVC) coated nylon or a polyester fabric.

Available in a wide range of weights and colors, the material used to make an airform is similar to the PVC membranes that are used for commercial roofing applications. This is a huge advantage because PVC coated fabrics are tough. They offer excellent weathering characteristics and resistance to harsh chemicals and industrial pollutants.

There are two basic domes that you'll build using airforms: DBS domes and EcoShells. Each uses the same airform materials, designs, and tools.

- **DBS Dome:** These can have a footprint an acre in size or larger, but will require professional expertise to build. DBS domes will be the all-hazards core of your community.
- **EcoShell I:** An EcoShell I is a poor man's DBS dome. It can have a footprint of up to 30 feet in diameter, and it is ideal for two-story, above-ground residences.

- **EcoShell II:** David South created this type for use in developing nations with warm climates. An EcoShell II can have a footprint up to 20 feet in diameter. For survival communities, these will be used primarily for small outbuildings and covers.

The major differences between DBS domes and Ecoshells are reusability and the use of an airform primer. Primer is used to prevent delamination which causes layer separation.

When constructing a DBS dome, the airform is a valuable and integral part of the structure and should only be used once. For this reason, it is highly advisable to use a primer when building a DBS dome.

On the other hand with EcoShells, an airform can be re-used one hundred times or more. For this reason, a primer is not required with EcoShells.

Airform Primer

After inflating an airform for use with a DBS dome, the first step is to tie the airform down securely. Then, primer is applied with a sprayer or with a hand roller on the interior surface of the airform before the insulation is sprayed on.

There are two reasons for using primer. The first is to create a tacky adhesive surface on the airform for the insulation layer, and the second is for the plasticizers that are used in high-tech PVC fabrics.

Plasticizers give the airform's PVC material flexibility and reduce brittleness but at a cost. Over time, plasticizers can migrate or outgas which cause blisters to form between the airform and the insulation. By applying a primer before you spray the insulation, you will lock the plasticizers into the airform material.

The development of a suitable primer became an important issue for David South. In 1995 he worked with the University of California at Santa Cruz (UCSC) to develop a primer product he called Monoform Primer. It was manufactured by Bayer Material Science and marketed as Bayblock Prime FR, which is available through Monolithic Constructors.

Bayblock Prime FR is an elastomeric coating. An elastomer is any elastic material that resembles rubber and returns to its original shape after a deforming force is removed.

Airform Equipment

When using an airform to build a dome, it must be inflated with the required positive air pressure for maintaining the airform's shape during construction. Consequently, all airforms will have an entrance built into them, which will be used for the fans and the airlock. Crews will enter and exit the inflated airform using the airlock.

- **Airlock:** With DBS domes, all work is done inside the airform and and the airlock is used as a construction crew entrance.

- **Mixer:** Whether you're making shotcrete or concrete, you'll need a mixer. Smaller mixers are affordable and work well for producing small batches. Whereas larger, more expensive mixers can deliver a continuous flow.
- **Loader:** Whether you are mixing shotcrete or concrete continuously or in batches, you will need to get it from the mixer to the pump hopper. A front-load skid-steer loader, like the tough little Bobcat, is ideal for this and many other construction tasks.
- **Pump:** You will need a concrete pump to build DBS domes, whereas with EcoShells hand troweling is an option. An affordable option is the GHP 1500 concrete pump by Monolithic Constructors. This is a 3 cu. yd. per hour shotcrete pump that was designed by David South for dome builders.
- **Fans:** With smaller EcoShell domes, you'll need a powerful fan to initially inflate the airform, but once that is accomplished, a smaller fan can be used to maintain the necessary positive air pressure inside the airform. With larger DBS domes, you'll use a pair of large fans to make sure the dome remains inflated, should one fail.

With any type of concrete dome, the concrete's reinforcement is essential because concrete has very poor strength as a tension material. Therefore, the correct type and placement of reinforcement is essential for helping the concrete absorb tension forces.

Reinforcement

After you've built a dome, the one thing no one will ever see is what determines the strength and longevity of your structures. These are the materials used and the manner in which you reinforced the structure. Therefore, it is essential you understand the power of basalt reinforcement for survival applications.

Basalt vs. Steel for Survival

The most commonly used reinforcement bar (rebar) available today is made of steel. This can be a bit misleading because there is steel, and then there is junk steel. Every time you see an 18-wheeler rolling down the highway stacked with crushed vehicles bound on their way to reclamation, you see junk steel; the primary source for most of the steel rebar used today.

With junk steel rebar, the stress cracks, caused by earthquakes or impact events, will allow water to intrude. Once water penetrates the shotcrete and reaches the steel rebar, the structure begins to fail. This is because water causes steel rebar to rust, and this will eventually result in catastrophic damage to the surrounding shotcrete.

Domes constructed with steel rebar will last 100 years under the best conditions. Is this enough for survival? No, because the only reason to use steel rebar is it is less expensive than basalt. However, the additional cost of basalt rebar far outweighs the cost. The reason for this, is earthquake ground movement and shaking.

Earthquake swarms can repeatedly stress structures and eventually create opportunities for water intrusion. Add the stresses of a series of significant earthquakes over time, and rusted steel rebar in a dome could very well be the difference between life and death.

Here are the benefits of Basalt reinforcement:

- It does not rust. A dome made with basalt rebar can last 1,000 years or more.
- It has three times the tensile strength of steel and one fifth the weight of steel.
- It is naturally resistant to alkali, rust, and acids.
- It is great for safety being non-combustible and fire-resistant.
- It has the same thermal expansion coefficient as concrete!
- It allows for more design flexibility by reducing the thickness and spacing.
- It offers superb electromagnetic shielding. Due to its paramagnetic properties, basalt does not conduct electricity or induce fields when exposed to RF energy.
- It is easier to handle. Basalt rebar is easier to cut and lighter than steel rebar.

In addition to steel and basalt, there is also a fiberglass rebar. If you cannot find basalt rebar and time is of the essence, only then is fiberglass rebar an option. While it does not rust, it cannot match the benefits of basalt.

There are several types of basalt rebar you can use. The ones you will likely want to stockpile include:

- **Basalt Rebar:** The term rebar is a contraction of "reinforcement bar." Rebar is used for reinforcing DBS domes, EcoShell I domes under 30 feet in diameter, sidewalks, foundations, and other such concrete applications.
- **Basalt 3-Ply Rope:** Basalt rope is a continuous strand of loosely twisted and drawn fibers typically used to reinforce EcoShell II structures under 20 feet in diameter. A 3-ply rope is preferable.
- **Basalt Mesh:** Mesh is ideal for road reinforcement, impact baskets, and utility structures such as planter boxes, fences, etc., and repairs.
- **Basalt Chopped Fiber:** Used to reinforce concrete, with all the benefits of basalt.

When you hold basalt rebar for the first time, you'll be impressed; steel rebar is much heavier and difficult to handle.

For example, you're building a 6-meter (19.5 feet.) wide EcoShell II dome in a developing nation. Labor, in these situations, is usually more available than materials and a single 100 meter (328 feet) roll of 3-ply basalt rope is all you would need to reinforce this dome.

Given that a 100-meter coil is one fifth the weight of steel, one man can easily lift and carry it on his back for miles to a job site if necessary. Try doing that with a similar amount of steel rebar of any diameter.

Rebar Sizes

Basalt rebar is typically offered in coils and sticks, and you'll use both. The sizing convention for rebar in America is based on imperial measurement which has metric equivalents.

- **Basalt Rebar Coils:** Used for smaller diameter rebar sizes between one-quarter inch in diameter up to one-half inch. They are imperial bar sizes #2, #3 and #4.
- **Basalt Rebar Sticks:** Used with diameters greater than one-half inch and is typically sold as ten-foot-long sticks. These are imperial bar sizes #5 and above.

Regardless of whether you are using basalt rebar coils or sticks, all concrete domes will use the same layout scheme for horizontal hoops, and vertical ribs. However, the type of basalt rebar used depends on the dome you're building.

For Win-Win survival community applications and based on dome type, here are the different forms of basalt reinforcement you'll use typically.

- **DBS Dome:** These are your larger domes. Larger domes will use the smaller #2 in basalt rebar with a closer spacing.
- **EcoShell I:** This type of EcoShell uses #5 basalt sticks or larger for domes up to 30 feet in diameter. With smaller domes, you use larger diameter rebar with wider spacing.

- **EcoShell II:** This type of EcoShell uses 3-ply basalt rope for domes up to 20 feet in diameter.

Another virtue of basalt reinforcement is shipping and handling. Because steel rebar is heavy and difficult to work with, it is typically shipped directly to a large project construction site by the manufacturer.

On the other hand, basalt rebar, regardless of the type, is much easier to handle, ship, and store. This makes basalt the best choice for survival community stockpiling.

A wide selection of basalt rebar samples can be purchased at basalt-mesh.com. It is advisable to have these and other construction material samples on-hand, such as the PVC- coated materials you'll use to make your airforms.

Also, making scale models of the domes you'll be building is helpful for training and recruitment purposes. This is especially true when explaining how shotcrete is used.

Shotcrete

An amazing thing about concrete is the many new amazing things that can be done with it.

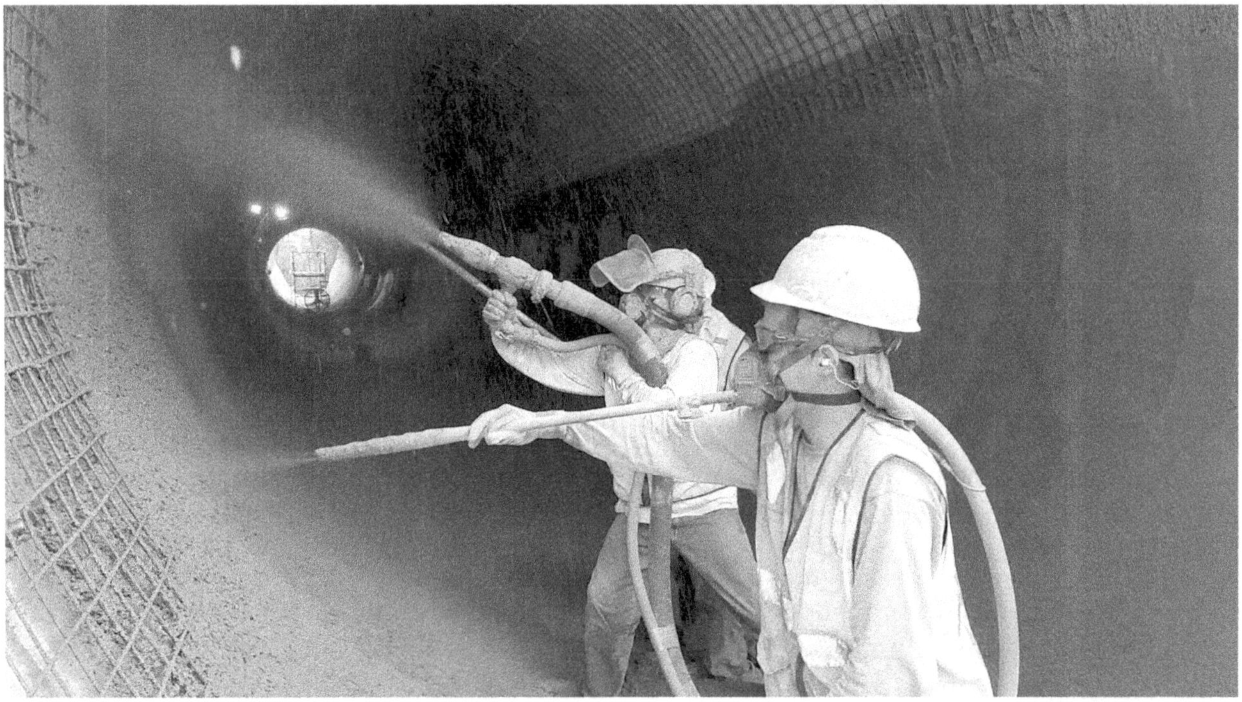

For centuries concrete has always been a strong and reliable construction material. Today, it can be optimized for countless applications by using various binders, additives, sealants, and paints. Those who use it have always sought new ways to make it better and stronger.

A good example is found in Roman concrete. The Romans were able to create buildings, monuments, and roadways, some of which are still in use today. Yet, no modern concrete can last as long, so why are we using Portland cement instead of Roman cement today?

The recipe for Roman concrete was lost during the beginning of the dark ages, and modern types of cement such as Portland cement were not discovered until the 18th century. Fortunately, thanks to modern concrete binders, we can do things today the ancient Romans would envy.

Binders (Admixtures)

A concrete binder or binding agent is any material or substance that can draw the cement together to make it stronger and for other properties as well. Also called admixtures, binders are additions to the shotcrete or concrete mix to achieve certain goals.

With any type of concrete dome, the binder of choice for your shotcrete mix will be fly ash from oil or coal. When mixing your shotcrete, you'll use a mix of 75% standard Portland cement, 25% fly ash, plus water.

Given that there is a wide range of modern binders, why something as simple as fly ash?

Fly ash costs less than other available components. It eliminates air holes, combines with the other chemical components, slows the hardening process, and makes a better, stronger concrete overall.

Fly ash comes as a fine powder that resembles Portland cement. It is chemically different than Portland cement, yet it has excellent cementitious properties. Consequently, when cement and fly ash are mixed together, they make a total, super-strong cementitious material.

There is another reason why fly ash is the ideal binder for building concrete domes.

When compared with simple cement and water mix, a shotcrete mix made with fly ash will harden slower due to the chemical and physical properties of the fly ash when it is used as a binder. Here is where this unique chemical reaction is beneficial when spraying shotcrete.

Spraying shotcrete on an airform is somewhat like painting a new car with different paints. It is done in a series of thin layers to avoid runs and other problems.

Similarly, fly ash slows the hardening process a little, which makes it easier to apply multiple layers of shotcrete, especially on larger structures.

Primers, Sealants, Paints

Primers offer a high-performance way to pretreat porous concrete or other materials such as airforms. A sealant is any substance that can prevent fluids from penetrating the surface of the dome structure itself and through joints or openings in materials.

Here is where the PVC material used by modern airforms offers an added advantage. When used in commercial roofing applications, it can be safely used with a wide variety of primers and sealants.

With uncovered above-ground domes like EcoShells, a good paint will give your dome UV protection and better temperature management while enhancing the dome's appearance.

One thing to remember is that there is no one-size-fits-all solution. Rather, what you're building, where you're building it, and when, will be numerous factors to consider when selecting primers, sealants, and paints.

For example, you are building a dome in Nevada. Most of the state is a barren moonscape, and water intrusion probably will not be at the top of your threat list. However, for those living in a wet state like Minnesota, water intrusion is a concern.

Here is where you would add additional waterproofing using a sealant. A good place to begin exploring for these options is with firms that offer sealants and other products for the pool and spa industry. One such firm is Aquron. Their web-site is aquron.com, and their aquatics division offers solutions for concrete swimming pools made with shotcrete or gunite.

Shotcrete or Gunite

When explaining the DBS dome construction method using shotcrete, do not confuse the term shotcrete with gunite. While gunite is technically a type of shotcrete, the difference is considerable.

- **Shotcrete:** A ready-made mixture of cement, water, and additives are sprayed at high velocity and pressure through a spray nozzle. The point to remember is that with shotcrete, the spray material is in a liquid state before it reaches the spray nozzle.
- **Gunite:** This type of shotcrete uses a dry cement mixture that is mixed with water manually by the operator at the nozzle end. As with regular shotcrete, gunite is sprayed at a high velocity and pressure.

While Gunite has its uses, it is not suitable for concrete domes. It requires a highly skilled operator, is prone to mix errors, and can result in an inconsistent coating and the formation of weak spots.

Concrete

Concrete is the most frequently used building material in the world. On the basis of tonnage, more concrete is used than twice the amount of steel, wood, plastics, and aluminum combined.

As with shotcrete vs. gunite, the terms concrete and cement are often confused.

- **Cement:** Usually provided in powdered form, cement is a component of concrete. Portland cement is the most popular in use today.
- **Concrete:** With basic concrete, Portland cement is typically mixed with water and aggregates (rock, sand, or gravel) and the cement is the sole binding agent. With more advanced mixes, admixtures such as fly ash may be used as a binder to achieve other desired goals.

Whether you are pouring concrete or spraying shotcrete, keep an open mind to new admixtures and concrete variants such as Hempcrete.

Hempcrete

Hempcrete is a mix of cement, water, hemp aggregate, and a lime-based binder. It produces a building material with excellent thermal insulating and acoustic properties.

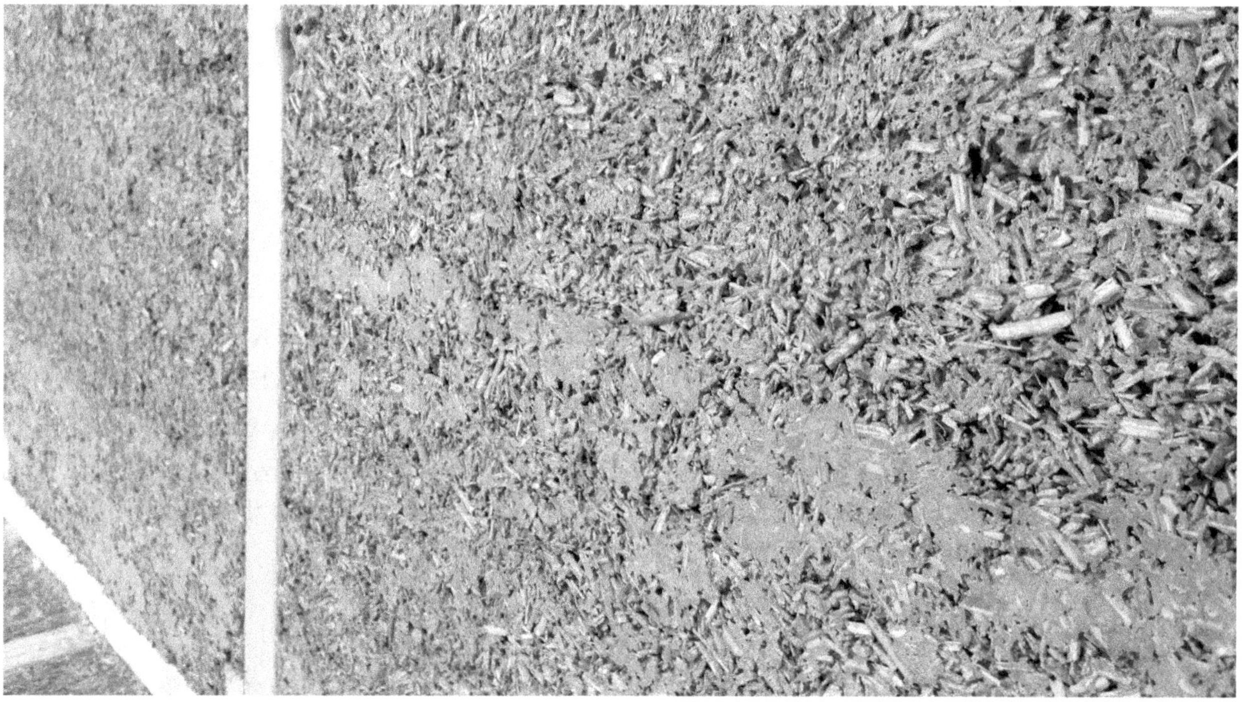

NOTE: Never use Hempcrete below-ground or with any load-bearing application.

For the interiors of an all-hazards concrete dome, hempcrete plays a vital survival role. It buffers temperature and humidity, prevents dampness and mold growth, and contributes to a comfortable and healthy environment.

Is hempcrete a stoner concrete so to speak? No, it is made from industrial hemp varieties with a THC level below 0.2% in the upper third of the plant.

Hempcrete is becoming more popular in America. However, Europe has been the Hempcrete leader for over two decades. This trend started after European leaders saw the potential for green development with Hempcrete. Consequently, hemp is now being used to develop thousands of products and derivatives, and the uses go far beyond construction.

Hemp is now adopted for use in many business sectors including textile, automotive, industrial design, food, medicinals, paper, cosmetic, paint, animal bedding and care, biomass and construction among others. Is this something new? No.

Industrialized hemp was a common crop in colonial-era America. It was used for such applications as paper, textiles, rope, and sailcloth. There is an urban legend that the United States Constitution was written on hemp paper. This is understandable because, until 1883, up to 90 percent of all paper in the world was made with hemp fiber.

However, famous 19th century Yankee Clipper sailing ships, the greatest commercial sailing vessels of their day, used hemp sailcloth and ropes and with great success.

During WW II, our government created a special, national licensing program for hemp farming, to supply rope and other war essentials. Farmers in the South were growing and harvesting hemp which was then woven into rope.

Some of that hemp rope made its way to the Alcatraz Federal Penitentiary on Alcatraz island off the coast of San Francisco, CA. There, hardened criminals were given a chance to join the war effort, and they did so, gratefully and with excellent workmanship.

Their job was to create hemp cargo nets for the troopships. Draped over the sides of the ship, soldiers would climb down these convict-made cargo nets, into the landing craft below.

Without a doubt, hemp was a great cash crop for the farmers during WW II and is becoming so once again; as modern hemp farmers once again enjoy the same profitability today. In fact, when you acquire your ranch property, you'll want to make sure that growing hemp (which is not psychoactive) can be permitted in that state.

10

Design Team and Infrastructure

In this chapter you'll learn to build an all-hazards property infrastructure that includes the main property road and thin-wall accessory structures. Then, you will work through the process of constructing an EcoShell II storage shed and an EcoShell I two-story residence.

Solving the technical engineering issues is what a design team does. Therefore, the goal of this chapter for community leaders is to help them to understand the construction process where they can point to any area on the property and competently say to a design team, "This is what I want here, and that is what I want there."

For the design team, the goal is to detail the process sufficiently for them to know how to engineer the solution. Later, we'll discuss several types of dome structures and their applications, but for now, an understanding of the basics is essential.

Your first task as the founder of a Win-Win survival community will be building your design team. You must assemble a competent design team and find the right person to lead it.

Building Your Design Team

The modern world, as we know it, is dominated by right angles. Our language, architecture, and worldview reflect that.

On the other hand, the language and worldview of a Win-Win survival community by necessity must be very different. It must reflect the mission of your church: to manage resources, raise children, and to be a shining light of hope for all.

To illustrate the subtle differences, let's use language as an example.

- Construction industry professionals say they apply shotcrete and build domes.
- Win-Win community members may prefer to say that they shape shotcrete and raise domes.

The point here is that land flows, bends and curves. For your community to survive and thrive harmoniously with land; right angles should be used judiciously.

Since we live in a world created by right angle thinking engineers and architects, is it logical to ask how one can get these professionals to embrace fully this novel, new worldview? There is no need to, and frankly, it would be counterproductive because this is something they work with daily.

Therefore, the first step in assembling a successful design team begins with recruiting the best right angle, licensed engineers, and architects you can find.

Technical Team Members

Vetting engineers and architects for your project design team is a straightforward process so let's begin with three recruiting givens:

- The church has acquired a ranch site with 400+ usable acres suitable for 100-150 members in permanent residence.
- Full funding to build a fully operational ranch has been obtained.
- This will be a complete, turnkey survival community design project.

Your technical team members will likely not be members of your church and that is perfectly fine as they are accountable and licensed contract professionals.

However, the team leader is a crucial decision. Given the unique worldview of a Win-Win survival community, were this author to make the call to fill this incredibly important role, who would that special person be?

A uniquely talented team leader with a Win-Win vision, who understands the construction process well enough to say, "This is what I want here, and that is what I want there."

Team Leader

Your team leader should be hand-picked and a member of your church. This is your best first choice. In any event, the team leader needs to come from outside the box. This is why your search for team leader candidates must begin on day one.

This position requires a fusion of vision, best-of-class right angle engineering solutions, and the graceful subtitles of a woman's touch. An ideal candidate would be, a woman in her forties with a family and a supportive husband. She would also be a skilled and creative person, such as a gifted custom jewelry designer.

By this stage of life, she would be well-settled and her family and professional skills would help her to manage the myriad of details the team will have to face. Sure, this makes sense, but why the jewelry criteria?

With survival everyone fights, everyone works, and everyone participates. The key to making it work is that men make it possible; women make it worthwhile; and children make it necessary. Anyone downrange of an armed woman defending her family is in deep kimchi.

This is why the overarching goal of the design team must create and nurture the idea of a supportive family, if your community is to serve as a shining light of hope for all.

Like custom jewelry, a Win-Win survival community design needs a vision that is beautiful and inspiring on the outside and strong on the inside.

Community Vision

Custom jewelry is about shapes, colors, form and function, and durability. When made well, its opulence will outshine its inherent strengths and complexity. Likewise, whether you're creating a necklace with matching earrings or a Win-Win survival community, it begins with a visionary and a vision.

For this design team leader, the land drives the vision process. It is the setting upon which all else is perched or embedded. Then various domes, outbuildings, and utility structures serve as a broad selection of gemstones in many different sizes, shapes, and colors.

As a jewelry designer, she will have a talent for presenting each gemstone in a way that enhances the overall effect. Like a well-designed piece of custom jewelry, her final design for the community will flow with the land, so that its beauty outshines its inherent strengths, livability, and convenience.

Like a sculptor who gazes upon a block of marble and sees a finished statue, she will look at the land and see the finished result as well. The rest is right angles.

With this grand and ambitious thought in mind, let's focus on infrastructure and how the design team will address essential infrastructure needs on your property and its roads.

Infrastructure

When creating a master design for a Win-Win survival community ranch, you'll need to build or reinforce existing property roads, sidewalks and walkways, and thin-wall accessory structures.

It is essential that every church property, whether it is a retreat or a ranch, has frontage on a public road that is maintained by a county, is free of, any easements and covenants, and must have more than one way into and out of the property. From there you'll use a system of property roads, sidewalks and pathways to ensure safe and reliable ranch access.

Property Roads

At its core, a Win-Win survival community is a food-production machine and there will be a steady stream of delivery vehicles and large trucks entering and leaving the property each day. Your property's main road needs to be able to handle heavy hauling.

It must handle a loaded dump truck or an 18-wheeler hauling a large piece of construction equipment. Therefore, you'll need a strong and resilient base, whether it is rock, concrete, or asphalt, to support your road's paving.

A sound property road will be critical to the success of your survival community, and a recent development, recycled concrete tire tracks, is just the ticket. This solution came about due to the amount of time, effort, and cost required for maintaining public roads, especially those with well-trafficked heavy hauling routes.

Recycled concrete tire tracks are incredibly cheap and easy to build; yet, they are amazingly durable. They will reduce your road construction costs by 20% and reduce road maintenance by 75% for roads paved with asphalt. Roads paved with concrete have a reduction in maintenance cost of 95% or more. In lieu of concrete or asphalt, you can use gravel with the findings compacted with a steamroller.

The secret ingredient is recycled tires.

This process begins with digging a trench that is approximately eighteen inches deep. While this is being done, you prepare discarded tires by cutting out their sidewalls. What remains is a cylinder comprised of the tire's outer tread.

You'll need lots of tires because you will lay them side-by-side in the trench.

Once the tire cylinders are in place, you finish the road base by filling it with crushed stone to the tops of the tire cylinders. Crushed stone is a widely used material in the construction industry, and there any number of suitable fillers.

After the trench has been filled, the road base is compacted, to prepare it for paving with more crushed stone, asphalt, or concrete. The type often favored by paving companies is crushed stone #57. Sized at approximately three-fourths of an inch, this type of crushed stone is ideal for concrete and asphalt driveways, landscaping, and French drains.

When concrete is used as the paving, weather safety is a concern, so be sure to add anti-skid surfacing. There are different ways to do this, and the oldest and simplest way with concrete is a broom finish.

After the concrete is poured, you pull a broom from one side of the wet concrete surface to the other. There are other options as well, and your design team will identify the best one based on your property's characteristics, local weather patterns, and community goals.

Once your main road is ready, you're ready to build the walkways and sidewalks.

Walkways and Sidewalks

When designing your communities, the first thing your team leader must set in stone will be a wheelchair accessible pathway specification.

Not only is this specification for the benefit of people in wheelchairs, but it also benefits parents with baby strollers. Remember, your church is a survival community, which means that you produce food and babies – and in that order.

An innovative team leader will invite someone who uses a wheelchair to introduce the design team to their world for a day. The objective is a good fusion of experience and practical ideas.

What is to be gained by this?

Imagine a dormant volcano unexpectedly erupts, and your community is fifty miles downwind and right in the thick of it. Consequently, a two-foot thick layer of ash blankets your property.

In this circumstance, moving about the property will be much safer on sidewalks and walkways that are wheelchair accessible by design. The difference between the two is:

- A walkway is a clearly defined footpath for pedestrians and can be used anywhere.

- A sidewalk is a type of footpath that borders a paved road.

One specification both hold in common is the width. They must be at least 36 inches wide to certify as wheelchair accessible, but then, isn't 36 inches a bit stingy? After all people in wheelchairs have families and friends; they need room to walk abreast of each other also. Therefore, always remember to make your footpaths family-friendly and extra-wide.

This is also a wonderful opportunity for our team leader to add beauty to the overall design. As her team resolves mechanical layout and paving issues, she can begin adorning and protecting these footpaths with various thin-wall accessory structure designs.

Thin-Wall Accessory Structures

So far, we've discussed domes made with inflatable airforms. As a first step in learning how to build them, let's begin with infrastructure accessories that are smaller, simpler and very useful. I call them thin-wall accessory structures.

Thin-wall accessory structures are used in combination with domes, footpaths, and such. There are three major differences between accessory structures and concrete domes:

- Accessory structures are shaped with crafted wood forms and not airforms
- The thickness of an accessory structure's wall is thinner than those of concrete domes
- They are open to the air and without insulation

When building a survival community, an overall look that is spartan and unappealing is not required in any way. There is nothing that says an accessory structure must be square. Rather, they can be almost any shape, and this offers a flexible way to build functional walls with cosmetically appealing shapes.

They can also be highly functional designs, such as an offset fence.

Offset Fences

Fences in our right angle civilization are predictably straight, even though during times of extreme weather, they can fail because they capture the wind like the sail of a sailboat.

The force of the wind not only pushes against the fence's reinforcement; it also pushes the body and weight of the fence against the reinforcement as well. This is why people often have to repair their straight fences after a big wind storm.

With a Win-Win survival community, avoiding this kind of damage is important, and offset fences are your best solution. Here is why:

- **Catching the Wind:** A straight fence catches the wind. During a weather event, high winds batter a straight fence's windward side. The only support comes from the wall's thickness and reinforcement. The reverse side of the fence is called the leeward side and offers little or no support.
- **Deflecting the Wind:** An offset fence is self-reinforcing. In a weather event, the windward side of the fence sets at an angle which therefore deflects the wind. Plus, the wall is reinforced by the offset on the leeward side of the fence. The result is a much stronger fence.

The first step in creating an offset fence is to decide on its basic pattern. We will use two common patterns, zig-zig and curved.

Zig-Zag Offset Fence

To start things off, let's assemble the necessary construction materials for our zig-zag offset fence:

- Concrete for post holes
- Shotcrete for the fence body
- Colored shotcrete or stain for the finish
- No. 4 basalt rebar sticks in 10' lengths for vertical reinforcement posts
- Sheets of basalt open-cell reinforcement mesh
- Softwood lumber for the wall form in various sizes from 1 x 3 inches and up
- ¼ inch sheets of 4 x 8 foot softwood plywood for the wood form

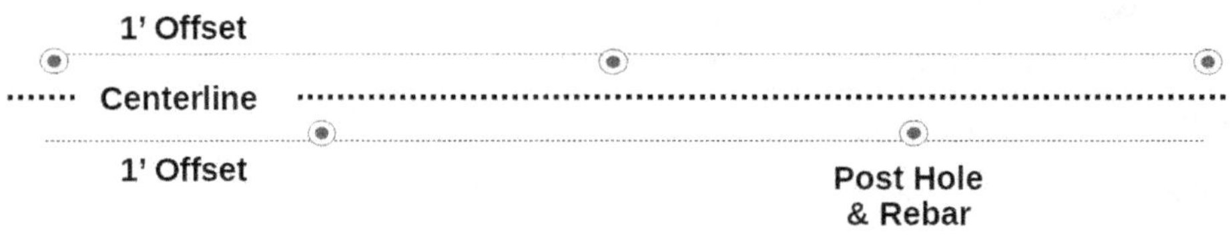
1' Offset
Centerline
1' Offset
Post Hole
& Rebar

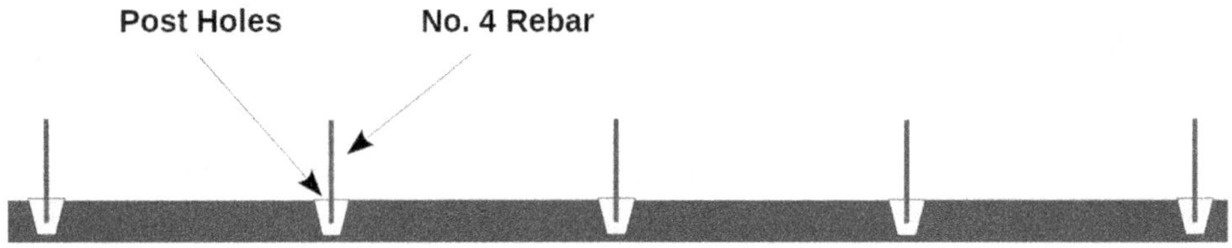
Post Holes
No. 4 Rebar

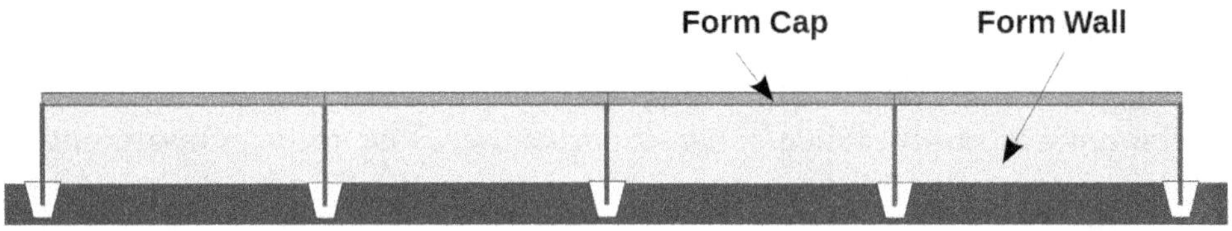
Form Cap
Form Wall

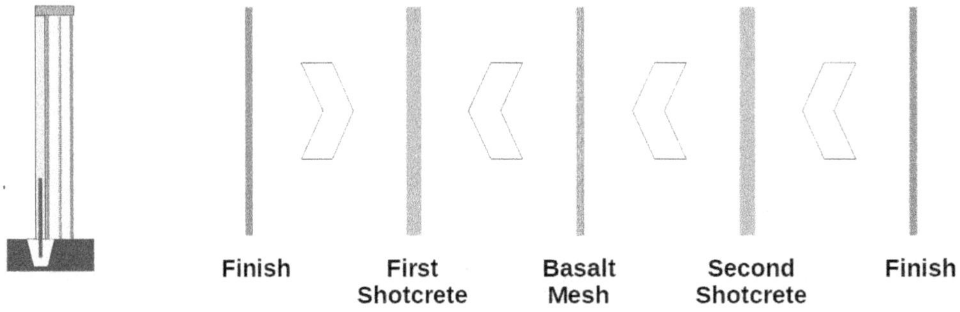
Finish
First
Shotcrete
Basalt
Mesh
Second
Shotcrete
Finish

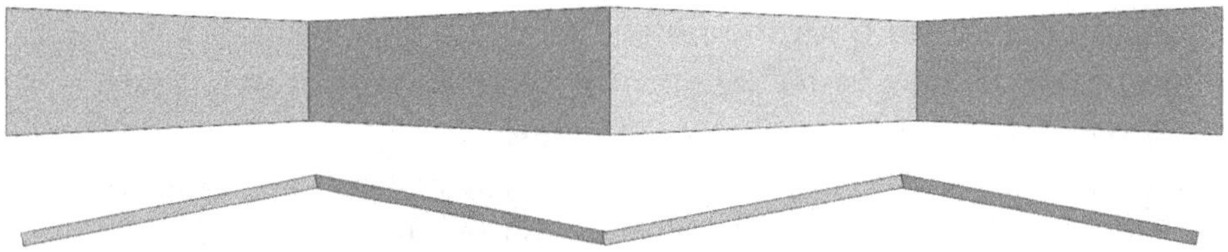

For the purpose of this discussion, let's assume you are building a thin wall 4 foot tall zig-zag offset fence. Here is a quick 10-step summary of the general process:

1. **Wall Placement:** The first requirement is to place the fence. A primary requirement is that it must deflect the wind; so, the first step is to determine the prevailing winds for the property. Then you decide where the fence should begin and end and its overall length and orientation.
2. **Wall Placement Chalk Lines:** Lay down three parallel chalk snap lines that run the full length of the fence. The first line is the center snap line. Then one foot to the right of the centerline you lay down the right offset line. Next, one foot to the left of the centerline, you lay down the left offset line.
3. **Wall Form Chalk Lines:** For the purpose of this example, the offset line to the left of the centerline is on the windward side of the fence. So, the first post hole will be dug on the leeward side of the wall which is on the right offset chalk line.
4. **Snap Form Chalk Lines:** Starting with the right offset snap line, mark an X on the ground for the first post hole. Then pin the end of the chalk line to the ground over that spot and draw it out to a length of exactly 8'. Keeping the chalk line straight and taunt, draw it to where it intersects with the left offset snap line and make another X for the next post hole. Then repeat the process back and forth between the offset snap lines to complete the process.
5. **Post Holes and Reinforcement:** Once your post hole markers are made, dig the post holes for the fence approximately one foot deep into the ground. After all the post holes are dug, fill them with concrete and stand the basalt reinforcement rebar in their centers. A No. 4 rebar is half an inch thick and ten feet long. For a short 4 foot fence, cut the sticks in half. This will give you one foot of rebar for the post hole and 4' of rebar for the wood form.
6. **Wood Form Setup:** You will use softwood lumber and softwood plywood to build a complete wood form. The softwood lumber is attached to the softwood plywood sheeting to create a shallow cavity into which you will spray the shotcrete to create a thin wall structure. Vertical stakes on the outside of the form will secure it to the ground. The result will be a form that looks like a narrow open-top cereal box that stands vertically on its edge.
7. **Spray Preparation:** To keep shotcrete or concrete from sticking to the forms, concrete professionals often coat the contact side of the form with a low-grade oil or form-release agent. These are typically brushed on to a medium thickness. Your design team will determine a suitable form-release agent or method.
8. **First Shotcrete Spray and Mesh Reinforcement:** Spray a layer of shotcrete into the form to a thickness of roughly 1" for a short fence. This will become the windward

side of the fence. While the first spray is still wet, cover the entire surface with sheets of basalt open-cell reinforcement mesh. When spraying shotcrete, the surface thickness will vary depending on skill and experience. Nonetheless, there must be no gaps between the basalt sheets after they are placed. Once the first spray is covered with reinforcement, you are ready to spray the second shotcrete layer over it.

9. **Second Shotcrete Spray:** With the reinforcement mesh in place, spray another 1" thick layer over the reinforcement mesh and the first spray. This will become the leeward side of the fence.

10. **Final Steps:** After the shotcrete sets up, remove the wood form. You can spray a fine layer of colored shotcrete on all sides of the fence or use a concrete stain to color the fence for a better appearance. A sealer is optional and highly advised.

While a zigzag offset fence is strong, it's basically a right angle solution. That being said, offset fences are ideal for all-hazard survival communities because they can be sculpted to flow with the natural layout of the land.

Given this, let's build the second variant, a curved offset fence with a small variation on the same materials and methods.

Curved Offset Fence

The difference between curved and zigzag offset fences is primarily the shape. Instead of sharp, stair step-like angles, you're creating an offset wall with gentle curves. This difference will impact how you set up your wood form.

Sheets of ¼" softwood plywood is also used for large circles where the arc is wide and gentle as in the case with a curved offset wall.

For best results and to add flexibility, score the plywood about every half inch on the outside of the form, opposite the interior spray side, with vertical cuts about 2/3 the depth of the board.

The form for a curved offset fence begins with vertical stakes used to create the overall shape. They will anchor the form so the plywood can be curved to shape.

Like a straight zigzag fence, a curved offset fence will be self-supporting, because the structure will still extend one foot to the right of the centerline and one foot to the left, for a total offset of two feet. After that, the rest of the construction process is essentially the same as with the zigzag offset wall.

Now that you know how to make two types of thin-wall offset fences, let's add a few curved planter boxes to our walkways to create a more beautiful and inviting outdoor living space.

Curved Planter Box

A curved planter box alongside a sidewalk or walkway not only adds the natural beauty of colorful plants to your outdoor living space; it can also serve a useful role in your community's food growing efforts.

For example you could plant "winter herbs." These herbal varieties fare better than others in chilly weather. This makes them the perfect herbs to grow and eat, and many also have valuable medicinal properties.

Winter herb varieties include rosemary, parsley, thyme, mint, Winter Savory, and Basil. You can also mix varieties, but make sure that you use species that work well with others. For example, Mint does not play well with other species, and it will take over your entire planter.

With curved planter boxes, the construction process is very similar to a curved offset fence. The difference is that the structure is an enclosure instead of being open on both sides. It will also be shorter in height. Herein is the key to applying the shotcrete and basalt reinforcement mesh at the bottom.

With offset fences, the bottom of the form is perpendicular to the ground.

With curved planter boxes, the first shotcrete spray, the basalt reinforcement mesh, and the second shotcrete spray all flare inward at the bottom towards the center of the planter box. A few inches is fine for the flare, and remember, the center must be left as open ground to allow for drainage.

Now that you've learned how simple it is to make offset fences and planter boxes, you've mastered some essential basics. With this it's now time to build domes.

11

EcoShells I & II

The differences between EcoShells and DBS domes are considerable. It begins with their appearance but also how they are constructed.

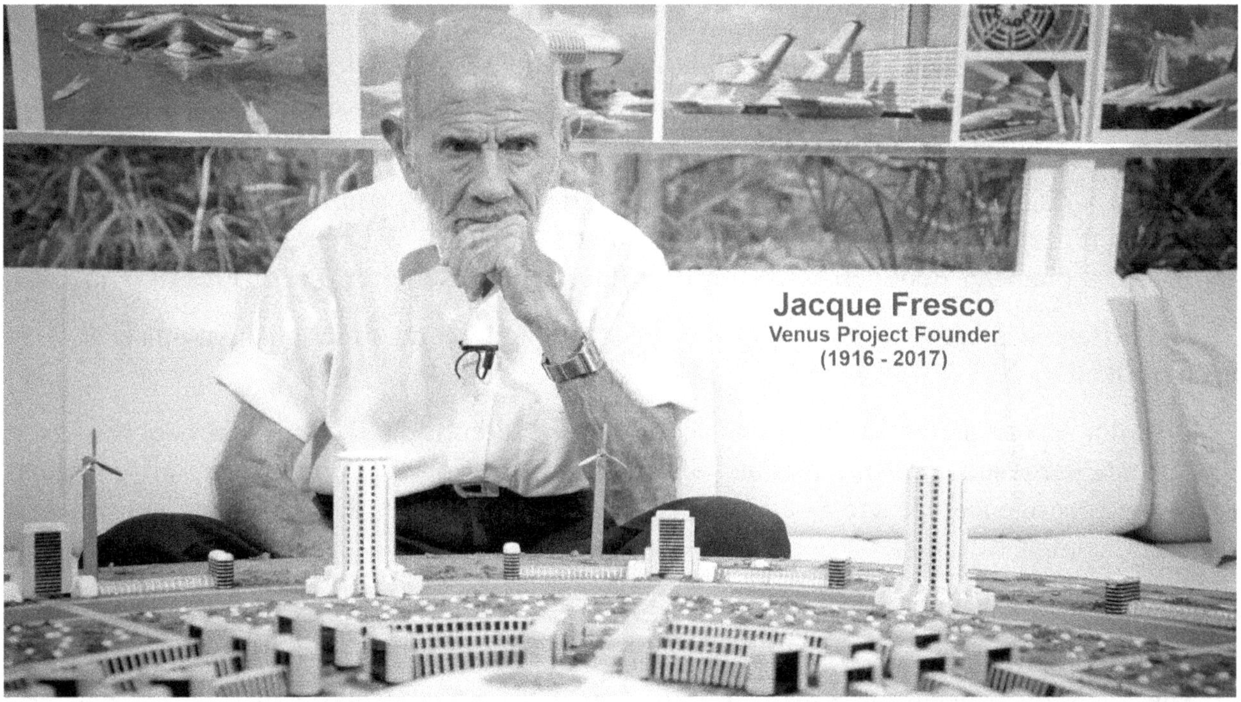

DBS domes can be massive in size and are futuristic-looking structures. To see a future world with domes, visit The Venus Project web site at www.thevenusproject.com. It was founded by Futurist, Jacque Fresco (1916 to 2017), a man of science with a great passion for the future of our species.

EcoShells, on the other hand, are smaller and appear similar to the grain silos throughout the heartland of the country. What creates this look is that EcoShells have tall vertical stem walls that are topped by a classic semi-hemisphere shaped dome.

The process begins with determining the dimensions of your structures, and how much land they will require.

Dome Dimensions

When designing your community, it is necessary to determine how much square footage is available with each dome's dimension and how much acreage is required. The www.square-footagearea.com website is a useful community design tool. You'll want to use their Area of a Circle Calculator.

For quick reference, here are the dimensions for the EcoShell sizes you'll most likely use, and the amount of land that is required to place them. Keep in mind, one acre of land is 43,560 sq ft. So, let's see how much land is required.

The maximum diameter for an EcoShell I dome is thirty feet, whereas the maximum diameter for an EcoShell II is twenty feet. Here are the EcoShell floor space and acreage dimensions:

- 10 ft diameter EcoShell I or II. 79 sq ft of floor space. Requires 0.001 acres of land.
- 20 ft diameter EcoShell I or II. 314 sq ft of floor space. Requires 0.010 acres of land.
- 30 ft diameter EcoShell I. 707 sq ft of floor space. Requires 0.020 acres of land.

The differences between the two dome types are significant, so let's take a closer look at each of them.

DBS domes can theoretically be one acre in size, and building them requires sophisticated designs and large amounts of materials. In order to make concrete domes more affordable as third-world residences, David South created EcoShells that significantly lower construction costs and complexity.

An EcoShell I can be as large as thirty feet in diameter. They are well-suited for the design and building of affordable two-story residences, in developing and industrialized nations.

The EcoShell II design is a major refinement of the original EcoShell I design, and was created by David South specifically for third-world family residences.

The criteria David used were established by the United Nations. It is a permanent residence for impoverished families of eight, living in a hot equatorial climate.

The specifications call for a diameter of 6 m (19.69 ft) with 28 m2 (304 sq ft) of interior floor space. That may seem small to us, but if you live in a tent or hut, an EcoShell II is a major step up.

Another important third-world criterion is the need to save on materials. Given the abundance of labor in these countries, a more labor-intensive design was possible. So how do the two types compare?

EcoShell I vs. EcoShell II

Here is how the EcoShell designs compare with each other and DBS domes:

- **Size:** With an EcoShell I, you can build a 30 ft diameter two-story permanent residence. With an EcoShell II, the largest dome you can build is a 20 ft diameter single-story permanent residence.
- **Stem Wall:** Stem walls are common to EcoShell I and II designs and offer a great way to create usable interior space within the dome interior. They offer excellent living space for above-ground EcoShells without an overcover.
- **Application:** There are three types of Win-Win structures: above-ground, above-ground covered, and below-ground. EcoShells I and II are solely for above-ground applications without overcover. DBS domes can be used for all three, but for Win-

Win communities, they're the only type used in above-ground covered and below-ground applications.

- **Dome Slab and Ring Beam Footing:** An EcoShell II that is up to 20 feet in diameter can be constructed on a simple concrete slab also called a "pad." However, an EcoShell I that is 30 feet in diameter will require a pad plus a substantial ring beam footing beneath it to provide necessary vertical load-bearing support for the shell. You will learn how to build both types of foundations in this chapter.
- **Safety:** Both EcoShell I and EcoShell II domes are strong structures that can withstand natural disasters, fire, termites, and rot. In terms of a dome's ability to resist penetration, an EcoShell II with a 3-inch thick shell can stop a typical NATO 5.56mm assault rifle bullet. An EcoShell I with a 4-inch thick shell is barely thick enough in most cases to stop a larger NATO 7.62mm caliber rifle bullet.
- **Relocation:** All DBS domes and EcoShells, are permanent installations with the sole exception of the 10-ft diameter EcoShell II outbuilding. These small, 10-ft diameter domes can be fitted with permanent lifting hooks for relocation as needed.
- **Insulation:** The EcoShell II is intended for residences in tropical climates, and do not provide the insulation needed for temperate climates. However, an EcoShell I can use an insulated shotcrete mix suitable for a permanent residence in a cool climate.
- **Outbuildings:** The EcoShell II is perfect for outbuildings. Your Win-Win survival community will use this type for outside kitchens, work areas, covers, storage sheds, pump rooms, garages, and such.
- **Shotcrete/Concrete Application:** Unlike DBS domes where shotcrete must be sprayed, the concrete for an EcoShell dome can be sprayed or troweled on. In third world countries where construction labor is much less expensive than materials, this is a big cost advantage.
- **Reusable Airform:** With DBS domes, airforms should not be removed and reused. This is why David South designed EcoShell airforms for reuse. In fact with proper handling and care, an EcoShell airform can be reused 100 times or more.

There are other aspects to building a concrete dome. One that applies equally to all types is the placement of service lines.

Service Lines

The term service line refers to the various services provided to the structure such as water, waste, power, and so forth. Regardless of the type of concrete dome you build, always remember these three cardinal rules:

- **Service Lines:** No service line, regardless of type, may have direct contact with any of the dome's shell material. Service lines must pass through a dome shell via rust-proof and water-tight conduits or service tunnels that incorporate safety precautions for maintenance, movement, and temperature.

- **Service Line Entry Points:** If water reaches steel or iron, it will rust and this will undermine the integrity of the dome. Therefore, the materials you use with service line entry points must be basalt, plastic or stainless steel. No matter the conduit or service tunnel used, carbon steel or iron must never come into direct contact with the shell of any dome.
- **Service Line Flexibility:** Service lines must never be fixed directly to a dome shell. If a service line is fixed to a dome shell, earthquakes can cause serious failures. Incoming and outgoing service lines must incorporate additional travel length and flexibility.

Now let's raise an EcoShell II, the simplest, easiest, and quickest of the domes to construct.

Before starting, let's review quickly the five stages of construction common to all domes.

Construction Stages

While there are significant differences between DBS dome and EcoShell designs, your team manager will manage the five-step process used to raise any of them.

- **Stage 1 – Foundation and Reinforcement:** The foundation must support the full weight of the dome, which is substantial on large domes. This determines the complexity of the foundation.
- **Stage 2 – Airform Setup:** All airforms share the same basic design. They are open at the bottom with a bead of basalt rope that seals around the edge and are fastened to the foundation in various ways.
- **Stage 3 – Shell Wood Framing and Services:** Wood forms are for doors, windows and services such as electric and water. These are installed before the concrete is applied.
- **Stage 4 – Shell Layers and Reinforcement:** Regardless of the type of concrete dome you construct, it will be constructed in layers and with ample reinforcement.
- **Stage 5 – Finish:** EcoShell airforms are reusable and are removed after the dome shell is complete.

We will use this 5-stage process to develop your understanding of our first EcoShell II storage shed construction project example, and in subsequent examples, we'll focus on the differences.

However, before moving on, one essential safety point.

Wind Monitoring

Before moving to our EcoShell I example, let's consider two important things the team leader or a designated safety observer must do to ensure the success of the project: Monitor the wind speed and any signs of deformation while inflating the airform.

- **Wind Speed:** Airforms are very vulnerable to damage when they are partially inflated. Therefore, never inflate a dome in winds exceeding 15 mph. 10 mph is better, and less than 5 mph is optimal.
- **Inflation Deformation:** As a general rule, it takes approximately thirty minutes to inflate a dome with a footprint of thirty feet. The inflation process should be carefully observed to ensure that the airform does not deform while inflating.

In our first EcoShell example, we will build a smaller 10 ft dome. For this project, one safety observer is adequate. For larger domes and depending on size, you should have two or more safety observers, and anyone can be taught this skill.

You will probably use inexpensive walkie-talkies, but please make sure that your observers also have loud police whistles. If they spot a problem and you hear a call over the radio or hear a whistle, you'll know to turn off the fans immediately so you can resolve the issue before proceeding.

Now, let's build an EcoShell II shed to store gardening implements.

EcoShell II Storage Shed Example

To illustrate a commonplace EcoShell II design for Win-Win survival communities, we will construct a utility shed that is 10' in diameter with 79 sq ft of floor space. It will have an 8-foot vertical stem wall topped by a classic, semi-hemisphere shaped dome with a low, 1:4 profile.

The size of this example EcoShell is important because permitting is usually required for outbuildings with less than 100 sq ft of floor space. Be sure to check local permitting rules for small outbuildings.

With a 10' EcoShell II, you also have the option to add built-in lift hooks and we'll be adding them to our example for extra measure.

Now, let's build our EcoShell II storage shed to hold our gardening implements with our five-stage process, beginning with siting of the dome.

Stage 1 – Foundation and Reinforcement

1. **Siting the Dome:** When choosing where to locate your EcoShell II, the soil beneath the slab must be dry, well-compacted, and must not contain any organic matter. It must also be well-drained, so that water does not undercut the dome slab.

2. **Foundation Wood Framing:** You begin by building a wood form in the shape of the dome's footprint. What you want is for the outside wall of the shell to be in continuous contact with the dome's slab, also called a "pad."

3. **Foundation Reinforcement:** No. 4 basalt reinforcement bar (rebar) is cut to shape to create a grid pattern for the slab. Because rebar should never lay on the ground, it is suspended before pouring; therefore, you must raise rebar off the ground by placing what are called chairs underneath them to keep the concrete level. Chairs come in various sizes and are available in polypropylene or steel and look somewhat like small candlesticks. Never use carbon steel. Only use the polypropylene chairs.

4. **Foundation Pour:** In this case, we'll pour a four-inch-thick slab. Before the concrete sets up, you will insert the reinforcement hooks. A unique feature of this size dome, is that you can add lift hooks before pouring the slab with a conventional concrete mix of cement, sand, stone, and water. Additional admixtures and sealants may be helpful.

5. **Shell Reinforcement:** With an EcoShell II design, basalt 3-ply reinforcement rope is anchored to the slab with a ring of 1/4" by 4" stainless steel hooks. Like candles on a cake, the hooks must circle the outer edge of the slab, approximately 2" inside of the outer edge, and embedded about 8" to 16" apart. Before inserting the hook into the concrete, make sure it has a stainless steel nut, washer, and another nut at the bottom of the hook. This will help to lock it into the slab.

6. **Optional Lift Hooks:** Use a 24" long length of No. 4 basalt rebar. You need to create a U-shape so that the parallel bars sit horizontally in the slab, with the U-shape part bent upwards for easy hook-on access. You'll need four equally spaced lift hooks extending from the outside edge of the pad, so the dome can be lifted and moved as needed.

Stage 2 – Airform Setup

7. **Inflate the Airform:** Once the slab has cured, you're ready to build the dome shell. Place the airform in the center of the slab, attach a large fan, and inflate the airform. After that, you can use a smaller fan to keep it inflated. In this example, our EcoShell II has an 8' stem wall and a semi-hemisphere dome top with a 1:4 profile, to accommodate a double-wide metal door.

8. **Interior Tie-Downs:** After the airform is fully inflated, it needs to be secured to the dome slab. This is done with short lengths of angle iron used as tie-downs on the inside of the airform after it has been inflated. Tie-downs are installed with the flat edge against the basalt rope bead at the bottom of the airform. The vertical edge of the tie-down needs to be 3.5" to 4" from the edge of the slab. Tie-downs are fastened to the slab with concrete screw anchors.

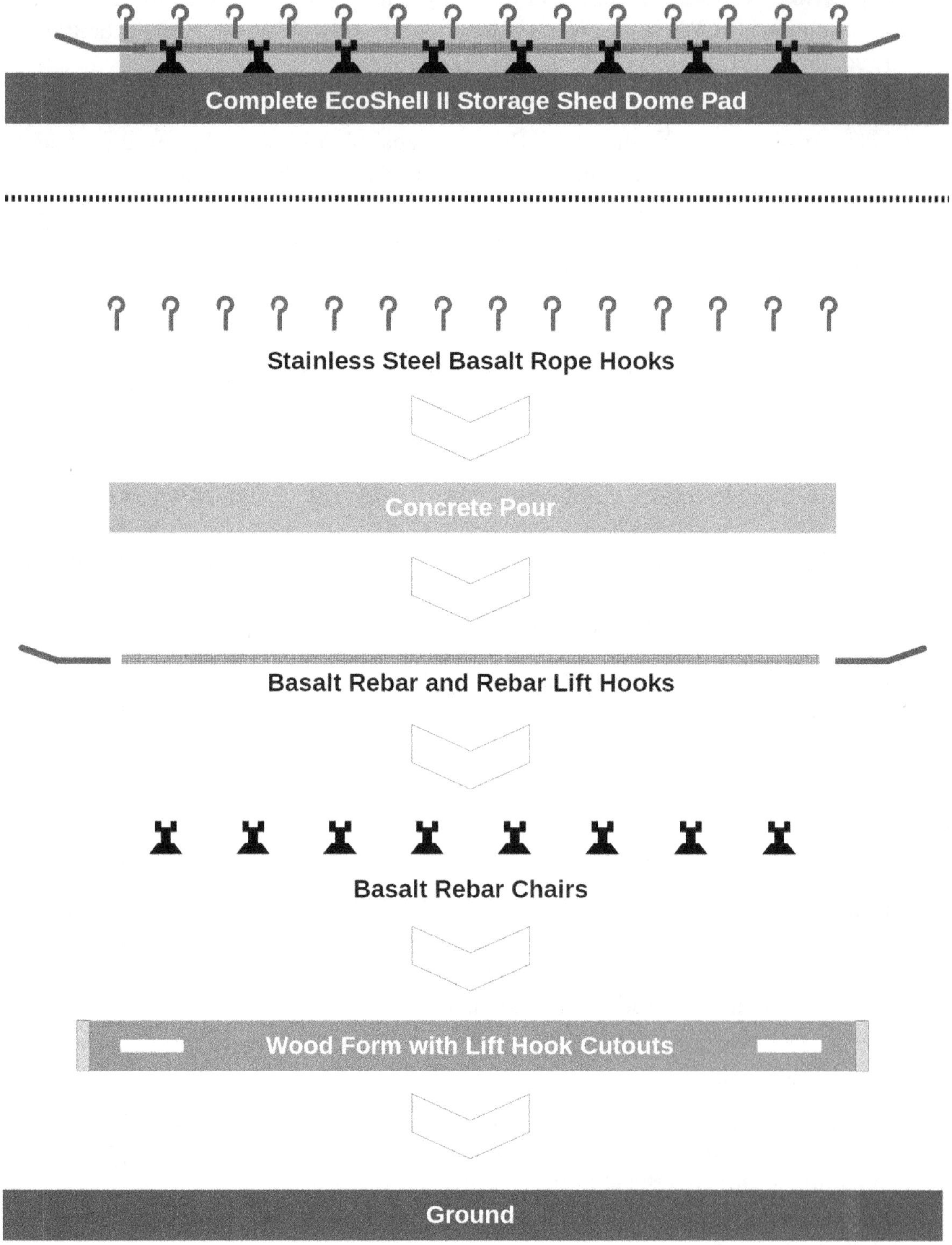
Complete EcoShell II Storage Shed Dome Pad
Stainless Steel Basalt Rope Hooks
Concrete Pour
Basalt Rebar and Rebar Lift Hooks
Basalt Rebar Chairs
Wood Form with Lift Hook Cutouts
Ground

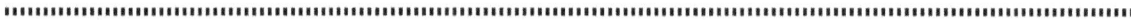

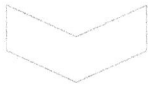

Stage 3 – Shell Wood Framing and Services

9. **Door Frame:** After raising the airform, you can add wood forms to define windows and doors. In this example, we'll add a double-wide door for easy access. Rebar and shotcrete are not applied inside a wood frame. After the shell has cured, the wood frame is removed so the finish work can be done.

10. **Outside Service Conduits:** If you are building a pump house or a lit garage for example, you'll want to build service conduits into the dome design. Conduits are created by drilling a hole through the side of a dome. You need special forms for service line entry points that allow you to run interior conduits before you apply the first shotcrete layer.

Stage 4 – Shell Layers and Reinforcement

11. **First Shotcrete Layer:** Once the slab has cured and the wood form for the door frame has been placed, you will spray a one-inch layer of shotcrete without reinforcement on the airform. It can also be troweled on.

12. **Reinforcement Hangers:** While this layer of shotcrete is still wet, you can embed small reinforcement hangers in it to add extra basalt reinforcement around window and door wood frames.

13. **Wrap the Rope:** The next reinforcement step is to overlay 3-ply basalt rope as reinforcement around the first shotcrete layer. Like lacing up a boot, you begin by wrapping the rope from one hook, over the top to the next hook and back again. Then you will wrap reinforcement rope using the reinforcement hangers described in the previous step around the wood forms. Never splice, cut, or knot the reinforcement rope.

14. **Second Shotcrete Layer:** After the reinforcement has been applied, you're ready for the second shotcrete layer. Spray or trowel on a two to three-inch, second layer of shotcrete.

Stage 5 – Finish

15. **Remove the Airform:** The tie-downs and concrete screw anchors are removed from inside the airform, and it is deflated and removed. EcoShell airforms can be re-used 100 times or more with proper care. This is a huge cost saving when building multiple domes.

16. **Finish:** After the dome is finished and cured, you can texture, paint, and seal it on the inside and outside. If you want the EcoShell interior to be cooler on hot sunny days, paint a white-colored lime wash on the exterior in multiple layers until it forms a solid color surface.

This now completes our EcoShell II example. Our next project is to build an EcoShell I two-story residence which is a larger dome and requires an all-hazards foundation.

All-Hazards Dome Foundation

In our previous example, a 10' EcoShell II storage shed, a simple pad with lift hooks installed to facilitate moving the dome was used. This was the goal for building 6-meter EcoShell II housing in the third world, and a single-slab foundation is sufficient for the load-bearing requirement.

Regardless of the type of concrete dome, if it has a diameter greater than 20', a more robust two-part foundation system is necessary. With a ring beam footing and slab, it can support the greater weight of a larger-diameter dome shell.

Note: This design is more complex than a simple pad, and requires excavation.

The load-bearing characteristics of a dome are very different from those of conventional two-story wood-frame structures. With frame houses, the second floor is an integral part of the load-bearing structure and must be constructed before the roof is put on.

However, with concrete domes, the second floor is not part of the load-bearing support for the roof. It is optional and can be added during interior finish after the dome has been constructed.

Interestingly enough, this creates a world of interior design opportunities where the sky is the limit. If you want the interior of your concrete dome to resemble a theme park attraction, you can do it.

Now, let's take a closer look at how to construct a ring beam footing for survival applications.

Ring Beam Footing

The critical part of an all-hazards dome foundation is the ring beam footing, and as the name suggests, this part of the foundation is an open concrete ring that encompasses the circumference of the dome structure. The size and width of the ring beam footing itself will depend on the dome type, size and location.

Wood forms are used to shape the ring beam footing, and this design is critical because the finished ring beam footing must support the entire dome shell as well as the outer edge of the dome slab.

The bottom of the ring beam footing is wider than the top and spreads the weight of the dome shell more evenly across the ground. The narrower section on the top of the ring beam footing supports the dome shell directly. A notch, on the inside edge at the top of the ring beam footing, provides an overlapping connection point for the slab.

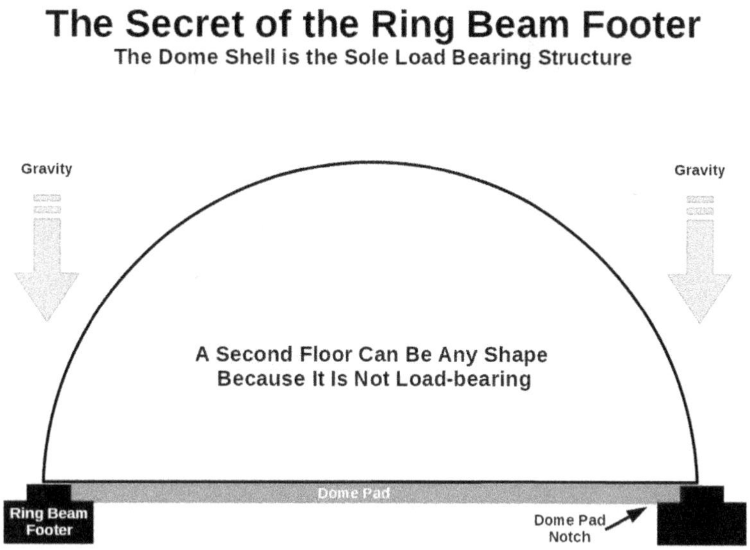
The Secret of the Ring Beam Footer
The Dome Shell is the Sole Load Bearing Structure
Gravity
Gravity
A Second Floor Can Be Any Shape
Because It Is Not Load-bearing
Dome Pad
Ring Beam
Footer
Dome Pad
Notch

With a conventional concrete dome design, a circular trench is dug for the ring beam footing, and the earth is heavily compacted. Once that is done, the ground inside the ring is smoothed and compacted so the slab can be poured. This works well for a conventional foundation, but there are concerns about the added stresses of groundwater incursion.

I expressed these concerns to David in 2016, and we developed an all-hazards foundation based on his standard design. With David's solution, the ring beam footing and slab remain the same. The change is a sub-foundation for drainage and earthquake mitigation.

Sub-Foundation Construction

When building any dome of any type, that is 20' or more in diameter, you want it to have an all-hazards sub-foundation for a Win-Win survival community.

With a conventional concrete dome foundation, the earthwork excavation is limited to a narrow circular trench for the ring beam footing. Inside of that, the soil is tightly compacted for the slab. Here is the process:

1. **Excavation:** With an all-hazards dome foundation, added excavation is necessary to accommodate the sub-foundation system layers. You not only excavate for the ring beam footing, but you also excavate inside that footing for an all-hazards sub-foundation with a depth sufficient enough to embed a slotted drain system. The final step in this part of the process is to excavate narrow trenches in the sub-foundation area for horizontal drain pipes.

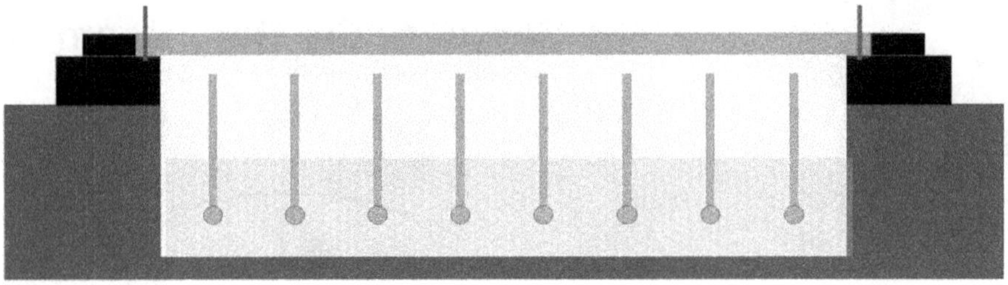

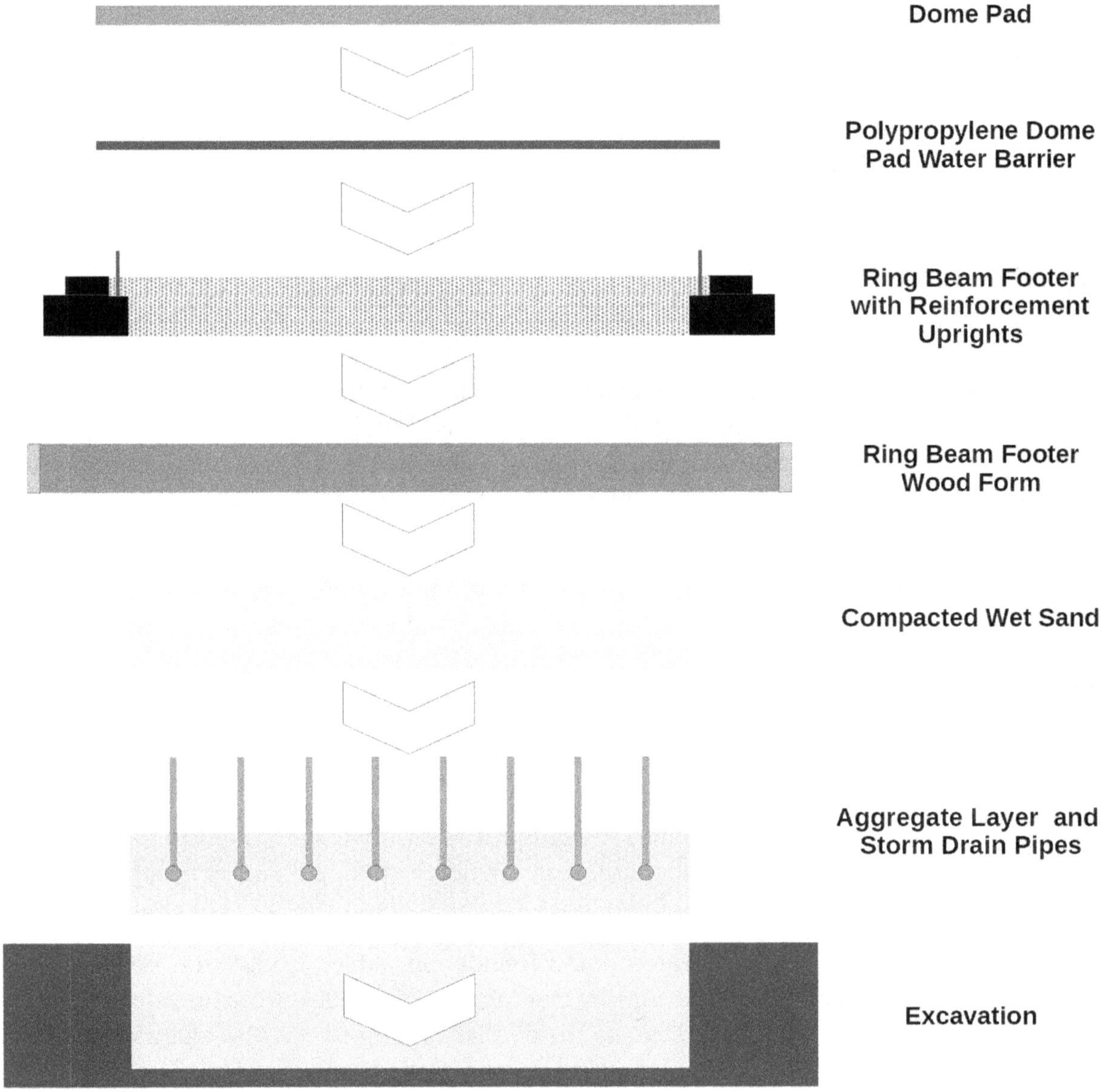
Dome Pad
Polypropylene Dome Pad Water Barrier
Ring Beam Footer with Reinforcement Uprights
Ring Beam Footer Wood Form
Compacted Wet Sand
Aggregate Layer and Storm Drain Pipes
Excavation

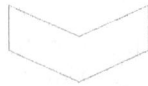

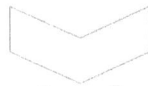

2. **Position Storm Drain Pipes:** Horizontal drain pipes are laid in the trench and run out and connected to a storm drain system. Vertical drain pipes with slits in the upper half are then inserted into the horizontal drain pipes to form an upside-down T-type connection. For best results, use ABS or PVC plastic drain pipes for optimal corrosion resistance.

3. **Slotted Storm Drain Cover:** Certified fill dirt is poured into the drainpipe trench and compacted. When finished, the upper two-thirds of the vertical drain pipes will be exposed, and the rest will be underground.

4. **Aggregate Layer:** When the slotted storm drain system is finished, a layer of smooth river rock aggregate is laid over the compacted earth to a height of no less than six inches above the tops of the standing drain pipes. When finished, all you will see is an even layer of smooth rock.

5. **Sand for Drainage and Earthquakes:** Sand is useful for drainage while helping to mitigate the effects of horizontal earthquake ground waves on the structure. Sand is poured over the river rock aggregate up to the bottom of the slab notch on the inside of the ring beam footing, and the sand is compacted. When finished, all you will see is smooth compacted sand.

6. **Polypropylene Dome Pad Water Barrier:** The next step is to lay down a polypropylene water barrier over the sand. This will help block weeds, ground moisture, and flooding due to a rising water table. It must be a single, heavy sheet of polypropylene with the exact dimensions as the slab. Lay it on the sand, so that its edges extend beyond the sand, into the ring beam footing's notch for the slab. When finished, you will see the top of the ring beam footing and the polypropylene covering the sand and the inside notch for the slab. The purpose of the slab notch is for the slab to overlap the inside of the ring beam footing so that the two join to form a single structure.

7. **Place Reinforcement Uprights:** Because this type of sub-foundation is only used with EcoShell I and DBS domes, basalt rebar sticks will be embedded in the soil beneath the ring beam footing. When completed the sticks for EcoShell I and DBS domes will stand upright like a ring of birthday candles. For an EcoShell I, the sticks are embedded upright, close to the outermost edge of the ring beam footing. With DBS domes, the sticks are embedded upright in the shelf-like, slab notch on the inside face of the ring beam footing.

When you've completed these seven steps, the remaining steps will be much the same as with the EcoShell II example above. We'll revisit these concepts when we construct our example EcoShell I and DBS domes, but for now, we are ready to build a two-story EcoShell I residence.

EcoShell I – Two-Story Residence Example

An EcoShell I is an in-between design that offers the benefits of the EcoShell II design and DBS domes. As in the case with an EcoShell II, the airform of an EcoShell I may be reused. The ability to trowel the concrete instead of spraying it, is a huge plus.

Another benefit is that an EcoShell I can be larger and taller than an EcoShell II. Also, both can be insulated for cool weather by using a special concrete mix.

An EcoShell I offers a Win-Win survival community a design option that is attractive and affordable. These above-ground residences are much more survivable than conventional wood frame residences, during high winds, earthquakes and other events.

To build the two-story EcoShell I silo-style residence used for this example, you'll need to rent a bucket aerial lift for work on the outside of the airform and an indoor aerial scissor lift for the interior work.

There are other key differences as well, but the major difference between this EcoShell I example and the previous EcoShell II storage shed is with the foundation; so let's take a closer look at that.

Stage 1 – Foundation and Reinforcement

1. **Siting the Dome:** When choosing where to site your EcoShell I, remember that it will be a permanent site. Also, it is likely that you will build a group of EcoShell I resi-

dential domes, which when finished, will look like the clusters of cabins seen with motels or resorts. Make sure there is ample acreage with supporting infrastructure and services.

2. **Earthwork:** You will need to excavate an all-hazards sub-foundation, and the basalt rebar sticks will be embedded in the ring beam footing. They must be on the outside of the airform; about 1" to 1.5" from the edge after it is inflated. This way the uprights connect the concrete shell with the foundation. Other earthwork requirements are for the service lines, and adding a nearby vertical or horizontal closed-loop field for your geothermal HVAC system.

3. **Ring Beam Footing Wood Framing:** You construct a circular wood form in the shape of the dome's footprint for the ring beam footing. The aim is for the outside of the shell to form a continuous outside surface with the dome slab. The actual size and shape of the ring beam footing will vary depending on the size and load-bearing weight of the dome.

4. **Sub-Foundation:** The layers of the sub-foundation system are placed and topped with the polypropylene dome pad water barrier.

5. **Footing Reinforcement:** After the sub-foundation is complete and the wood forms are in place, the interior of the footing is reinforced with basalt rebar.

6. **Shell Reinforcement:** With EcoShell I designs, vertical uprights of No. 4 basalt rebar are embedded vertically in the earth inside and from beneath the ring beam footing. Once positioned, the uprights will stand roughly 4' tall, and after the airform has been inflated, they must stand one and a half inches outside of the fully inflated airform.

7. **First Foundation Pour:** You'll use a conventional concrete mix of cement, sand, stone, and water to pour your ring beam footing. Additional admixtures and sealants are helpful. This will also lock the uprights into the footing, so the foundation connects directly with the dome shell.

8. **Safety Caps:** In the event of a slip or fall, an upright reinforcement bar can injure a worker. There are plenty of plastic caps on the market, but David South came up with a simple, inexpensive solution using large wood cabinet knobs. Drill out the center of the knob to the size of the rebar and then stick it on top of the upright.

9. **Slab Reinforcement:** Once the sub-foundation is complete, it is time to add reinforcement for the slab. No. 4 basalt reinforcement bar (rebar) and rebar chairs are placed over the polypropylene dome pad water barrier. Be very careful to avoid trips and falls during this stage.

10. **Slab Pour:** You'll use a conventional concrete mix of cement, sand, stone, and water for pouring your slab. Additional binders and sealants are helpful.

Stage 2 – Airform Setup

11. **Place the Airform:** Once the foundation has cured, you're ready to raise and shape the dome shell. Place the airform in the center of the slab.

12. **Fans and Airlock:** Attach two large fans to the airform for inflation. To ensure the dome does not deflate during construction, each fan must be able to inflate and maintain the shape of the airform. You will also add an airlock to enable workers to enter and exit the airform without a loss of positive air pressure inside the airform during construction.

13. **Raise the Airform:** Be sure the airform is centered on the slab and that your observers are ready to make sure you properly inflate the dome. Since this is a two-story airform, having an inflation observer in the bucket of an aerial lift is advisable.

14. **Tie-Downs:** After the airform is fully inflated, it is secured to the dome slab in the same manner as the EcoShell II example previously described.

Stage 3 – Shell Wood Framing and Services

15. **Door and Window Frames:** After raising the airform, you can add wood forms to define windows and doors, using the same method described in the previous EcoShell II example.

16. **Outside Service Conduits:** You'll want to build service conduits into the dome using the same method described in the previous EcoShell II example.

Stage 4 – Shell Layers and Reinforcement

17. **Vertical Reinforcement:** After the airform has been inflated and framed, you're ready to add reinforcement for the entire shell using the uprights. The uprights are used to anchor vertical loops made of basalt rebar sticks.

18. **Horizontal Reinforcement:** Once the vertical reinforcement loops are in place, you will hang horizontal loops of rebar and tie them to the vertical reinforcement loops. This will vary with the size of the dome. A general rule of thumb is, you want to create an eight-inch square pattern with the vertical and horizontal loops. You will also need to reinforce the wood frames for doors and windows.

19. **Inside Service Conduits:** Electrical, communication and fire safety outlets must be strategically placed throughout the dome interior, and the junction boxes will face the interior. They will be mounted to the structure via a stainless steel conduit, designed to protect the wiring throughout the inside wall of the structure without compromising the integrity of the concrete shell.

20. **First Shotcrete Layer:** Once the reinforcement has been placed, spray or trowel on the first layer of shotcrete on the airform. The shotcrete needs to be approximately 1.5

inches thick, so the airform is covered to the inside edge of the reinforcement uprights. The uprights also need to be exposed to the outside. Once this is done, you are ready to add an insulation layer.

21. **Shotcrete Insulation Mix:** To insulate an EcoShell I residence shell for a cool climate, you want to use a regrind Styrofoam shotcrete insulation in pieces no wider than 3/8". This mix produces a weaker concrete with a moderate R-value insulation rating. Here is the typical mix ratio for a EcoShell I dome:

    - (6) 5-gallon buckets of Styrofoam
    - (4) 5-gallon buckets of sand
    - (2) bags of Portland cement
    - (10) gallons of water

22. **Second Shotcrete Layer:** Spray or trowel on a two to four-inch layer of the Styrofoam shotcrete insulation mix onto the shell. In a warm climate like Arizona, three inches should be sufficient, but if your community is in Minnesota, you'll want the full four inches. When this layer sets up, you'll be ready for the final layer.

23. **Third Shotcrete Layer:** The final layer will be one-half-inch thick and use the standard formula of three parts Portland cement and one part fly ash from oil or coal. This will lock in and protect the insulation layer. Optionally, you can use colored cement with this final layer, where powder or liquid pigments are added to the standard shotcrete mix before it is applied.

Stage 5 – Finish

24. **Remove the Airform:** The tie-downs and concrete screw anchors are removed using the same method described in the previous EcoShell II example.

25. **Finish:** After the dome is finished and cured, you texture, paint, and seal on the inside and outside. If you want your EcoShell to stay cooler on hot, sunny days, use a white-colored lime wash. Apply the wash in multiple layers until it forms a solid color surface.

Now you have an above ground EcoShell I shell that is ready for interior and exterior details. While it will not be a true all-hazards structure, it is able to survive a lot.

What role can two-story EcoShell I residences serve in an all-hazard community design? As a close-knit collection of above-ground survivable residences, that are situated near an above-ground, covered all-hazards community center.

12

DBS Domes and Overcover

Previously, we defined three types of Win-Win survival community structures: Above-ground, above-ground with cover, and below-ground. In "Chapter 11 – EcoShells I & II" we built two above-ground structures, an EcoShell II storage shed and an EcoShell I two-story residence.

EcoShells are rated as survivable structures because they are exposed to the environment without all-hazards overcover protection. Therefore, in this chapter we are going to build upon the concepts presented in the previous chapters and construct an all-hazards church retreat community center that is adjacent to a small group of EcoShell I, two-story residences.

When you have completed this chapter, you will understand the overall construction process for DBS domes for church retreats and church ranches, and how they play a pivotal role in a layered, all-hazards strategy.

Layered All-Hazards Strategy

Typical prepper strategies center on a single, highly-fortified shelter. On the other hand, a Win-Win survival community uses a layered, family-friendly, all-hazards strategy with different structure types and three levels of protection:

- **Survivable:** Above-ground EcoShells offer basic survivability for earthquakes, wind, and water-driven natural disasters. They can also withstand impacts from pistol and smaller caliber assault rifle bullets.

- **Highly-Survivable:** Also referred to as hardened structures, these DBS domes are highly-survivable structures with overcover. They offer excellent protection from solar radiation, volcanic ash fall and ejecta, and 100+ lb stony meteorite impacts. They represent a good balance between safety and livability for permanent residences.
- **All-Hazards:** This DBS dome type is a multi-purpose, all-hazards service dome. For normal operations, they serve as mechanical rooms and passageways between other domes. They are built with twice or more the protection of a highly-survivable structure; they provide the maximum protection during extreme short-term events. With an optional impact basket, they can withstand a 200 lb stony meteorite impact.

The equivalent of an all-hazards DBS service dome is a modern day safe room, or what is also known as a panic room. These rooms are heavily fortified and installed inside conventional residences or businesses.

Within Win-Win communities, DBS service domes are an all-hazards shelter equivalent of a safe room. Consequently, when an adult instructs a youngster to "go play," any playroom they choose to go to will be in one of the safest structures in the community.

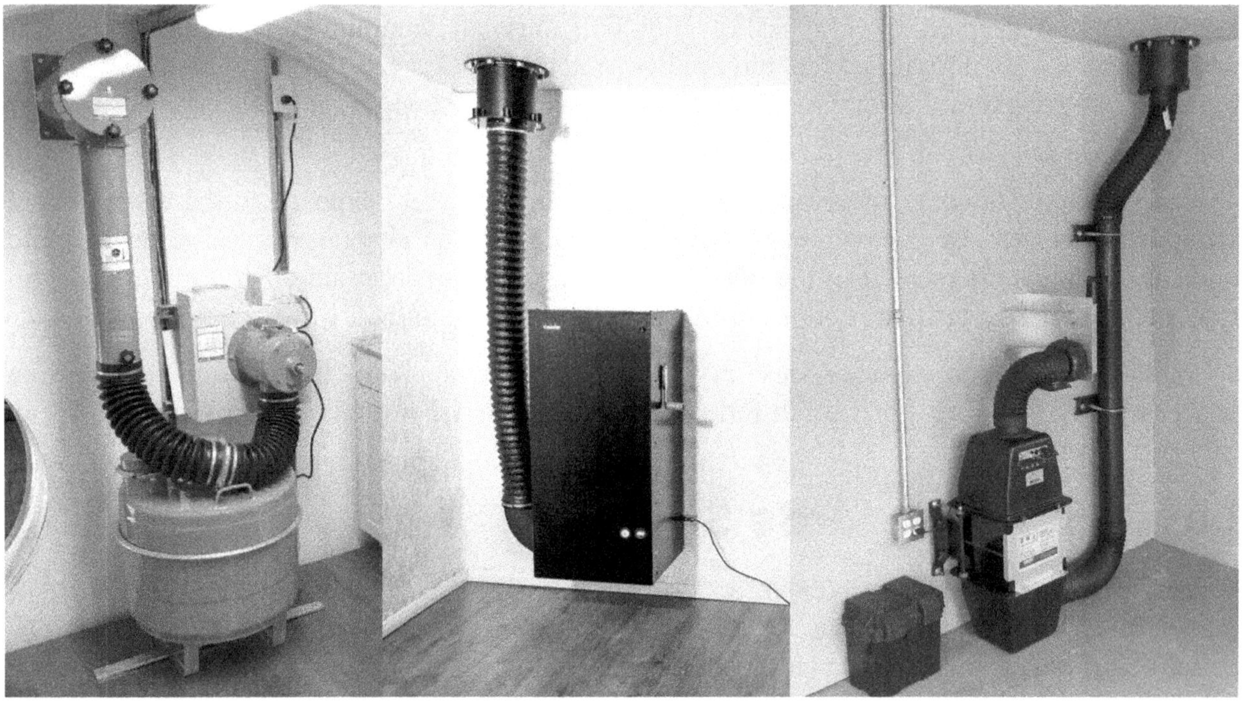

While it is more expensive to construct an all-hazards service dome, it pays for itself in savings. For example, Nuclear, Biological, Chemical (NBC) air filtration systems are a must. They cost approximately $10,000 each.

Stand-alone domes must have their own filtration systems. However, a single filtration system installed inside a service dome can service multiple, attached domes. A backup NBC system is always advisable and by centralizing your mechanical systems, the savings can cover the cost of extra cement and reinforcement.

Then comes the overcover. This is the final stage of the DBS dome's earthwork and looking at it sideways, one could imagine it as a layer cake made with layers made of clay, certified clean fill dirt, basalt aggregate, and cover soil. It protects a DBS dome from radiation and provides impact shielding. It also serves as a moisture and abrasion barrier as well.

Before learning about this final stage of the earthwork, it is necessary to understand the entire earthwork process as it applies to preparing a construction site for a DBS dome.

DBS Dome Earthwork

At the outset of construction, extensive earthwork will be required as part of the dome's foundation and overcover.

Whether you are building a Win-Win survival community retreat or ranch, DBS domes will be constructed above-ground and below-ground with an all-hazards foundation and overcover. There are different options with both.

Overcover Rule No. 1
Cast No Shadows

Shadows with Hard Edges are Like "X" on a Treasure Map

Structures that Cast Sharp Shadows are Easy to Spot

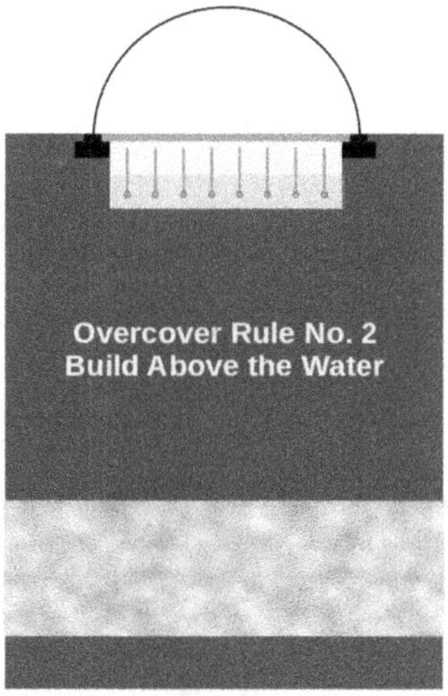
Overcover Rule No. 2
Build Above the Water

100 Year and 1,000 Year Events are About Permitting

A Win-Win Must Plan for a 12,000 Year Event (Noah and the Flood)

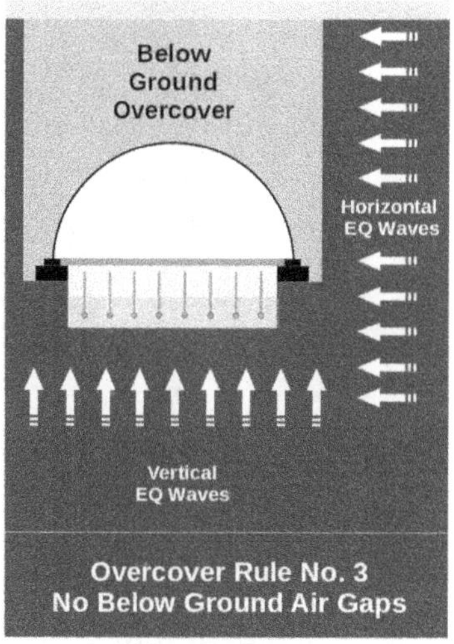
Below
Ground
Overcover
Horizontal
EQ Waves
Vertical
EQ Waves
Overcover Rule No. 3
No Below Ground Air Gaps

Vertical EQ Waves
Air gaps can create stress failures.

Horizontal EQ Waves
Waves must pass through and around the dome. Air gaps create deadly sway.

Regardless of the overcover used, there are three basic rules to keep in mind:

1. Cast No Shadows
2. Build Above the Water Table
3. No Below Ground Air Gaps

Follow these rules for maximum overcover protection and to minimize surveillance concerns.

Above-Ground with Overcover

When looking for suitable property for a church retreat, remember the three golden rules of premium real estate: location, location, location. To see how that works, let's imagine that we need to build a church retreat in NW Minnesota.

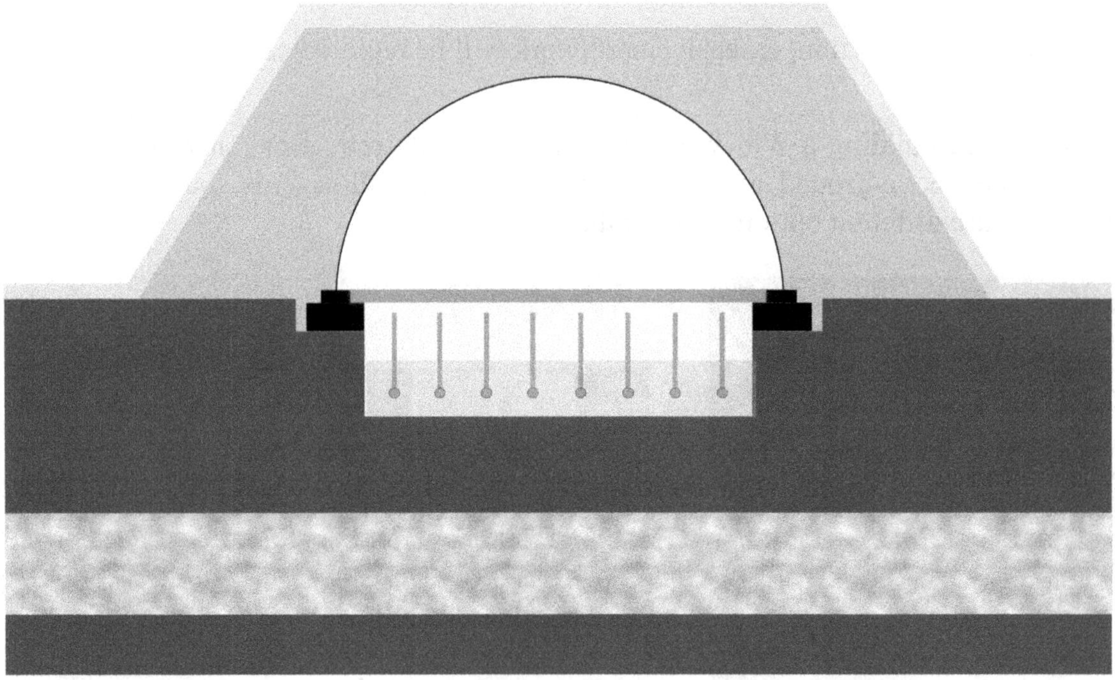

For our example church retreat in NW Minnesota, we will discuss three common options for DBS domes with above-ground cover. They are:

- **Open Ground:** The DBS dome is constructed on open ground with excavation as needed for the all-hazards foundation. No other excavation is required, but since the domes would be fully exposed on all sides, this option requires the largest volume of overcover. If you use the open-ground option, digging a large pond on the property (if you can permit it) is a great way to get fill dirt for the overcover.

- **Partial Height Excavation:** Assuming a dome has a height of 20 ft. high; you will excavate to a depth of ten feet plus the additional depth as needed for the all-hazards foundation. The excavated fill dirt and top soil can be used then for the overcover.
- **Embedded Between Knolls:** A knoll is a small hill or eminence with a rounded top that is sometimes called a hillock. Knolls typically occur in multiples. By siting your structures in the low area between two knolls, your earthwork requirements are similar to the open ground option but with limited excavation. More importantly, you save on the overcover as well.

Of the three options, partial height excavation and embedded between knolls are your best overall options. The finished structures blend well with the natural contours of the land.

Now that we've done flat, let's go vertical.

Below-Ground

Let's assume that your church retreat is located in a hilly area. Realtors call this kind of property, "vertical land" because it is on or next to a hillside or a mountain.

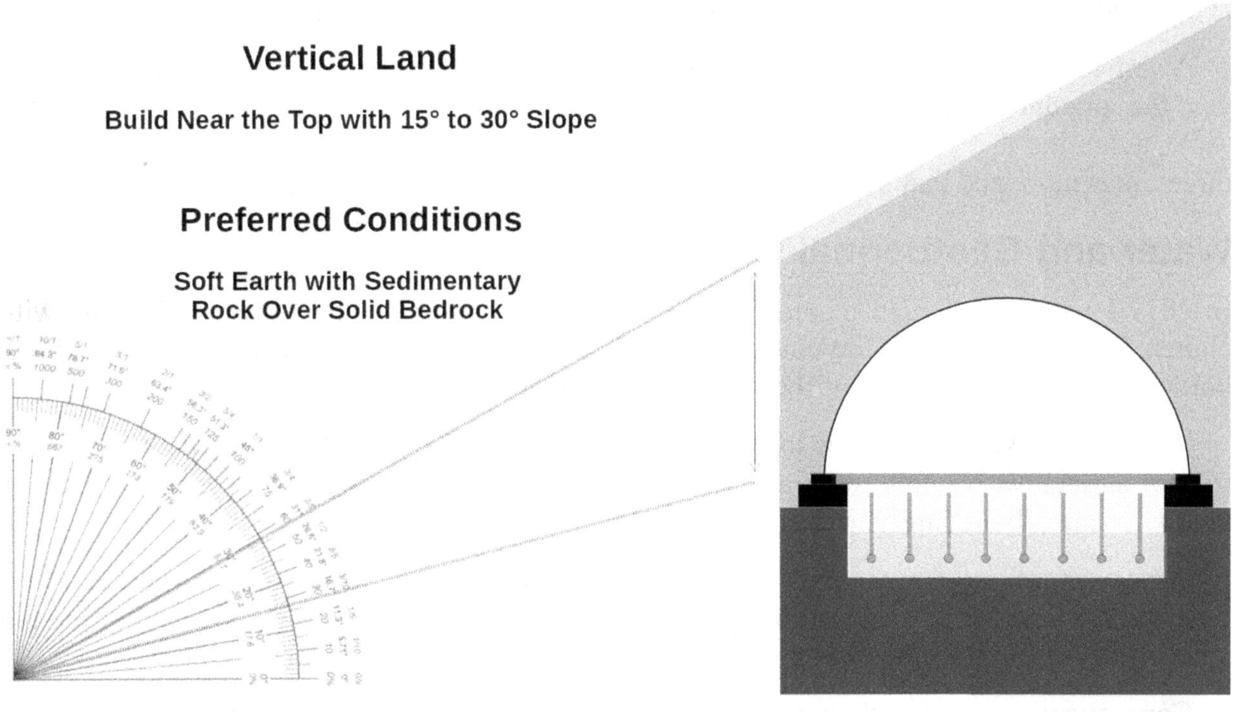
Vertical Land
Build Near the Top with 15° to 30° Slope
Preferred Conditions
Soft Earth with Sedimentary
Rock Over Solid Bedrock

When I was crisscrossing the country and visiting these types of properties, I would often ask the realtor, "Is this property above the 12,000 year floodplain?" The usual reaction was a blank face as they grappled with the question. They knew about 100-year and 1,000-year flood plains, but a 12,000 flood plain always seemed to stump them. After the gears turned in their minds for a while, they would eventually admit that they had never heard of a 12,000 year flood plain.

That is when I would answer, "Of course you have. Didn't you learn about Noah and the Flood when you were a child?" Always a perfect gotcha moment.

Was this an irrelevant trick question? Not at all, because when building below ground on the side of a hill or mountain, the ideal place to locate your dome structures in on the top third of a hill, or well up the side of a mountain. Why? Because, this is how humanity has done it for thousands of years and long before the invention of flood insurance.

Visit old communities in Europe and elsewhere and what do you see? Towns are built on a hill top or on the side of a mountain, and the farm areas are located in the valleys below. As the old saying goes, "Old tricks are the best tricks," and this one has worked for centuries. Why reinvent the wheel? Rather, you need to do the same.

When evaluating "vertical land" for a retreat or a ranch you want to locate your below-ground structures on a 10° to 45° slope. The ideal "vertical land" will have a slope of 15° to 30°, and it will have soft earth over bedrock and be well above the water table. You should avoid land where you have to excavate into igneous rock, shale, or sandstone.

A simple question to ask is, "Are explosives required to prepare the site?" If the answer is yes, the amount of time it will take to complete your earthwork will be approximately the same, assuming that you add extra manpower and technology. In the end, you'll spend two to three times more and that's not all of it. Another cost to consider will be drilling.

Water and Geothermal Wells

In 2017 I led a small field reconnaissance team in the areas around Eureka, Montana with church volunteers Duane Brayton and Dee C. Located a few miles south of the Canadian border, this northwest region of the state is a highly desirable prepper area.

We visited several properties locally and a pattern quickly formed. Land suitable for a retreat or a ranch with ample water and soft soil was prohibitively expensive; the best parcels of land were already in family trusts for over a century.

What was left is what we called a "folly of dreams." Some men, often corporate types, dreamed for years of retiring and living the big sky life in Montana. They dreamed of buying a large tract of land without really understanding the geology and complexities involved.

Consequently, building their retirement mansions would burn through their savings at an undreamed of rate until further development efforts became unsustainable. Or, until their wives told them that they had their fill of paradise and were headed back to the city. The guys would always fold on this one, and list their big sky dream property for sale.

Another big problem for big sky retirement dreamers, was that they often bought "vertical land" on alluvial shale with water tables that were 900' deep and production rates were not impressive as a rule.

But the larger concern is electrical power. Having to pump water up from 900 feet requires a lot of electrical power. It was not uncommon to see a 480 VAC service panel used with irrigation pumps in order to get a reasonable volume of water.

When the grid fails, so will these properties; because when you have to truck water up a mountain, the whole big sky dream goes out the exhaust pipe.

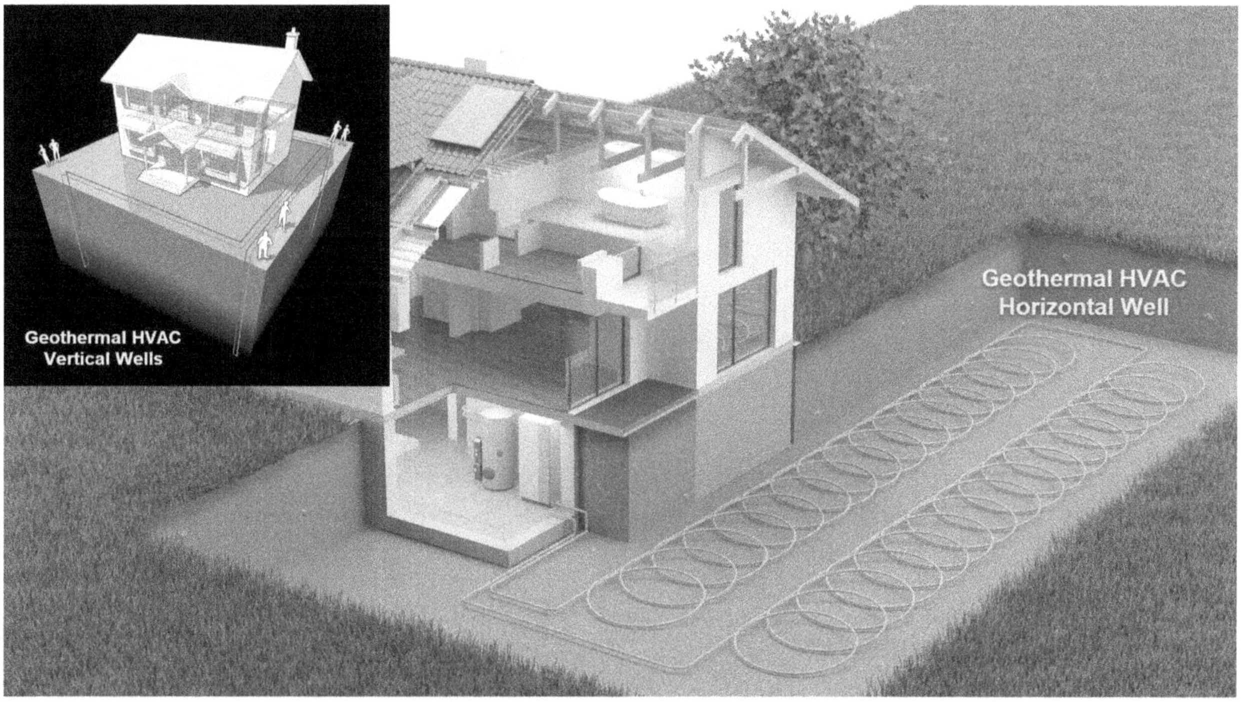

Another critical concern is that igneous rock or shale can make it terribly expensive to drill geothermal heat pump wells. If you are using vertical wells, they will need to be 150'ft to 300' ft deep depending on your area, and you will need to drill several of them with a significant amount of distance between wells.

Roads and Walkways

When excavating the side of a hill or mountain to clear an area for a DBS dome with overcover, you will also need to create new roads and walkways on the property.

When evaluating land, consider the type and its contour because this will determine your infrastructure development costs and efforts. This is why you want land that offers good terrain for roads and walkways.

Gentle curves are nice, and offer plenty of vehicle ambush sites but is this the best way to go? Not really. A well-equipped sniper fire team, with Barrett M82 .50 caliber shoulder-fired semi-automatic sniper rifles and a clear line of sight, can do the same job with far less risk and much fewer personnel. Spare the curves, and buy a pair of M82s.

Another advantage of straight roads is when heavy equipment must be brought to the construction site. Afterward, there will be normal daily truck traffic as well.

The upshot is this, when buying "vertical land" for a church property, you need to work with experts. Not only will you want technical experts such as geologists and design engineers, but you'll also want a security specialist to advise you on how to create a defensible community as well. We'll discuss this expert later.

Service Lines

A Win-Win survival community is a self-supporting entity, and while a retreat will be limited in scope and size, a farm or a ranch can become quite large. When evaluating "vertical land" keep infrastructure in mind, because you will need to provide services such as waste, water, and communication to your structures.

With an all-hazards design, all service lines are below ground with ample cover. Remember, if you buy the wrong kind of land; expect these costs to be triple that of what they normally would be.

Once you've acquired your land and completed your infrastructure and preparatory earthwork, you are ready to raise your DBS domes and here is the good news. No matter the shape or size of a DBS dome, they all are constructed in the same way.

Let's revisit the five major construction stages to illustrate the key differences between DBS dome and EcoShell designs.

Construction Stages

There are significant differences between DBS domes and the EcoShell designs and in the previous chapter, we introduced the five EcoShell construction stages. Now, let's apply them to a DBS dome, to see how the five stages change:

- **Stage 1 – Foundation and Reinforcement:** Extensive earthwork will be required with DBS domes before and after constructing an all-hazards dome foundation. The basalt rebar sticks will be embedded in a different position on the ring beam footing.
- **Stage 2 – Airform Setup:** All airforms have the same basic design. However, fastening a DBS dome airform to the foundation is very different from EcoShells.
- **Stage 3 – Shell Wood Framing and Services:** Wood forms for doors, windows and services such as electric and water are built before the concrete is applied. With a DBS

dome, the forms are added to the inside surface of the airform. With EcoShells, the forms are added to the outside of the airform. Either way, they must be reinforced.

- **Stage 4 – Shell Layers and Reinforcement:** The insulation and shotcrete are applied to the inside of a DBS airform. The opposite is true with an EcoShell I.
- **Stage 5 – Finish:** A DBS dome airform becomes a permanent part of the shell. It will become the bottom layer of the overcover system, which provides protection from radiation, water, abrasion and impact.

When designing your community, it is necessary to determine how much square footage is available with each dome dimension and how much acreage is required before you break ground.

DBS Dome Construction

A DBS dome is a tried-and-true design. It is tough, flexible and can be used to create structures theoretically as large as an entire acre in size. The DBS domes for a basic Win-Win survival community center are typically 44 ft and 60 ft in diameter.

An aerial scissor lift for the interior work inside the dome shell is required. Depending on your project plan, you may also need to rent an outdoor boom aerial lift to work outside the dome shell.

And with that, congratulations Dear Reader! You're now ready to build a DBS dome; so let's look at the construction process to raise a complete, DBS dome shell.

Stage 1 – Foundation and Reinforcement

1. **Siting the Dome:** When choosing where to site your DBS dome, remember that it will be a permanent site. Make certain there is suitable land, ample acreage, supporting infrastructure and services.
2. **Earthwork:** You will need to excavate deep enough for an all-hazards sub-floor with an extra-large ring beam footing. This will also include the service lines as well.
3. **Foundation Wood Framing:** You begin by building a wood form in the shape of the dome's footprint for the ring beam footing. The aim is for the outer wall of the dome's shell to have a continuous contact with the surface of the dome slab.
4. **First Foundation Pour:** Pour your ring beam footing using a conventional concrete mix of cement, sand, stone and water. Additional admixtures and sealants are helpful.
5. **DBS Dome Reinforcement:** With DBS domes, vertical uprights of No. 4 basalt rebar are embedded in the ring beam footing. The ring of uprights should be about five inches from the inner edge when the airform is inflated.
6. **Safety Caps:** In the event of a slip or fall, an upright reinforcement bar can injure or impale a worker. Commercial rebar caps are available, or you can make you own using wooden door knobs. Drill out the center of the knob to the size of the rebar and stick it on top of the upright. Another alternative is to use short lengths of cut rubber tubing to cover the end of the rebar.
7. **Sub-Foundation:** The three layers of the sub-foundation system are placed and topped with the polypropylene dome pad water barrier.
8. **Slab Reinforcement:** Once the sub-foundation is complete, it is time to add reinforcement for the slab. No. 4 rebar and chairs are placed over the polypropylene dome pad water barrier. Be careful to avoid trips and falls during this stage.
9. **Slab Pour:** You'll use a conventional concrete mix of cement, sand, stone and water for pouring your slab. Additional binders and sealants are helpful.
10. **Lower the Uprights:** Once the foundation has set up, you're ready to bend the uprights to the slab floor. Make sure they are all pointing to the center of the slab and once they are all down, cover them with heavy plastic sheeting for worker safety. After this step, you are ready to position and raise the airform.

Stage 2 – Airform Setup

11. **Place the Airform:** Once the foundation has cured, you're ready to raise and shape the dome shell. Place the airform in the center of the slab and draw it out so that it covers the slab.

12. **Anchor the Airform:** With airforms, a basalt rope is sealed inside the edge of the airform to provide a mounting bead. On DBS domes, the bead on the outer edge of the airform is positioned around the edge of the foundation to a depth of about three inches below the top. Then, a thin stainless steel metal strap is screwed completely around the entire circumference of the airform just above the bead. Stainless steel concrete screw anchors are then driven through the strap and airform into the foundation to seal the airform for inflation.

13. **Fans and Airlock:** Once the airform has been anchored, you will attach two large fans for inflation. Each fan must be able to inflate and maintain the shape of the airform. An airlock is used to allow workers to enter and exit the airform without a loss of positive air pressure during construction. Once this is done, you're ready to raise the airform.

14. **Raise the Airform:** Be sure the airform is centered on the slab and that your observers are ready to make sure you properly inflate the dome. For large domes, having an inflation observer in a bucket aerial lift is advisable.

Stage 3 – Shell Wood Framing and Services

15. **Door and Window Frames:** After raising the airform, you can add the wood forms to the inside of the airform to define the placement for the windows and doors.

16. **Outside Service Conduits:** You'll want to build your service conduits into the dome using the same methods described in the previous EcoShell II example.

Stage 4 – Shell Layers and Reinforcement

17. **Prime the Airform:** The airform is a permanent part of the structure with DBS domes, and it will need additional protections. Spraying a coat of primer on the inside surface of the airform creates a tacky adhesive surface for the insulation layer.

18. **First Insulation Layer:** The first 1.5 inch thick layer of polyurethane foam insulation is sprayed onto the inside of the airform.

19. **Embed Reinforcement Hangers:** After spraying the first layer of insulation, insert short lengths of basalt reinforcement sticks, also referred to as "pigs." These must project horizontally toward the center of the dome.

20. **Second Insulation Layer:** The next 1.5 inch thick layer of polyurethane foam insulation is sprayed onto the inside of the airform over the first layer and hangers. After

the insulation fully hardens, the pigs are used to mount vertical and horizontal reinforcement hoops.

21. **Raise the Uprights:** The uprights integrate the dome shell with the foundation and provide the first ring of vertical reinforcement hangers. When raised, they should be about two inches away from the inside surface of the polyurethane.

22. **Vertical Reinforcement:** After the airform has been inflated and framed, use the uprights to anchor the vertical reinforcement loops for the entire shell. The vertical loops need to be about one to two inches from the insulation.

23. **Horizontal Reinforcement:** With the uprights and hangers in place, you can hang horizontal loops of rebar on the pigs and tie them to the vertical loops to create a complete reinforcement grid. Also remember to reinforce wood frames for doors and windows.

24. **First Shotcrete Layer:** Once the reinforcement has been placed, spray the first layer of shotcrete on the airform. It needs to be between 1.5 to 2 inches thick so that it covers the inside edge of the reinforcement grid.

25. **Inside Service Conduits:** You will want to have electrical, communication, and fire safety outlets strategically placed throughout the dome's interior. These service lines will be mounted to the reinforcement grid through stainless steel conduit and the junction boxes must face the interior.

26. **Second Shotcrete Layer:** When the first layer of concrete is ready, spray on another two to three inch, second layer of shotcrete.

Stage 5 – Finish

27. **Empty the Airform:** Remove the fans and airlock and construction equipment. You now have a completed shell.

28. **Inside Finish:** After the dome has cured, you can texture, paint, and seal on the inside. Some prefer the inside surface to be rough instead of smooth because it offers a natural cavern look-and-feel. To smooth the surface, remove the rebound. Rebound is the concrete back splatter that occurs during spraying.

29. **Outside Sealer:** The airform is a permanent part of the DBS dome survival structure. It also serves as a primary water barrier. Before overcover is added, consider painting the exterior of the airform for more protection. Check with the airform manufacturer for specific guidelines, as some types of overcoat may damage the airform.

This completes the process of raising a DBS dome shell. Regardless of the type, shape, or size, you now know enough to build any dome structure you want on a church retreat or ranch.

All-Hazards Community Center

This takes us back to "Chapter 6 – Plan B Basic Concepts" where we introduced the idea of an all-hazards community center for a church retreat – a 44' service dome, a 60' residential dome and a 60' community dome with a full kitchen.

Community Center

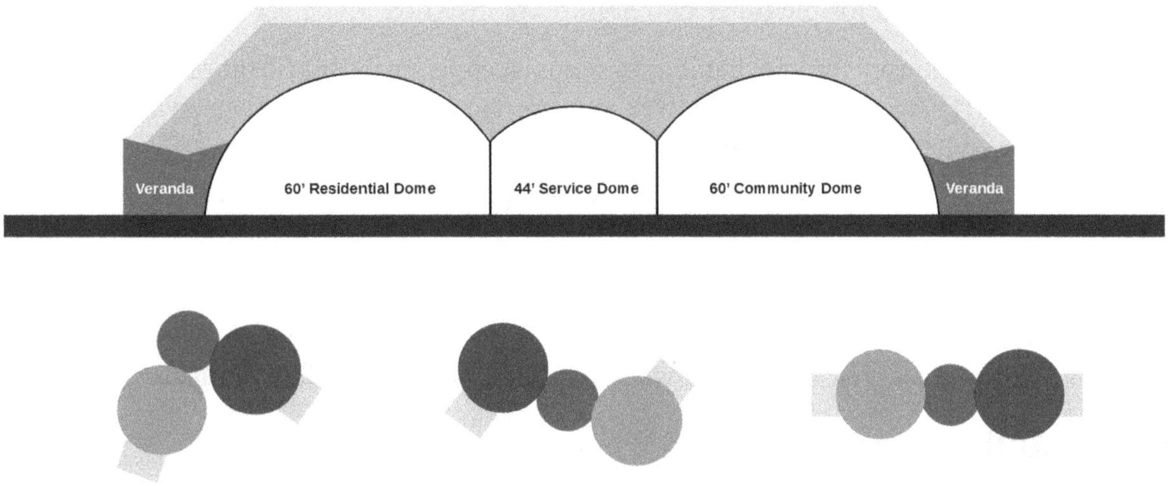

Flexible Configurations

Instead of being constructed separately, these three community center DBS domes will be designed as a single shared-wall cluster. The ability to share walls eliminates the need for separate passageways. It also speeds construction.

In this example, we are creating a three-dome cluster, with a 44' service dome straddled between two 60' domes, with shared walls. The result is that a single airform is used for all three domes and so the cluster is constructed as a single unit.

I spoke with David South about this, and asked him if there was a limit to the number of domes in a cluster. He told me that the largest cluster he had built was in France, and it was a single airform, consisting of 17 domes. This is more than any Win-Win survival community will ever need.

Let's have a closer look at the three domes in our cluster and an accessory veranda structure.

Service Dome

The community center is a shared wall cluster of DBS domes with radiation and impact shield below ground and with an overcover protection shield for above-ground applications.

At the heart of this system are multi-function structures I refer to as service domes. When youngsters are instructed to "go play" by an adult they will know to go to the upper level of the nearest service dome as quickly as they can and to wait there for an adult to arrive.

A service dome offers a single point of entry for outside service lines. Consequently, the mechanical systems used for the other two domes are installed in the service dome.

A service dome houses the mechanical systems such as an NBC filtration ventilation system, geothermal HVAC, emergency power system, survival gear, and survival supplies. It also functions as a passageway between the other two shared wall domes.

In our example, we will raise a classic, semi-hemisphere 44' diameter DBS dome with a 1:2 profile. This means it will be 22' tall and the ground floor will have 1,520 sq ft of usable floor space on the main floor.

In addition to that, a second floor or loft will serve as the "go play" room. It will be a bright and colorful play area with many wonderful distractions for the youngsters.

Residential Dome

The residential dome will be a classic, semi-hemisphere 60' diameter DBS dome with a 1:2 profile. It will be 30' tall and the ground floor area will have 2,827 sq ft of usable floor space on the main floor. Two floor domes with tall ceilings offer calming and spacious living areas.

As mentioned in Chapter 6, smaller private sleeping quarters are on the first floor and an open dormitory with bunk beds is on the second floor with storage areas for young adults and children.

A critical concern with this dome, as with the others, is that biological life forms generate considerable heat and humidity. Managing the heat is a simple matter for the HVAC system. The dome shell itself serves as an excellent thermal battery which means slow temperature changes as conditions change.

However, dealing with humidity is not as easy. A sudden influx of people bedding down for the night will strain the HVAC system unless there is also a separate dehumidifier, which is a complex and costly solution.

An excellent and inexpensive alternative is to use hempcrete partitions in the residence dome. Hempcrete is a bio-composite made of the inner woody core of the hemp plant mixed with a lime-based binder. Popular in Europe for insulating homes in extremely cold climates, hempcrete has superb benefits. However, it is not suitable for load-bearing applications or for direct contact with the ground.

In terms of dome interiors hempcrete:

- Is non-toxic and there is no off-gassing or solvents
- Has high mold resistance and offers an extremely healthy living environment
- Has high vapor permeability for superb humidity control
- Is highly resistant to fires and pets

Instead of conventional drywall, use hempcrete for partitions and walls. In a DBS dome, hempcrete offers a highly effective way to stabilize sudden humidity level fluctuations. It can also be colored with a wash for a very aesthetic appearance.

When the dome fills up with members and guests, the increased humidity they release into the air is absorbed by the hempcrete, and then slowly released over time. This way, the HVAC system can easily manage humidity spikes without the need for separate dehumidifiers.

Community Dome

Like the residential dome, the community dome is a classic, semi-hemisphere 60' diameter DBS dome with a 1:2 profile. It will be 30' tall and the ground floor area will have 2,827 sq ft of usable floor space (not including a full or partial second floor).

The purpose of the community dome is to provide a spacious and comfortable space for church meetings and social events. For example, the community center dome can offer the following features:

- **Full Kitchen:** A full kitchen with professional quality gas stoves and electric appliances suitable for preparing meals for thirty. The gas stoves are powered by methane biodigesters.

- **Small Performance Stage:** Opposite the kitchen, a small stage with a piano or electronic keyboard for leading sing-alongs and member performances.

- **Folding Tables and Chairs:** A storage area under the stage is used for folding tables and chairs and exercise mats.

- **Large, Wall-mounted Projection Screen:** The addition of a large projection screen can turn the community center into special events profit generator for the church.

- **Audiovisual Equipment Loft:** A good place to mount lighting, projection and sound equipment is in a small loft above the kitchen area with ample room for a technician.

These are a few of the possible amenities you can add to your domes. Once you've finished building your DBS dome cluster, you're ready for the final step – overcover.

DBS Dome Airforms and Overcover

If domes were belly buttons, an EcoShell is an outtie and a DBS dome is an innie. With an EcoShell, the shotcrete is applied to the outside of the airform, whereas, with a DBS dome, the shotcrete is applied to the inside of the airform. When a DBS shell is finished, the airform covering it, is all that you will see.

This brings us a thorny vulnerability when it comes to DBS dome airforms and overcover.

In the early days, David South would remove the airforms so they could be re-used and thereby save clients' money. Regrettably, this proved to be a tricky process. Damage could occur to both the airform as well as the outer surface of the dome shell.

He consequently decided that airforms should no longer be removed from large domes, but rather, be left in place as a permanent water barrier. This solved one problem, but as is often the case, it created another – degradation of the airform.

Airform Degradation

Airforms can be made with a Butyl or polyvinyl chloride (PVC) coated nylon or polyester fabric. Either way, these materials are tough stuff but they suffer from the same Achilles Heel, ultra-violet (UV) radiation from the sun.

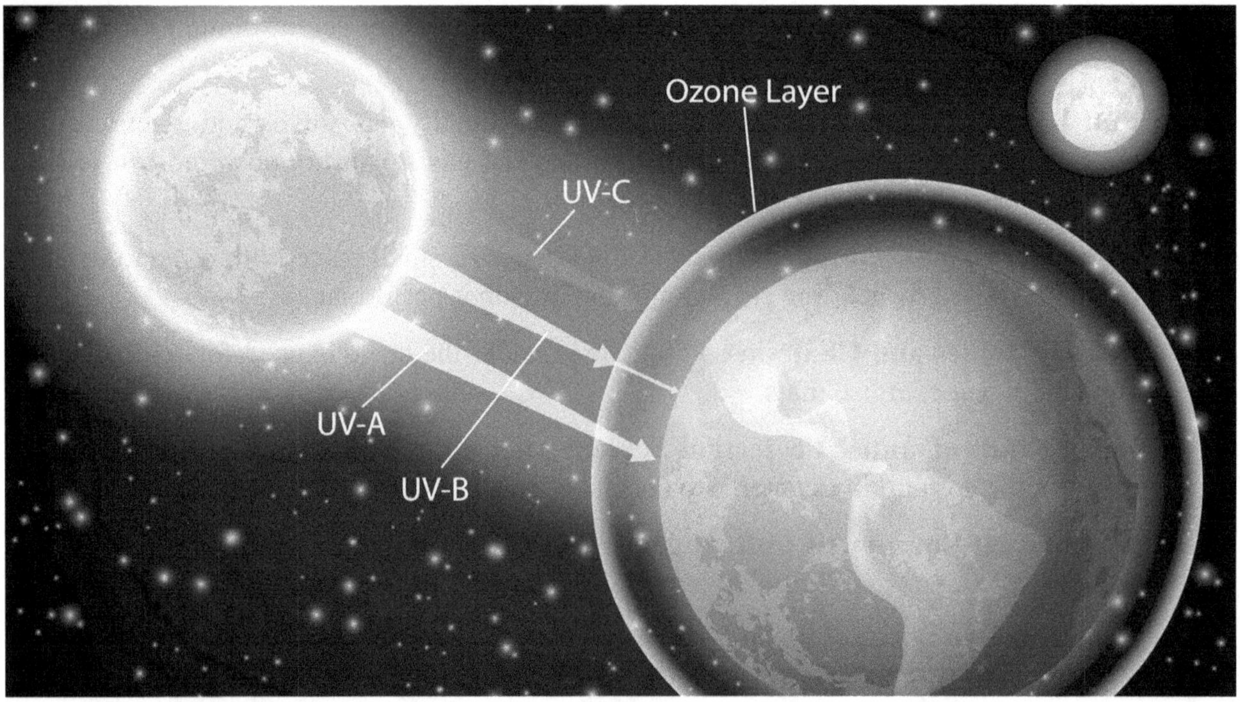

This Achilles Heel produced two major developments of value to Win-Win survival communities:

- **EcoShells:** With EcoShells, UV radiation is not a problem with EcoShells because the airforms are removed after the dome shell has been constructed.
- **Overcover:** With overcover, the need to protect airforms from UV is eliminated.

This is good news for us, but for David, the issue of UV protection has always dogged him.

Look at it this way. A DBS dome made with basalt reinforcement will last 1000 years but not its airform. The useful lifespan of an unprotected airform is twenty to twenty five years. UV radiation will eventually degrade the PVC causing it to fail.

Herein was David's conundrum with DBS domes; a relatively long-lived concrete shell with a short-lived airform. While preventing UV exposure with above-ground structures was impossible, what was possible was a way to mitigate the damage and prolong airform life-span. This launched David on a long and noteworthy journey of discovery.

UV Mitigation

David's first DBS dome UV mitigation effort was to cover DBS domes with ceramic tile. This was affordable and easy to work with for DIY projects. However, cold weather causes ceramic tile to crack; so this material proved unsuitable.

David's second mitigation effort was porcelain tile. This was more expensive than ceramic tile, and it required the services of a professional installer.

Porcelain tile is far superior to ceramic tile. It does not crack, has an extremely low water absorption rate, and is more durable in areas of heavy usage. This explains its current popularity for use with swimming pools, bathrooms, kitchens and other areas of high traffic.

What David learned was that a DBS dome airform covered with porcelain tile would last about thirty to thirty five years, about ten years longer than an unprotected airform. That was a positive step in the right direction, and the next would be better.

David's third DBS dome UV protection effort was a metal cladding. A typical metal roof will last anywhere from 30 to 50 years. However, when premium metals such as stainless steel, titanium, zinc, and copper are used, the cladding can last well over 100 years.

The downside is that given the physical size of a large dome, a roof lasting 100 years can be prohibitively expensive. This brings us back to David's conundrum. He could build a 1,000-year dome with a 100-year airform, but only at a heavy price.

With a Win-Win DBS dome with overcover here is what you get. A dome that can last 1,000 years with an airform that can also last 1,000 years. Here's the best part, with a Win-Win, this is a buy one get one BOGO bonanza.

Now how does that work?

Plastics do not biodegrade like organic matter, as the plastics used in the airform will degrade and eventually fail as a result of long-term exposure to UV of approximately 1,000 years.

A DBS dome with overcover will never see sunlight for 1,000 years; therefore, there is no UV-radiation to degrade the material. This is a great solution but also creates another problem. Airform failure due to abrasion.

Abrasion Barrier

With a DBS dome, ground temperature is a critical factor. While an EcoShell I is insulated with a special concrete mix, a thick layer of insulation is required for above-ground covered and below-ground DBS domes due to the properties of the overcover.

It is important to keep in mind, that the ground temperatures, soil type, moisture content, and other elements will determine the actual temperatures at any given depth for your DBS dome. A good rule of thumb to follow for ground temperature is for 6' below the surface, the temperature is roughly 55° F, and at 12' below the surface, it is approximately 50° F.

13

Overcover

The overcover is the final stage of the dome earthwork, and it is comprised of layers of natural clay, certified clean fill dirt, basalt aggregate (or tailings), and cover soil. When done properly, it provides a dome significant protection from radiation and impacts.

Once a newly constructed dome or dome cluster is ready for overcover, there are two types.

- **Highly-survivable:** 6' thick shield with four layers of natural materials.
- **All-hazards Overcover:** 14' thick shield composed of the same materials, including an optional impact basket as described in this chapter.

Before any overcover is applied, the concrete must be properly cured which requires 30 days.

Short-change the process by applying the overcover too soon and the dome's concrete shell will be compromised which will result in shrinking or cracking.

Therefore, it is only after the dome shell has properly cured that you are ready to apply the overcover, as part of a structured, all-hazards overcover protection strategy. One based on three principal threat categories.

All-Hazards Threat Categories

With all-hazards overcover protection, the three principal threat categories are natural in origin and are as follows:

- **Solar Radiation:** The Sun is just now emerging from a Maunder Minimum, also known as the "prolonged sunspot minimum." As we approach the threshold of the next solar maximum, this is of concern because the solar maximum that followed the Maunder Minimum in 1715 was very strong. If the same holds true today, we'll likely see higher levels of UV radiation, X-rays, Gamma rays, and plasma from solar storms.
- **Earthquakes:** Horizontal ground movement from large seismic events is the force that causes conventional buildings to sway and fail above ground. Below the ground, these same forces can cause a vertical stem wall to cave like in a conventional basement. Keep the upcoming Solar Maximum in mind, because since January 2013, more earthquakes of all magnitude have been recorded each month than in all of recorded history. Worse yet, this lengthy uptick in activity appears to be unabated.
- **Impact Events:** A meteorite is a piece of rock from space that strikes the surface of the Earth, and when several of them strike together, it is a meteorite swarm. During periods when large numbers of fireballs are observed, individual impact events are more likely, as are meteoroid swarms. In fact since January 2013, more fireballs are observed each month and this trend is also increasing without relief.

Therefore, there are risks that can be seen by everyone. However, there are less obvious risks too, and both can blindside you with equally catastrophic results.

The takeaway here is that you cannot protect 100% from all threats, which is why you use a balanced, holistic approach when designing a survival community.

Holistic Strategy

It is easy for a myopic focus on the large threats that you face to lead you to invest great sums of money into building impressive survival structures at the expense of smaller threats that are more likely to occur.

Let's use a small threat example to illustrate the point.

Assuming a kitchen volunteer forgets to wash his or her hands before helping to prepare the evening meal, and there is fresh fecal matter on his or her hands, what could happen?

The feco-oral route of transmission is one of the main modes to spread some of the world's most serious infectious diseases. All it takes is for one thoughtless act of negligence to negate the principal goal of hardened structures. That being, to stay alive.

A holistic solution mitigates this risk.

With a holistic solution, avoid a myopic focus on a few threats and balance all of the perceived threats to your community with your available options and funding capacity.

How will a holistic solution address the threat in this feco-oral transmission example?

For the price of a sack of Portland cement, you can buy an OSHA-Kitchen Safety Handwashing Sign for the bathroom. Due to its importance and the serious implications it has to the health of the community, you make this a mandatory safety regulation.

Given that you're buying signs, get another one that warns, "Watch for Falling Rocks."

Meteorites

Solar radiation and earthquakes are straightforward threats to assess. However, impact events are a bit harder to assess. This is because when a meteorite impacts the Earth, the amount of destructive energy released depends on the mass, velocity, and trajectory of the impactor and to a certain extent – a collision of Murphy's law and dumb luck.

When researching asteroid impact events, there are countless pages and videos about extinction level and near-extinction level events.

How well can you endure something like that with a structured all-hazards strategy? Let's be realistic. If an asteroid large enough to be a city-killer strikes your Win-Win community, the impact event will be catastrophic. On the other hand, a smaller impactor can still be quite destructive. Such was the case in 2003.

2003 Impact Event

On Tuesday, September 23, 2003 at 4:00 PM local time, a stony 44 lb (20 kg) meteorite crashed through a two-story house in New Orleans. It struck and penetrated the roof of the house and destroyed an antique wooden desk on the second floor. It then punched a hole through the second floor and into a downstairs bathroom, where it also punched a hole through the foundation and shattered into pieces beneath it. The largest fragment found was approximately the size of a grapefruit.

Now let's assume the same impactor hits one of your church structures. We'll begin with the domes we learned about in "Chapter 11 – EcoShells I & II."

If that 2003 impactor had struck the EcoShell I two-story dome residence described in that chapter, it would have easily penetrated the concrete shell due to the Styrofoam-concrete mix for insulation. This would result in extensive damage, if the interior of the dome is showered with impact fragments.

However, any dome, with an all-hazards overcover, would have been completely unfazed by the 2003 New Orleans impactor. Why? Because this is what happens, when you have a holistic solution to threat protection and use a structured all-hazards strategy.

Structured All-Hazards Strategy

A classic cinema quote from *The Hunger Games* (2012) film was, "May the odds be ever in your favor." This was a clever and obvious way of assuring the public that the Games were fair. It contained a less-subtle message for the contestants. Only one of them would survive.

With those kinds of odds, *The Hunger Games* were like playing a game of roulette in Las Vegas, and only one contestant would walk away from the game alive. Contestants essentially had to bet their lives on 00, which pays 35 to one.

They all knew the odds, and if the ivory ball landed on their number, they'd live. If not, they'd die a glorious death. Glorious for the audience, that is.

Herein is the saving grace of a structured all-hazards strategy when playing the odds; it levels the playing field with a simple, useful statistical rule of thumb.

Playing the Odds

The Casino game Roulette, which means "little wheel" in French, has been popular with casino-goers since the 17th century. When allocating resources to protect against various threats, the game offers a useful strategic planning guide.

If you're feeling lucky, a "straight-up" inside bet on 00 pays 35 to one, and if the ivory ball lands on your number, you're a winner. If not, you lose. This all-or-nothing strategy is not well-balanced, and it leaves you exposed to a wide range of lesser and greater threats.

When playing Roulette, you can mitigate this risk by placing “outside” bets as well. These do not involve a specific number such as 00. For example, a bet on a color, (red or black) pays one to one, and you have a fifty-fifty chance of doubling your money. In addition, there are many inside and outside betting options with various risks and payouts.

When betting against all of the potential threats facing your community, survival planning is not about winning a fortune. It is about walking away from the game – alive!

For this reason, a winning overcover all-hazards threat strategy uses all available resources to “cover as much of the table” as possible with a simple combination of lower-risk, “outside” bets.

With a Win-Win survival community, how you play the odds begins with categorizing the principal threats.

Survivable

To be rated as survivable, a dome must offer basic protection from earthquakes, wind, and water-driven natural disasters. It should also be able to withstand impacts from small and medium caliber pistol and rifle ammunition.

This is the rating for above-ground EcoShell I and II domes, where the standard shell thickness varies between 3” to 4” depending on the application. In the case of an insulated EcoShell I though, the Styrofoam shotcrete mix reduces a concrete shell’s armor performance.

Highly-Survivable

Also referred to as hardened structures, a highly-survivable structure offers excellent protection from solar radiation, volcanic ash fall and ejecta. The goal of overcover is to enable the dome to survive meteorite showers from multiple impacts of 100+ lb stony meteorites.

For current commercial applications, standard dome thickness is approximately 4” overall. However, by increasing overall shell thickness to 6”, you increase its armor strength by 50%. This increased thickness also offers the option for a flatter dome profile.

For example in terms of armor protection, a dome with a 1:3 profile and a 6” thick shell will be 142.5% stronger than a similar diameter dome with a 1:2 profile and a 4” shell.

All-Hazards

DBS service domes are the all-hazards shelter equivalent of a safe room or panic room. They have a 1:2 profile and a reinforced 8” shell and serve as hardened underground bunkers.

During extreme short-term events, a service dome offers twice the protection of a highly-survivable structure.

During normal operations, all-hazards service domes have a dual-use role. On the lower level, they serve as service line entry points, mechanical rooms, and as passageways between other domes. In the upper area or loft, is a "go play" safety room for youngsters.

This brings us to the thorny vulnerability of dome airforms in general because this applies to service domes as well. Airform failure due to abrasion from earth movements.

Abrasion Barrier

Very large earthquake (VLE) swarms are a fairly recent phenomena. We've tracked them since 2018. This trend began with large swarms consisting of thousands of small earthquakes off the coast of Hawaii during the months of June and July 2018.

In 2019, similar VLE swarms occurred in the USA along the West Coast in Alaska, Southern California, in the China Lake region, and the Cascadia Subduction Zone region from northern California to Canada. VLE swarms present a serious risk to Win-Win communities.

It does not matter whether your community is located in an area that historically has a low risk of earthquakes. That can change in a heartbeat., If VLE swarms suddenly beset your community properties and you've covered your domes with unscreened fill dirt, you may have unseen damage.

With a VLE swarm, sharp rocks in the unscreened fill dirt can work their way down until over time they begin to grind against the airform surface. The subsequent result is that the airform will likely see a partial failure of its integrity.

This is why special care must be given to the raw materials used to build your overcover layers. When using a comprehensive overcover strategy, it starts with the right materials.

Overcover Materials

With overcover, simple works best. You're not doing something exotic, like using gold foil to protect the electronics of a spacecraft. Rather, you're old school about this because your solution is something an ancient Roman architect would appreciate.

Here is the material mix:

- **Natural Clay:** In terms of half-life radiation shielding, finely screened clay is approximately 25% more effective than compacted dirt.
- **Basalt Shielding:** The basalt aggregate shield layer is your primary protection layer. It helps to protect from both radiation and small impact events.
- **Soil:** Layers of finely screened soil are used between the clay and basalt.

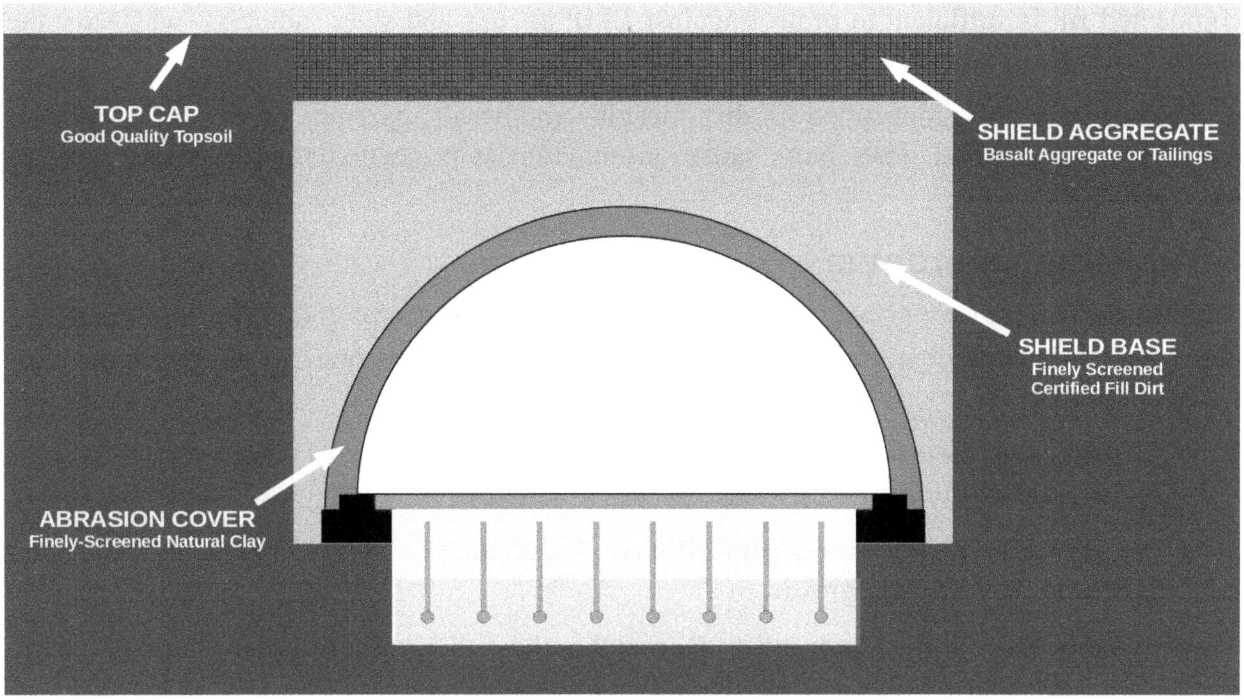

When it comes to the basalt shielding, some maintain that inch-for-inch, basalt is as effective as iron or steel and offers several times more protection than compacted dirt. Also, tailings are as effective as aggregate but cost significantly less. This same basalt shielding is also an effective protection from meteorite impacts.

As to what happened during the New Orleans impact event that occurred on September 23, 2003, after punching through the roof, a desk on the second floor, and a bathroom on the first floor, it finally shattered to pieces beneath the foundation.

Why there? The foundation was reinforced concrete, and the impactor was fragmented by the rebar and concrete. Here is where the dome's two shield layers offer a unique combination of impact protection.

The basalt aggregate layer is a dense field of hard rocks. This will cause stony meteorites to begin breaking apart just as the 2003 New Orleans impactor did after it penetrated the home's foundation.

Impactor fragments with enough velocity and force to make it through the aggregate layer will be captured in the shield base layer underneath it. A further backup to that layer is the clay cover beneath it and then, the dome shell itself.

Therefore, our four-layer overcover is either 6' or 14' thick depending on dome type; which raises an obvious question. Conversely, if a 5' thick overcover comprised solely of compacted fill is sufficient to protect against EMP attacks and solar radiation, why have the additional expense of an overcover comprised of different material layers?

The answer is this: compacted fill dirt plus clay and basalt aggregate creates an all-hazards overcover with several times more radiation and impact protection than a simple layer of compacted dirt.

Structured Overcover

This brings us back to "Chapter 6 – Plan B Basic Concepts" where we first introduced the idea of an all-hazards community center for a church retreat. The center is a three-dome cluster consisting of:

- **All-hazards Service Dome:** A 22' high, semi-hemisphere, 44' diameter DBS dome with a 1:2 profile.
- **Highly Survivable Residential Dome:** A 30' high semi-hemisphere, 60' diameter DBS dome with a 1:2 profile.
- **Highly Survivable Community Dome:** Another 30' high semi-hemisphere, 60' diameter DBS dome with a 1:2 profile.

By using a combination of different dome diameters with the same 1:2 profile, produces a 14' height difference between the top of the 44' all-hazards service dome and the larger, highly-survivable, 60' residential and community domes.

Let's see how this height difference works for our community center.

Overcover Strategy

Regardless of the dome type or size, the earthwork is a 4-layer overcover. Here are the layers, beginning with the first, which serves as the last barrier of protection for the dome airform:

- **Abrasion Cover:** 60' domes are covered with a 1' layer of finely-screened natural clay to create an abrasion cover against grinding due to earth movements. For service domes, a well-packed, 2' layer is used.
- **Shield Base:** A well-packed, 1' layer of finely-screened certified fill dirt is applied over the clay to support the next layer. For service domes, a well-packed, 6' layer is used.
- **Shield Aggregate:** A 2' layer of basalt aggregate or tailings is applied over the shield base. This shield is for radiation from solar storms, EMP weapons, and impact events. For service domes, a well-packed, 4' layer is used.
- **Top Cap:** A well-packed, 2' layer of good quality topsoil suitable for planting. It serves as a natural-appearing surface for the overcover.

As you can see, the overcover for the all-hazards service dome is significantly greater.

- The height of a 60’ dome will be 36’, including the 6’ overcover.
- The height of a 44’ service dome will be 36’, including the 14’ overcover.

As to the weight of the overcover. A standard DBS dome with a 4” shell can support over 30’ feet of earth, rock, and clay. For extra impact shielding, the impact basket option offers increased protection without changing the overcover height.

Service Dome Impact Basket

An optional service dome impact basket can be incorporated into the top 2’ of the 6’ shield base layer for service domes. The sole purpose of an impact basket is to increase the meteorite anti-penetration properties of the overcover.

With stoney meteorite impact events, a service dome with an optional impact basket can theoretically double the level of protection for the dome structure and occupants within.

In “Chapter 13 – Overcover,” we discussed a meteorite impact event that occurred on September 23, 2003, when a stony 44 lb (20 kg) meteorite crashed through a two-story house in New Orleans. It struck and penetrated the roof and both floors of the house

It punched a hole through the second floor and into a downstairs bathroom. However, after it pierced the foundation, it shattered into pieces beneath it. The largest fragment found in the soil below the foundation was approximately the size of a grapefruit.

What caused the New Orleans impactor to shatter was the combination of concrete and reinforcement in the foundation. This same principle is employed with an impact basket.

The reason for using an impact basket is not to prevent deep earth penetration by a meteorite such as the New Orleans impactor. Instead, it will fragment the impactor into smaller pieces, which will have considerably less energy for deep earth penetration.

Depending on your final design, an impact basket can theoretically double your overcover protection from meteorite impact events. Likewise, it will raise the cost of your overcover.

Nonetheless, you have the freedom to initially plan your overcover without this option during the planning stages. If you change your mind, you can easily add this option during the construction phase.

It will require a minor shield base modification, followed by the construction of the impact shield itself. When completed, the impact shield will be the immediate layer below the shield aggregate layer, which is your primary protection from solar radiation.

Shield Base Modification

An impact basket is incorporated into the upper level of the overcover without changing the overall height.

This option uses a well-packed layer of certified fill dirt to a height of 4', thereby allowing the top 2' for the impact basket.

Unlike the other layers in your overcover design, an impact basket requires a 2' high pit to be formed as part of the shield base.

For optimal protection, the impact basket pit needs to extend 10' outwards from the dome's footprint. Therefore, a 44' wide service dome will require an impact basket trench that is 66' wide.

Impact Basket Materials

The downside of an optional impact basket is the added construction cost. On the upside, the good news is that you will already have on-hand most of the materials required, such as sand and recycled tires.

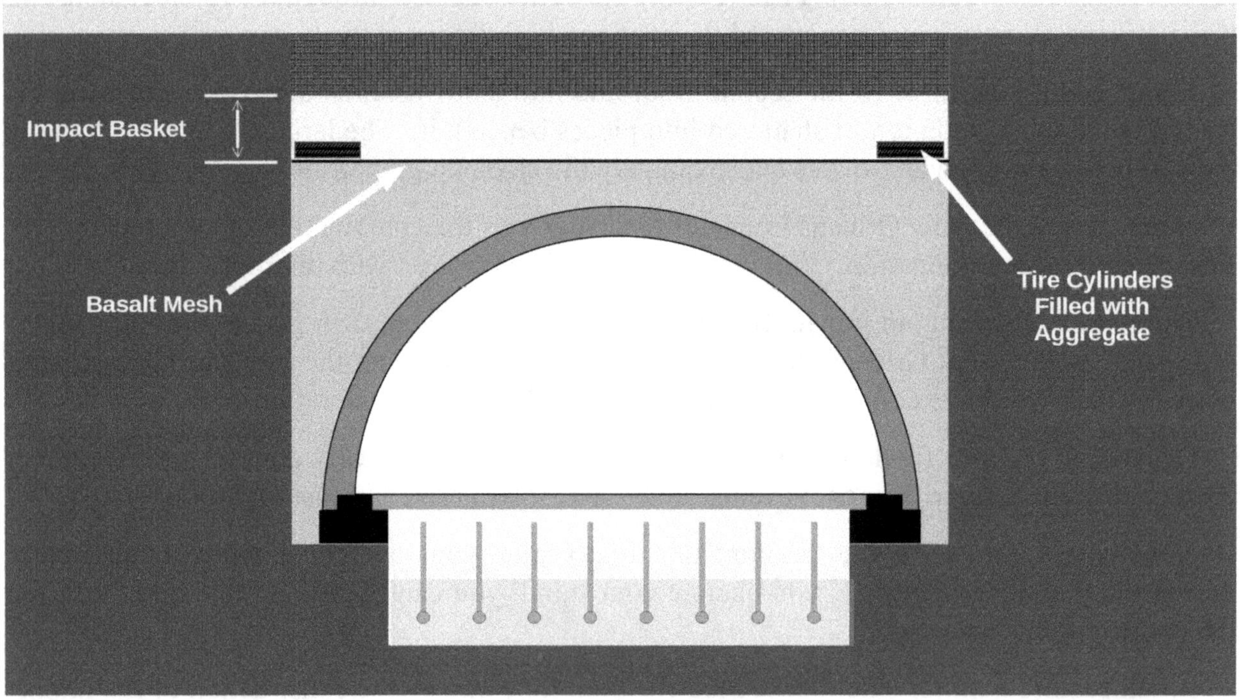

In "Chapter 10 – Design Team and Infrastructure," we discussed the need for highly-survivable infrastructure, including a main property road paved with mechanical concrete using recycled tires cylinders.

With a road, the base uses an 18' deep trench for the recycled tire cylinders filled with aggregate. After this, the trench is paved over with concrete, asphalt, or compressed aggregate.

When adding impact baskets to your service dome overcover, you'll use the same recycled tire cylinders with a 2' trench. Instead of using aggregate to fill the trench, you will use sand.

Given that you will already use recycled tire cylinders and sand for other purposes, you'll need to order more for your impact basket. You will need to special order basalt roving and road reinforcement fiber mesh for your impact baskets.

There are many different basalt road mesh types with different width, thickness, and open-cell spacing options that come on rolls up to 328ft (100m). The roll length dimension is critical because you'll need to cut it into 66' lengths to ensure a strong impact basket.

Please note, if you are tempted to use inexpensive iron or steel reinforcement instead, remember, it will rust and degrade. On the other hand, basalt will last for centuries.

And finally, you'll need to order plenty of basalt roving which is used to fasten the recycled tire cylinders to the basalt road mesh.

Impact Basket Design

Your design team will incorporate an impact basket into the overcover based on your design goals. However, regardless of the final design, should your service dome survive an impact event, it will need to be repaired.

When this manual repair requirement is factored in, overcover repairs can be made using using shovels and wheelbarrows. The same holds true for the impact basket. It must be capable of being repaired just as easily with hand tools and manual labor.

The key component in your impact basket will be your 66' long lengths of basalt road mesh which are required for even the most minimal design. There are two basic options:

- 4-sided Mesh Square: Requires two, 66' lengths.
- 6-sided Mesh Hexagon: Requires three, 66' lengths.

Recycled tire cylinders are the principal components for impact shock absorption. In the most minimal design, you will use a simple basalt road mesh without tire cylinders.

For added shock absorption, tire cylinders are woven into both ends of a 66' long length of basalt road mesh with roving. During an impact event, they will work much like the shock absorbers in your car, which are used to lessen the effect of jarring bumps so as to give you a smoother ride.

Once you've laid down your lengths of basalt road mesh with or without impact shock absorption, the entire 2' trench is filled to the top with wet, compacted sand. After the sand dries, you are then ready to apply the shield aggregate layer over the shield base layer with its impact basket.

IMPACT BASKET CONFIGURATIONS
(Effectiveness Varies with Design)

125% Protection

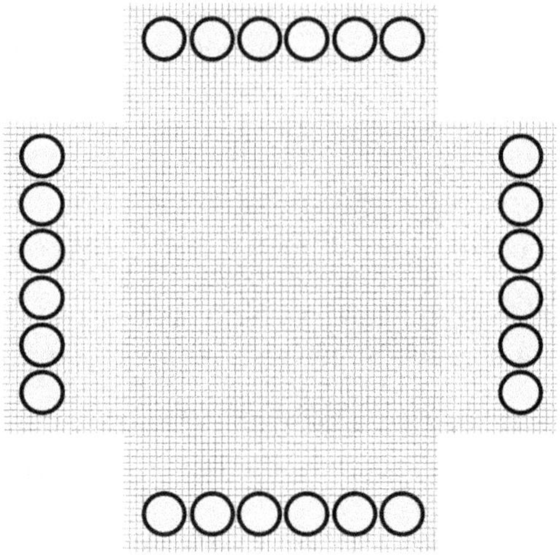

150% Protection

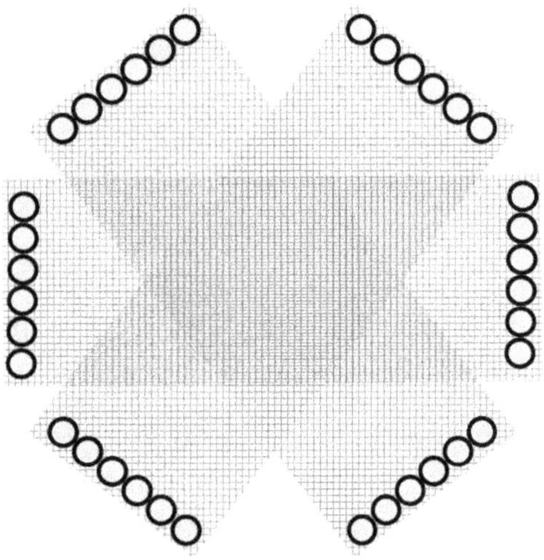

175% Protection

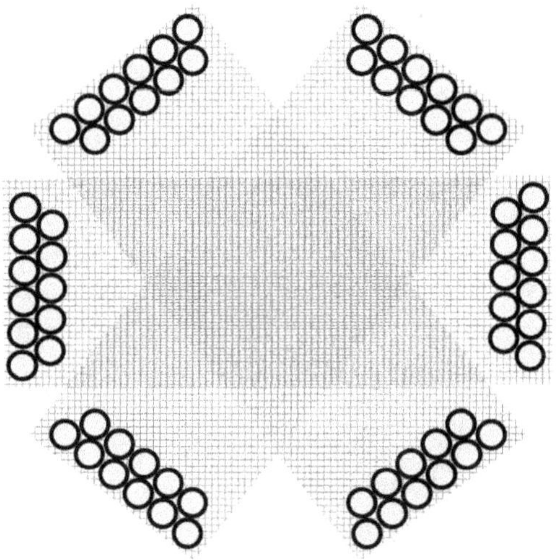

200% Protection

Design Configurations

The final amount of impact protection you'll gain from the addition of an optional impact basket will depend on how it is designed and the materials used.

In other words, there is not a one-size-fits-all solution. Rather, it will likely be a trade-off between cost and protection. So to illustrate the possibilities, let's use four examples ranging from 125% to 200% protection over a standard design.

With all four designs, the mesh square is laid directly on the bottom of the trench on top of the certified fill dirt used by the shield base. The entire trench is then covered with sand fill.

Here is how the four designs compare:

- **125% Protection:** A simple 4-sided mesh square which is laid directly on the certified fill dirt at the bottom of the trench and covered with sand.
- **150% Protection:** A 4-sided mesh square with a single row of tire cylinders bound together with roving at each end. The mesh and tires are covered with sand.
- **175% Protection:** The impact basket uses a 6-sided mesh hexagon with a single row of tire cylinders woven together with roving at each end and filled with sand.
- **200% Protection:** The impact basket uses a 6-sided mesh hexagon with a double row of tire cylinders woven together with roving at each end and filled with sand.

Before discounting the simple 125% design, you may want to consider using it for your residential domes, which use a 1' deep shield base layer. Instead of using certified fill dirt for these domes, substitute the fill dirt with a 1' deep, simple, mesh and sand impact basket.

Impactor Risks

The two largest factors in the risk-reduction effectiveness of an impact basket are the design discussed above and the type of meteorite, of which there are basically three. Let's briefly discuss them in terms of which ones a community is most likely to experience.

- **Stoney Meteorites – 95% Probability:** The impact shield is primarily designed for this type. They are generally composed of approximately 75 – 90% silicon-based minerals, 10 – 25% nickel-iron alloy, and have trace amounts of iron sulfide.
- **Iron Meteorites – 5% Probability:** You could say iron meteorites are nature's version of an armor-piercing anti-tank round. They typically feature an iron content of approximately 90 to 95%, with the remainder comprised of nickel and trace elements. Your impact shield will be marginally effective with this type.
- **Stony-Iron Meteorites – 2% Probability:** The least abundant of the three main types, the stony-irons, account for less than 2% of all known meteorites. They are

comprised of roughly equal amounts of nickel-iron and stone. Your impact shield will be moderately effective with this type.

The bottom line is that the actual size of the impactor can be of less a consideration when factoring in its type. In the end, it comes down to luck and your construction budget. With this in mind, let's see how all this works using an example based on an impact event where your service dome takes a direct hit from a stoney meteorite

Impact Basket Example

For this example, let's follow the path of a 200 lb. stoney meteorite from the moment it strikes the top surface of your service dome overcover and comes to a stop before it can penetrate the dome shell.

As stated previously, an impact basket is to increase the meteorite anti-penetration properties of the overcover. It is optimized for stoney meteorites and does stop them. However, it help breaks them apart at a safe distance from the dome shell.

This example shows how an optional impact basket uses energy displacement and micro-fraction to achieve this end.

We will follow the sequence of events for a 200 lb. stoney meteorite that impacts the overcover with a 6-sided mesh hexagon and a double row of tire cylinders for shock absorption.

- **Top Cap Layer:** The top 2' layer of the top cap is comprised of quality topsoil. The impactor will pass through this layer first. The impact energy will be primarily focused on the leading edge of the meteorite.
- **Shield Aggregate Layer:** As the meteorite passes through this layer, micro-fraction will then substantially weaken the impactor's integrity.
- **Impact Basket – Step 1:** The meteorite strikes the sand at the top of the impact basket. This step refocuses the impact energy on the meteorite's leading-edge, increasing the energy displacement and micro-fracturing process.
- **Impact Basket – Step 2:** The meteorite impacts the basalt mesh. Like the concrete foundation and reinforcement discussed in the 2003 impact example, the overlapping layers of basalt mesh will force a sudden energy displacement, and micro-fracturing will begin shattering the impactor into smaller pieces.
- **Impact Basket – Step 3:** The use of tire cylinders woven to the basalt mesh with basalt roving will further mitigate the impact shock by increasing the energy displacement and micro-fracturing process. At this point, the meteorite is dragging the impact basket with it.
- **Shield Base Layer:** As the meteorite punctures the basalt mesh in the impact basket, it is fragmented into smaller pieces, each with substantially less energy.

The result of all this is that the 200lb stoney impactor in this example will be deprived of the energy needed to pierce the remaining 4' of the shield base layer and will come to rest there, leaving the structure below intact.

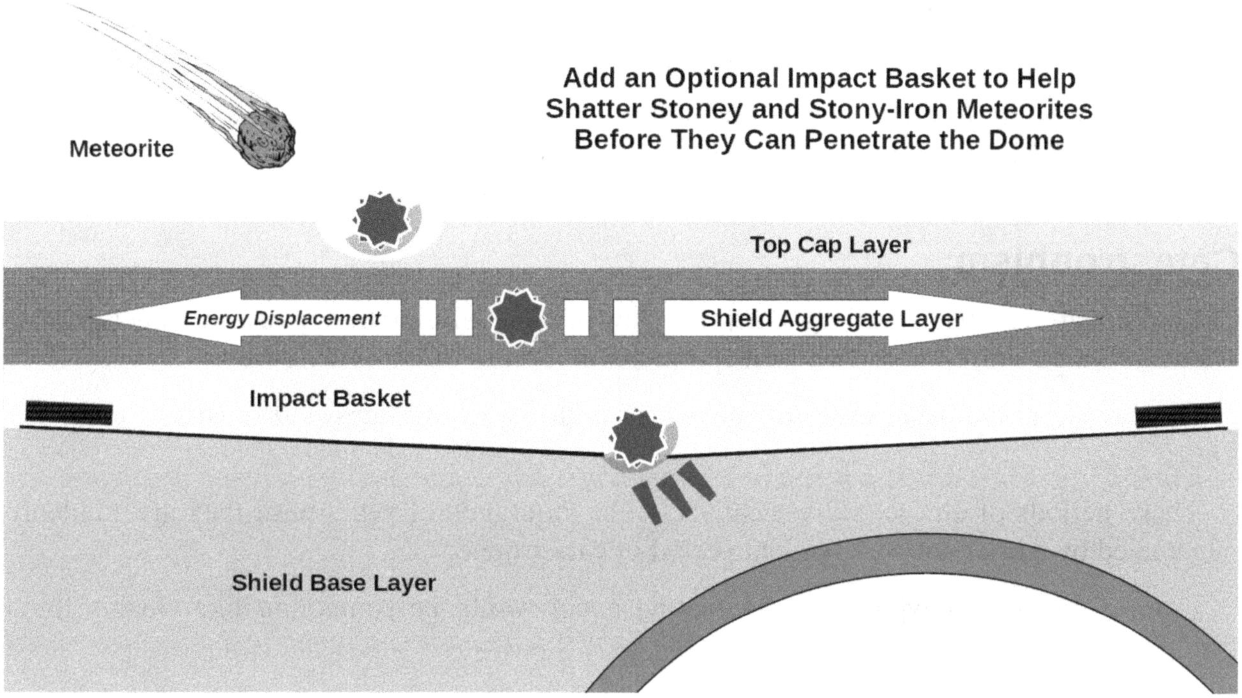
Meteorite
Add an Optional Impact Basket to Help
Shatter Stoney and Stony-Iron Meteorites
Before They Can Penetrate the Dome
Top Cap Layer
Energy Displacement
Shield Aggregate Layer
Impact Basket
Shield Base Layer

After the danger passes, the community can then repair the damaged overcover using simple hand tools and materials on-hand.

Whether you incorporate an impact basket into your overcover or not, what about all that dirt and basalt aggregate? Is there a dual-use? Yes.

Soil Banking

If we were to use a golfing analogy to describe where we are in the overcover strategy, one could say that we're still waiting to tee-up for the front nine. This is where it is about surviving the worst that man and nature can throw at us. After that, it's time to play the back nine, and with a Win-Win survival community, we're talking about soil banking.

Soil banking is a long-term soil storage strategy that addresses the need to provide a useful source of soil and fertilizer capable of supporting life following a catastrophic period. Yes, it is extremely long-term but what a magnificent insurance policy for success it makes.

A soil banking strategy gives Win-Win survival community design planners a way to "kill two birds with one stone." Protection in the short term and food production in the long term after things return to normal.

Heads up. Let's take a necessary moment and examine our beliefs about the evolution of life on this planet.

All of the . . .ologies, . . .isms, and institutions that define our modern cultures were created during a period of historical quiescence. What we believe today may not necessarily put us in a good position to survive a catastrophic tomorrow.

Soil banking may rankle one's sensibilities, but it will essential to the survivability of communities. The basis of this is an old scientific explanation for evolution called catastrophism,. This is something every Win-Win leader needs to understand.

Catastrophism

Catastrophism was the prevailing scientific view of the evolution of life on our planet prior to Darwin. Stated simply, catastrophism spurred evolution in the following way.

Quiescence is the usual order of our world with the normal ups and downs of everyday life.

These periods of quiescence typically last for thousands of years until they are suddenly punctuated by a brief and very violent period of catastrophe.

From a creation viewpoint, a punctuating event would be something like Noah's flood from the Old Testament.

Catastrophism worked well for science until Darwin's theory of evolution circumvented the scientific peer-review process, and that's when it got the boot.

What prompted this rush to expediency? Darwin's theory provided science a way to completely disengage from the creation narrative of the Church. Here is why.

Darwinism, also referred to as uniformitarianism or gradualism, posits that evolution is a slow and prodigious process.

Catastrophism and creationism, on the other hand, maintain that life on our planet is shaped largely by brief periods of violent events, which disrupt the usual quiescence of our world.

The only difference between the two is that catastrophism measures the passage of time in scientific terms; whereas creationism measures it according to an interpretation of scripture.

For the purpose of survival planning, catastrophism is the most practical of the three because it explains the evolution of life on our planet without the distortions of political and religious agendas.

Without these distortions, new survival-related understandings of old events like Noah's Flood are possible.

Noah's Flood

The Biblical deluge account of Noah and the Flood is only one, of the over one hundred other deluge accounts in the wisdom texts and narratives, from the many other cultures across the globe.

With that in mind, let's ponder on how another Noah's Flood in our future could play out.

Preceding the deluge there will be a period of extreme solar storms, volcanic eruptions, impact events, and forest fires. Then the skies of our planet will descend into a "nuclear winter" as soot and ash are hurled into the stratosphere. This will result in a partial block of direct sunlight and make it very difficult to grow crops on the surface.

Once things begin to settle down, our planet will want to cleanse itself, and like us, nothing beats a nice long shower to do exactly that. The ensuing rains of a lengthy, global monsoon will cleanse the earth, which is why you need to build your domes with all-hazards foundations.

Fair-is-fair. Now let's go pick on the scientists.

Deccan Traps and Chicxulub

Scientists have usually balked at the Biblical account of Noah's Flood. They cite that there simply is not enough water on the surface of the planet to sustain such an event.

However, when you read the other deluge accounts of ancient cultures, a different pattern emerges. Perhaps, the flood was not a flood, but a series of global tsunamis caused by a planetary pole shift event. And yes, scientists will probably balk at this before they shrug their shoulders and walk away.

Hence, the only kinds of catastrophic events scientists will embrace are those with ample, deep-time, geological evidence. Well then, let's play the geology card.

From a scientific viewpoint, there were two catastrophic events that occurred 66 million years ago, the eruption of the Deccan Traps in India and the Chicxulub impact near the North shore of the Yucatán Peninsula in Mexico.

There are scientists who maintain that these events occurred simultaneously and on opposite sides of the planet. This, they argue, was the actual cause for the dinosaurs' extinction, a one-two knockout punch from a hellish, global conflagration due to ejecta, ash, and soot.

Kids think dinosaurs are fun, but fact is, we'd be slow moving happy meals for them so it's best they remain in the fossil record. Preferably, without us.

Therefore, after ejecta, boulders, and a heavy layer of ash fall on your community, the only thing between you and that fiery hell is your overcover. This is when knowing you have 14' of clay, soil and basalt aggregate over your head is good thing.

A wonderful thing about catastrophism, is how it helps you to mentally prepare; as this evolutionary model hearkens back to an ancient Persian adage, "This too shall pass."

While a global tribulation may last a few years or for a decade or more, it will eventually pass. This is the message of catastrophism and why it can give us hope that one day in the future; after years of much misery and suffering, we will reach the backside of the crisis.

The best way to ensure the success of this future is to plan your defenses using applied catastrophism.

Applied Catastrophism

With applied catastrophism, you are balancing short-term and long-term resource management strategies based on the premise that the community must not only survive a catastrophic event; it must also be able to rebuild a quality life, afterward.

With this expectation, any effort to preposition valuable materials for the future is essential, and those resources ideally are going to be close at hand. This brings us to the materials in your overcover, the soil and basalt aggregate or tailings.

Let's assume there has been a terrible solar storm, and your side of the world is facing the sun when the plasma from a CME strikes and the radiation scorches the life out of the topsoil. It leaves the top 12" to 18" of soil incapable of supporting life.

During the crisis, your community will handily survive the destruction because this is what it is designed to do. But what happens after you determine that the crisis has passed? Can "normal life" resume with above-ground gardening and farming?

Where applied catastrophism shines is that it tells us that a catastrophe will be relatively short-lived; after which, normal life can be re-established during the subsequent period of quiescence. In a very real sense, applied catastrophism demands that you prepare for better times as well.

Here is where your overcover can become a useful source of soil capable of supporting life when better times arrive in some distant tomorrow. But for today, you need to consult with an agronomist before selecting the soil for your shield base and top cap.

Agronomy is the science of soil management and crop production, and you want to find a competent, local agronomist to consult with on the overcover regarding soil banking for three of the four layers as follows:

- **Shield Base:** This layer is finely screened certified fill dirt. Although surface soil will have been irradiated by solar storms, this buried dirt will escape most of that. After the crisis has passed and quiescence has returned, it can then be excavated and used as amendable starter soil.

- **Shield Aggregate:** The basalt aggregate or tailings are removed and crushed into rock powder, which is then used to fertilize and amend vast amounts of land.
- **Top Cap:** After the shield base and shield aggregate layers are removed for reuse, the top cap can be re-applied over the clay cover. The end result is that the dome structures will not be as tall as before, but they will look essentially the same and still offer a reduced but valuable level of protection.

When working with your agronomist, explain these goals so that he or she can guide you to the best local sources of fill soil and basalt aggregate with a specific goal of soil banking for the future.

Another important issue to discuss with your agronomist will be the final overcover layer. The top cap.

Top Cap

The soil of preference for a simple top cap is topsoil. Topsoil is very dark and sometimes black in color due to the biological life within it. There are roots from vegetation, earthworms, and insects. The amount of sand and clay in the soil will vary by region, but as a rule, topsoil will have moderate texture.

Topsoil is not the only soil you'll use; so when evaluating the soil on your property for overcover, a simple ball test is used.

Pick up a handful of soil and ball it your hand and use the following criteria to classify it:

- **Clay Soil:** The dirt clumps into a sticky ball when handled that is hard, crusty, and difficult to work with.
- **Sandy Soil:** The dirtball will be granular and crumbly, and it will easily break apart.
- **Loam:** This soil is fluffy because it contains roughly equal amounts of sand, silt, and clay. The dirtball will form a solid shape that can easily be broken apart.
- **Topsoil:** The difference between loam and topsoil is that topsoil contains more decayed organic material than loam. Sandy loam makes for the best topsoil.

Soil that is intended for food production, whether it is the native soil or soil purchased from a third party, needs to be sampled and analyzed on a regular basis by a reliable laboratory in consultation with your agronomist.

This is why your agronomist and design engineers will play a key role in helping you to decide which type of cap you need for your overcover.

There are four basic overcover types:

- **Native Cap:** Overcover with the original site soil and fauna, regardless of soil type. One year after the overcover has been applied; there should be no significant, discernible difference between the overcover and the land surrounding it.
- **Flat Cap:** The simplest of all caps to apply, a single layer level on top of the overcover, used for growing in sunlight and controlled conditions, such as, hoop houses for raised bed gardening and hothouses. These allow for longer growing seasons and protect plants from heavy winds, stormy weather, and volcanic ash.
- **Terrace Cap:** A terrace cap is essentially a stepped series of smaller flat caps. When building on sloped land, a terraced cap follows the natural contours and elevation of the land and is ideal for growing in sunlight under controlled conditions with maximum results.
- **Permaculture Cap:** The term permaculture describes a holistic set of design principles centered on enhancing natural ecosystems and creating a robust rainwater harvesting system. When properly designed, a permaculture system is self-sustaining; human intervention is not required to maintain it.

And with this Dear Reader, you have mastered all of the basic concepts you'll use to design and construct your church retreat and ranch infrastructure and structures.

Part III – EcoTech Farming and Ranching

14

Feeding 1,000 Martians

Now that we've covered the basics of dome construction, it is time to address how to finance your church properties through the production of high-demand, all-natural organic fresh foods. The actual product mix will vary depending on the property type, its location, and the market demand.

The principal goals are:

- **Church Retreat Goal:** A retreat will have 4+ acres of usable land and produce enough food to feed 50+ church members in residence and generate income sufficient to cover basic operating costs.
- **Church Farm Goal:** A typical farm will have 40+ acres of usable land and 100 members in residence. The goal is to produce enough food to feed 10 times the number of church members in residence and to cover basic operating costs.
- **Church Ranch Goal:** A typical ranch will have 400+ acres of usable land and 150 members in residence. As with a farm, the goal of a ranch is to produce enough food to feed 10 times the number of church members in residence and to cover basic operating costs.

The ultimate goal is to develop and successfully implement technologies and methods that will enable a future Win-Win community to feed 1,000 Martian pioneers each day and finance the expansion of the church ranch and the acquisition of new church properties.

Hold the presses. Martian pioneers? What's with this Mars angle and this ultimate goal of a Win-Win survival community to feed 1,000 Martian pioneers?

Colonization is an essential requirement for the survival of our species and this is one side of the same coin. You colonize in order to survive and if you cannot survive, how can you colonize?

This is why future generations of off-world, Win-Win pioneers are necessary. They'll grow up in a culture with advanced all-hazards food production techniques and technologies, where members are loyal to their mission and to each other.

Another way to look at this is with the race to space.

NASA was the only show in town for the longest time, but future space exploration reminds us of the early days of the automotive industry. There are the few players who remain today, and the many who failed. Those who failed include familiar names such as Hudson, Oldsmobile, Packard, Pontiac, Rambler, and Studebaker.

Today, we have another large starting lineup of companies aiming for their slice of the future, and these include: Ariane, Bigelow Aerospace, Blue Origin, Boeing, Firefly, Lockheed-Martin, Rocket Lab, Space Adventures, SpaceX, Spaceflight Industries, ULA, and Virgin Galactic.

Whoever makes it to a future time when we have the ability to colonize other worlds, space companies will be competing for the one singular distinction. To be the first to construct a kilometer-long colony ship to the stars.

For these companies, Win-Win communities will a ready source of paying passengers, and they will not be traveling in steerage, either. The bottom line is that a Win-Win survival community that can feed 1,000 Martian colonists will be a financial goose that lays golden eggs for any firms seeking to capitalize on the largest ever expansion of the human race.

Adopt this mindset, and survival is no longer a matter of lurching from one fear-driven expedient solution to the next, and for what God only knows. Rather, your community members will share a clear vision of a Star Trek future, humanity's next majestic leap forward, and how their descendants will play a vital role in it.

Given a clear view of the future, the burdens of the present will be like a game of golf. Everyone suffers on the front nine; so our children can go to the stars on the back nine. Now that's worth living for.

Let's tee up with EcoTech farming and ranching.

EcoTech Farming

Going to other worlds is an essential requirement for species survival, and Win-Win communities will produce future generations of off-world colonists who understand essential food production techniques and technologies.

A Win-Win survival community will grow food in traditional ways, and also in new innovative ways that some might say "pushes the edge of the envelope," but which is exactly what you need to do in order to feed 1,000 Martian pioneers each day.

The cutting edge, of this food production method, is an indoor aquaponics-based farming strategy I've named "EcoTech," which is an all-natural ecology that is hosted within a technosphere.

For the purpose of this discussion, the term technosphere describes a diverse technological environment that is designed to host an all-natural ecology. The goal of EcoTech farming is to create a stress-free, natural environment for plants inside a man-made growing structure.

A brilliant example of an effective EcoTech solution is in the science fiction film, *The Martian* (2015). Matt Damon is astronaut Mark Watney in the film. Though fiction, this film is based on solid facts, and what Watney faces offers a very credible survival scenario.

While slogging through a sudden Martian storm to the launch vehicle, Watney's spacesuit is damaged by flying debris and sand from the storm. His shipmates do not receive a signal back from him, and thinking him dead, they must lift off before they are marooned.

While there are many excellent articles about the science decisions Watney makes in this film, they tend to miss the most important decision. The day after he is marooned on Mars, Watney makes the conscious decision to survive. Remember, that with survival, commitment is half of the battle or more.

Watney determines that he needs to feed himself until help arrives, and there is not enough packaged food for that on hand; no matter how much he might ration himself.

A botanist by profession, he chooses science over rationing and finds a sealed package of raw potatoes that were set aside for a special meal. With potatoes in hand, he guts out his habitat and builds the first indoor grow on Mars.

After creating a sealed growing environment inside the habitat, Watney covers the floor with Martian dirt and lays out his rows. Then, he removed manure packets from the crew's toilet waste bin and used the contents to make humanure (human manure.)

In a repetitive planting cycle, he spoons a dollop of humanure into the dirt, tops it with a piece of raw potato that has an eye on it, covers it with dirt, and waters it. In due time, he is able to grow enough to sustain himself and becomes the first human to grow potatoes on Mars. Even after his habitat experiences a catastrophic decompression due to an airlock malfunction, he still has a supply of harvested potatoes.

With this in mind, let's consider the ecology and technosphere aspects of the film's Martian scenario.

- **Ecology:** The ecology was utterly simple, all-natural Martian dirt, water, raw potatoes, and humanure. For the potatoes, Mars offered a controlled habitat with no competitors or pests to deal with. Spud heaven.
- **Technosphere:** Watney's EcoTech solution also produced an ingenious mix of existing and ad hoc technologies and fixes to control the temperature, humidity, oxygen levels, carbon levels, and to make water.

This was an inspirational story and it has a solid basis. If you get to watch the movie, the first thing you might wonder is: Assuming Watney's habitat had been a below-ground DBS dome, what would be the crisis? There would be none.

Nonetheless, there is a point to be made here.

Watney only had to farm for one Martian; whereas, your church must farm for 1,000 Martians.

Therefore, due to the factors of scale, some aspects of the EcoTech farming methods discussed in this chapter will be more sophisticated than the Watney Mars EcoTech solution.

Nonetheless, there is one incredibly inspiring line in the movie when Watney says, "I'm going to science the shit out of this." This brings us to the analysis method I used to create the EcoTech concept. It is something I call "Follow the Photon."

Follow the Photon

In February 1997, I was contracted by Lockheed Martin Commercial Space Systems, Sunnyvale, CA, as a networking systems analyst to work on a civilian adaptation of a Cold War spy satellite. My assignments were with three of the satellite control ground stations in the system. One of them turned out to be the most technically interesting of my entire career.

Encrypted satellite-to-ground command and telemetry communication systems are very complex. What was needed was an end-to-end explanation of the system for future controllers.

As I began sorting through the volumes of manuals and specifications, I could see it was still a work in progress. Hence, reconciling all that would take an inordinate amount of time.

So there I was, sitting at the control console, looking at the blinking command prompt on the monitor before me, and pondering the situation.

After a while I asked myself, "What if I could follow a single photon of light, from the command prompt on the monitor in front of me, all the way up to the spacecraft's onboard payload computer and back to the ground station command console?" (What is a photon? From the Greek, phos, phot = light, photons carry light through space.)

Now that was an interesting question, but could I do it?

I fetched a cup of coffee and stepped out for some fresh air. As I sipped my coffee, I noticed the huge satellite dish used by our command station, and that is then, I knew I could do it. The first step was to find the command input that would initiate a process beginning with a keyboard, going through the satellite dish and then all the way up to the spacecraft itself, and back.

The project engineers were a bit nervous as they watched me pulling up floor panels and squeezing behind tightly-packed equipment racks. Undaunted, I followed my little photon everywhere it went and with a keen attention to detail.

I hand-tracked each cable connection, every device, and everything that happened to the data packet carrying my little photon of light as it wove its way out to the satellite dish transmitter, then to the payload computer in the spacecraft, and back.

To this day, I still marvel that these complex communication systems work, but they do, and so did following the photon. It was a huge success with the engineers and the controllers.

I would have never dreamed that years later I would follow the photon once again. Only this time, the solution to feeding families in space would not begin with space technology. It would begin with space geology.

Families in Space

In 2010, while researching material for another book, I interviewed another author on an unrelated topic for my podcast. It was during our pre-production meeting when he told me that he had recently completed a space colonization study for NASA.

He explained that he had led a think tank comprised of medical and survival professionals to examine the issues future families would face if they were to be self-sustaining in space. This would be the case whether these colonists were colonizing another planet or an L5 space habitat in a stable orbit along the path of our Moon's orbit.

We discussed many issues and there were a lot of thorny ones for sure. However, their study was successful in identifying several critical issues and it was peppered with the caveats and opposing explanations which are typical of the scientific process.

The three major study issues did resolve with pristine clarity though, and we'll use them as our first EcoTech talking points.

Space Fertilizer

One of the technical problems the test subjects successfully addressed was the one for fertilizer. This was an important win, because fertilizer in space is just as important as it is here on Earth. Remember, Watney used humanure to fertilize his potato crop in *The Martian*.

The study participants found that a combination of worm castings, worm tea, chicken, and rabbit manure worked best.

The good news about worm castings is that wormeries are perfect for indoor small spaces, which makes them ideal for EcoTech. Compost worms such as Red Wigglers – *Eisenia fetida* and Redworms – *Lumbricus rubellus* are used, and produce highly-desirable, solid, and liquid fertilizers.

Worm castings are the solids. They are heavy, and you can make a ball of worm castings in your hand that will clump much like clay. Consequently, worm castings can be better than compost in some ways.

Worm tea is the liquid fertilizer produced by wormeries and also called "Worm wee," "Worm elixir," or "Worm juice." Worm tea is a highly prized fertilizer, and your community can use what you produce, or opt to sell it on the open market for a considerable profit.

Chicken manure is the third part of the mixture, and like worms, chickens are also profitable, but not all chicken breeds are suitable for indoor EcoTech farming. This is because size matters.

With standard chickens of various breeds, processing age determines the type:

- **Broiler-fryer:** Age – 7 to 13 weeks. Weight – 1.5 to 4 pounds.
- **Roasters:** Age – 3 to 5 months. Weight – 3.5 to 7 pounds.
- **Stewing:** Age – 10 months. Weight – 4 to 7 pounds.

These birds are stellar above ground performers and great earners. However, standard chickens proved to be too large for feeding families in tightly confined space; so efforts were focused on finding a suitable breed to feed families in space. They chose Cornish hens, a crossbreed of White Rock and Cornish chickens.

Standard chickens can feed 3 to 4 people, whereas a Cornish hen is a single portion bird. Their processing age is 5 to 6 weeks, and their weight never exceeds two pounds.

In terms of egg production, standard chickens are the hands-down winners, but in terms of manure and meat volume, Cornish hens produce more than standard chickens over time.

How does this stack up for Win-Win survival communities? You can raise any kind of chickens you want. Full size birds and Cornish hens included above and below ground.

- **Above-Ground:** Your community can raise a mix of penned and free-range breeds on any property.
- **Below-Ground:** Penned breeds that produce the most eggs are obviously desirable. They will be raised in a special-purpose farm dome.

Then there are the rabbits. They have a healthy weight ranging from 2 to 11 pounds and are highly adaptable for feeding families in space. There are many breeds to choose from, and the wild breeds are typically smaller than domesticated breeds, also known as bunnies.

As a rule of thumb, rabbits are ready to butcher about 10 to 12 weeks after birth, and all breeds provide nitrogen-rich manure. Depending on the species and sex, benefits include milk, wool, fur, and pelts. Some produce meat favored for human consumption, whereas others are betting suited for use as dog food.

Rabbits are incredibly prolific, which is why special military operations teams sometimes bring male and female rabbits along as they begin a long-duration mission lasting several months. By the time the team reaches its designated operating area, there is already a litter of rabbits on the way, and within weeks a safe and reliable supply of fresh meat.

Prime Innovators

When I asked the NASA consultant, what he thought was the most astounding finding of his study; he chuckled and said, "The children."

They observed that it regardless of the type of growing system used in the study; the children were amazing systems engineers and could master them all. They proved to be first-rate problem solvers because they were totally tuned into the ecology of each system.

I asked him how they reported this to NASA. He replied that they found the children to be the prime innovators when it came to optimizing food production. Based on that, their recommendation for space colonists was to let the children run the grows and for the adults to support them.

In other words, if you need to define an EcoTech problem, get an adult. If you need to solve it, get a 10-year old. Why is this? Because it was a 10-year old who first identified a very big problem.

Mineralization

The whole conversation was fascinating, but one comment would prove to be his most profound statement of all. He said, "We found mineralization to be a problem."

Search the term "mineralization" on the Internet and you'll see the definitions are diverse and complicated; so for the purpose of this discussion, let's use a simple definition.

For the purpose of supporting a space colony, mineralization is about getting essential minerals into their bodies.

This is not easy, since it takes time for geology to wear down mountains, turn rock into dust, and then have the snow melts and rains wash it all down to the lowlands. This is how nature begins the process of making perfect soil. Then along comes modern agriculture and mankind makes a perfect mess of it.

To illustrate the point, below are the first two paragraphs of an article presented to the US Senate:

> "Do you know that most of us today are suffering from certain dangerous diet deficiencies which cannot be remedied until the depleted soils from which our foods come are brought into proper mineral balance?
>
> The alarming fact is that foods—fruits, and vegetables, and grains,—now being raised on millions of acres of land that no longer contain enough of certain needed minerals, are starving us—no matter how much of them we eat!"

A quick question for you, dear reader. In what year was this article read to the Senate?

- 1983
- 1999
- 2004
- 2011
- None of the above.

The correct answer is E, none of the above. This article was presented to the US Senate in 1936 by Senator Duncan Fletcher. It is titled the *Modern Miracle Men* by Rex Beach and was based upon Dr. Charles Northen's Proper Food Mineral Balances.

The modern Red Delicious apple serves as an appropriate example for what goes wrong when you deplete your soils and breed for commerce.

The red delicious apple was first recognized in 1880 in Madison County, Iowa. As one of the 15 most popular apple cultivars in the United States, it is a huge commercial success today. Fruit distributors have designated the red delicious apple as a "decorative fruit," and no wonder, they taste like sweetened cardboard.

The reason is that red delicious apples have been cultivated for one-year of shelf life, which is like whispering sweet nothings in a commodity broker's ear. Consequently, the commercial red delicious apples we see in stores today are grown in depleted soils, picked green, and allowed to begin ripening in the back of an 18-wheeler.

The next time you visit the produce section of your local grocery store, hold a red delicious decorative apple in your hand and reflect on Dr. Charles Northen's warning. Then, remember this one critical point as you put it back on the shelf.

Mineralization is the command input for all EcoTech systems.

Inputs vs. Outputs

Why do we have red delicious apples that taste like sweet cardboard? After WWII the "Green Revolution" began and was well on its way by the 1960s. Since then industrialization has redefined the ways in which we manage our crops and yards. Therefore, in terms of Win-Win survival communities, how we solve food production problems is not the main goal.

We're solving problems each day, or at least we think we are, but for whom and who picks up the tab? Thanks to vast amounts of man-made fertilizers and pesticides, the runoff has created vast ecological dead zones in our oceans. It was not for nutrition but for the single-minded goal of profit, and the results are:

- **Genetically Modified Organisms (GMO):** GMO has proven itself to be a scientific evil. Whether we use Monsanto Frankenfoods on Earth or in space, we'll self-destruct as a spacefaring species.
- **Monocropping:** Used extensively with corn, soybeans and wheat, monocropping is science's misguided solution for the pests. It replaces natural diversity with monocrops. This results in damage to soil ecology and makes it vulnerable to pesticide-resistant pests and competing plants.
- **Truck Farming:** Fruits and vegetables are bred to financial goals, and picked green before they fully ripened for the sole purpose of profitability. It makes one wonder how many nutrients are available with exposure to diesel fumes.

The result is modern science sending us, in the end, a mixed story about minerals and human nutrition. As much as 85% of all American farm soils, by some estimates, are depleted of minerals and elements.

If our descendants are to colonize space, we must stop digging this output-oriented hole and change direction with input-oriented thinking. This includes NASA as well.

One reason NASA is struggling with the task of feeding families in space is that their thinking is not centered on nutrition. Their focus is on other scientific goals which outweigh all other concerns. Food for them, is principally something you put in a tube or package. This becomes a side project for a community only focused on science.

This strategy works for exploration, but for permanent colonization NASA should go back to the drawing boards. With colonists food will be the central focus of their lives, and science will be the side project.

However, when you scrape away the happy speeches, the only reason NASA is interested in growing food in space is to save fuel. It takes a lot of rocket fuel to push a ten-year supply of food for 1,000 colonists through space. All other considerations are just that, other considerations.

This brings us to our existential need for plant-derived minerals. It is critically important that food production and nutrition be returned to its central place in our lives. It has been for most of humanity's existence and needs to be again. This brings us back to our mineralization command input.

Plant-Derived Minerals

The enzymatic process inside our bodies demands minerals, which is why minerals are necessary for virtually every metabolic process that occurs.

The process of mineralization begins with geology. This is how Mother Nature gifts us with minerals to nourish our bodies. However, geology is only the first step in this process of nourishment and how it provides us with metallic minerals.

Unfortunately, our bodies do not understand metallic minerals that well and they struggle to absorb them. A good example is found in inexpensive grocery store multiple vitamins. The labeling is great and the claims are impressive, but in the final analysis, our bodies only absorb 10% to 20% of the supplement.

You can observe this yourself. When taking inexpensive daily multiple vitamins collect your waste and liquefy it. You will discover the undigested remains of your multiple vitamins mixed in with your manure. This brings us to a critical term, bioavailability.

Bioavailability defines the extent to which a nutrient or medication can be used by the body.

Most inexpensive grocery store multiple vitamins made with inorganic metallic minerals passes uselessly through our digestive systems and into our toilets.

Therefore, any discussion of mineral bioavailability is not about the mineral itself. It begins with converting the minerals from a metallic state to a state suitable for proper human bioavailability.

This may sound theoretically intriguing, but is there a benchmark of success? Something we can point to and say, "This is the good stuff."

The Good Stuff

Capitalism gifted us with depleted soils, but it also gifted us with the solution. We can buy something that Mother Nature wants us to receive freely: plant-derived bioavailable minerals. These products are marketed as colloidal minerals, a combination of these bioavailable minerals.

Colloidal mineral products are derived from prehistoric plants. They provide a combination of plant-derived bio-available minerals that have a particle size that is equal to or less than one micron in size. That is roughly 1/7000th the size of a red blood cell.

These plant derived minerals are extracted from humic shale using cool, clear water, and then processed through a complex array of special filters. Humic shale is like the forest floor; it is comprised of very compacted dry leaves and sticks.

How does this translate to nutrition?

Of the 115 known elements, naturopathic physicians and holistic researchers maintain that the human body requires 84 of them. Of course commercial interests opposed this narrative and have used fear tactics, such as the arsenic scam, to cloud any discussion.

Corporate spinmeisters post articles everywhere on the Internet with fear-based warnings about the arsenic contained in colloidal mineral products. To promote this further, they point to the product labels and tell us to see for ourselves. But what are we actually seeing?

Propaganda spin always uses a bit of truth to make itself palatable. Yes, arsenic is bad for your health but only in sufficiently large amounts.

Colloidal minerals do contain arsenic, but at levels considerably lower by percentage than the arsenic found in the soils currently used to grow our foods and in the ground beneath our homes. Therefore, the issue is not about spin or markets; it is how to mineralize your space-based EcoTech grows with rock dust.

Rock Dust

Rock dust is used by farmers and gardeners to amend their soils with minerals. There are different types of rock dust, and the minerals in them begin as inorganic particles in a metallic state.

Since mineralization is a broad topic, for the purpose of space colonization, the following four factors are useful in evaluating each type of rock dust:

- **Sourcing:** Common deposits and rare deposits. Sources of rock dust can be as common as the basalt quarries spread across the country or from rare, specialized deposits. As a rule of thumb, igneous rock dust is common; whereas rock dust from rare deposits of sedimentary and metamorphic rock are uncommon and usually come from a single source.

- **Plant-Available Minerals:** The mineral composition of rock dust varies by type. Igneous rock sources have a broader range of minerals than sedimentary and metamorphic rock sources such as glacial rock dust.

- **Long-term Continuous Use:** With common basalt rock dust, there are no concerns regarding heavy metals and continuous use is fine. However, there may be concerns with the concentration of heavy metals in rock dust from rare sedimentary and metamorphic deposit sources which raises doubts about long-term continuous use.

- **Nutrient Release Rate:** How long does it take for all the metallic particles in the rock dust to fully dissolve so plants can uptake their minerals? Generally, rock dust from common deposits such as basalt will require two or more years for complete mineralization. Rock dust from the rare sedimentary and metamorphic deposits will only take a few months.

To see how families living in space can best use rock dust, let's put these four factors into play for a mission to send 1,000 of them to colonize Mars.

We begin with the colony ship that will make a one-year journey to Mars. As it is being constructed in orbit around Earth, one of the first modules to be built will be the compost module. Whether you are acquiring a property for a retreat or a ranch, the first order of business will be to start your composting work.

Enough soil is transported to the compost module to get the process started along with a three-year supply of rock dust. Which type of rock dust will you stockpile in the module? One sourced from a sedimentary or metamorphic rare deposit because they have a much faster nutrient release rate?

Whoa! Why not start with basalt rock dust? And why just a three-year supply for the colonization compost module? On March 20, 2006, NASA inserted the Mars Reconnaissance Orbiter into orbit around Mars, and it imaged a huge outcropping of basalt near Marte Vallis.

Interestingly, the data suggests that ancient releases of water from aquifers beneath the Martian surface in Marte Vallis could have been 100 times the flow rate of the Mississippi River. Assuming these aquifers still exist in some small measure, Marte Vallis could be an ideal, single-source location for soil, basalt, and water.

Therefore, it is important to begin composting in space by using Glacial Rock Dust or any other rare deposit rock dust with a relatively short nutrient release rate. This way everyone enjoys delicious, nutritious, fresh foods grown onboard during the journey.

When they get to Mars, they'll be able to use the wonderfully rich growing soil and fully stabilized aquaponics grows in their space ship to get things started. At that point, colonization's job number one will be find water, and basalt for long-term continuous use.

This brings us to a command input, and we will use it to follow the photon from the rock pile to the dinner table.

The Mineralization Process

As mentioned previously, mineralization is the command input for all EcoTech systems, and in a manner of speaking, if the colony cannot get rocks into their heads, they'll fail.

Once the mineralization command input is executed, here are the five basic steps of the mineralization process:

1. **Soil Amendment:** The rock dust is spread on the soil.
2. **Plant Uptake:** Plants uptake the metallic minerals from the rock dust and digest it.
3. **Plant Digestion:** When digesting a mineral, the plant adds a hydrogen atom, which totally changes the molecular structure of the metallic minerals.
4. **Plant Transformation:** As a result of the plant digestion, metallic minerals in the rock dust are transformed into bio-available "food state" minerals. The plants are now ready for consumption with their "plant-derived minerals."
5. **Consumption:** A human or animal eats the plants containing "plant-derived minerals" with an absorption rate of 80% to 100% which all the cells in our bodies need to work optimally.

Remember eating metallic minerals is very inefficient because your body struggles to absorb them, and they may actually poison you. This is why you will use plants to digest the metallic minerals for you. Now, let's execute our mineralization plan.

Mineralization Command Input

To imagine the process of mineralization used on your church properties, you begin with, as I call it, an "uptake soil bed".

An uptake soil bed can be located above ground or below ground, and this will also determine the types of plants you use to digest the minerals to make them bio-available.

Uptake Plants

A pioneer plant species, like the dandelion, is a good place to start for an above-ground uptake plant. Yes, we treat them as weeds in America and spend a king's ransom to get rid of them. The dandelion is very useful in other parts of the world as a vegetable and also for making herbal medicine.

The advantage of using pioneer species for your mineral uptake requirement is that they are a hardy species. They can survive in poor quality soils due to their adaptations, which include long roots and root nodes full of bacteria. Mother Nature uses them to colonize ecosystems and to enrich the soil; thus it can support the secondary plant species.

For below-ground grows in more confined areas, mushrooms can serve the same purpose.

Now, let's start our follow the photon example using an above-ground uptake soil bed.

Follow the Photon

Imagine that you are standing before a tilled row in your uptake soil bed and holding a handful of rock dust. Look at the rock dust in your hand and imagine that you see a tiny sparkling light buried within it. This is the photon we'll follow and track through the ten stages it will take to feed 1,000 Martians.

1. **Dusting:** Using the recommended amounts and procedures, you dust your freshly tilled, uptake soil bed.

2. **Planting:** You plant dandelions and fertilize them.
3. **Growing:** Water your beds and use natural solutions to free them of pests.
4. **Harvest:** If you harvest early, you can eat the plants but not if later.
5. **Compost Add:** Chop the harvested plants and add them to your compost pile.
6. **Compost Enhancement:** A great way to give your compost pile a boost is to cover it and then locate a chicken coup next to it. The chicken manure adds a lot to the compost as the chickens eat a veritable banquet of seeds and little critters. Every romp on the compost pile will be a paradise buffet for the birds.
7. **Wormery:** Use the compost material as media for your wormery. You can add chicken egg-shells and coffee grinds to your worm beds for extra measure, but never add dead organisms or citrus. Worms are magnificent underground architects. They basically eat whatever is in front of them. What comes out of them are castings and tea, which you can use or sell as you see fit. A good use for the castings and tea is also in the grow beds where you raise plants for use in fish food.
8. **Feed the Fish:** The only natural way to get minerals into an aquaponics system is with the fish. A wormery not only provides a lot of castings and tea; it also provides a lot of worms. These you will feed to the fish in your aquaponics system along with a fish meal that is comprised of worms and plants from your fish food beds. But you must remember that what you feed your fish depends on the species, and some of them can be finicky eaters.
9. **Fish Fertilize the System:** There are two biological keys to doing aquaponics. First, the bacteria lining the walls of your aquaponics system, and the second is the manure that they produce. How you process that manure will depend on the growing system you employ, but the end result is the same. The plants get what they need to grow fantastically well.
10. **Harvest and Enjoy:** When the plants are ready for harvest, do so and enjoy. They will be fresh, tasty, and nutritious. And this concludes our follow the photon example, well almost.

What's the last stop for our photon? We'll find it in our manure, after we do our business, just like those inexpensive multiple vitamins.

That is unless we need to use humanure to grow potatoes on Mars like astronaut Mark Watney did in *The Martian*. (Which is *<u>STRONGLY</u> NOT RECOMMENDED!*)

15

EcoTech Farming and Ranching

Growing food for survival and future colonization with modern technology means that we need a food-centered lifestyle and encompasses both mission requirements. Satisfying these requirements begins with learning how we will feed ourselves and our descendants.

Before organizing a food production methodology, the first step is to encourage a community mindset for creating effective ecologies with a synergistic combination of plant and animal species.

At the top of this food chain is the predator, Homo sapiens, and interestingly enough, Homo sapiens is Latin for "wise man."

The second step is to examine the present-day conventional wisdom that dominates our push-button world of instant gratification.

Organic Family Farming

We salute small-scale, organic family farmers today for finding new ways to build a good life by giving their customers the very best with only a few acres of land. What a joy it is to see these young families creating a new world of nutrition opportunities.

But the mainstay of modern production remains within the domain of highly mechanized corporate farming and their hundreds and thousands of acres under cultivation. While we still refer to them as farmers, they no longer fit the traditional definition of the term. Rather, they are industrial-scale commodity producers, and many of them now refer to themselves as commodity producers.

It comes down to family farmers vs. commodity producers. How are the two different?

Whether you're a small-scale organic family farmer working a few acres of land or a commodity producer with thousands of acres, what you plant depends on the market you serve.

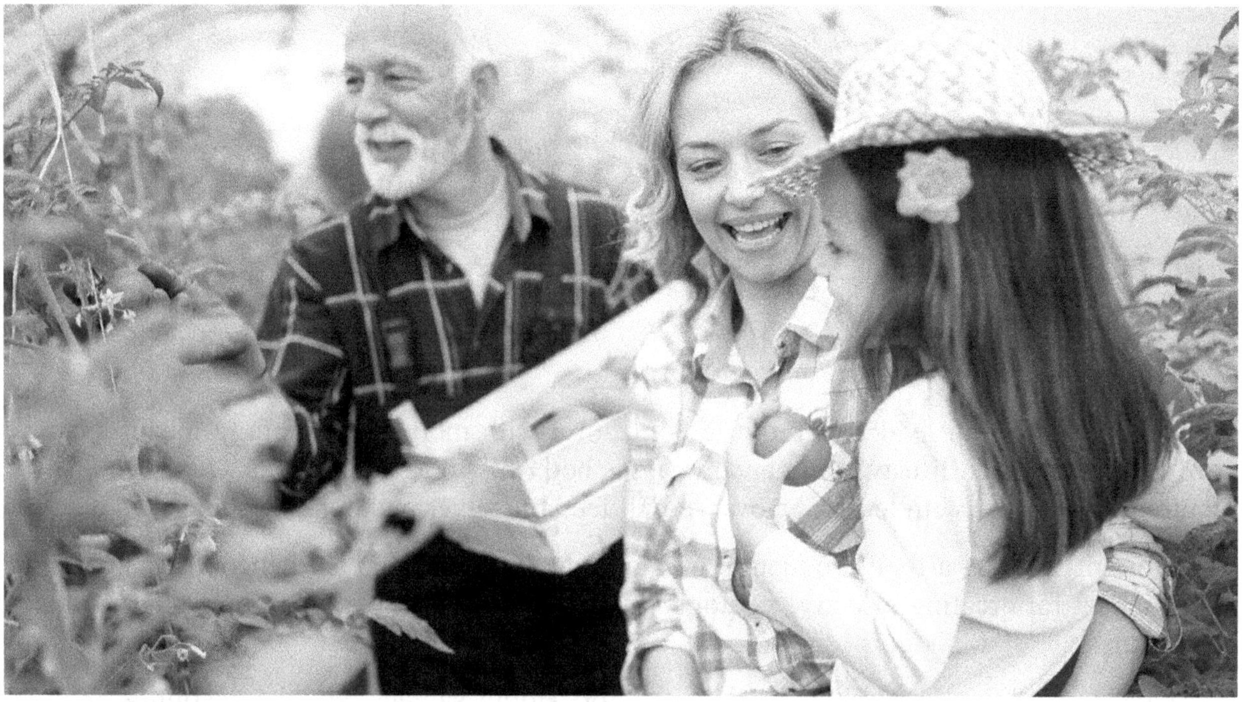

This is a predictable financial model for the present day. But what about living through a catastrophe, rebuilding after, and then going to the stars? Will this financial model address these needs as well?

No, because when crops are grown around external market demands, every species of plant or animal is treated as a separate revenue stream. Therefore, even food producers must go to the store to buy what they are not producing themselves. Herein is the problem.

An aquaponics farm for example only grows iceberg lettuce, which is a low-nutrient demand high-value cash crop, with a 90 days-to-maturity harvest. This results in four harvests per year or continuous harvesting on a weekly or monthly basis. This is why a successful aquaponics operation can pay like a stuck slot machine. You hit a pay line with every harvest.

However, if these lettuce growers personally want to enjoy their own product at their family's meals, they'll need to go to a store to buy ingredients for the salad dressing. But how does this work in a survival situation?

If you try to survive on the iceberg lettuce, you'll have to eat a lot just to get a few net calories. A better source of net calories will be the salad dressing, if the grocery store has not been forced to close during a major disaster.

This is not to say an EcoTech survival model cannot also be financially successful. It can, thanks to the unique quality and diversity of products. Later, we'll discuss a powerful way to monetize this model, which is at its core, a food sovereignty solution.

Food Sovereignty

According to conventional wisdom, food production is market-driven. However, it is not a suitable pathway to success for the noble goal of feeding 1,000 Martian colonists. A different model is required. One based on morality and service to others.

A Win-Win survival church is that model. It is a gathering of like-minded people with a sense of mission to serve God's will for humanity with morality, science, and common sense.

A useful model was established by a grassroots international movement of peasant farmers, indigenous communities, and middle-scale producers called La Vía Campesina.

Founded in 1993, La Vía Campesina created the "food sovereignty" model in 1996. 81 nations worldwide currently support this movement.

The basic tenets of the Vía Campesina food sovereignty model are well-suited to a Win-Win EcoTech framework for survival and space colonization. With this combination, pioneers can:

- Eat food produced through ecologically sound and sustainable methods,
- Participate in the production of healthy and culturally appropriate food, and
- Work with like-minded others to promote sustainable agriculture.

In short the La Vía Campesina and Win-Win EcoTech models offer a food-centered family approach that puts the nutrition needs of families above the self-interested profit motives of markets and corporations. Here on Earth. But what about up there?

A food sovereignty model for space colonization uses a non-terrestrial way of calculating risk and return.

The *risk* is that you starve to death before you can *return* to Earth alive; the odds of that will depend on who comes to your aid – or not.

Service to Self

Conventional preparedness is pretty much a me-and-mine, philosophy. You get you and yours to safety and then solve any problems as they develop. Will you go to ground, knowing what happens afterward? No.

You go down into a dead hole in the ground, eat dead food, and worry about dying.

From the first to the last of its events, a cataclysm can last months, years, or even a decade or more. Consider this: In such a prolonged environment where the world about you howls and writhes with pain, how will a service-to-self model provide you with any comfort or succor?

Perhaps the answer is summed up in a lyric from "The Wreck of the Edmund Fitzgerald" by Gordon Lightfoot.

Does anyone know where the love of God goes
When the waves turn the minutes to hours

What's the meaning here?

If you survive for the sake of survival, there will be the initial back-patting and victory laps, but uncertainty will grow over time. As you watch supplies dwindle, the minutes will turn into hours. Sure, they will get you through the cataclysm, but then what? Hunter and hunted?

After nagging doubts set in, all will huddle in fear dreading the eventual sound of picks and shovels overhead as angry, starving people labor to dig you out and take what you have.

This is why preparation is not about a person, place, or thing. It is building the future by changing how we think about a service-to-others survival mindset.

Survival State of Mind

For as long as humans have tilled the soil, farming methods have been passed down from one generation to the next. This blessing of history is seen in the successive generations of farmers who continue the tradition by growing on family lands with long-established methodologies. That said, surviving a cataclysm and colonizing space is not about winning a ribbon at the state fair.

A more suitable historical reference would be much older, about 10,000 years older.

It was a time known as the Neolithic Revolution, and in evolutionary terms, it was a turning point for our species. Before then our ancestors lived as hunter-gatherers in much smaller numbers.

Those were the days of an abundance of resources to meet basic needs, and in terms of personal freedom, they afforded a relative amount of free time to spend in leisure. That is, if a guy with a bigger club didn't clobber you, or something with huge teeth didn't eat you. If you could dodge those types of obstacles, the rest would be gravy.

You may wonder, what is the fundamental difference between humanity today and our hunter-gatherer ancestors?

Perhaps the answer to that question is locked away in an elusive engram embedded within the collective memory of our species and which dates back to this unique period of Neolithic personal freedom. We can see evidence of this stone age engram today in those called early adopters.

Early Adopters

On the upside, our Neolithic ancestors were opportunists who were free to roam the countryside in search of sustenance. The downside was sometimes they didn't find it, and this probably wore on a few of the younger hunter-gatherers. Enough was enough, and they decided to find something a little more reliable.

In Silicon Valley, the technical term for these dauntless young Neolithic hunter-gatherers is "early adopter." Early adopters are the people with an affinity for innovation; they precede the much larger market of mainstream adopters who follow them.

In a manner of speaking, our young Neolithic hunter-gatherers joined with like-minded others to launch Stone Age 1.0, and they did a remarkable job of teaching themselves how to cultivate crops and to domesticate animals.

The Neolithic Revolution was humanity's first technology revolution. For the very first time in the history of our species, someone asked the one question that would forever change the course of human events. "Is there an easier way to do this?"

This timeless question brings us to the present and the current Holy Grail of science, finding Earth-like exoplanets for future colonization. This narrative is no longer the stuff of science fiction. We've gone beyond that. Today, our species has a serious collective drive to spend vast sums in a search for someplace to explore, so we can continue human civilization.

This is how it has always worked. It has propelled humanity from the Stone Age to the Space Age; we've never once stopped being opportunists and never will. However, what we do about it is what makes the difference.

Some take the low road and some take the high road. Although the high road is more difficult to navigate, it does have one very desirable advantage. Light traffic.

For a Win-Win survival community, the calling to the high road is balancing service-to-self with a predominant service-to-others orientation and the building of a sustainable, multi-generational view of the future.

Generations

When it comes to a positive survival state of mind for your community, the goal of feeding 1,000 Martian colonists will be the reason Win-Win community members get up in the morning for another bleak day of hardship.

They'll make a difference for other survivors and doing this will give their lives meaning, hope, and the spiritual strength to work wonders.

Imagine this scene.

Church members are going about their daily activities of survival such as planting seeds, harvesting crops, and home-schooling children. At the same time, they are also on the lookout for any problems future generations would face on new worlds. When they discover one of these problems, they share their findings with others and ask, "Is there an easier way to do this?" And they'll find it together. This is what immigrants and pioneers do.

America is blessed as a nation of immigrants. Those who came before us endured long and difficult journeys to reach these shores, whether voluntarily or involuntarily, here they stay.

Most came to escape tyranny and poverty with the hope of making a better life for themselves and their children. It was this very hope that helped to give them the courage to sell all they had for the price of steerage on a steamship.

As they gathered at the rails of their ships in New York Harbor, it was this hope that warmed their hearts as they gazed upon that magnificent Lady Liberty with a torch, who welcomed them to their new home.

They had hoped for streets paved with gold but knew in the end that they would march down the gangplanks into a hard life of cold-water flats and dehumanizing sweatshops. Despite these experiences, they pushed on.

What gave many the strength to continue on? It was the hope that their children and their children's children would enjoy a good life in a free country, where opportunity is the taproot of democracy.

There is another point to be made here. With each new generation, there are new challenges, needs, and opportunities. Will the parents naturally focus on these needs? My bet is the answer is still "Yes!"

Multi-generational Phases

A Win-Win community will be a collection of families, including the childless, as well as those who walk alone. Therefore, instead of defining the future in terms of generations, a more inclusive paradigm, multi-generational phases, is needed.

By organizing your efforts into phases as opposed to generations, you see those who will follow as going through a succession of phases, where any number of generations may be required to complete each phase.

There is no universal strategy in developing phases; each Win-Win community must identify these phases in their own way. Once an initial lexicon of phases has been defined, let it grow and evolve as you learn new things and master new skills.

To illustrate the idea, below is a simple three-phase example:

- **Pre-Catastrophic:** The first step to feeding space colonists, with natural, delicious, and nutritious food, is to prove it first on Earth. This begins with creating a vibrant and determined food sovereignty culture.
- **Catastrophic:** The ability of the church to provide large quantities of fresh food to survivors through charity food banks will provide opportunities for vital mutual-defense and support alliances. It will also give members a noble reason to quell the despair of survivor guilt.
- **Post-Catastrophic:** Valuable survival knowledge will be gained by each Win-Win community during a catastrophe. The ability for them to spread the word about discoveries and inventions via HAM radio will be an essential tool for defending the community and to help launch a new and more evolved next civilization.

We'll discuss HAM radio in greater depth later, but you may wonder what HAM radio has to do with food production? Where is the connection?

Here is the connection. If your community is great at producing food but you choose to ignore the need for two-way communications, signals intelligence, and radio discipline, your community will be ripe for plunder during the worst of times, and many of your members will perish.

Why? We bipedal types are not only an opportunistic species; we're also an invasive species as well.

EcoTech Ark

An invasive species is one that is introduced into an environment outside of its native range. When our descendants set foot on new worlds, they and all the lifeforms they have with them will be an invasive species. Therefore, a Win-Win community must see itself as a survival ark for the colonization of other worlds.

A modern survival ark will have something in common with airplanes and ships. They will have manifests that detail lists of passengers, crew, and cargo. Ergo, all that a future generation will have to work with in space, is they take with them.

Planning for space travel begins by creating an EcoTech ark manifest. The first order of business is to create a manifest of the desired plant and animal species. If our choices are reckless and self-serving, the environmental harms that are happening in our world today will go to space with us. Ergo, humanity could become invasive bringers of death.

Bringers of Death

An example of bringers of death is found in the Florida Everglades. In recent years, it has been overrun by various species of large constricting snakes, like pythons and yellow anaconda. Often released into our environment by unthinking pet owners, they are only the tip of the iceberg.

Naive Floridians have also thoughtlessly released exotic aquarium fish into the wild, and now the state is straining to cope. The list of invasive fish species in Florida now includes Asian Swamp Eel, Blue Tilapia, Brown Hoplo, Clown Knifefish, Jaguar Guapote, Lionfish, Mayan Cichlid, Sailfish, Snakehead, and Suckermouth Catfish.

If future colonists go into space with the same reckless stupidity, how will we know?

One day, mission controllers on Earth will announce something like, “Telemetry tells us the colony life support equipment is still working, but we’ve lost all contact with the colonists. No one is answering our hails. We suspect mass starvation.”

Failed Stewards

Humanity, especially since the advent of the western Industrial Age, is well-experienced in trashing environments for profit. Time and again, we take what we want until there is nothing left worth stealing, and leave a terrible mess. So the search for new exploitation opportunities continues. Instead of becoming better at preventing these reckless outcomes, we’ve become better at hiding the truth. A classic example is the McDonald's fish sandwich.

When McDonald's first introduced the Filet-O-Fish sandwich in 1962, they were made from Cod and very delicious. Consequently, Cod fisheries were dangerously depleted to satisfy consumer demand. In the process of this folly, a new fish species solution was found.

When fishing for Cod, fishing nets have to descend through a layer of the water column favored by Pollock, a fish species that schools above the Cod. Pollock were considered a “trash fish” in those days due to its oily flavor. Fishermen would separate them from the Cod and toss them overboard as by-catch.

This caught up with McDonald's a few years ago, and they switched from Cod to Pollock and promoted their Pollock Filet-O-Fish sandwiches as being tasty. No matter how they spun it, there was no way to put a happy face on this; so corporate spinmeisters soon avoided mentioning Pollock. Instead they diplomatically say that their Filet-O-Fish sandwiches are “Sourced from sustainable fisheries.”

This is an example of bad species stewardship by McDonald's. Just imagine, if they had promoted their original Filet-O-Fish sandwiches in 1962 as “Delicious Cod, sourced from sustainable fisheries.” Maybe an entire species would not have been brought to the brink of collapse if they had. But they didn’t. The problem with species trashing like this is that it promotes even worse behaviors.

So what do we do about it? Do we continue to play along and take this kind of bad stewardship with us to the stars?

What will come of that? Bad stewards in space will lurch from one destructive exploitation failure to the next until the vacuum of space settles the matter in a cold, deadly and violently unforgiving way.

What does this mean for a Win-Win survival community with a goal of feeding 1,000 Martian colonists? If they go to space for exploitation, they will also eventually fail.

This is why Win-Win leaders must of necessity be opportunists but always, responsible stewards for the future.

Responsible Stewardship

The first act of responsible stewardship for our communities will be to create and maintain an ark manifest that includes each species selected for colonization including us, homo sapiens.

A good way to start this process is to create an EcoTech Biosphere and Technosphere Task Force (EBT). This task force will be a combination of individual resources that are assembled for a particular tactical need, with common communications and a leader.

EBT Mission Goals

The initial mission goal of your EcoTech Biosphere and Technosphere Task Force (EBT) will be to develop an integrated plan for your church ark species manifest which will require two skill sets:

- **Biosphere:** All of the plant and animal species used in an EcoTech system and their environmental requirements. The biosphere is an all-natural ecology of plants and animals, and EBT task force members responsible for designing the biosphere will focus on the relationships between organisms and their environment.
- **Technosphere:** The technology used to host a biosphere for the purpose of creating a stress-free environment for all of the desired species in a biosphere. The EBT task force members responsible for designing the technosphere have a very singular goal, to provide a stress-free environment for the species within the biosphere, so that each day is another day in paradise.

Conceptually, there is no overlap between an EcoTech biosphere and its technosphere. The two concepts are defined by clear boundaries.

For example with aquaponics, the boundary is the surface area, inside your aquaponics system, where it contacts the water in the system. At this point the bacteria needed to process the fish waste will flourish and form what one could think of as a thin biological membrane. Without this vital membrane, the fish waste will kill the fish.

This brings us back to the definition for EcoTech: an all-natural ecology, hosted within a technosphere. The term "hosted" speaks to an essential EcoTech concept.

EcoTech Hosting

In current use, hosting is a term more closely associated with the Internet. It conjures up visions of endless equipment racks filled with a Christmas tree of blinking lights and miles of cables interconnecting a maze of devices.

However, this also generally describes how technologically modified environments are created and maintained. Therefore, if we take that vision from Internet server farms to agricultural farms, the imperative is exactly the same, to make money.

The goal of modern industrial agriculture is not to grow or raise nutritious commodities. It is to quickly grow commodities in large quantities. As far as all those essential minerals and nutrients that everyone needs, it is assumed that modern technology will invent synthetic fertilizer solutions at a much lower cost than doing it right the first time.

How does this play out? For the plants, it is a steady diet of synthetic fast food fertilizers. The result for consumers, is a steady diet of synthetic fast food nutrition. It is no wonder that we spend a fortune on supplements each year.

Nutrition-oriented Discipline

Compared to drug store supplements, EcoTech hosting is a nutrition-oriented discipline. It offers a more upscale vision, and for some it can be spiritual.

One way to think of EcoTech hosting is by comparing it to how we travel today. Inexpensive roadside motels offer cheap rooms and lots of road noise. Conversely, expensive hotels provide a more enjoyable experience. Hosting for them is about making your stay comfortable and pleasant, while making you feel appreciated.

When designing your technosphere, your goal is the same. You want to create an all-natural biosphere where each day is another day in paradise for the species that exist within it.

The good morale and the productivity of your teams will help you create this paradise.

When organizing your EcoTech Biosphere and Technosphere Task Force, each team member will participate based on their ability and preference.

Some will prefer to focus on the biosphere and others the technosphere. The leader will get them together and provide enough time and information about what is expected. They can then decide which team they want to be on. Once the teams are formed and everyone is ready to begin, the first thing to decide is who is coming to dinner? In other words, a species manifest.

Species Manifest

Before a Win-Win survival community breaks ground, it must begin to build its species manifest with a detailed list of all the plant and animal species expected. This species manifest must be deemed an ever-evolving work in progress from day one.

Great care must be taken when selecting the species that you bring to your properties and eventually to space because farmers currently select species to serve market demand.

A Win-Win survival community does not exist to survive market demand. It exists to survive the hardships of post-catastrophe and to provide a template for survival for eventual space colonization. Therefore, it must create a holistic species plan that focuses on complete needs-based diets and recipes.

Grow-to-Diet

A Win-Win community by definition is self-sustaining and can transition through different growing environments with a grow-to-diet strategy. This becomes the foundation of your community's farming and ranching operations.

This strategy must encompass different types of diets in support of the diverse needs of a community and its cultural food preferences. It must also be consistent with a community's financing strategy.

In "Chapter 1 – Surviving With Our Heritage", we introduced two Win-Win survival community funding strategies: incremental self-funding and turnkey funding.

Incremental self-funding is a bootstrap strategy for those founding a church in small financial steps, whereas turnkey funding is a single lump sum investment. In this book, we will use two basic diets that are equally applicable to both strategies.

- **Survival Diet:** Living through a cataclysm means frequent hardship, stress, and physical exertion. Active adults will need 3,000+ high-quality calories each day in warm climates and even more in cold climates during these intense periods. Therefore, an optimal survival diet needs to address a variety of circumstances, growing climates, seasons, and nutrition demands.
- **Space Diet:** Traveling to other star systems for the purpose of colonization will take generations, and they will need fresh food on the way there. There will be less physical activity in space when compared with survival, unless something sudden and deadly happens.

The major difference between the two is the growing climates. It varies on earth. It is more constant in space, and the environment will be maintained with temperature and humidity setpoints.

The favored setpoints on the International Space Station (ISS) are based on a Mediterranean-like climate. Using this as a model will enable a lighter, more varied, and flavorful diet to brighten the tedium of long-duration space travel.

A short description of these two diets could be summed up in two questions.

- **Survival Diet:** "Hell of day, and I'm hungry enough to eat the back end of a hobby horse. What's for dinner?"
- **Space Diet:** "What are we in the mood for tonight? Greek or Italian?"

Seriously, when a community selects and plans its diets, the stars are the limit; as long as those choices support a nutritious food-centered lifestyle.

Food-Centered Lifestyle

Previously, in "Chapter 14 – Feeding 1,000 Martians," the movie *The Martian* was used to establish the goal of feeding 1,000 Martians a day. Matt Damon played astronaut Mark Watney, who also happened to be a biologist, and he used that knowledge to create a food-centered lifestyle.

Had Watney been an astronaut with little or no knowledge of biology, the movie's plot would have been about starving to death on Mars. Why? Because feeding yourself is not something you want to have to learn during a crisis. Therefore, what does a food-centered lifestyle entail?

Every member of the community must work a few hours each day in the hands-on business of growing food. This is critical because most Americans today have a hands-off mindset about how food is produced, and this ignorance will be deadly for future survivors and colonists.

This is not new because Hippocrates of Kos (460 BC to 370 BC) first sounded this warning. Referred to as the "Father of Medicine," he established the medical doctrine of "Primum non nocerum (First do no harm)." Sadly, this is no longer universally administered as an oath by modern medicine.

Nonetheless, Hippocrates gives a simple and powerful axiom for survival health:

"Let food be thy medicine and medicine be thy food."– Hippocrates

To find the right recipes begins with a search for multi-cultural food wisdom, and there is no place like home.

Survival Diet

Surviving a cataclysm means hardship and limited choices. What is needed is a health-promoting and satisfying diet for changing circumstances.

The survival diet model is based on the diet and recipes of America's pioneers during the 18th and 19th centuries.

Today we enjoy our modern comforts and it is difficult to imagine the lives of early pioneers. Let's consider how this played out for the women. They spent entire days staring at the east-end of a west-bound team of oxen, and then they had to prepare an evening meal for some very hard-working and hungry people.

These amazing pioneer women rose to the challenge and made it work. Then in a wonderful gesture of love for others, they passed this knowledge on through treasured cookbooks.

As you read these cookbooks, what strikes you first is how American pioneers were continually on the lookout for health opportunities. When you read their 18th and 19th centuries recipes, you'll see three powerful survival advantages:

- **Foods that Heal:** Pioneers tended to their pains and miseries with food. They did not have modern pharmacies in the new lands; instead they took the wisdom of Hippocrates with them. "Let food be thy medicine and medicine be thy food."
- **Simple Ingredient Lists:** They took a few simple ingredients with them, such as salt, flour, and coffee. They walked the Earth like hunter-gatherers for the rest and availed themselves of every species opportunity for sustenance and health along the way.
- **Simple Preparation:** Pioneers did not have modern all-electric kitchens. They worked long, hard days and cooked with cast iron cooking implements over wood stoves and open fires. Pioneer recipes were not as complex as our modern recipes.

Hands down, the pioneer diet was generally healthy and soul-satisfying, when there was enough of it.

We are blessed with a treasure trove of American pioneer recipes free for the downloading on the Internet and in public libraries nationwide. A veritable cornucopia of survival wisdom.

A Win-Win survival community will be well-served with a library stocked with shelves of cookbooks from all over the world. In a recovering post-historic world, heirloom seeds will be shared and bartered, and knowing how to prepare what grows from them will be helpful.

Win-Win survival community member residences and community centers will have all-electric kitchens that are designed to feed a small number of people. But it's one thing to feed a family and quite another to feed 1,000 Martians. How do you reconcile the two? Your grow-to-diet recipes need to be cooked-to-recipe in an authentic manner.

Authentic Preparation

For large-scale Win-Win survival community food preparation, commercial kitchens based on Pioneer recipes necessitates a return to the 19th century for an authentic food preparation model. It is found in the antebellum mansions of the Deep South.

The term antebellum means before the war and this type of architecture dates from the American Revolution to the beginning of the Civil War. Today, if you visit a southern city like Shreveport, Louisiana, you will see a number of these incredibly beautiful mansions.

They all have their differences, but the one thing they all have in common is that none of them have a kitchen – inside that is.

Antebellum kitchens were known to catch fire easily; so they were often built as separate outbuildings at a safe distance from other the buildings on the plantation. Consequently, when a kitchen caught fire, no effort was made to extinguish the flames other than to contain the fire. They would just let it burn.

After the structure was reduced to ash, the cast iron door hinges, cooking implements, stoves, and so forth were removed and cleaned for reuse. While this was taking place, timber was ordered for a new outbuilding, and within a week or so, a new kitchen was in full operation again.

This "'old school'" strategy proved to be highly effective, and it is easy to implement today.

To prepare your survival diet, build an above-ground EcoShell I without insulation for an authentic pioneer type kitchen.

Inside, you will design and build a cast iron kitchen, with wood stoves that are powered by bio-fuels, such as wood and pressed pellets. Your electricity demand will be dramatically less for cooking, as will your dependence on propane and natural gas.

For added power production, design the stoves in the pioneer kitchen with boiler tubes that capture the heat that would otherwise be vented, to heat water to run a steam-powered generator. An added benefit is that the kitchen can be used as an emergency power generation system as well.

If there is a fire with a Win-Win pioneer type kitchen, most of everything inside is cast iron and concrete; so grease fires will be your principal concern. If a fire starts, do not be a hero; get out and let it burn out. Then clean up the mess and get cooking again.

On the other hand, if a fire starts while in space, it will turn into a God-awful crisis. It is why captains use frequent fire drills to keep crews on the ready should disaster strike.

Space Diet

In the controlled environment of the International Space Station (ISS), there is no weather. Rather, there are setpoint ranges. This is the range of temperature and humidity levels that provide the most comfortable environment for travelers.

For the purpose of a Win-Win survival community, the benchmark setpoint ranges on the International Space Station (ISS) are the command input models for growing a space diet on Earth. They are:

- **ISS Temperature:** Nominally kept between 72° F and 78° F (22.2° C to 25.5° C) and adjusted as needed for crew comfort.

- **ISS Humidity:** Nominally kept in a range between 40 percent and 70 percent.

In short, the ISS has a Mediterranean climate range of temperature and humidity levels. Air temperature is critical with aquaponics because it regulates the water temperature.

Therefore, the ideal Win-Win community Mediterranean setpoint for aquaponics technospheres is 72° F (22.2° C) with 50 percent humidity. This setpoint is also perfect for growing premium organic medicinal cannabis, and we'll learn more about that later.

If one were to define the diets in seasonal terms, a survival diet is a heavier winter-like diet; whereas, a diet for space is more summer-like.

Given that preparing a survival diet requires cooking with cast iron cooking implements over wood stoves or open fires like the pioneers, what about in space?

Cooking in Space

Does a space diet require commercial scale, all-electric ovens, microwave ovens, and the like? This is a key question for engineers since the first thing they need to address is the energy demand for cooking. In addition there are the air handling systems needed to remove heat, smoke, and humidity from within the spacecraft.

On Earth the problem is the same for energy and environmental demands in an off-grid community that produces its own power.

The solution to this conundrum is having an ample supply of sunlight here on Earth and in space to cook. Given present solar technology, that effectively limits the range to the orbit of Jupiter for space.

Comets do not begin to outgas until they are inside the orbit of Jupiter; therefore, a Jupiter solution is a solar oven, like those from GoSun. To learn more, visit their site at www.go-sun.co.

On Earth and in space, this will eliminate excess energy and environmental demands. With a bit of creative research, your community can find a wealth of Mediterranean recipes for your space diet. Then you experiment with them and adapt them to commercial-scale solar oven cooking.

Best of all, the goal of eating fresh food on long space journeys will no longer be concerned with fuel consumption. Rather, it will be about holistically feeding the body, soul, and mind.

What does this mean, then? We can actually have a Star Trek future, and it begins the day you call for volunteers to research survival and space recipes. Your community will have a blank canvas and a free hand to paint natural solutions with a broad brush; so imagine the fun to be had, and the excitement of creating an entirely new field of food wisdom.

That's the plan for now and who knows? Hopefully, future spacecraft will not be limited by food vs. fuel trade-offs. Rather, someone will invent a new type of propulsion system that provides ample opportunities to grow fresh food in space and to bring domesticated animals as well.

That's right folks; we're talking about livestock in space, whether in livestock pens or as frozen embryos. Still, raising ranch animals is less about modern science and more about Stone Age 2.0 practicality.

Farming and Ranching

A simple definition for ranching is that it is about raising livestock. This works well enough today, but in terms of EcoTech farming and ranching, it creates more questions than answers.

To illustrate the point, let's make a ranching choice, and our task for this example is to choose three species from the following four: Horses, mules, donkeys, and dogs.

This choice is not as easy as it may appear. It becomes challenging because since everyone loves dogs, this shifts the focus to the other three species. And where does this leave us?

Mules and donkeys get along with dogs about as well as opposing divorce lawyers, and that's a problem.

Horses and dogs are domesticated as companion animals, and as long as the dog is respectful, they'll get along.

Given that we tend to like dogs and horses pretty much the same, we now have a cinematic Thunderdome conundrum scenario. Two species enter, and one species leaves. The one that does is either a mule or a donkey, but not both.

Moment of truth, Dear Reader. Here it comes.

You can plow the ground with a mule or a horse, but you can't plow with a donkey.

Arrivederci, donkey.

That's a shame because donkeys are useful creatures and great guard animals. Ask any predator that has survived the kick of an irate donkey. But is there a point to this? Yes.

Someone from the city will say "Horses and mules work for me." Slam dunk. Problem solved. When compared with horses, mules are easier to work with and live longer. Also when compared with donkeys, mules are more intelligent and less obstinate. Done deal. Move on.

Whoa there city dweller! On second thought. Why are we talking about donkeys again?

Once the last of the mules you originally acquired for your ranch expires and there is no one to sell or trade for another mule, you're at a dead end. Mules are a hybrid mix, and to breed replacement Mules, you need a male donkey and a female horse. And did you know that they are also sterile and therefore unable to reproduce?

That changes things. If you're a city dweller starting up a Win-Win survival community, how do you fix this? You don't! From day one, you begin by recruiting someone who can. This brings us to the EcoTech differences between farmers and ranchers.

Farmers vs. Ranchers

For the purpose of EcoTech farming and ranching, a difference between them is how farmers and ranchers view their relationship between the land and their animals:

- A rancher sees the land as a vast home for his animals.
- A farmer sees the animals as assets in a well-organized system.

Size is really the major difference though. Retreats have 4+ usable acres, farms have 40+ usable acres, and ranches have 400+ usable acres. One could say that ranches are put together like panoramas whereas farms are put together more like table-top picture puzzles.

Both views are valid and equally necessary for successful ranching and farming. However, where the two begin to differ is with mechanization:

- Farmers work more than ranchers and favor the heavy use of mechanization for maximum market output. So, the technosphere is their primary focus.
- Ranchers are far more conservative about mechanization because their main priority is the welfare of their animals and so their primary focus is the biosphere.

Now, we arrive at the real difference. The one that sets the right tone for EcoTech farming and ranching.

- A farmer is always a farmer.
- A rancher can be a rancher or choose to be a rancher who also farms.

This is why the optimal mindset for a Win-Win survival community is to be ranchers who also farm. This requires two ranch operating groups: Farming operations and ranching operations.

The benefit of this balanced mindset is an objective and holistic view of technosphere and biosphere integration and interoperability issues.

Can you find this mindset online or in a library? No. It only exists in a living culture.

Ranching Operations

Modern mechanized farming depends on stable sources of fuel, machinery and replacement parts. Therefore, the day the nation's power grid fails for any reason, is the same day your mechanized farming operations begin to fail. This results in rationing, and vehicles will be held in reserve for crucial farming tasks and community defense.

This is why the command input for your ranching operations will be horses and the culture that supports them. From that starting point, all the other livestock and draft animal considerations can be easily and quickly determined.

Therefore, you need to explore living horse cultures, and a good place for this is with Pioneer re-enactors.

Pioneer re-enactors provide a powerful living culture because they devote great care to authenticity and the pioneer experience. They are an invaluable resource of wisdom, tips and leads about the practical uses of horses, other draft animals and suitable livestock.

But of equal importance, they'll be heavily immersed in the supporting technology, which means 19th century horse-drawn wagons, plows and such.

You will not need rocket scientists to build this old school technology. Rather, you'll need a wainwright for building wagons and a wheelwright to make and maintain the wagon wheels. Likewise, you'll also need saddle makers, horse trainers, blacksmiths, and others.

Here you'll find a real advantage with these living horse cultures. They are all interconnected in some manner; if you share and respect their values, they're happy to share their knowledge with you.

Also, after your community acquires a ranch property, explore the area for a nearby Native American tribe and do not hesitate to reach out to them. Their living culture wisdom can offer great insights into horse culture and the healing and nutrition properties of local plant and animal life. Likewise, if there is an Amish community nearby, reach out to them for their knowledge as well.

If you think you're too clever to bother with all that and you shoot from the hip, you'll be a flop, and you'll know it by the look on their faces. Why go there? Instead, showing good listening skills and sincere respect for their knowledge and traditions will serve you well.

Also, recruit a special person to your community to serve as a liaison. Ideally, someone with an understanding of how to survive in a post-mechanization world beset by dangers.

Here is where you need someone to represent you, who possess a talent that is respected among all horse cultures including Native Americans. On such person is a horse whisperer.

Find a Horse Whisperer

People who work with horses do so as a lifestyle choice. They typically come from some horse background, or perhaps they were city kids who dreamed of working with horses while riding the bus to school each day. A modern lifestyle choice for a few.

Back when all Americans knew how to live without electricity, most everyone knew how to live with horses too. This is important; because after the national power grid fails, we will need to transition into a modern version of the agrarian age.

Therefore, horses are the command input for EcoTech ranching operations, and each ranch will have its own unique needs and features, which will ultimately shape its choices for horses, draft animals and livestock.

Regardless of location-specific animal concerns, the common criteria will be:

- No show animals. Best-of-class work animals only.
- The ranch is also a home for the animals.
- Extreme event emergency overcover.

When it comes to horses as the command input for your EcoTech ranching operations, the person for the job will be a good barn manager. The maestros of large barn and stable operations, they orchestrate the daily lives of each animal with a keen eye for detail.

Is finding a barn manager your mission as a church founder? No. The first person you really want to recruit for your ranching operations will be a horse whisperer. These are unique individuals, who interact with animals in a holistic way. One, that in a manner of speaking, connects them with the animal's soul-spirit.

Here is where a horse whisperer will make a unique survival difference because they are effective at calming and healing traumatized animals. Living through extreme events will be hard on man and animals alike, and there will be a need for this skill. Plus, there is another useful benefit as well. No one can break a green horse faster than a horse whisperer.

Our modern living horse culture is well-connected and broad; so let your horse whisperer be your guide to this culture. And while you're at it, let them do most of the talking. That is except for when you have your checkbook in hand, and you explain your community's species rules.

EcoTech Species Rules

The goal for surviving a cataclysm on Earth is to create a nourishing and sustaining future for space colonization. As a key part of this, the EcoTech species rules for selecting plant and animal species are:

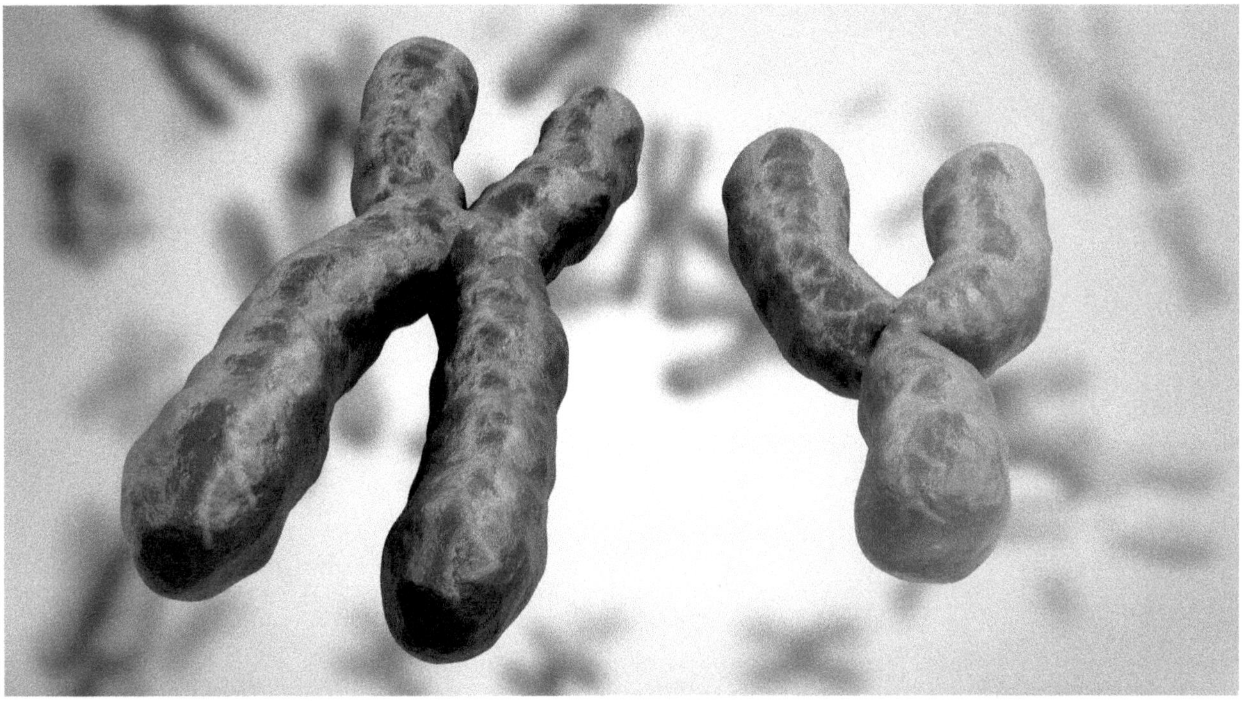

- **Authenticity:** For animals, best-of-class working breeds and food breeds. For plants, everything begins with organic heritage seeds and cuttings. No GMOs.
- **Diversity:** Because a Win-Win community grows-to-recipe, it is essential that the species plan offers the most diverse range of useful species possible.
- **Resilience:** Plant species that are durable, and disease-resistant, and can handle extremes in the environment are essential. Less resilient species should only be grown for special requirements. Animal species must have a strong constitution and be able to thrive on their own.

Once you've got your first slate of species ready to go, it's time to get right-angle about it.

16

EcoTech Planning

The planet Mars offers a poignant message about species survival. It was once beautiful like Earth, and then something very terrible happened. This is why the Moon and the Planet Mars are just intermediate waypoints on amazing journeys to the stars for future colonists.

However, the first step in the journey is not capital intensive, high input commodity production, where farm fields are laid out so farm machinery has wide pathways for their tires.

The first step is to build a productive and organic farm with permaculture and rain water harvesting.

America has a severe issue with freshwater waste. The excessive pumping of groundwater has over-stressed aquifers in arid regions of America and elsewhere.

We've known for decades that we are pumping the water out of the aquifers faster than nature can replace it. Yet, we just keep doing it anyway.

Aquifer depletion can affect a single well and it can likewise affect a larger aquifer system that underlies several states, like the Ogalalla Aquifier.

The results of groundwater depletion vary, and none bode well for the future. After the nation's power grid fails for any reason, water access will be an even larger problem. How about having to pump water from 1000 ft or more instead of 250 ft?

Is it possible to find a Win-Win ranch with an initial strategy based on present-day mechanized farming practices with the assumption that the community can transition it to an

EcoTech model at a later date? Yes, it is possible, but it is a slippery slope to capital intensive truck farming.

GMO Danger

If you initially found your Win-Win ranch and it has a strategy based on present-day GMO commodity farming practices, the industrial genie will be out of the bottle, and it will not be a blessing. It will be the proverbial "tail that wags your dog." It will set the stage for eventually abandoning your community's food sovereignty goals.

It also sets you up to fail if you try to farm the same crops organically. If your farm adjoins a farm with GMO crops and seeds or pollen from those fields are carried into your fields by the wind, you've got another problem.

Should wind-borne GMO pollen from your neighbor's fields be found in your field or pollen from your farm be found in a neighboring GMO farmers field, by law you have one of two choices. Lose everything fighting a vicious army of corporate GMO legal raiders or sell out to the blackmail.

At that point, you can talk about food sovereignty until the cows come home, but not as a functional Win-Win survival community. Where will this lead? Should things go sideways, time will become your enemy and put into play the most difficult judgment call of all. Imagine finding yourself in a survival situation where you've got enough seeds to start over but not enough time and starvation is setting in.

Do you eat your GMO seeds to keep everyone from starving to death, knowing full well that they are coated with an insecticide to insure that pests do not eat the seed before it germinates?

Or do you plant them knowing that between planting and harvest, many members of your community will starve to death. Then what happens to the few who live to see that last harvest? What will they do after that? Learn to eat ground worms, grass, and tree bark as an alternative to GMO death seeds?

What brings you to that point of sadness? Commodity farming is driven by large-scale output and the market needs to output enough produce to fill a fleet of 18-wheel trucks. The result of this output-oriented strategy is the depletion of minerals from the soil, poisoning of land and water with industrial chemicals, and the excessive over-pumping of aquifers.

EcoTech planning is an input-oriented strategy.

Input vs. Output

EcoTech planning is about the responsible stewardship of land based on an input-oriented strategy. The goals are threefold:

- Less water
- Less land
- Less heavy mechanization

With an input-oriented strategy, the goal is to find a sustainable balance between resource inputs and market outputs. The fulcrum for this balancing act lies between the biosphere and technosphere sides of your EcoTech planning efforts.

- **Biosphere Output:** Because your Win-Win community is growing-to-recipe, the selection of plant and animal species will depend on the contents of your designated recipes. Here is where output drives the process. You need to figure out what you want to produce and the quality and volume of the product required.

- **Technosphere Input:** The goal of your Technosphere team members is to determine how to maximize the inputs required for the desired biosphere output. This needs to be done in a holistic manner consistent with responsible stewardship of the resources.

An input-driven holistic system view of your Win-Win property's farming and ranching operations will create a sustainable system, for survival both during and after a cataclysm on Earth, as brave families take their first steps to ensure the survival of our species.

Input-driven Holistic System View

Everything has to start somewhere, and with EcoTech planning, command inputs will determine your overall farming and ranching strategy. Therefore, when looking from above, the differences between input-oriented farming and market-driven output-oriented farms are quite striking.

When using an online map program like Google Earth, market-driven farms and ranches appear orderly and well laid out. However, change that to a boots on the ground view and what you'll see are unsustainable market-driven solutions, which in the absence of a functioning power grid and fuel will fail.

With EcoTech farming and ranching, every plant and animal in your species manifest must play a vital role as an interconnected element within a recipe-driven, holistic off-grid food production system. Therefore, the first step in creating this system is to define your command inputs.

Defining Command Inputs

EcoTech command inputs are the launch points for your various EcoTech farming and ranching operations, and there is a simple way to identify them. You look for a SPOT, a single point of truth.

Conceptually, the SPOT method is much like working a picture puzzle.

Every puzzle enthusiast knows that each piece of the puzzle will somehow eventually connect to a corner piece. So, their command inputs are the four corner pieces and finding them is a straightforward process. They open the box and pile all the puzzle pieces on a tabletop and sort through the pile to find the corner pieces, which are then the first to be placed. After that, they use the corner pieces to work the puzzle from the outside in.

With EcoTech planning, a similar process is used; once you find a SPOT, the rest of the pieces will fit together and bless you with a multitude of knowledge resources.

SPOT-on Knowledge Resources

The odds are 100-to-1 that any survival need or idea that comes to mind has likely been tried by someone. They've probably posted a wonderful smartphone video on the Internet telling what they've learned. Watching these videos will inspire you.

Likewise, there are those who go to the next step and write and publish books about what they've learned.

These books can be somewhat helpful and here is an easy way to classify them:

- **Get 'er Done:** A quick start do it yourself (DIY) book with simple directions and procedures. These books are typically a first effort; so if the formatting is a little odd and there is no alphabetical index, do not let these issues sway your decision.

- **Need to Know:** Ideal for conceptual planning and design. These books identify crucial concepts, technologies, and methods. They play an essential role in helping you make steady improvements in your EcoTech strategies and engineering designs.
- **Useful Reference:** Anything else of interest that may prove useful at a future time. If you wonder whether or not the information in the book is worth the price, you're putting the cart in front of the horse. Rather, ask yourself, "Is my life worth the price of this book?" Then decide accordingly.

What you'll come to admire most about these knowledge sources is the love that inspires them. Love for families, love for the land, and a noble passion for what they do. Should a 10-minute amateur video yield only one useful idea; it is still worth watching, if for no other reason than to experience the passion.

Immersing yourself into this wonderful world of food production culture will inspire you in ways you cannot begin to imagine.

However, terminology can be an issue, because it is so diverse. Therefore, once you identify a SPOT, the process of connecting the rest of the puzzle depends on establishing common terms and definitions.

EcoTech Terminology

Win-Win communities need to use a consistent terminology that reflects common usage as much as possible. For example, two terms in popular use which can be problematic are "garden" and "farm."

At one time, the difference was clear, but in recent years, the emergence of small-scale organic farming has blurred the difference. Even agricultural experts struggle to offer a clear difference and for good reason.

When we think of survival gardens, the victory gardens Americans planted during WWII to supplement their war rations come to mind.

This is a good place to begin, because of the Green Revolution which began after WWII. The result of the revolution is today's vast fields of GMO monocrops, such as corn or wheat, that are worked by armies of air-conditioned farmers who ride massive GPS-guided farm machines.

All of this should make one wonder, "How much rocket fuel will it take to transport a farm equipment dealership to Mars?" Even worse, it could force nations to launch a new Dr. Strangelove crisis, where all sides race like maniacs to close the Mars-tractor gap.

Now that we've had a moment of fun, let's get EcoTech practical with a few necessary definitions. The first is the EcoTech difference between ranches and farms.

Ranch or Farm?

In the eastern half of the US, people think farms. In the Western half of the country, they tend to think ranches. This begs an obvious question. Why are large Win-Win properties called ranches in this book?

Win-Win properties are called ranches for the following reasons:

- **Location:** The ideal location for a Win-Win ranch is at an elevation of between 2,000 to 4,000 FASL (feet above sea level) with an ideal size of 400+ usable acres. This affords Win-Win communities a desirable survival altitude for ranching and farming.
- **Land Use:** More ranch acreage will be used for grazing and herding than farming operations. Assuming your ranch has 20 acres under cultivation, you will also want to stable up to twenty draft animals and horses. 2.5 acres of land are required for grazing per animal, for a total of 50 acres. Therefore, the largest need for land will be for ranching and grazing operations.
- **Herding:** Due to the large amount of land required for livestock grazing, horses and vehicles are used to herd them from one area of the ranch to the next. If the ranch property borders Federal land with grazing rights, this can open considerable ranching opportunities.

Another way to determine whether you have a farm or a ranch is with movement. On farms, livestock is typically restricted to enclosed areas such as pastures and paddocks. With ranches, livestock can free-range on large tracts of land as well as be restricted to enclosed areas.

The upshot is this. If you have free-ranging livestock, you'vc got a ranch; no matter how much produce you farm. With a Win-Win property, you do it all; so this is why it is called a ranch.

Let's discuss the basic Win-Win terminology for farming and livestock properties.

Property Terminology

With farming fertile soil, water, and a good growing season are essential. Therefore, a prospective property for a church ranch has two essential criteria, and the terms for them are:

- **Latitude:** The closer your property is to the North or South Pole, the shorter the growing season, because sunlight is less direct. The growing season begins later due to the low angle of the Sun, which means it takes longer for the soil to warm during the spring months. Generally, the ideal latitude range for a Win-Win ranch in the Northern Hemisphere is between 30° and 50° North.
- **Elevation:** As a rule of thumb, the height threshold for high-altitude farming is 5,000 FASL (feet above sea level). High altitude farming has three specific challenges. The

amount of light the plants can receive, water availability, and soil nutrient availability. In general, the ideal elevation range for a Win-Win ranch in the Northern Hemisphere will be between 2,000 and 4,000 FASL.

You may wonder, given that there are successful high-altitude farms, should one ignore beautiful, high-elevation properties above 5,000'? Or, more specifically, can a Win-Win community succeed with high-altitude farming? Yes, it can because the goal is eventually to feed 1,000 Martians. However, this raises a nagging issue regarding atmospheric surface pressure.

The range of pressures on Mars is equivalent to those on Earth at altitudes of between 19 to 37 miles high. The point is, whether you are farming at 5,000' or higher, you darn well better know exactly what you're doing. The risks of high-altitude farming are high, and even worse, the crops are more susceptible to UV light damage from extreme solar weather.

Before you buy a property above 5,000 FASL, you'll need to recruit church members who grew up on high-altitude farms, and the more, the better. Otherwise, if you try to learn how to farm above 5,000' as you go, you may wind up hoping to God that you can grow enough potatoes to survive, in the same way Watney did in The Martian.

Instead of pondering that, let's go find some land to buy.

Property Location

When searching for a suitable church property, the ideal one will have the right location, geology and water sources. Yet, when it comes to searching for church properties, the command input is the politics of the region where the property is located.

Politics, as a command input, will drive your property searches to areas where permitting is reasonably manageable and affordable and will not create costly and time-consuming impediments.

Here are a few basic command input guidelines to help you refine your property searches.

- **Avoid Blue States:** Never attempt to permit in a blue state without full political support at the state government level. The bureaucracies and their permitting processes are fraught with delays, uncertainty, exorbitant fees and regulation. Red states on the other hand, are usually more amenable. Once a red state-licensed engineer signs off on your construction plan, the rest of the process can typically be completed in a time-and-cost efficient manner.
- **Avoid Metropolitan Areas:** Regardless of whether you're in a red state or a blue state, large cities and metropolitan areas will be difficult due to land availability, costs and permitting. Another problem: properties adjacent to large metropolitan areas could be overrun quickly by starved and desperate city-dwellers during a cataclysm.

- **Rural Counties in the Red States:** Generally, remote rural counties in red states offer the best options in terms of land availability, cost, and project permitting.
- **Unincorporated Areas:** The best properties to search for in rural red-state areas are those situated in unincorporated areas of a rural county. They will not be governed by a local municipal corporation, which means one less regulatory layer.
- **Public Access Road:** The access roads to your retreat or ranch must offer two ways to enter and leave the property from a public road. Repairs, snow plowing and other maintenance concerns with private roads can be problematic. It is best to have direct access to a public road maintained by the county.
- **No Easements or Covenants:** Properties with preexisting easements and covenants can embroil your church in lengthy and costly legal disputes. Think of easements and covenants as land mines. They're all good until you step on one.
- **Moving Water:** Water is life and your community and farming operations will need a lot of it, so properties with natural springs, ponds and lakes are best. The ideal location will have a year-round creek, or stream that has a continuous flow rate of at least 15 gallons per minute (GPM) is suitable for hydroelectric power. The higher the flow rate, the better.
- **Amendable Soil:** Growing crops on a sand dune is an interesting notion for science fiction buffs, but the ideal property will have a nice rich organic loam ready for planting. More likely, expect to begin with a soil that is less than ideal. If so, the soil must be amendable.

Above all else, the most important thing that you can do to ensure you acquire a suitable property for your church is to work with a local realtor. Someone who has been working in the market long enough to know where the "cow chews the cud," as they say in Texas.

Your best choice for a realtor will be an established professional of high integrity with a personal interest in what you are doing.

As for the commission, the land acquisition costs for a Win-Win church property are about ten percent of total costs for a fully developed property. Therefore, when working with your realtor and other professionals, be firm and fair, and use the correct terminology to express your interests and concerns when evaluating prospective properties.

Farming Terminology

Although most of your ranch property is used for ranching operations, the most intensive use is with the farming operations.

Never forget, a Win-Win survival community is a church that farms and teaches farming.

Relevant farming terms are:

- **Truck Farming:** Truck farmers grow some vegetable crops on a large scale, for distant markets and their fields can cover vast tracts of land. Win-Win communities are not intended to serve as mechanized truck farms. Rather, they use small fields and indoor farming for sustainable opportunity farming.
- **EcoTech Opportunity Farming:** Opportunity field farming employs EcoTech sustainable planning to work around disasters, extreme weather, and shorter growing seasons.
- **Garden:** Gardens are unprotected and can be as small as a planter box or it can be up to an acre in size.
- **Community Garden:** Large, protected gardens that have work and social out-buildings. One-eighth acre is a good reference size for a Win-Win community.

With opportunity farming, your community will use high-risk open field farming to grow fodder and forage among other things:

- **Fodder Crop:** A broad agricultural term to describe foodstuff grown for domesticated livestock such as cattle, rabbits, sheep, horses, chickens, and pigs.
- **Forage Crop:** A more narrow ranching term to describe foodstuff grown for free-ranging livestock like horses and cattle.

A simple way to distinguish the two is that forage is typically used with free-ranging livestock. Whereas, fodder grown for domesticated livestock is kept in enclosed areas

Livestock Terminology

For thousands of years, our species has refined the art of domesticating and raising livestock, and so must Win-Win survival communities. One particular need will be draft animals like horses and mules. Here are some basic horse and livestock-related terms:

- **Barn:** A building used for storage or keeping animals such as cattle.
- **Pen:** Any small enclosure area used to contain domesticated animals, such as sheep or cattle.
- **Pasture:** Land on which livestock is kept for feeding, and which may or may not be enclosed.
- **Paddock:** A small enclosure or field of grassland, especially for horses.
- **Stable:** A ranch building or facility set apart from the rest and specially adapted for the lodging, feeding, and training of animals with hooves, especially horses.
- **Horse Corral:** A fenced-in enclosure for livestock, especially for horses.
- **Horse Round Pens:** A circular corral or pen, used for training, exercising, and breaking horses.

If you're a vegetarian, you may wonder if ranch animals are really all that necessary. Are you a vegetarian who enjoys cheese and eggs cooked in butter? Practice your "yee-haw," because you're a cowboy or cowgirl rancher who also happens to be a vegetarian.

If we are to survive on Earth and also go to the stars, we need to take the foods we've come to love and cherish with us. Your community will be like a modern off-grid Noah's Ark. It will not look like one though.

Off-Grid Organic Farming

As you search for church properties online, you'll use map applications with satellite imagery of rural areas. These images will be dominated by farm fields that use center pivot irrigation. What you'll see is something resembling a chaotic checkerboard, and every checker is the same color, dark green.

Center pivot irrigation is a common feature of mechanized farming. It was invented by Colorado farmer Frank Zybach in 1940 and has been widely adopted by American farmers as a high-efficiency water distribution technology. However, it is also highly grid-dependent.

If the nation's grid collapses, farmers will use generators to power their irrigation systems. But what happens when they run out of fuel? Their plan B will devolve into a spasmodic series of ad hoc workaround solutions, which in the end, will fail without direct and immediate government assistance.

Meanwhile, how will things be going for Win-Win survival communities as their mechanized, grid-dependent counterparts struggle to save their crops? To paraphrase a popular saying, "It will be another day at the EcoTech operations," because Win-Win communities will utilize several types of above-ground and below-ground EcoTech technospheres, from high-risk above-ground open fields to all-hazards below-ground aquaponics.

Technosphere Design Criteria

A technosphere is any coherently-organized growing environment. It can be as simple as an in-ground raised bed or as complex as a massive, below-ground aquaponics system. The discussion of an above-ground farming technosphere's design begins at ground level.

One may ask, are simple soil beds for gardens and fields a type of technosphere? The answer is yes. A technosphere is any coherent, man-made structure that alters the natural state of the environment, regardless of the materials or methods used.

Your technosphere design team will need to address the following criteria for every technosphere on church property, regardless of type or use:

- **Water Demand:** Water is life and must be conserved and used judiciously even during times of plenty. A successful water discipline regime will also serve to inspire the sound management of other vital resources.
- **Energy Demand:** Farming requires energy. Thankfully sunlight is freely available, but not so are other energy sources such as electricity to power a well pump. For this reason, off-grid technosphere farming designs need to have off-grid, energy-efficient solutions.
- **Interoperability:** Each part of an EcoTech system must interact and function in a holistic manner with every other part of the system. Standards and consistent methods are necessary.
- **Harvesting:** The number of harvests you can plan on, depends on your biosphere and technosphere choices. There are three types: seasonal, extended season, and continuous. Seasonal field crops are unprotected and subject to the environment. Greenhouses offer extended growing seasons and weather mitigation. For continuous year-round harvesting, above-ground hothouses and below-ground aquaponics are reliable producers.
- **Risk Mitigation:** For a Win-Win community, a catastrophic risk is the total loss of a crop with no chance of salvage. Loss prevention and mitigation cannot be left to chance; you must be proactive in assessing and managing crop loss risks due to severe and extreme events.

A good example of risk mitigation is found in *The Martian*. When the habitat airlock failed, causing explosive decompression, this exposed the interior of the habitat to the Martian environment. As a result, the habitat's Earth-like atmosphere blew out, and Watney's indoor potato garden was completely destroyed.

Fortunately, Watney managed to salvage enough potatoes to keep him alive until his rescue. How long could Watney survive on potatoes alone? Who knows, but he would ultimately encounter deficiencies in Vitamins A, B12 and E and calcium and selenium.

For those who want to try the Watney diet, a word to the wise. Potatoes are slightly toxic too and the poison is in the stem and leaves. However, trace amounts can be found on the potato itself, and if they are not removed, they can make you sick if you eat enough of them.

The point is responsible risk mitigation is preventing catastrophic crop losses. This is a responsibility that is shared equally by everyone involved in the EcoTech planning process.

Crop Loss Threats

There is a diversity of ways in which a Win-Win community can farm, ranging from small to large. Examples include the curved planter boxes we made in "Chapter 10 – Design Team and Infrastructure," or an open field of hemp or sunflowers. What both have in common is that they are virtually unprotected and vulnerable to sudden, catastrophic loss.

Farmers worry about a lot of things. There are three crop threats that top their list and are a similar concern for above-ground technospheres:

- **Animal Pests:** Deer, rabbits, and squirrels fall into this category. Be mindful of crops such as alfalfa, corn and winter grains that can trigger animal feeding frenzies.
- **Insect Pests:** Every backyard gardener learns very early that there are insect pests for just about every plant. If you grow it, something will eat it. Beetles, grubs, and slugs among others will eat their weight and more in plant matter in a day.
- **Severe Weather:** Frost and hail are perpetual crop loss concerns and this will play a role in selecting what to plant. For example borscht is a popular Russian soup because beets, the principal ingredient of borscht soup, are highly frost resistant.

There are numbers of ways that farmers have to deal with these threats and you need to know them because your above-ground farm operations will be exposed to these and other extreme threats as well.

Extreme Threats

A conventional mindset pushes concerns for extreme threats to the fringe, where it can be ignored. When it comes to extreme threats, modern mechanized farming follows a market-driven, plant-and-pray strategy that delegates the risk of extreme threats to someone else like a hedge-fund manager.

The principal difference between those pushed to the awareness of extreme threats and those that have conventional awareness is, no matter how much denial, mockery, humiliation and shame is cast upon those in awareness by family and friends, they still know what they know. Nothing can change that.

These people come from every walk of life and what those who deny their awareness fail to understand is why they are aware in the first place.

Awakening Experience

The ability to comprehend the scope of extreme threats is either the result of a disciplined approach, a triggered experience, or an awakening experience.

Soldiers in war and first responders typify a disciplined approach. Their training teaches them how to take action without long periods of contemplation. Whether they agree with a given concern or causality, they prepare for all-hazards events with an open mind.

Those who have awakening experiences as the result of a catastrophic trigger event, undergo something very different from a disciplined approach because this kind of awareness is something you cannot train for and it can occur in several ways.

Triggered awakenings begin with an existential crisis that confronts the experiencer with the need to be foresighted. Like the creases on a pair of pants, a trigger event is not something easily ironed away.

This was the case for David B. South and myself during the 1989 Loma Prieta earthquake in San Francisco. After a triggered awakening like that, you never look at the world in the same way again.

However, beyond a disciplined approach, or a triggered experience, the single greatest life changing event of all is a paranormal awakening.

Paranormal Awakening

A paranormal awakening is triggered in people through profound dreams, visions, and premonitions that leave an indelible memory.

No matter the age, sex, or walk of life, most experiencers report asteroid impact events, tsunamis, and wars. When they share these experiences with others, most are mocked into silence.

Win-Win survival communities need to employ the same practical view of these paranormal experiences as the KGB and the CIA have done, because arrogant mockery often results in a catastrophic waste of valuable intelligence.

Intelligence agencies made extensive use of psychics and remote viewers during the Cold War. The Russians favored psychics and the Americans favored remote viewers.

In either case, both agencies were equally practical. They viewed paranormal experiences as worth exploring for the intelligence and the intelligence was collected. Then they processed it.

A Win-Win survival community needs to employ this strategy because paranormal awakenings are often prophetic harbingers of possible future events.

Prophetic Harbingers

A prophetic harbinger is a benign sign that you are on the timeline of a prophecy event. Therefore, when evaluating experiences, use these three rules for a true prophecy:

- True prophecy always includes a benign harbinger.
- The purpose of the harbinger is to warn you to prepare.
- Be aware of the prophecy, but do not live in expectation of it.

These prophetic awakening harbingers are often haunting for experiencers. When they recount their experience, note the information, but do not dwell on it.

As Yoda, the Stars Wars character, says, "Always in motion is the future," because you're always looking at possible futures. Therefore, the future is not cast in stone, and one of the reasons we incarnate in this life is to learn how to become better at changing it.

What you really want are the experiencer's sensory impressions, because paranormal awakenings are accompanied by real-life sensory impressions.

Many, for example, report seeing orange-black skies in their dreams and visions. Others go a step further. They not only see orange-black skies; they feel the wind-borne grit on their skin and can hear the wailing of the afflicted. For them these experiences are IMAX-real and unforgettable. They happen time after time, and in many cases, often begin in early childhood.

If it only happens once, it could be seen as a fluke. But when you start to hear the same thing from many different people, gather the intelligence and seriously evaluate it. What you find might surprise you.

Is this kind of intelligence valuable? It was to our ancestors. In every clan or tribe, there were those with a paranormal gift. It wasn't always accurate, but it was often more valuable than educated guesses. So, these people were respected – not mocked and silenced.

What can you learn if you open your mind to true prophecy? One example is that everything you think you know about the December 21, 2012, Mayan Calendar prophecy, is wrong.

Dead wrong!

The Mayans Got it Right

December 21, 2012 has been written off as the single most humiliating non-event in the history of entertainment television, and according to the pundits, the ancient Mayans got it wrong.

The pundits got it wrong.

December 21, 2012 was not the prophetic end of the world. It was the benign harbinger of a prophecy that was to be fulfilled.

Media hype, foolish mockery, and ego aside, what was this all about?

The Mayans, like other ancient cultures, used unique and unequivocal celestial alignments as their harbinger signs. December 21, 2012 was a harbinger date and the ancients were sending a benign warning to the future. When a very rare celestial harbinger alignment was observed, it would be a sign that humanity is standing at the threshold of a prophetic event.

This actually happened, and Dear Reader, you can do one of two things. Roll your eyes or see where the science and the numbers lead.

An honest review of planetary and solar system phenomenon since December 21, 2012, reveals the following:

- **Extreme Weather:** The global effects of extreme temperature on worldwide crop production has not been quantified yet. Prediction models are failing because of a steep increase in the global number of crops lost due to extreme weather since 2012. Type the following Internet search string, "climate change crop failures." You will see how extremes in weather are devastating the Third World, and we're not immune to this.
- **Extreme Space Weather:** Solar storms and UV exposure are critical factors regarding survival. Our sun is near the end of a Maunder Minimum. After this prolonged sunspot minimum, there will be a solar maximum. Historically these can be severe at the outset. This will affect weather and create a whole host of issues, but the one that you'll have to deal with each day is the UV light exposure.
- **Extreme Fireballs:** A fireball is a large meteor that streaks across the sky with a smoky trail. The total number of fireballs observed in North America in 2012 was 2,100. In 2013 it was 3,500. In 2018 it was 5,800. These increasing overall numbers portend threats big and small. A type of fireball called a bolide is big enough to explode, and can release as much energy as an atomic bomb. Small is bad too. A violent unexpected shower of meteorites can pulverize crops, exposed structures, people, and livestock.
- **Extreme Volcanism:** In 2012, the average number of active volcanoes erupting over a period of 12 months was between 50 to 70. In 2018, this was the number of active volcanoes erupting each month. The concern is that large scale eruptions can put down a thick layer of ash that will destroy unprotected above-ground crops and structures.
- **Extreme Seismicity:** The total number of earthquakes of all magnitudes in 2012 was 19,403. In 2013 it was 89,565. In 2018 it was 160,281. A major earthquake will cause extreme events like tsunamis and wildfires. Broken roads and bridges will also block vehicle traffic with heaps of concrete debris.

Most see these disturbing trends but fail to act. If you're a born-hard pioneer, you see what you see and take action, and this brings us to EcoTech Engineering.

17

EcoTech Engineering

An EcoTech system is an all-natural ecology that is hosted within a technosphere. This inside-out view of issues has allowed us to focus on the various diets and recipes that will define your community species manifest.

EcoTech engineering creates these systems using an outside-in problem-solving approach to survival and colonization farming and ranching. Now you will learn how to do it.

It begins with a simple question. What do severe events have in common with extreme events? Ask an EcoTech engineer for the answer, and he or she will point to a sign that says, "DC-3 TOUGH. When in doubt about the stresses—overbuild."

Severe vs. Extreme Events

When financing your construction efforts, two terms that you will often hear are severe events and extreme events.

Contractors will tell you that preparing for severe events is the most cost-effective strategy; whereas preparing for an extreme event will needlessly drive construction costs up.

Let's see how that works; an excellent case for us is the Fukushima Daiichi nuclear disaster.

On October 11, 2011, a 1,000-year extreme event generated a massive earthquake and tsunami. This resulted in hydrogen explosions at the Fukushima Daiichi power plant in Japan and three nuclear cores subsequently melting down.

Not because the Japanese government was unaware of the risk of a 1,000-year extreme event.

They were and had been so from the very beginning.

When the plant was first designed, the engineers offered financiers two choices. They could build for a 100-year severe event risk or spend a lot more and build for a 1,000-year extreme event risk.

At the time, a political decision was made to build for the 100-year event because it was a cost-effective strategy, instead of the vastly more expensive 1,000-year extreme event design. How smart was that? Today, Japan's yen-pinching nuclear volcano is slowly poisoning the Pacific Ocean and nothing can be done to stop it.

This is the difference between severe vs. extreme event engineering. Therefore, who wants extreme event engineering and is willing to pay for it? Survivors and future colonists, that's who, and they'll do it with overcover and opportunity.

Extreme Event Engineering

Farmers love to make things grow, while engineers love to make things fail. In terms of EcoTech engineering, this is a match made in heaven.

It's easy for engineers to build technospheres to host various biospheres, all with a single hosting goal in mind. Every day is another day in paradise for the biosphere lifeforms within it.

It's harder though for engineers to keep an extreme event from smashing it all to pieces, or at the very least, to mitigate the event enough so that the damage can be repaired quickly.

This will keep your EcoTech engineers up at night, and what will they ponder? The difference between severe and extreme events.

In "Chapter 13– Overcover," we introduced an earthwork overcover strategy for DBS domes that uses several feet of natural clay, basalt shielding, and soil to provide all-hazards protection. For EcoTech engineers this is the gold standard because all-hazards food production is job number one.

Below-ground commercial aquaponics and indoor farming technospheres will be the tent poles for the entire food production strategy, and this strategy provides great opportunities for above-ground opportunity farming as well.

Opportunity Farming

All-hazards commercial aquaponics and indoor farming will be a community's money machine prior to a cataclysm.

Once a below-ground farm is fully operational, it will become the core of a holistic Win-Win food production system and a stable revenue generator as follows:

- **Below-Ground Aquaponics Farming:** Primary ingredients, such as fish, fowl, and vegetables that are commonly called for in your grow-to-diet recipes, will be grown in low-risk, below-ground aquaponics and indoor-farming technospheres. Allow your engineers six months to fully stabilize the entire system. After that, the system can be tweaked in planned, incremental steps that help avoid unnecessary complications.
- **Above-ground Opportunity Farming:** Above ground there is greater exposure to extreme events. However, growing in a variable-risk environment provides additional opportunities with greater flexibility and speed.

Each above-ground variable-risk technosphere will have its own unique risk to return equation. You'll use them to grow the other plant species called for in your grow-to-diet recipes.

This is an opportunity farming strategy. It is growing above ground in an open environment where crops are subject to catastrophic loss resulting from extreme events.

An example of this is open-field farming, which makes it a good place to start.

Open Field Farming

This is an easy way to farm for seasonal production. You mark off a field, plow it up, and broadcast the seeds by machine or by hand. Then, add fertilizer and water and nature will do most of the work.

A technosphere is any man-made or man-fashioned coherent structure that alters the natural state of the environment, regardless of the materials or methods used. Therefore, a simple open field such as this is an extremely basic technosphere.

However, when you build a supportive and protective environment around the field, it becomes a more complex technosphere. Nonetheless, it is still an unprotected, high-risk, high-return opportunity. Only highly-survivable plant species should be grown in this manner.

Examples of resilient field crops include hemp for insulation, clothing, medicinal oil, and fodder and sunflowers for seeds and oil. These crops are extremely useful, but from an EcoTech perspective, they will play a supporting role in a Win-Win survival community's grow-to-diet strategy. The primary field farming role is with in-ground raised bed farming.

In-Ground Raised Bed Farming

In-ground raised bed (IGRB) farming is where crops are planted in well-defined rows with pathways between the rows for agricultural machinery and draft animals.

A difference between IGRB and field farming is in how the seeds find their way into the soil. In general, seeds are broadcast with field farming, as mentioned earlier. With in-ground raised bed farming, seeds are drilled or implanted into the soil.

A superb IGRB reference model for EcoTech engineers is *The Market Gardener*, by Jean-Martin Fortier.

In *The Market Gardener*, he shares the non-mechanized cultivation methods he developed to build a profitable family farm on just one and a half acres with in-ground raised-bed farming. How profitable? He reports yearly earnings of up to $100,000 per acre with what could be called semi-mechanized cultivation.

There are many inspiring reasons for Fortier's success, but the one from an EcoTech opportunity farming viewpoint is his use of land.

Fortier In-Ground Raised Bed Model

The Market Gardener book is a must-have. It provides a foundation for above-ground opportunity farming, because soil is the command input for above-ground opportunity farming.

JEAN-MARTIN FORTIER
the market gardener
A SUCCESSFUL GROWER'S HANDBOOK
for SMALL-SCALE ORGANIC FARMING
Foreword by Severine von Tscharner Fleming, The Greenhorns
Illustrations by Marie Bilodeau

It goes without saying that farm equipment the size of a recreational vehicle is not suited to the confines of a small-scale farm of a few acres. These vehicles require pathways that accommodate large farm equipment tires.

Fortier designed his method around how Third World farmers, who cannot afford large farm equipment, maximize land use. What he has done to make his farming method profitable stands as a classic model for technosphere engineering, and it's incredibly simple.

Instead of laying out rows that accommodate four-wheel farm tractors with tires ranging from a 9" rim to a 54" rim in size, the solution was to reduce the number of wheels.

Fortier uses light weight two-wheel farm equipment like self-propelled two-wheel tractors, rototillers, and rotary harrows instead of heavy four-wheel farm equipment which require large low pressure (fat) tires to minimize soil compaction.

By eliminating two (fat) tires, he enhanced his land usage with the following row layout. In-ground raised beds for growing are 30" (75 cm) wide, while the pathways between them are 18" (45 cm).

Therefore, we'll express Fortier's preferred row ratio as 30-18, with the understanding that it reflects his unique goals as an organic market gardener in a northern climate.

Row Ratio

Is the Fortier 30-18 row ratio the best for EcoTech IGRB farming? No, and for two reasons. This ratio limits the plant species that can be cultivated and it does not allow for the use of draft animals.

Fortier's choice of 30" (75 cm) - in-ground raised beds still stands as a cardinal rule. It offers optimal harvests plus access to useful small-farm technologies. However, before delving further into row ratios, there is one thing to consider with two-wheel farm equipment.

Be careful when choosing equipment with electronic ignition as they may be vulnerable to an EMP event. What you want are machines with analog ignition systems like the Magnetron ignition systems used in popular lawnmowers. This old-style analog-type ignition system will survive an EMP event. Or you can choose diesel power if you can find it.

As everything eventually wears out, once your mechanized farming implements can no longer be repaired or fueled, what will you have to work with? This is a serious question, because Fortier's 30-18 row ratio does not address the survival need to continue farming after a catastrophic event is essential.

For this reason, the EcoTech row ratio must allow for more survival options. This is why a EcoTech 30-30 row ratio offers the following survival benefits:

- **More Planting Choices:** Fortier grows to market and must be careful in his choices of the species he plants. He favors plants that grow low-and-narrow in the row bed. His

30-18 row ratio is ideal for semi-mechanized, grow-to-market two-wheel farming methods with a limited planet species range. An EcoTech 30-30 row ratio offers a much broader range of available plant species.

- **Tall-and-Wide:** Win-Win survival communities will need to plant a diversity of species. It will of course have the low-and-narrow species. But there are also tall-and-wide species, like corn and tomatoes. While this can be done with an 18" pathway, field access will become an issue; whereas 30" will provide an adequate pathway when planting tall-and-wide species.
- **Draft Animals:** In a post-catastrophic world, spare parts and fuel for mechanized farming will be hard to come by. The use of draft animals will help to prolong the life of farming equipment and fuel.

Here is the principal difference. When Fortier laid out his farm, he did not anticipate using draft animals, so his farm is laid out for hand-operated farm machinery. In a post-catastrophic world, UPS no longer delivers replacement parts to repair broken machines; that would certainly present Fortier with a serious challenge.

Conversely, an EcoTech 30-30 row ratio allows the use of mules and most horses, which is why a Win-Win ranch needs draft animals. The point here is, in a post-catastrophic world, survivors will be operating in the Stone Age 2.0 mode, and they'll need them.

Another thing Fortier failed to consider when laying out his farm besides draft animals is what firefighters call "topping." Topping occurs when high winds drive fire across treetops, which often results in a firestorm and we need to look at this, because it goes directly to the essential topic of risk mitigation.

Risk Mitigation

On the back cover of his book, *The Market Gardener,* Fortier presents a perfect tagline for Win-Win survival community opportunity farming.

Grow better, not bigger!

This says it all in just four words. Yet, there is a pronounced difference between market gardening and Win-Win opportunity farming, namely efficiency and the environment.

- **Fortier:** Small-scale organic farming is about the efficient use of land and water in a relatively stable environment.
- **Win-Win:** Opportunity farming is about the efficient use of land and water in an environment that is susceptible to sudden and catastrophic crop loss.

A good way to illustrate the difference found in Fortier's book is to see an aerial view illustration of his farm in chapter four that lays out all the structures, grows, and so forth. When you find this illustration, note the closeness of the trees bordering the entire farm.

This reveals what an EcoTech design team will see as a huge red flag.

This practice of bordering farms with trees began decades ago as an effective and inexpensive way to provide protection from high winds. However, long-term drought causes dieback in the upper branches of a tree. This is when the risk of topping during a firestorm can occur.

Drought-stricken trees wither from the top down. Ergo, the canopy of the trees that border the property turns into a ready source of fuel.

Topping occurs when winds are strong and all it takes is for one tree upwind of the rest to catch fire. Then, winds will drive the fire from treetop-to-treetop at fantastic speeds, potentially overtaking anyone in the middle of it.

For a small organic farm like the one Fortier describes, the loss of crops due to a fire is one thing, but equally bad is that this kind of fire will devastate vital buildings and machinery within the tree border. If this happens to Fortier, he may live to file an insurance claim; but if it happens to a survival community, dig graves.

It is therefore better to surround growing operations with zigzag, thin-wall fences. They will serve as a self-reinforcing wind barrier, and create gaps in the vegetation for a fire break. To help protect crops, farming overcover such as hoop houses can be used.

Farming Overcover

When we think of row farming overcover today, hoop houses come to mind. Those are the polyvinyl tunnels that look like Quonset huts draped over the crop rows. There are also the floating row covers that lay gently on the plants to give them a thin-skin layer of protection.

All of this is the result of the introduction of plastics following WW II, and yes, we are all aware of the many downsides of plastic.

However, farming overcover is an area where plastics have become a huge game-changer in the course of human history. We're talking about major gains in productivity here, and yet, the growth of plastic overcover is rooted in the age before it.

It was the age of glass, and for EcoTech engineers, the benchmark model for an above-ground technosphere is the glass overcover used by the Conservatory of Flowers in Golden Gate Park, San Francisco, California. It was one of America's first high-technology technospheres with glass glazing.

Glass Glazing

Glazing is the process of setting panes or sheets of glass in frames, such as in the windows that surround the Conservatory. The word glazing is derived from the Middle English, for "glass," and this describes the culture which bore the technological roots of this historic landmark

Founded in 1878, this magnificent Victorian greenhouse is constructed of whitewashed glass and wood. It is a designated historical landmark. It also serves as a useful EcoTech model for three reasons:

- Electrification: On August 25, 1895, the Conservatory was wired for electricity to power an electrical environmental control system. In its day, that was rocket science!
- Earthquakes: Although the 1906 and 1989 earthquakes devastated San Francisco, the Conservatory was relatively unharmed.
- Diffuse Lighting: The diffuse lighting created by whitewashed glass avoids hot spots and shadows. It also allows plants that favor the sun to coexist with those that favor shade.

Over the years, the Conservatory was repeatedly damaged by fire, and wind, and always restored. Having visited this Conservatory on several occasions, I was always amazed at how it was relatively unfazed by the 1906 and 1989 earthquakes.

Yet, it wasn't until I heard what David B. South had to say about storm protection and picture windows that it clicked. David said, "A 3-foot-wide picture window is ten times as as strong as a 5-foot-wide window." This is why none of the windows in David's own DBS dome home are more than 3 feet wide.

If you ever get the chance to visit Conservatory of Flowers in San Francisco, keep that in mind, because while the overall structure is very large, the panes of glass used to cover it are relatively small.

Another thing is the use of whitewashed glass. As you stroll through the Conservatory, be mindful of how the light passes through these panes and casts itself upon the biosphere within. There are no hot spots. There is only softly diffused light.

Pane, Panel, and Film

The term "pane" is closely associated with glass, such as the glazing we see in our homes, glass hothouses, and greenhouses. However, glass is not recommended for EcoTech overcover. Even when glass is tempered to make it safer and stronger, it is much too heavy for above-ground EcoTech opportunity farming use.

Bottom line, forget the glass. Go with plastic and with EcoTech engineering.

The primary EcoTech above-ground overcover will be either of two basic categories:

- **Panels:** The term panels is associated more with glazing plastics, which can be as clear as glass, but much safer and stronger. The point to remember about glazing plastics is that panels are rigid and must be set within a framing system.
- **Film:** Plastic films used for overcover are rolled out like saran wrap and can be attached to a simple hoop structure or laid directly upon the crops.

When evaluating plastic films, always remember the trade-offs between material strength and light penetration. Thicker plastic films, like those rated for strong frost protections, are stronger but do not let as much light through, while the reverse is true with thinner plastic films.

Realistically, plastic films offer marginal protection from extreme events, at best. They should only be considered for the same reasons farmers use them today, to protect row crops from pests and to help extend the growing season.

With in-ground raised-bed farming, commercial-grade plastic film hoophouses offer extreme event advantages.

Plastic Film Hoophouses

As the name implies, a flexible plastic film is formed into a tunnel held up by hoop rings. This allows you to tend your crops inside an overcover that can be quickly placed as needed and taken down when not. Commercial grade hoophouses are handy and they offer a good level of overcover protection for in-ground raised-bed farming operations.

Commercial grade hoophouses are designed to stand up to severe weather events such as heavy snow, frost, and high winds, plus they offer the strongest and thickest material available. These are desirable features for sure, but plastic film is more susceptible to the heat from hot volcanic ash and wind-driven embers from fires than glazing plastics.

The bottom line with plastic film is that it is useful for severe event protection, but in terms of extreme events, overcover made with glazing plastics is what you need.

Glazing Plastics

Glazing plastics came about in the years following WW II and offered a first in the recorded history of humankind. For survivors and future colonists, you can forget glass because glazing plastics are the ticket. There is a broad range of glazing plastics to choose from.

The thing about plastics is that the number of choices can be a bit overwhelming; certain plastics are good for certain things. The command input with glazing is light. The first decision is whether to use clear or diffuse overcover, which applies to both glass panes and plastic panels.

The purpose of clear glazing is to let the light in. Given that we could see high UV light levels during extreme events; this is a red flag concern for growing food. However, clear glazing plastics can be very useful for the processing and preparation applications. Two such practical uses are:

- **Space Kitchen:** Large panes of clear glazing plastic can be used to create an enclosed above-ground solar oven kitchen, where the ovens can perform at their peak levels.
- **Sun-Drying:** Mushrooms will play a key role in your below-ground, indoor farming operations. By building an enclosed above-ground sun-drying room, you can fill the drying tables with freshly harvested mushrooms. The UV light will promote the production of Vitamin D during the natural drying process.

For indoor farming, glazing plastics with diffuse light is the preferred material and here is what you want in an EcoTech above-ground technosphere panel:

- **Diffuse Light:** With diffuse lighting, the structure will be placed with a north-south orientation; the light will fill the interior throughout the day without hot spots and shade.
- **Panel Type:** Panels made with fluted twin-wall glazing plastics offer excellent strength and insulation. To make these panels, two flat sheets of plastic are joined in the middle with vertical flutes of plastic, which create an interior air space. This insulation gives the panel a thermal barrier effect, so that as the temperature drops quickly at night, these insulated panels will slow the temperature drop, thereby reducing biosphere stress.
- **Size and Weight:** Plastic panels can come in a myriad of sizes, but you must standardize on one size that must be small and light enough that a single 100-lb person can handle it.
- **UV Protection:** Look for plastic glazing with UV coatings for added protection. A good indicator is a warranty. Look for products with a minimum, 5-year warranty.

One thing about shotcrete and glazing plastic, you can create artistic masterpieces, like the magnificent Victorian style of the Conservatory of Flowers in San Francisco. The possibilities are endless. Nonetheless, with EcoTech engineering, beauty must take a back seat to survivability. The answer will be EcoTech Go-Grows made with diffuse glazing plastics.

Go-Grow Technospheres

With a Win-Win survival community, below-ground DBS domes provide a true, 1,000-year extreme event engineering. A different strategy is required above ground due to the higher exposure to extreme events. It must incorporate strength, mobility, and adaptability in order to adapt growing opportunities as they evolve.

However, when we look to the business marketplace for solutions, on the one hand, there are cheap, made-to-fail, flimsy, do-it-yourself (DIY) designs for hobbyists, while on the other hand, commercial solutions are designed to provide protection from severe events—but not extreme events.

Therefore, with the current offerings, what we have are a myriad of options for glass and plastic glazing products, none of which are viable extreme event survival choices.

Are there off-the-shelf commercial extreme event solutions? A few, though extreme event engineering is more of a specialized field serving governments and wealthy interests. This is why market-driven companies often use terms that help to differentiate themselves from their competitors.

Those with years of experience in dealing with this market-driven terminology will have sorted it out over time, but what about those who have not? Instead of market-driven terminology, Win-Win survival communities will invent new, needs-driven solutions for above-ground EcoTech farming.

In the spirit of this, I have coined a new EcoTech term, "go-grow."

As the name implies, go-grow is not about traditional farming where you plant the same acreage for years or generations. A go-grow is purely about opportunity farming. When you see an above-ground opportunity to grow something, you go and "go grow it."

You can do it in a field or an in-ground raised bed, but the most survivable option is indoor farming with an overcover structure designed to adapt quickly to adverse changes and evolving needs. As the Marines say, "Improvise, Adapt, Overcome!" You begin with whatever is currently available in commercial severe events technologies, and then you: "Improvise, Adapt, and Overcome!"

When your EcoTech engineers begin designing go-grow technospheres, they'll have to work with what is available. Like the Marines, they'll grumble about having to make do with hand-me-downs, but in the final analysis, they'll produce a winning go-grow modular system.

Go-Grow Modular System

The key to the go-grow concept is a highly-survivable, modular system design. When needs arise, and the conditions permit, you raise a new go-grow or reconfigure an existing one. To create Go-Grows, EcoTech engineers begin their design efforts using existing indoor growing models.

One such model is found in the Conservatory of Flowers in the Golden Gate Park, San Francisco, California, as previously discussed.

For EcoTech engineers, the Conservatory provides three important lessons:

- **Forget Glass:** What was available in 1878 was whitewashed glass that the Conservatory founders used. Had glazing plastics been available to them, as practical people, they would have used it.
- **Less is More:** A less-is-more strategy is one of the principal reasons why the Conservatory can survive major earthquakes. The Victorian style used small panes of glass, which have two benefits. First, smaller panes of glass are stronger than larger panes and are better at resisting high winds and projectile impacts. Second, the additional wood framing required for these smaller panes gives the overall structure much greater strength.
- **Sitting Target:** Any permanent above-ground structure is a sitting target during extreme events. The Conservatory is a beautiful permanent structure, but it is fully exposed to the destructive forces of extreme events. Sometimes, you just need to get out of the way of what is coming.

This explains why the Conservatory can survive major earthquakes but is still vulnerable to heavy damage due to fire and wind. Historically, the solution for these extreme events has been a combination of replacement materials and massive contributions of cash to keep the Conservatory open. Yet, in a post-catastrophic world, there will be no funding drives and no way to find replacement parts. In the end, the structure will be abandoned altogether or its components used for other needs. For a Win-Win community, this is not acceptable.

This is why the engineering process must incorporate the time-proven technology of the Victorian age with a space-age technology model. One such space-age, severe-event model is found in Solexx greenhouse designs.

Solexx Greenhouse Model

Hobby gardeners love to work with greenhouses made with plastic panels and there are a wide range of greenhouse kits on the market to choose from.

The ones to focus on are the more expensive offerings with better plastics and structural designs.

For EcoTech engineering, a highly useful model is by an American company called Solexx. They have models for the hobbyist, as well as commercial hothouses and greenhouses made with multi-walls and diffuse glazing plastics.

Like David B. South, they also share a lot of knowledge on the Internet. An excellent first step is to visit them at www.solexx.com to learn more about their technology. Another firm to investigate is Palram Americas at www.palram.com.

Severe Weather Designs

Solexx makes lightweight technology solutions that meet severe weather requirements. Their engineering method is optimized for strength and protection.

Their high-end hobbyist greenhouses provide superb and lightweight severe weather designs with shatterproof protection against wind and snow. When evaluating their technology, here are the essential criteria:

- **Glazing Plastic:** The Solexx material is available in various thicknesses. A 3.5 mm panel is available for hobbyists, whereas their professional-grade version is 5 mm thick. This professional-grade twin-wall plastic glazing is stronger than the competing 8 mm polycarbonate offerings. Only the fluted professional twin-wall 5 mm Solexx panels or 8 mm polycarbonate panels are suitable for EcoTech farming.
- **Severe Weather Rating:** They are designed to handle severe weather such as 70 mph winds and heavy snows. With regards to EcoTech engineering, Solexx is a good start-

ing model provided it is upgraded to survive extreme events, such as 100 mph winds and heavy volcanic ash falls.

- **Composite Framing:** Composite materials are quickly gaining popularity among bridge builders. Bridges are stronger and will last longer with these specially formulated plastics. Solexx uses a similar composite plastic for framing.
- **Ground Anchoring:** A big advantage with composite framing is the ability to add ground anchoring to hold the greenhouse steady in high winds. With Solexx, grounding anchors are screwed deeply into the soil and connected via metal wires to the composite frame. Simple but effective.
- **Portability:** A fully constructed 8-foot Solexx hobby greenhouse is so light, a 100-lb woman can pick up the entire greenhouse herself, and walk with it to a new location. In terms of EcoTech engineering, this is a HUGE advantage!
- **Ergonomics:** Solexx designs are well thought out. Unlike cheaper designs that basically offer little more than a thin, plastic enclosure, Solexx builds strong overhead hanging rods and benches into their designs.
- **Durability and Safety:** Solexx pays close attention to the things that can make a big difference, such as doors that do not come unhinged and louver air vents to reduce biosphere stress.
- **Pathway:** With in-ground raised bed farming, an in-ground raised bed row ratio of 30-30 is recommended for Win-Win communities. The Solexx design provides for a 36”- pathway through the greenhouse center for wheelchair access. This width also offers easier access and the use of wheeled interior carts and bins.
- **Extendable Designs:** If you start with an 8’ long greenhouse and design to expand your indoor operations, you can seamlessly extend the first greenhouse with another 8’ section for a completely enclosed greenhouse, 16’ long and so forth.

The fantastic thing about this technology is how light it is, given its strength. It’s almost beguiling. If you remember seeing a Samsonite luggage commercial from the early age of television, you’ll chuckle when you visit their web site. There you will see images of large, portly fellows dangling from the greenhouse’s overhead hanging rods. So yes, one could say that Solexx is Samsonite tough.

For all of these reasons, after you form your church one of the things you will do is acquire one or more off-the-shelf Solexx hobby greenhouses and study their modular severe-event design features. You want your people to have hands-on experience working with and in these severe-event greenhouses. Then, they can use this experience as a jumping-off point to create a more robust modular design.

Extreme Events Designs

As with the in-ground raised bed model in *The Market Gardener*, Solexx is a first step to creating a more robust EcoTech overcover with considerable above-ground protection from extreme events. Using the Solexx features discussed above, the four points your EcoTech engineers need to focus on are:

- **Glazing Plastic:** The size of Solexx panels is optimized for a balance between affordability and severe weather protection. Smaller panels mean more framing and for improved extreme event protection, and the Conservatory model of smaller panes with a more robust framing system proves it.
- **Composite Framing:** The Solexx method affixes panels to the frame with screws so that raising their greenhouses is cost-effective, strong, and relatively easy. However, fiddling with screwdrivers during an extreme event is not the best way to make quick panel replacements. Rather, you need a simple but strong quick-release panel mounting system that facilitates rapid setups, takedowns, and repairs. The quick-release aim is 1-1-1 rule: one person, one panel and less than one minute to do it.
- **Ground Anchoring:** Stronger ground anchoring than what is provided in the current Solexx designs is required for extreme events. For extreme events, the ground anchoring should be effectively doubled. Also, like zigzag thin wall fence posts, your ground anchors should also be anchored in concrete.
- **Extendable Design:** A modular system will feature a standardized combination of construction components. It needs to allow for ad hoc changes to the overall system to serve a grow-to-diet strategy.

These four points are great initial steps; the fifth step is earthwork, as part of an overall modular go-grow design.

Glazing plastics and earthwork? How does this work, and what do you call it?

Go-Grow Revetments

The term, revetments, has different definitions and the most common usage describes a concrete or stone facing to sustain an embankment. Professional concrete pumpers use shotcrete spraying to do a lot of this and you may need to do some as well, depending on the property.

However, a different kind of revetment provides a more useful model to base your go-grow strategy on. They are the military aviation revetments we see used on military airbases. They are fortified three-wall structures used for parking combat aircraft with bomb loads.

It is one thing to lose a few aircraft and another to lose an entire squadron; without this protection, all it takes is for one missile to accidentally ignite. Then, like a firestorm jumping from one treetop to another, the secondary detonations from the initial event can destroy the rest of the squadron.

Consequently, the engineering goal for aviation revetments is to separate combat aircraft from one another with a series of containment areas large enough for one or a few aircraft. The primary purpose of these revetments is to contain blast forces should a weapon accidentally detonate.

This way, the damage is limited to the aircraft within a single revetment containment area, which will block the spread of blast forces to aircraft in adjacent revetments, thereby containing the destruction.

The risk containment benefits of aviation revetments make them an excellent model for above-ground indoor go-grow farming operations, where containment and mitigation are equally necessary.

As an example, you have a side-by-side cluster of greenhouses without a go-grow revetment. In the event of sustained 100+ mph winds, the result will likely be catastrophic for these vital farming operations.

It only takes the first upwind greenhouse that faces the wind to fail, and a wind-borne hail of devastating projectiles will damage or destroy those greenhouses downwind. This additional debris projectiles will cause a lot of additional damage.

On the other hand, like a properly designed aviation revetment, a go-grow farming revetment will contain the damage, and you may save enough of your go-grow operation. The crop loss is mitigated and damaged technospheres can be repaired and returned to service.

Go-Grow Revetment Design

When designing an above-ground overall farming system, the great thing about go-grow revetments is that simple works best. Any windbreak material that can withstand repeated 100+ mph winds that contain flying debris should be used and earthwork fits this requirement.

To illustrate the go-grow concept, let's assume that your church is going to build a community center like the one first introduced in "Chapter 6 – Plan B Basic Concepts," an above-ground covered all-hazards community center.

This design uses two 60-foot DBS domes that are connected with a service dome for a dormitory and a community area, and all are under an overcover of dirt, aggregate, and clay.

One advantage of building this way is you can use any orientation relative to the Sun; so let's assume you have a free hand in deciding where to place your multi-dome cluster.

With field and raise bed farming, an east-west orientation provides the best use of sunlight. However, go-grow greenhouses with diffuse lighting will perform best with a north-south orientation.

Therefore, the command input for revetment design is the prevailing winds. They will determine placement for your multi-dome cluster and adjacent go-grows.

Now let's use an example to illustrate the concept.

Example Revetment

For this example, we'll assume the prevailing winds are northerly. This means the multi-dome cluster will be laid out lengthwise with an east-west orientation. The side of the structure that faces the wind is the windward side. The opposite side is the leeward side.

On the windward side, the slope and height of the overcover provide an advantage because a covered DBS dome cluster, like a community center, will be at least twice the height of the go-grow greenhouses on the leeward side.

With this orientation, extreme winds will blow on the windward side of the overcover and its earthen flank will harmlessly absorb flying projectiles.

Additionally, its gentle slope will direct extreme wind forces up and over the top of the overcover, much like the way air moves over the airfoil of an airplane wing. In this way, a good portion of the wind's force will pass over the go-grow greenhouses in the revetments below, thereby preventing or mitigating damage due to wind velocity and projectile impacts.

Remember, go-grow is about the opportunity, and here is where you have a great two-for-one payback with this type of revetment. A go-grow revetment needs a long back wall. From that, smaller, perpendicular partition mounds extending straight out from the overcover.

This example configuration offers two notable benefits:

- **Back wall:** The reverse slope or leeward side of your DBS dome cluster overcover will serve as the back wall for your go-grow revetment.
- **Risk Mitigation:** The protection from smaller partition walls will mitigate catastrophic loss with protection from easterly or westerly winds due to unusual or extreme weather.

When the go-grow revetment is complete, it will have strong protection against the greatest wind threats. The open side of the go-grow complex will face south, which in this example is the least threatening. This is where you close in your go-grow operations with a series of EcoTech II storage domes, such as those discussed earlier.

With this in mind, let's look at the go-grow houses inside the revetment containment area.

Go-Grow Modular Grows

The difference between the greenhouses and hothouses today is that hothouses are basically greenhouses with heaters. Nevertheless, the terms greenhouse and hothouse are confusing for some, and this is more a historical issue than one of technology.

The term hothouse was popularized during the Victorian era, with heated glasshouses like the Conservatory in San Francisco. A good historical hothouse example was in Russia prior to the Bolshevik Revolution of 1917.

At that time, Russians were using hothouses to grow pineapples in Saint Petersburg, Russia, in the dead of winter. This is impressive when you consider that Saint Petersburg is situated about seven degrees below the Arctic Circle.

The message here is twofold. The first is that pineapples are tasty, so why not include them as treats? The second is that go-grows are about growing opportunities for a complete diet and not markets.

Therefore, your EcoTech engineers will need to assess all of your community's various indoor farming requirements and technologies. Using this data, they can then create a unified system design with structured multi-cropping modules and associated support systems.

Preventing Structural Failure

Greenhouses come in many shapes, and the ones you do not want for above ground go-grows will have stem walls. Like with a classic DBS dome, you want a dome-like structure with a 1:2 profile.

With the Solexx composite framing method, panels are on the outside of the structure. Panels are screwed into the composite frame, far enough from each other to slide in an H-channel and U-trim panel sealers.

This is an excellent solution for go-grow structures. However, Solexx hobby greenhouses are designed to stand against 70 mph winds, whereas EcoTech engineering requires that the structure withstand 100 mph winds. That difference of 30 mph is huge.

Therefore, your primary building component will be an inline building module shaped like a Quonset hut or hoop house with framing for 3' x 3' panels. To illustrate the need for this panel size, let's compare the two different panel sizes: 3' x 3' panel vs. a 4' x 8' panel.

Here is the scenario. A projectile traveling at 100 mph hits the panel hard enough to penetrate or damage it. Once this happens, the panel is subject to peeling, once the wind's forces get underneath it and begin to peel it away.

If the 4' x 8' panel fails due to peeling, the wind can force its way into the structure, and explode the cover. The failure will be catastrophic. This is why storm shutters are used over windows in areas prone to hurricanes.

With a 3' x 3'square panel, the wind creates problems in the structure, but the cover will be designed to hold. The failure will be mitigated, thereby allowing for emergency repairs.

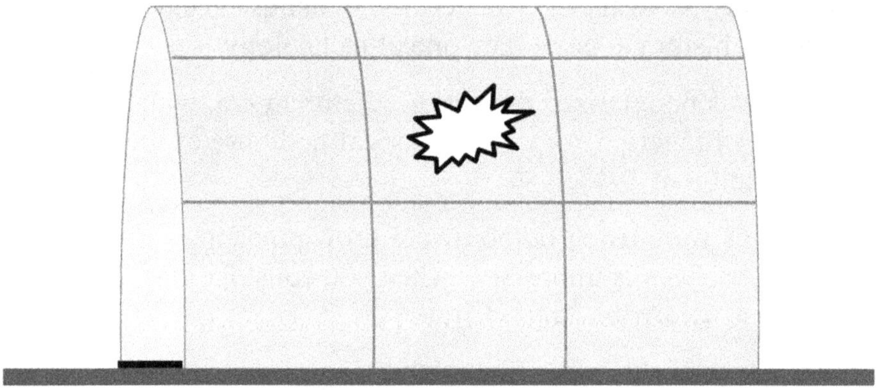

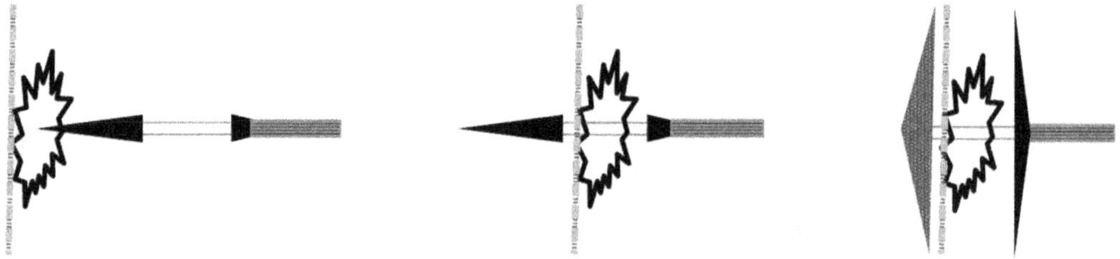

Here is where your EcoTech engineers can devise an umbrella-like emergency repair patch. Once a panel has been penetrated, the emergency device is poked through the hole and then triggered, so that it unfolds over the panel area and is forced against the structure by the wind.

These are the kinds of EcoTech design considerations that you will bring to the other elements of the go-grow, such as modules for corners, connecting tunnels, drip irrigation, air filtration, emergency lighting, and so forth.

When you're finished with your designs, you will have to acquire a large standardized stockpile of panels and fittings. You want your EcoTech engineers to design new and re-purpose existing go-grows in a virtually endless number of ways. One such design can incorporate hobbyist small-scale aquaponics.

Aquaponics Technospheres

The early use of aquaponics-like systems dates back to the 16th century Aztecs. However, commercial aquaponics, as it is done today, is truly a space-age farming solution. It began in 1979 with Dr. James Rakocy and his team at the University of the Virgin Islands, where they developed the deep water culture (DWC) technology which is in popular use with commercial growers today.

As we discussed in "Chapter I5 – EcoTech Farming and Ranching," there is no overlap between an EcoTech biosphere and its technosphere. Rather, they are distinctly defined with a clear boundary. The boundary for the aquaponics biosphere is wherever the bacteria that lives on the surface area inside your aquaponics system contacts the water in the system.

In terms of EcoTech engineering, your aquaponics technospheres will be the structure and the team that actively creates your primary food production, and money machine, as well.

Here, we need to introduce a difference between church retreats and a church ranch that typifies the survival planning process.

Failure is the greatest teacher, but only if you pay attention, because survival is about learning what hurts and what works. The goal being, to learn enough about what works, before what hurts kills you. This is why your church retreat is where your members go to make mistakes, and the ranch is where they use what they've learned from their mistakes.

What will you use at a church retreat to learn about aquaponics? There are several ways to do small-scale aquaponics and the best choice for most beginners is the flood and drain system. They are much easier to build than DWC commercial systems and are an excellent way to learn and perfect your techniques.

Just keep in mind that small-scale systems are far more sensitive and less forgiving than the more complex large-scale aquaponics systems.

Water is the command input of aquaponics, and if you're not mindful of that, do not be surprised to see your fish floating belly up one morning.

In the next chapter, we'll discuss how you can fund your church ranch by building a premium, cannabis-ready aquaponics facility. A PCR (Premium cannabis-ready) facility is a pure, all-natural organic growing environment.

Premium cannabis is a pure organic product that is well tolerated by cancer patients who've become averse to powerful chemicals being introduced into their bodies. Pound for pound, no other agricultural product, including truffles, sells for more. On the other hand, recreational cannabis with its exotic fertilizers sells for one half or one third as much.

So here is what you do. You get an early start with hobbyist aquaponics.

First, buy a get 'er done book for hobbyists. A fine option is *Aquaponics for Beginners* from www.howtoaquaponic.com. They have a great startup solution for beginners. Their book is tied to their online website with lots of information and resources. Once you've done that, you can order a suitable Solexx greenhouse with a heater if desired and all of the materials needed to build your first hobbyist experimental indoor aquaponics grow.

When you're ready to explore the world of large-scale all-hazards commercial aquaponics, a must-read book is *Aquaponics Gardening*, by Sylvia Bernstein. This book will transition you from hobbyist to commercial aquaponics. We'll get into this in greater detail in the next chapter, but for now here is one thing to remember. Aquaponics works and it will be your community's money machine, but it is never as easy as "just add water."

18

EcoTech Aquaponics

In "Chapter 15 – EcoTech Farming and Ranching," we defined the difference between farmers and ranchers in terms of how they view the relationship between their land and their animals:

- A rancher sees the land as a vast home for his animals.
- A farmer sees the animals as assets in a well-organized system.

The optimal mindset for a Win-Win survival church ranch is that of a rancher who also farms because aquaponics is the most challenging form of farming done today. One that demands a thoughtful and diligent approach to creating and maintaining a reliable commercial-scale survival aquaponics system.

The command input for aquaponics is water, and on a larger scale farming with a grow-to-diet strategy requires multiple biospheres and technospheres. From a system-level point of view, this is what defines an EcoTech aquasphere.

EcoTech Aquasphere

In water sports, the term aqua sphere refers to four main events: swimming, diving, water polo, and synchronized swimming. The goal being, to rule the aqua sphere by winning all four events.

With commercial-scale EcoTech survival aquaponics, the goal is similar. You must win all of the events to rule the aqua sphere. What does that look like for survival farming?

In EcoTech engineering terms, the "aquasphere" is the overall scope of a large-scale survival aquaponics complex system, with multiple interlinked technospheres and biospheres.

When you watch aquaponics videos on the Internet by hobbyists and small-scale farmers, they often share their mistakes and what they've learned.

On a small scale, these mistakes are disappointments, but on a larger scale, they can be disastrous, which is why hobbyist mistakes are worth our attention.

Common Mistakes

Hobbyists love to grow-on-the-cheap by finding ways to invest the least amount of money and time for the greatest return. They tend to push the edge of their technology envelope, as pilots like to say.

For a Win-Win community, grow-on-the-cheap is not the same as growing-to-survive. Therefore, in order to survive, one cannot afford the grow-on-the-cheap mistakes small growers and hobbyists often make. A few of the problems commonly reported are:

- **Water Quality Issues:** In a large aquaponics system with thousands of liters of water, changes in water quality issues, such as pH, salinity, and ammonia levels, happen more slowly due to large volume dilution, which gives you more time to respond. Conversely, smaller systems contain less water. Negative changes in water quality propagate more quickly and with greater impact.

- **Shock from Rapid Change:** With aquaponics, air temperature is used to set the water temperature, and each species of fish has its own temperature range. What hobbyists fail to understand is that small-scale, thin-wall plastic fish tanks will heat and cool much faster than in the natural environment and this can lead to a catastrophic thermal shock from rapid temperature changes. However, with below-ground large-scale aquaponics, the thermal properties of a DBS dome will slow temperature changes. It takes roughly 12 hours to make a significant change in air temperature; therefore there is plenty of time to take corrective measures.
- **Oxygenation:** Fish require oxygen in the water, and after beginners have to restock their fish a few times, they catch on and fix the problem. Large-scale growing systems are more proactive and use discrete water quality sub-systems.
- **Concentration of Components:** An aquaponics system is a combination of subsystems, where each one uses different components to perform specific roles. Likewise, each requires space and energy. This is why hobbyists and small-scale aquaponics gardeners and farmers search for ways to have the components in their systems serve multiple roles. Unfortunately, this approach can result in a self-defeating destabilization of the entire system.

Rather, imagine your EcoTech aquasphere as a world-class sporting event. In order to dominate, you must win in each sub-system, and the rules are different for each.

To illustrate, let's use our follow-the-photon approach and embed our photon of light into a single drop of water that we can follow through the aquasphere.

Where does this water drop come from? Look up.

Rainwater Harvesting

Water is the lifeblood of your aquasphere. The above-ground technosphere for your aquasphere is, among its other roles, a rainwater harvesting system. While you can use well water or city water, they are problematic.

The concern with well water is hardness since it is often high in carbonates and magnesium. With city water, it is the man-made substances like chlorine, fluoride and particulates which are a problem.

These water sources must be properly treated if used. But, why start out with a third-best solution when the first best solution is free? It's rainwater and with a neutral pH of 7.0, there is nothing better for aquaponics.

To collect rainwater, you need a harvesting system large enough to support your needs.

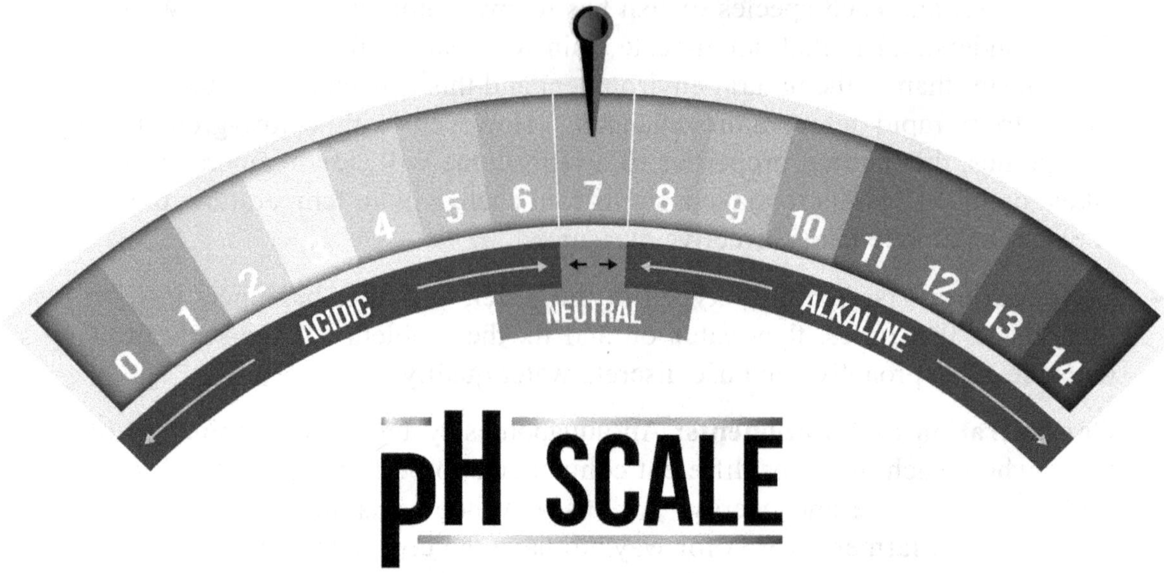

Take note: plants and animals have specific preferred pH ranges. If you use cement to build your rainwater harvesting system, it will destabilize your system. The water will leach calcium carbonate from the concrete which results in an unacceptably high pH over time.

pH Management

Aquaponics pH management is essential for creating a stable aquasphere. The pH scale spans zero to 14. Zero is on the acidic side, and a substance like battery acid has a pH of zero.

On the opposite end of the scale, 14 is on the alkaline side, and a substance like a liquid drain cleaner has a pH of 14. The middle value between the two is a neutral pH of 7.0.

Natural pure rainwater has a pH of 7.0, but it needs sand filtering to remove any particulates captured in the rainwater. When designing your filtration system, remember that with a severe event, such as a firestorm or a volcanic eruption, the first rain to fall will contain high levels of particulates.

A good way to minimize this problem is with a diversion system that would allow rain to fall for a sufficient length of time so that the bulk of particulates would be flushed before the water enters the filtering system. The amount of initial rainfall diversion would vary depending on circumstances.

From the rainwater harvesting system, we follow our photon on the next leg in its journey—the fish tanks.

Fish Tanks

Also referred to as rearing tanks, the two options for fish tanks are Plexiglass acrylic aquariums and round Polyethylene fish tanks. Plexiglass aquariums are well proven, and this plastic is stronger than glass, lighter, and more difficult to break, plus it offers much better viewing clarity. While glass aquariums cost a lot less, the big concern is that drilling holes in tempered glass for system connections can cause it to crack or break.

Aquariums are well-suited for raising young fish, called "fry." At this early age, they start to eat on their own. This stage lasts for a few months, and after the fry enter the juvenile stage, they begin to develop into adults. Be sure to have your fish tanks fitted with built-in viewing windows.

When starting out, experiment with various solutions until you find what works best for you, but no matter the solution, there is one undeniable fact of nature. Fish produce solid waste and ammonia, and for their survival, you must deal with it efficiently.

So, let's follow our photon of light to the next stage of its journey. As we depart the fish tanks, the next destination is a solids filter sub-system, a clarifier.

Clarifier

Getting fish waste and solids out of the aquasphere is essential. It can accumulate and cause plant-killing clogs in your hydroponics sub-systems. To accomplish this, a clarifier, also known as a "solids" or "mechanical" filter, is used. Its purpose is the yucky task of getting fish poop and other solids out of the aquasphere. Thankfully, that is a fairly easy thing to do.

There are different types of clarifiers, and in this case, the clarifier is a tank with a separator standing upright in the center of the tank.

As our photon of light enters the clarifier, the separator forces the water column to the bottom of the tank where the solids can settle to the bottom. Free of the waste, the water then rises up through the clarifier on the other side of the separator and out of the tank.

The collected fish waste in the clarifier is drained into a mineralization tank, where it can be collected and then used as fertilizer for soil gardening and farming.

After the solids have been removed, our photon of light is now being carried by our drop of water, from the clarifier to another sub-system, the biofilter.

Biofilter

In the fish tanks, the fish consume protein in their food, which they break down in their gut. Likewise, bits of undigested fish food in the system are broken down by the bacteria which line the interior surfaces of your aquaponics technosphere.

The biofilter uses the process of nitrification. With aquaponics two main goals are: to provide plants with the nitrates that they need to grow and also to prevent ammonia build-up that would kill the fish.

Although the topic of biofiltration can be quite complex, it is not beyond reach. When it comes to aquaponics, all you need is a keyboard and a serious desire to science the heck out of it. You'll do that in good time, but for now, let's test some water.

Water Testing

There are quite a few affordable do it yourself (DIY) tests for water quality. An acceptable test panel for aquaponics will include pH, ammonia, ammonium, nitrite, and nitrate. Like the gauges in your car's dashboard, these tests will tell you whether you are within acceptable safety guidelines. Of all the tests, the one for ammonia is the first result you'll want to see.

Ammonia and ammonium are made by the fish and the bacteria in your system. Ammonia (NH3) is very toxic and, at low levels deadly to fish. Ammonium (NH4) is also toxic for fish but in higher concentrations. It is important to remember that while plants can uptake NH4, they cannot uptake NH3.

With nitrification, ammonia is oxidized by bacteria in a two-step process. The process begins with a bacteria that converts ammonia into nitrites. Then a different bacteria continues the process by converting nitrites into the nitrates needed to fertilize the plants in your system.

After checking the ammonia level, the second test result you'll want to focus on is pH because there is an interesting relationship between ammonia and pH. The lower the pH level, the lower the ammonia level will be. Conversely, the higher the pH level, the higher the ammonia level will be.

With these things in mind, let's look at the kinds of test panel results you'll want to see with a stable and productive aquasphere:

- **pH:** Safety range of 6.2 to 6.8 pH with the optimal range being is 6.2 to 6.4 pH.
- **Ammonia:** Zero is the goal.
- **Ammonium:** No more than the fish can handle, and which the plants will uptake.
- **Nitrite:** Zero is the goal. It is a deadly go-between from ammonia to desirable nitrate.
- **Nitrate:** This is what your plants need, and fish can handle high levels of it.

This brings us back to our photon of light and now we find it in a biofilter sub-system, which like a clarifier, is very simple. The bacteria, you will depend on to create a productive aquasphere, resides on the interior surfaces in your aquaponics technosphere, where it contacts the water in the aquasphere.

Biological Surface Area

There is a critical term in aquaponics, the biological surface area (BSA). The BSA represents the amount of surface area inside your system on which bacteria can live.

In a very real sense, much of an aquaponics system is an integral part of a natural biological filter. However, speed is a problem. A simple biofilter like this is much too slow to respond. You need a dedicated biofilter and here is where we now find our photon.

A dedicated biofilter forces the ammonia in the water to pass through a small media-filled tank with a massive BSA. Typically, the preferred media for this is clay pebbles, or Lightweight Expanded Clay Aggregate (LECA), which are widely used by aquaponics hobbyists and farmers.

Whatever media you chose, if you've engineered a proper biofilter, it will produce clean, non-toxic, nutrient-rich water for the plants. Let's now follow our photon of light out of the biofilter and into a hydroponics sub-system.

Hydroponics

In terms of overall physical size, hydroponics sub-systems are the largest and there are a variety of growing methods, with an important distinction to be kept in mind. With a dedicated hydroponics system, man-made fertilizers and other chemicals are required.

Hydroponics systems that are a sub-system of an aquaculture system, have an organic way to fertilize the plants. Let's review a few important hydroponics growing methods:

- **Nutrient Film Technique (NFT):** This is the ideal system for above-ground go-grows. Two methods are available: vertical plane production and traditional horizontal systems. It is a portable design that uses PVC plastic channels with openings for planting baskets. A thin film of nutrient-rich water is run through the channels. The plant's roots stay in the water, while the remaining plant is exposed to the air for oxygenation. If the plants in an NFT system die, the bacteria in the system also die.
- **Media Beds:** Media beds provide the ability to grow most anything, but they are immobile installations. They require a lot of media, like clay pebbles or less expensive gravel. Their advantage is that with media beds, you can stand small trees. They offer a lot of flexibility when creating a grow-to-diet plan for use above and below ground. The disadvantage is that media beds are also the most labor-intensive.
- **Flood and Drain:** Also known as ebb and flow, this small-scale aquaponics method employs a media bed where you flood and then drain the system. It is the simplest and the one most favored by hobbyists. In a Win-Win community, you'll principally use flood and drain media bed systems for experimentation and classroom training.
- **Deep Water Culture (DWC):** Nothing typifies large-scale commercial aquaponics more than DWC. This growing method will be your main producer of leafy green vegetables and herbs. This method relies on large Styrofoam rafts with holes in them for the planting baskets that float on the water surface of the large tank of nutrient-rich water. DWC tanks are about 12 inches deep and at the bottom will be a forced-air, PVC pipe system for oxygenating the water.

An important thing to keep in mind is that while you can grow the same plants with one or more hydroponics methods, there will always be those that perform best with a specific method. Be sure to factor that into your grow-to-diet recipe planning.

Now that our little photon has passed through the hydroponics sub-system, the next stop on this journey is the end of the line—the sump.

Sump Tank

Hobbyists build gravity-fed systems to keep them affordable and reliable and sumps are the Tail-End-Charlie in the design. Sumps are the lowest components in a gravity-driven, downhill system, and here is where you will purge small amounts of old water to continually make room for fresh water from your rainwater harvesting system.

Here we find our photon tucked inside a water drop that has passed all the way through the system to this final stage in the process. It can now be purged to make room for fresh rainwater, or it makes the cut so to speak and will be pumped from the sump all the way back to the fish tanks for the next complete cycle.

Now that we've identified the basic concepts, where does aquaponics fit in with a Win-Win survival community's grow-to-diet strategy?

Grow-to-Diet

The key criteria for a successful grow-to-diet strategy will be the time-to-harvest of each plant species required by a grow-to-diet recipe. Here is where EcoTech shines, as it offers a wide range of farming and ranching options:

- **Above-Ground Ranching:** Livestock such as cattle and sheep are raised for meat and dairy, and a slaughterhouse will be necessary to butcher the animals for meat-based recipes. There will also be other product options such as bone broth.
- **Above-Ground Field Farming:** This opportunistic form of EcoTech farming has the highest risk exposure to severe events, but presents unique opportunities such as orchards for fruit trees and nut trees, sunflowers for cooking oil, and so forth. For example you can grow a few acres of strawberries in the summer; then you can the fruit to make year-round treats.
- **Above-Ground In-Ground Raised-Bed Farming:** Some crops are not well suited to aquaponics and need to be grown in soil. Yes, you do see people attempting to grow potatoes with aquaponics, but the mixed results they get do not always justify the effort. The same holds true with other rootstock vegetables such as carrots, onions, and beets, or plants that require highly acidic soil such as cranberries. For best results, grow these in soil.
- **Above-Ground Go-Grows:** These highly-survivable plastic greenhouses provide the flexibility to support side-by-side growing with both soil and aquaponics. They are ideal for growing specialty herbs and other recipe ingredients. When an opportunity presents itself, a go-grow can be erected and put into operation in a day, making them highly-survivable.
- **Below-ground Farming:** A single underground DBS dome cluster is used to create a separate backup system for mineralization. They can use mushrooms as the uptake plants, wormeries for producing worm casings and tea, and various species of worms as fish food. For grow-to-diet strategies, raising rabbits and chickens for meat is the primary role. The secondary roles also include, fish food, fertilizer and pet food and other such by-products.
- **Below-ground Aquaponics:** The basic design creates a symbiotic environment suite that uses two 60' wide DBS domes. One 60' dome is for aquaculture. Fish are raised for diet recipes and to produce fertilizer for the system. The other 60' dome is a hydroponics sub-system where plants are grown without soil.

When choosing the best growing method for any particular species, the inherent flexibility of EcoTech farming methods provides more than one way to grow any plant species. A good example is potatoes which, as we said above, should be grown in soil.

Potatoes are a popular staple of many diets and especially pioneer recipes from the 18th and 19th centuries. Rich in starch they've become the world's fourth most important food crop, after maize, wheat and rice and are ideal for situations where you have a lot of labor and little land.

The GMO potatoes, we see in the store today are essentially insulin-triggering sugar balls. Look for creamy-texture organic, heritage varieties and use in moderation.

Since potatoes are a soil crop, how will you satisfy the recipe demand? Not with hydroponics. Rather, you can grow more than you need using open fields, in-ground raised-beds, and go-grows. Open fields and in-ground raised beds make sense, but how do you farm potatoes in a go-grow?

With go-grows, a proven solution is to grow potatoes in large barrels. This is DIY simple. You cut 55-gallon plastic drums in half and use the bottom half for growing potatoes. You'll stand a slotted drip irrigation pipe in the center, anchor it with metal wire, and then fill the barrel with compost and soil and plant your potatoes.

Now comes the interesting question. You need to irrigate and fertilize the potatoes in your go-grows, so where does it come from? You'll use a mix of surface water and nitrate-rich purge water pumped up from the sumps in your below-ground aquaponics system. Some amendments for salinity may be required, but as long as there is a useful level of nitrates, you're good to go.

Another water condition for your go-grow potatoes will be the pH. Potatoes thrive in soils with a pH lower than 6.5. The target range is 5.0 to 6.0 pH, so to amend high pH water, add citric or acetic acid in the form of vinegar to lower the pH. If you're a potato, what's not to love? If you're building your Win-Win community with a turnkey funding strategy, this works.

On the other hand, if you're building your Win-Win community with an incremental funding strategy, you may be in need of a high-value, cash-crop to finance your construction efforts. While salad greens offer a great way to achieve this, the top-dollar earner is only possible with a premium cannabis-ready (PCR) aquaponics system.

PCR Aquaponics

In "Chapter 1 – Surviving with Our Heritage," we introduced the two funding models in this book. The turnkey model is where the capitalization is a single lump sum investment. With the incremental strategy, capitalization occurs with a series of small bootstrap investments.

Both models are based on the same all-hazards, below-ground aquaponics technosphere goal. That is to build and license a medicinal-grade premium cannabis-ready (PCR) commercial farm, whether you will grow cannabis or not.

What is the advantage of having the ability to grow medicinal cannabis for cancer patients who are averse to the synthetic chemicals and fertilizers commonly used to grow recreational cannabis?

- **Downside:** There is no crop more difficult to grow than premium cannabis.
- **Upside:** A PCR strategy enables you to grow virtually any crop in the all-year safety of an all-hazards environment.

This raises the next logical question. If you are growing plants for diet recipes instead of cannabis, what is the functional difference between the two? There is no difference. Both will be PCR grows. The only difference will be in how the technospheres are organized.

For the purpose of this book, we will discuss the following:

- **Grow-to-Diet Aquaponics:** A PCR system can provide large volumes of quality fish protein while supporting multiple hydroponic sub-systems with a variety of plant species.
- **Monocrop Aquaponics:** Commercial farming tends to follow the monocrop model, where each component of the system is designed to provide an optimal growing environment for a single plant species.

With EcoTech farming, there are two basic farming cluster types: open-interior and microclimate clusters. Both types can be sized for multiple requirements, narrow or wide.

Open-Interior Clusters

An example of a useful open-interior cluster is a caterpillar structure that was built by David B. South in Italy, Texas, where he established his company. It was located thirty miles south of the Dallas-Fort Worth metroplex on Interstate 35 East.

Near the highway, David built a large multi-dome open caterpillar cluster for his Bruco manufacturing subsidiary. He fabricates plastic fabric airforms, compost covers, tension tarps for machinery, pond liners, and other applications there.

The Bruco facility uses an open caterpillar design, where the cluster is comprised of an in-line series of seven 60' wide DBS concrete domes with a 1:3 profile. The result is a single cavernous interior with a spacious working area.

With an open interior cluster such as the Bruco caterpillar design, seven domes were raised with a single airform to create shared walls without inner partitions. Each shared wall occurs approximately every 34 feet and the resulting overall dimensions are:

- **Width:** 60’
- **Length:** 240’
- **Height:** 20’

What David has found over the years is that domes that are 60’ and larger are needed for commercially-viable results. A smaller 40’ dome can technically work but not profitably.

Conversely, a larger 100’ dome also creates other concerns, like the need to build a multi-story interior with freight elevators and so forth.

If we picture David’s Bruco caterpillar open-interior cluster as a string of pearls, the dimensions of each of the seven DBS domes in the Bruco cluster will be:

- **Width:** 60’
- **Length:** 35’
- **Height:** 20’

With a 1:2 profile, the height is 30’ instead of 20’ with a 1:3 profile.

In terms of usable interior space and the amount of overcover required, a dome with a diameter of 60’ and a 1:3 profile is your best overall size.

Micro-Climate Cluster

The isolated environments of micro-climate clusters provide the highest level of safety and control in below-ground grow-to-diet EcoTech indoor farming.

Unlike an open interior cluster that has a cavernous space, like the Bruco caterpillar, a micro-climate cluster is larger overall, but has less usable interior space. The effective size is:

- **Width:** 60'
- **Length:** 45'
- **Height:** 20'

The domes in a micro-climate cluster require isolation; this is achieved with interior walls and airlocks.

This limited isolation helps to prevent cross-species issues and optimizes the environment for specific species. It also provides a safe and reliable way to use any combination of indoor farming methods.

In review, the two types of clusters discussed up to now are:

- **Open Interior:** A single continuous interior with no shared walls.
- **Micro-Climate:** Interior spaces are separated by walls and airlocks.

Flexibility is the crucial factor in the actual design of interiors so that they can be rapidly reconfigured as needed for different farming goals. When used in a below-ground farming facility, these two types are connected together with corridors.

This brings us to the third type of cluster. One that is designed to work all on its own.

Stand-alone Cluster

A stand-alone cluster is designed around a single growing climate. Corridors within the cluster are not required with this cluster type. Rather, it employs a mix of open interior and micro-climate spaces with shared walls and airlocks.

In essence, one could think of a stand-alone cluster as a small scale single climate facility with aquaculture and multiple hydroponic domes. It offers a fully self-contained design and is also scalable. This configuration is well-suited for space travel and early colonization.

It is important to remember that stand-alone clusters are mono-climate solutions because the ambient air temperature is what drives the water temperature in the aquasphere.

No matter how you develop your property, you'll eventually want to use all three cluster types for your various aquaponics farming operations.

Aquaponics Farming

If you're wondering whether commercial-scale aquaponics is impossible without agricultural rocket scientists, here is the good news. Unlike ranching which requires a living culture, when it comes to aquaponics, you can figure out the science fairly easily. The adage is, "There is a formula for everything and for everything, a formula."

This means that right angle engineer, who couldn't grow weeds if they tried, can become a successful aquaponics farmer. That is if they follow the DC-3 Rule: when in doubt about stresses, overbuild.

In contrast to that, small-scale and hobbyist aquaponics farmers are on a perpetual quest for efficiencies. Instead of the DC-3 rule, they favor solutions that require the least amount of floor space, power, equipment, and cash.

They figure out cost-cutting shortcuts and make their first efforts with great hopes. That is until their quest to do more with less destabilizes their system; then they are in crisis mode.

Here is an example. A small-scale aquaponics grower sees that his fish are being overwhelmed by parasites. To remedy the situation, he adds salt to the system that increases salinity, treats the fish for freshwater diseases, and promotes the formation of a healthy slime coating.

However, the amount of salt added causes a problem. In order to achieve the desired result, the salinity level in the overall system must be doubled or tripled. While increased salinity helps the fish, this stresses the plants because plants are averse to elevated salinity levels.

Therefore, isolation is critical when building all-hazards aquaponics systems for survival.

All-Hazards Isolation

It is one thing to lose a single crop to an unforeseen event and another to lose all of them. This is why isolation is the key to making large-scale survival aquaponics survivable.

While all-hazards isolated designs are more expensive to build, the advantage is that each compartment or sub-system can be isolated.

To illustrate the concept, here are some useful isolation techniques to consider:

- Crops are started from seed or cuttings only.
- Female and male plants are isolated to prevent cross-breeding.
- Fish are isolated from plants in separate domes.
- Fish tanks are set up in parallel with a split system, as opposed to serially.

In addition to isolation, another issue that aquaponics farmers struggle with is, the number and type of fish in the system.

Commercial aquaponics farmers are always looking for a fish and plant balance, where X pounds of fish will fertilize X pounds of plants, and there are several variables to consider. An example is young fry. Pound for pound, they will consume more food and produce more nitrate than the adult fish.

Why do commercial aquaponics farmers struggle with this balance? The answer has less to do with science and more to do with the expense of farming fish.

With EcoTech PCR aquaponics, you will grow and produce your fish feed. Unlike commercial growers who often donate harvested fish to local charities, survival communities need to produce all the protein they can. Therefore, you want to farm as many fish as possible in your aquaculture domes.

Water chemistry is what determines the amount of fish fertilizer you need from your aquaculture dome in your hydroponics sub-systems. Excess fertilizer is used as elsewhere, such as above-ground go-grows and in-ground raised bed farming operations. In other words, nothing goes to waste. It's all good.

For all this to work smoothly, you need a complete environmental control system.

Operational Monitoring

The easiest way to monitor the health and status of an aquaponics system is to find dead fish floating belly up in your aquaculture tanks. That may be fine for a hobbyist, but not for survival. You monitor the following criteria:

- **Air Temperature:** Air temperature controls the water temperature. It does not matter how complex a combination of interlinked aquaculture and hydroponics subsystems is, ambient air temperature is always going to be the tail that wags the dog.
- **Air Humidity:** This is a serious concern for hydroponics subsystems. When plants are young seedlings, higher temperatures and humidity levels may be more beneficial.
- **Air Circulation:** This is another serious concern for hydroponics sub-systems. Air movement must always replicate a natural environment. Instead of a big fan blowing air over the plants in one direction, oscillating fans should be used to create more natural air circulation patterns.
- **Air Filtration:** Fungus and molds are a constant concern, even in a highly isolated environment. A good solution: UV light filters to control the threat.
- **Oxygen Level:** The ability to control oxygen levels in the environment is an essential requirement for all below-ground DBS domes, regardless of application.
- **Carbon Dioxide Level:** Like oxygen, the ability to control carbon dioxide in the environment is also an essential requirement for all below-ground DBS domes, regardless of application.

- **Natural Cycle Lighting:** In terms of the growing cycle, plants take their cues from the sun and seasons, therefore lighting requirements will vary from species to species. Some crave darkness or shade and others love the light. Most vegetables and flowering plants need 12 to 16 hours of light daily, depending on their stage of growth. A general rule of thumb is to give your plants at least 8 hours of darkness each day.
- **Water Temperature:** When adding fresh rainwater to your aquaponics sump, the water temperature must be identical to that in the sump. Treatment tanks will normalize water temperature and prevent thermal shock for plants and fish.
- **Water pH:** The ideal pH for aquaponics is slightly acidic, which is similar to the pH levels found with blood and saliva. When pH levels are too far out of range, a system can be catastrophically destabilized.
- **Water Dissolved Oxygen:** Oxygen levels are extremely important for fish and the nitrifying bacteria. If oxygen levels are too far out of range, your system can destabilize and your fish will die.
- **Water Ammonia:** In farming with aquaponics, the difference between ammonia (NH3) and ammonium (NH4) is plant uptake. NH3 is a gaseous form of ammonia that cellular life-forms cannot uptake. It is a deadly poison; it only takes a small amount of NH3 to kill. Conversely, plants can uptake NH4 and fish can tolerate relatively high levels of it.
- **Water ORP:** Oxidation-reduction potential (ORP) is a useful test. As discussed previously, ammonia is first converted to nitrite, which then is converted into nitrate through the bacterial process of oxidation. When ORP is used together with pH and temperature, you have an excellent trio for monitoring the system.
- **Water Turbidity:** When the water in an aquaponics system becomes cloudy or hazy, the turbidity could be due to issues with your clarifier, biofilter, or you're just feeding the fish too much, and food particles cloud the water. The water in an efficient, well-maintained aquasphere will be as clear as that from a natural pond or stream.

Granted, there are a lot of things to monitor, but thankfully, commercial automation can be used to significantly enhance your environmental monitoring efforts for both air and water.

Automated Monitoring

In "Chapter 17 – EcoTech Engineering," we discussed the Conservatory of Flowers in Golden Gate Park, San Francisco, California, which was founded in 1878. In 1895 it was wired for electricity to power one of the first electrically-powered environmental control systems in America.

Environmental control systems have come a long way since then. With commercial automation, you can monitor the health and status of your aquaponics system in real-time. This is a huge advantage; it gives you a timely way to isolate problems and to make any necessary repairs.

Industrial air and water monitoring systems are built to high standards and can be integrated with computerized control systems. The following automation is suggested:

- **Air Monitoring:** Temperature, humidity, smoke, carbon monoxide, and carbon dioxide.
- **Water Monitoring:** Dissolved oxygen, free ammonia, temperature, turbidity, pH, and ORP.

An advantage of all-hazards below-ground aquaponics is that EMP protection is built in to the system. Nonetheless, when designing an automated monitoring system, make it DC-3 tough. Which means it needs to be redundant, including the sensors in the system.

System Redundancy

A good example of what happens when a critical automation system is designed without redundancy is the Boeing 737 Max 8.

In tragic crashes on October 29, 2018 and March 10, 2019, 346 passengers and crew died and for the same cause. An onboard computer system, the Maneuvering Characteristics Augmentation System (MCAS) wrested control away from the pilots and crashed both aircraft.

In both cases, the cause was a faulty sensor. Or to be more specific, the angle of attack sensor used by the MCAS system. Note that the sensor is used in the singular form, because unlike the other systems on the 737, MCAS was designed without redundancy—purely for financial reasons.

The point is that a Win-Win survival community cannot risk failure due to a deadly, penny-pinching scheme similar to Boeing's deadly MCAS debacle!

Therefore, you need triple-redundant control system as follows:

- **Primary System:** This is the system you'll use each day. It will be connected to a failover system via an electronic heartbeat. This simple, continuous signal, sent from one server to another, tells it all is well.
- **Failover System:** The failover server is identical to the primary system. When it no longer receives a coherent heartbeat from the primary server, the failover server automatically takes control of the system and sends an alarm to the operators.
- **Manual System:** In the event of a catastrophic failure of the primary and failover automation, control can be maintained indefinitely through a fully-functional manual control system.

Will doing all of this prevent you from a 737 Max 8 crash? Not if you're pinching pennies as Boeing did with a single-sensor configuration.

This is why you need two sensors for each air and water monitoring role. Even for a nominal system, both sensors will send the same data within allowable tolerances.

When one sensor begins sending anomalous data or ceases to function, an operator warning is issued, and the system continues monitoring the stable sensor.

Should both sensors cease to function; an alert is sounded and the system is then blocked from making changes without operator input.

With this, we have covered the essentials for constructing a Win-Win below-ground farm and aquaponics facility with a premium cannabis ready (PCR) design.

For those of you who have ever taken flying lessons, this is when your instructor tells you, "You're going to solo today." Or in other words Dear Reader, you've learned enough to do this on your own and congratulations, you've just soloed.

Now it is time to take your skills to the next level, learning how to master EcoTech cropping so you can get your pioneer flying license.

19

EcoTech Cropping

In "Chapter 1 – Surviving With Our Heritage," we introduced two Win-Win survival community funding models:

- **Incremental Funding:** A bootstrap strategy for founding a church with a series of small-capitalization investments from founders and other sources.
- **Turnkey Funding:** One or more funding sources fund a Win-Win church with one or more properties in a single lump sum investment.

The option to grow-to-market with high-value cash crops such as premium cannabis or salad greens is applicable to both models.

Grow-to-Market

If a Win-Win church is funded without the burden of debt and prior to the onset of a cataclysm, a Win-Win community may still require a market-driven revenue source to fund operations before it can launch a complete, grow-to-diet EcoTech farming and ranching strategy.

Examples of commonly grown commercial food species include:

- **Specialty Lettuces:** Arugula, Butterhead, Endive, Looseleaf, Radicchio, Romaine and Watercress
- **Edible Flowers:** Basil, Chives, Cilantro, Dill, Lavender, and Thyme

With a grow-to-market cropping strategy, you will grow two or more commercial food revenue crops for fine-dining establishments and organic grocery stores.

The ability to specialize plant species is why monocrop farming can generate substantial revenue. This is because specialization enables ideal growing conditions throughout the various growth stages of a crop species, which in this case, is premium cannabis.

Premium Cannabis

Leafy greens and herbs are proven money-makers, but the most profitable commercial species for a monocrop strategy is premium medicinal-grade cannabis.

On a pound for pound market basis, here is how lettuce and premium cannabis compare:

- **Profit:** Pound-for-pound, premium cannabis is more profitable than truffles.
- **Nutrient Demand:** Lettuce is a low-nutrient crop, whereas premium cannabis a high-nutrient crop. In order to meet high nutrient demands, more fish are required.
- **Growing Risk:** Hemp is the non-psychoactive version of cannabis, and is a weed. Plow a field, broadcast some seeds and fertilizer, irrigate, and nature does the rest. Not so with premium cannabis. Each growth stage is fraught with high-tech peril, which is one reason why it commands such a high price in the market. It is hard to grow well.

- **Labor Demand:** Premium cannabis is a very labor-intensive crop. Whether you use it to fund your operations or for medicinal use, when people cannot keep food down for any reason, it is a proven, non-pharma alternative.

The first question to ask about growing premium cannabis with aquaponics is: are there any licensed, successful models for this currently in operation in the United States and Canada?

Yes! Do an internet search using the query "cannabis aquaponics" and you will see a vibrant world of innovation and success with growing premium cannabis.

There are many growers who are doing amazing things; one interesting industry trend is what these firms are doing with the fish raised in their premium cannabis aquaponics system.

After harvesting their cannabis for top dollar, these growers donate large quantities of fish, typically Tilapia, from their aquaculture systems to local charity food banks. Perhaps this idea was inspired by Ben & Jerry's Ice Cream, but one thing is for certain, it does show that growers care about people. And yes, it's also great for public relations.

One particular firm in Canada, a licensed producer called Green Relief, serves as an excellent benchmark model for EcoTech farming and ranching. Located near Hamilton, Ontario, the company is situated in a climate adverse to cannabis, which necessitates growing indoors.

The firm built a large bunker-style concrete structure with a soil overcover. They now produce high-valued premium cannabis on a continuous harvesting basis. Their aquaculture is based on tilapia and their hydroponics sub-system employs the DWC aquaponics method (Deep Water Culture.) They grow their plants on Styrofoam rafts. Now that we know what they're doing, why are they doing it that way?

Growing cannabis is big business and their aquaponics facilities are very large and complex. Yet, they still accepted the increased startup costs, which are much higher than a conventional soil-based strategy. The reason? The numbers work. To illustrate the point, let's compare the two strategies using the same criteria.

Soil-Based Strategy

The following criteria are based on the soil-based licensed cannabis grows in the Sierra Nevada foothills region of Northern California, where the weather is ideal for this species.

- **Harvesting:** Small growers typically have a single harvest in a normal season. Larger growers will use hoop houses and lighting to extend the growing season so they can achieve two harvests in a single season.
- **Fertilization:** In areas like Yuba and Nevada Counties in California, cannabis fertilizers can be as exotic as pricey high-tech rocket fuel. It is not uncommon for growers to spend up to $50,000 a season to fertilize large grows for maximum production.
- **Insects and Pests:** Crops grows above ground and in the open are the most difficult to protect. When we think of insects and pest we tend to think small, but big is bad too. If deer can get to your cannabis grow, they will feast on the leaves, buds and seedlings. So, like a goat herder, you need dogs, as in big dogs, with big appetites.
- **Water Demand:** Cannabis is also a thirsty plant and requires a lot of water to grow. Given that each plant can generate $1,500 or more in wholesale products at harvest, they need to be watered by hand each day and with great care.
- **Planting Density:** Farmers think in terms of acres. Cannabis growers are high-tech gardeners and their focus is on the plants. Hence, they need open pathways to care for their plants each day, and so land usage becomes a secondary consideration.

Presently, large growers are forcing out the small growers through licensing and permitting restrictions that favor them. Therefore, small growers do three things to stay in business:

- **Discretion:** They are permitted and happy to be small. If they get a license to grow 99 plants, they'll plant half that, and what they do plant will be five-star organic quality. This is how they stay profitable.
- **Off the Radar:** As the old saying goes, "Out of sight, out of mind." If a county official can see your cannabis grow from the road, you're in deep kimchi. This is why savvy growers use sheltered areas that are virtually impossible to seen at ground level.

- **Privacy:** Governments are not the only ones who fly drones, which is why savvy growers plant in irregular patterns that visually blend in with the surrounding foliage.

The takeaway is that even with permitting, the best way to grow cannabis is to do it both legally and out of public view. With aquaponics, that's exactly what you get, so let's revisit the same criteria above to see how the numbers work.

Aquaponics Solutions

When financing your Win-Win ranch with PCR aquaponics, the numbers will work in a way everyone can appreciate.

- **Harvesting:** With aquaponics, you can continually harvest on a year-around schedule. You stagger the planting and harvest to schedule (i.e. weekly, monthly or quarterly).
- **Insects and Pests:** Plants grown indoors are shielded from pests and competition. This reduces plant stress which results in crop yields 25% or more over those grown in soil.
- **Fertilization:** By definition, aquaponics is an organic method of fertilization. The cost is only a few hundred dollars per harvest for electricity and fish feed. The fish you raise and sell will pay for your fertilizer production and then some.
- **Water Demand:** Aquaponics uses 10 percent as much water to grow the same amount of product as is required with soil. A good rainwater harvesting system will supply your aquasphere's needs. Make sure that rainwater harvesting is allowed in your area. If not, you can use properly treated city or well water.
- **Planting Density:** How many plants of the same species you can plant within a square yard or meter defines the planting density. With aquaponics, the typical density is 125% to 150% of that for soil. For cannabis it is closer to 200%.

Here is an interesting side note. For those who live in places like the Sierra Nevada foothills, renting local moving trucks comes with a unique experience. Many smell from cannabis, because small growers rented them to cure their crops in after harvest. This is not the best way for you to be known in the community.

Now that we have covered the basics for building premium cannabis-ready (PCR) aquaponics all-hazards facilities; now, let's go build one.

PCR All-Hazards Facility

An example all-season, continuous harvesting monocrop cannabis facility using 60' diameter DBS domes with a 1:2 profile can be organized into multiple micro-climate clusters with shared interior walls, and airlocks as follows:

- **Mineralization Cluster:** A 3-dome cluster used to produce mineralized fish feed.

- **Aquaponics Six-Pack:** Two 3-dome clusters serving three roles: aquaculture, hydroponics, and curing. From above, it looks like a six-pack of canned drinks.
- **Processing Cluster:** A 3-dome cluster for processing and packaging.
- **Service Corridor:** The service corridor is a single continuous vertical prolate ellipsoid configuration with a 1:2 profile. It is a 15' high helmet-shaped (vertical prolate ellipsoid) structure running the full length of the facility. The service corridor incorporates below-floor and overhead areas for service lines.

Using the service corridor as a centerline for our facility:

- **To the Left:** Nine domes in three clusters, mineralization, aquaculture, cannabis curing dome, and processing.
- **To the Right:** One cluster of three hydroponics domes with optimized environments for nursery, vegetative, and fruiting plant growth stages.

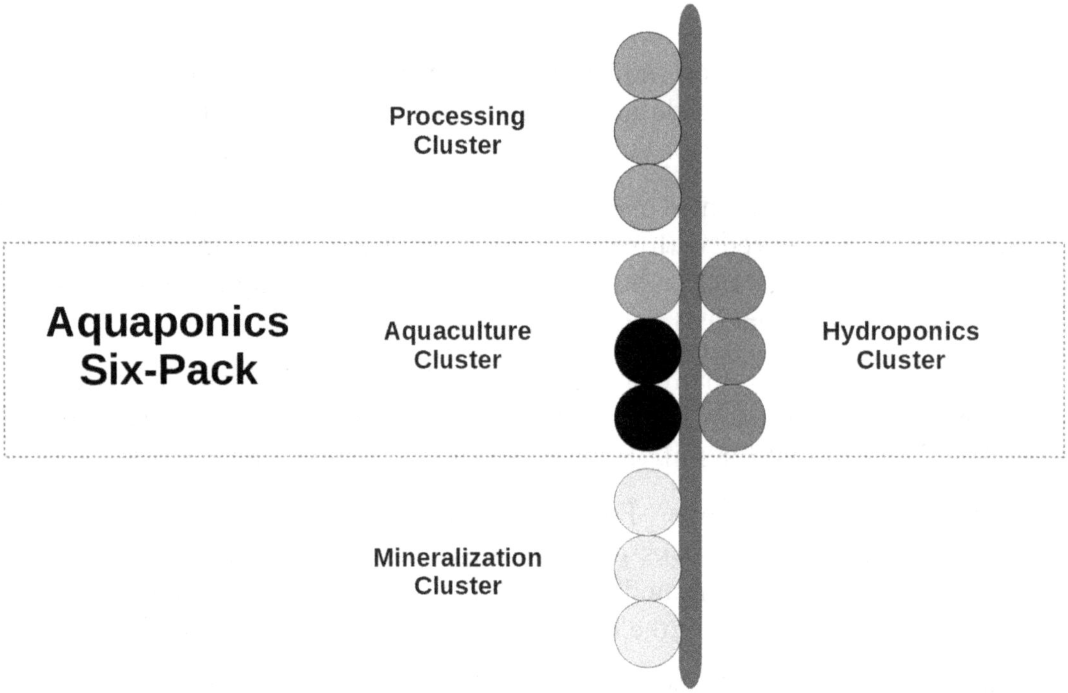

The service corridor, along with administrative work areas like control rooms, will use the same temperature and humidity setpoint ranges as used on the ISS (International Space Station):

- **ISS Temperature:** Nominal range is between 72° F and 78° F (22.2° C to 25.5° C)
- **ISS Humidity:** Nominal range between 40 percent and 70 percent.

- **Optimal Setpoint:** The optimal comfort setpoints are 72 degrees and 50% humidity.

Other facility considerations include air pressure, flood drains, and service lines as follows:

- **Air Pressure:** Airlocks are also used to connect adjoining domes and clusters to corridors an air pressures may differ. Isolation is essential to reliable operations, and this will help to maintain environmental integrity.
- **Flood Drains:** You can expect local permitting codes to require drainage. This is because a DBS dome with overcover will likely be viewed by county permitting departments as a basement. There is no one-size-fits-all solution, so local code compliance requirements will drive your eventual facility design.
- **Below-Floor Service Lines:** While your aquaponics system will have its own sumps, this system must also be able to handle flooding. This is why you should install raised floors in your domes so that you have easy access to the water, drainage, waste, and aquasphere service lines in the facility. Note: all aquaculture lines must be insulated.
- **Overhead Service Lines:** The helmet shape of domes will provide ceiling space for electrical service lines, communications lines, control rooms, mechanical rooms, passageways, overhead electrical and HVAC service lines and conduits.
- **Facility Access:** Each end of the service corridor, can serve as loading docks and secure entrances into the facility.

Using this example configuration, let's look at each dome in the facility beginning with those to the left of the service corridor.

Mineralization Cluster

The mineralization cluster is where fish feed and fish meal processing occurs. It uses one dome for mushroom beds.

Mushrooms are well-suited to below-ground rock dust mineralization uptake. After harvest, the mushrooms become organic feed for the wormery dome. Worm wee and castings offer lucrative secondary revenue streams.

Adult worms are harvested and used as mineralized fish feed. Also, in this cluster's third dome, all feed sources, including harvested fish, are processed into the different types of fish needed for the two species grown in the aquaculture cluster.

Fish feed options for juveniles and adults include blood worms and red wigglers, for example. However, with tiny fish fry, a different type of feed is required; one viable option is to make fish meal from fish and plant matter. For example, you feed catfish meal to the tilapia fry and visa-versa for the catfish fry.

Three things to remember are:

- Never, cannibalize a species by feeding it to itself.
- Fish are picky eaters.
- Experiment on the small, before you build.

Before breaking ground on a facility, you need to prove to yourself that you can grow feed for fish fry before you turn the first shovel full of dirt.

PCR Six-Pack Aquaculture Cluster

Beyond the mineralization cluster and to the left of the service corridor, we have two domes in then cluster dedicated to aquaculture and the third reserved for cannabis curing.

- **Tilapia Aquaculture Dome:** A favorite with cannabis growers, Tilapia are hardy and reproduce well. Juveniles and adults will thrive on blood worms raised in the mineralization cluster.

- **Catfish Aquaculture Dome:** You cannot afford to lose a crop, which is why you need a Plan B. In this case, a separate backup aquaculture dome with a different fish species. Catfish are also a popular retail fish. They are hardy and reproduce well.

- **Cannabis Curing Dome:** Curing is the most fragile phase of the harvest for cannabis plants. You must not force the curing process as many recreational growers do. Rather, for true organic medicinal-grade products, it must occur naturally.

After the plants are harvested, a warm and moist environment will mitigate harvesting shock. Then, as the plants dry, the temperature and humidity setpoints can be normalized.

Six-Pack Hydroponics Cluster

When growing cannabis underground, the domes in your hydroponics cluster need to simulate three different above-ground environments:

- **Nursery Dome:** An optimized environment for young seedlings and clones. The plants at this stage may require higher humidity levels and warmer temperatures.

- **Vegetative Dome:** Mid-summer warmth and longer lighting cycles are needed for young adults grown. Here is where the bulk of the plant growth occurs.

- **Fruiting Dome:** Cooler temperatures and shorter lighting cycles are necessary environmental queues because they stimulate the plants' fruiting process. This third stage is when female plants produce the 'good stuff.'

Of the three domes, the most critical one in the six-pack is the nursery. In this dome, seedlings and clones are grown. Mature plants used for cuttings are raised here.

Processing Cluster

Beyond the curing dome, the second farming cluster is where cured plants are processed into various products. They include:

- **Cartridges:** Oil-filled vaping cartridges
- **Concentrates:** Hashish, hash oil, and rosin
- **Edibles:** Foods and beverages made with cannabis
- **Extracts:** Oil and distillates
- **Flowers:** The buds favored for their quality by those who smoke
- **Prerolls:** Cigarettes made from flower trimmings
- **Seeds:** Commercial cannabis is harvested before the plant goes to seed
- **Topicals:** Used for localized, topical pain relief in roll-ons and creams.

What is missing from the list above are seeds, so let's address this. When people buy recreational cannabis off the street, they often get "bag seeds." Never use them.

Seed Genetics

With cannabis, it's the ladies who do all the heavy lifting, as the males do not flower.

Once seedlings grow to a stage where sex can be determined, the males are largely culled out, save for a few for breeding.

If you want to grow premium plants from your own seeds, keep in mind that clones of successful cultivars are the best way to begin. Be sure to do your due diligence on this.

To launch a brand new grow, clones and seeds need to be sourced from a reliable genetics supplier, such as the House of Dankness in Denver, CO. Their collection includes some of the most sought-after cultivars in the world.

Because the ability to be self-sustaining is essential to the EcoTech model, no matter how you start your grow, organize your own cultivation program as well, starting with the cannabis plants in the fruiting dome. You'll use a few of these as your clone mothers and making your own clone mothers is fairly simple.

Prior to harvest, a few carefully selected mature plants are allowed to fruit and then go to seed. After that, they can be harvested for products and seeds.

You now have a working configuration for growing grow-to-market premium cannabis, so let's design a similar grow-to-diet configuration.

If you think this was complex, hang on to your hat, Dear Reader. Monocropping cannabis is rather easy, when you compare it with cropping a comprehensive EcoTech grow-to-diet strategy.

Grow-to-Diet

Here is where it all starts to come together for survival and colonization. Your all-hazards below-ground farming and aquaponics complex will be the beating heart of your community's overall grow-to-diet system, thanks to EcoTech species rules and micro-climate control.

EcoTech Species Rules

In "Chapter 15 – EcoTech Farming and Ranching," we introduced the EcoTech Species Rules for selecting plant and animal species as follows:

- **Authenticity:** For animals, best-of-class working breeds and food breeds. For plants, everything begins with organic, heritage seeds, and cuttings. No GMO.
- **Diversity:** When a Win-Win community grows-to-recipe, it is essential that it grows, processes, and consumes the most diverse range of useful species possible.
- **Resilience:** Plant species that are hardy, disease-resistant, and which can handle extremes in the environment are essential. Less resilient species are only grown for special requirements. Animal species must likewise have strong constitutions and be able to thrive on their own.

These rules define the scope of your grow-to-diet strategy as you chose your diets and recipes. Implementing those choices requires multi-climate control.

Multi-Climate Control

With grow-to-diet aquaponics, hydroponics and aquaponics domes are paired, so the ambient temperature in both domes is identical. In this way, they function as part of a unified environment, where the ambient air temperature determines the water temperature.

In your aquaculture dome, the command input is the fish species for two reasons:

- **Thermal Shock from Rapid Change:** Fish are more sensitive to rapid temperature changes than plants.
- **Hydroponics Sub-systems:** A single, high-production aquaculture dome can support multiple hydroponic growing methods and structures.

Tilapia, is the most popular fish species for commercial cannabis aquaponics growers, although some states ban tilapia as an invasive species.

Tropical/Subtropical

Tropical climates vary from warm to hot, are moist year-round, feature lush vegetation, and are located from the equator to 23.5° North (the Tropic of Cancer).

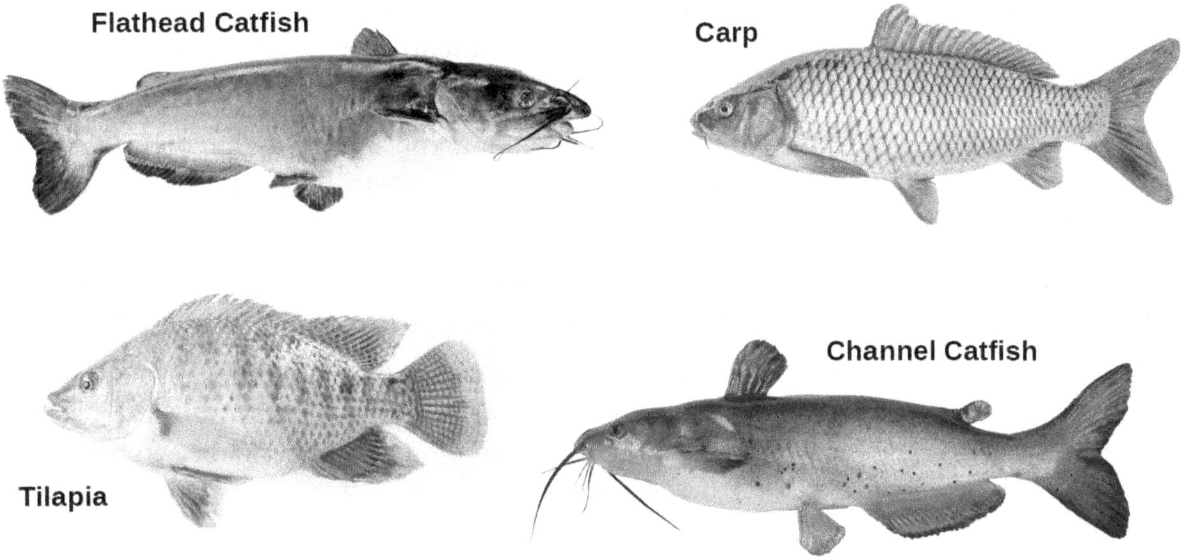

Above the tropics, from 35° to 66.5° are the subtropics. Subtropical climates typically experience hot summers and mild winters and, on rare occasions, see frost. Fish species that can thrive in both climates are:

- **Carp:** The ideal temperature is 84° F and the tolerance range is 75° F to over 88° F.
- **Channel Catfish:** The ideal temperature range is from 82° F to 89° F, and the tolerance range is 55° F to over 90° F.
- **Flathead Catfish:** The ideal temperature is 85° F and the tolerance range is 81° F to over 90° F.
- **Tilapia:** The ideal temperature range is from 70° F to 85° F and the tolerance range is 50° F to over 90° F.

Plants that grow well in subtropical climates include avocado, carob, cherry tomato, kiwifruit, mango, pomegranate, and sweet potatoes.

With a tropical climate, you have a wonderful range of popular species such as allspice, banana, bay leaf, cacao, coffee, dates, fig, ginger, green tea, breadfruit, guava, mango, monk fruit, mulberry, papaya, peach, pomegranate, star fruit, tea, and moringa.

Temperate

Most of America is located in the temperate zone, which is above the subtopics and ranges from 35° to 50°. With a cooler temperate micro-climate, you can use a different solution mix. Instead of growing-to-diet, you grow fodder for livestock.

With smaller ranches, the benefit is that you can reduce the amount of land for grazing with aquaponics fodder supplementation. But more importantly, what happens if there is a catastrophic natural event with harsh consequences for your ranching operations?

Granted, you'll lose animals, but if you lose them all, you'll have nothing left to start over with. Rather than blithcly waltzing down this path to catastrophe, the smart thing is to be situationally aware (SA).

With SA, you experience the world about you through your five senses, just as you did as a child. You actually see the world as you find it, or "in situ," as archaeologists would say.

Then review this SA experience using your adult mind, by projecting your SA observations through time and space to a future outcome. This is a way for you to establish your awareness, formulate a plan, and then act upon it, even though it may not be the best one. In time this worldview becomes a sixth sense of sorts, and you won't need to think about it. You'll just do it.

Who is the most capable to respond smartly when things go sideways? Your ranching operation team members and when the need presents, finding them will be easy. They'll already be where they are needed and doing what needs to be done. In this case, it will be moving the livestock to overcover protection domes specially constructed for this purpose; this is where they are watered and fed with supplemental fodder grown in your below-ground, all-hazards aquaponics facility.

You also get a nice bonus with a cooler temperate micro-climate. The cooler ambient temperatures give you access to a wide range of very delicious freshwater fish species, and topping the list are trout. Specifically, those that taste good, and here are three trout species to consider:

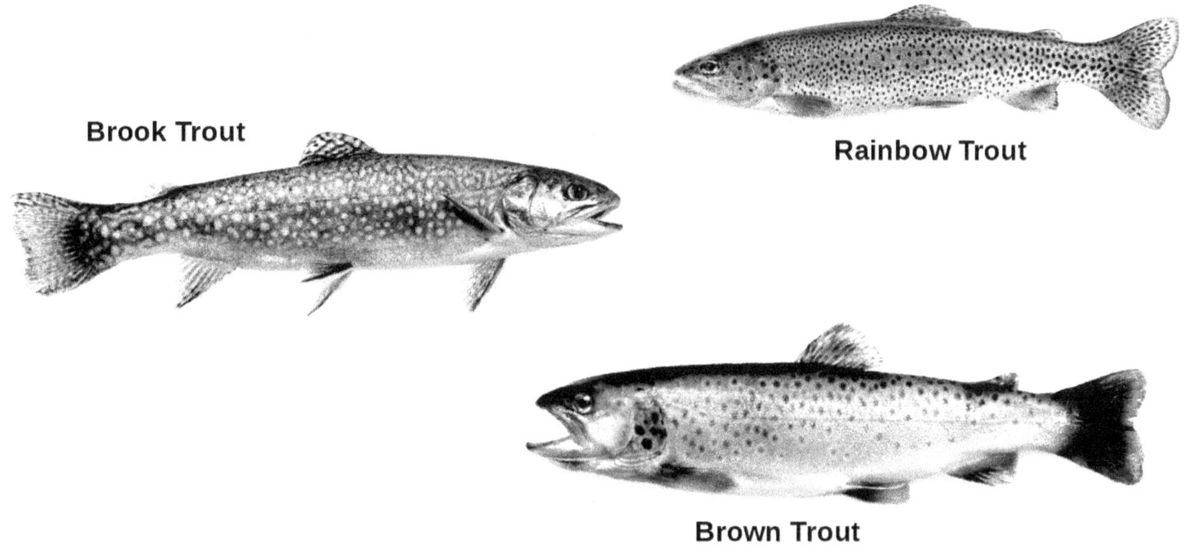

- **Brook Trout:** Ideal temperature is 58°. Tolerance range is from 44° F to 70° F.
- **Brown Trout:** Ideal temperature range is from 56° F to 66° F. Tolerance range is 44° F to 75° F.
- **Rainbow Trout:** Ideal temperature is 61°. Tolerance range is from 44° F to 75° F.

The colder temperatures in your hydroponics domes that trout like will also be ideal for growing fodder plants like wheatgrass and barley. A reasonable goal is to grow one ton of fodder or more per day with a well-balanced system.

With aquaponics, you can farm a single fish species, like the commercial cannabis aquaponics growers who favor the use of tilapia. While that species is a good monocrop choice for them, with a grow-to-diet strategy, we must remember that diversity is an EcoTech species rule.

It is wise to experiment with a mix of species in your fish tanks. Catfish are bottom feeders and get along well with other species like Smallmouth Bass, which prefer to swim above them. That could be a good adult pairing.

Water crustaceans such as crayfish are another option. Crustaceans do not grow as quickly as fish, but when an ammonia level alert registers a spike, you'll be glad to have a few of them in the fish tank.

Spikes like this are often caused by a dead fish decomposing somewhere in the system or a blockage in the system caused by undigested fish feed. For crustaceans, this is Manna from Heaven, and they'll be happy to take care of it.

With an aquaponics-based, grow-to-diet strategy, you literally have a world of opportunities to organize your diet recipe choices around.

On that note in the last chapter, you soloed. Well, Dear Reader, congratulations, you've just earned your wings. Now it is time to kick the tires, light the fire, and see how all this looks from above.

20

EcoTech Supersystem

Now it's time to examine this notion of growing food for survival and colonization from a high-level and top-down view. When you do that, what you see is a supersystem.

Supersystem is a technical term used to describe a network of communications, transportation, or distribution. When applied to an EcoTech supersystem, it is a network of technospheres, biospheres, and aquasphere. Therefore, our working definition is that a supersystem encompasses all the life-forms and resources within the boundary of a property.

From an EcoTech supersystem perspective, an aquasphere represents all of the water systems and water sources within the property boundaries. This includes rainfall and aquifers, which is why a dedicated aquasphere team or working group is necessary.

This is a definition that your right-angle engineer can work with, but does it work for the rest of us? This begins with a conscious decision to the question, "What does it mean to your church to have a food-centered life?"

Mediterranean

Unlike the tropical, subtropical, and temperate growing zones, Mediterranean climate zones are very localized.

The Mediterranean climate is characterized by dry summers and mild, wet winters. The name comes from the Mediterranean Basin where this climate type is the most common.

Generally, most of the Mediterranean climate areas are between 30° to 45° north of the Equator in western North America, Southern Europe, and south of the equator there are small areas in South America, Southern Africa, and Australia. These climate areas are usually found along the western sides of continents.

A Mediterranean micro-climate works equally well for both the survival and space diets. There are many species that can thrive in this climate.

Two fish that were a regular part of the American pioneer diet were crappie and bass. Both are good eating and played a significant role as a protein source for American pioneers.

- **Black Crappie:** The ideal temperature is 70° F and the tolerance range is 60° F to 75° F.
- **Smallmouth Bass:** The ideal temperature range is from 65° F to 68° F and the tolerance range is 60° F to 73° F.
- **Koi:** The ideal temperature range is from 65° F to 68° F and the tolerance range is 34° F to 90° F. This is good species for small-scale flood-and-drain systems in residences and facility meeting areas.

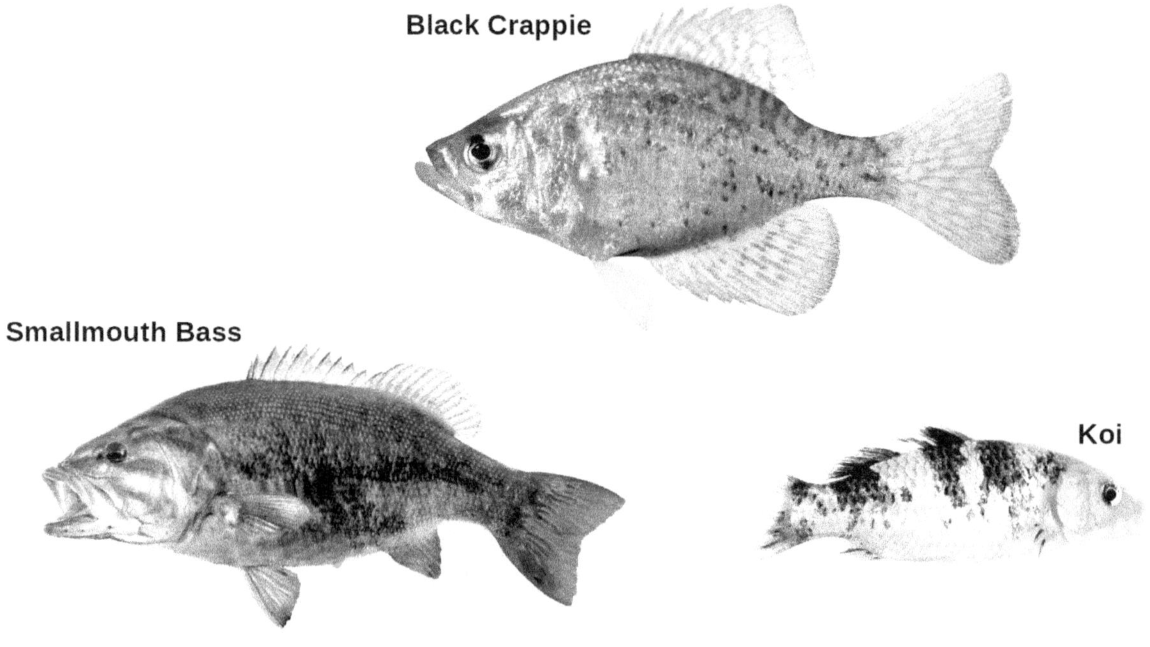

Plants that grow well in Mediterranean climates include: olives, figs, dates, citrus, grapes, tomatoes, avocados, legumes, cereals, grains and vegetables.

Feeding 1,000 Martians

We are going to create a supersystem that grows food in an all-hazards environment. The short-term goal is to feed ten people for every church member who resides on a ranch. In contrast, the long-term goal is to survive on earth and colonize space with a healthy diet.

With this in mind, it's time to explore the ideas presented in "Chapter 14 – Feeding 1,000 Martians" by demonstrating the feasibility of the concept with the goal of feeding 1,000 Martians. With an ambitious goal such as this, there as several steps.

What is the first step?

If you're a dreamer, it is your dream. There is a beautiful lyric in the show tune, "Happy Talk" from the 1949 hit musical, South Pacific, that says it best:

"You gotta have a dream;
If you don't have a dream,
How you gonna have a dream come true?"

I'm a dreamer, and I'm going to share my dream with you for future generations. This brings us to the next step in this discussion, creating a food-centered life.

A Food-Centered Life

In modern literature, the concept of a food-centered life is often about pancake breakfasts to raise money for a volunteer fire department, food tourism, or social events. We're told that food today is an expression of infinite associations for our many pangs of hunger, including physical, social, and emotional alike. Oh please!

Let's put this 21st century consumer society claptrap into context.

You will need to define a food-centered life for a survival community before a cataclysm happens. This is not to make a dramatic point. It's about preparing for the worst beforehand.

One example is Fukushima Daiichi. Since 2011, it has become a nuclear volcano, and each day is it pumping deadly radiation into the Pacific. There is nothing that can be done to stop it. Radiation does not dissipate; it accumulates.

The reactors that failed were the GE Mark 1 design. On September 11, 2017, EnviroNews, a nuclear authority, in an article by engineer and whistleblower Arnie Gundersen had this to say:

> "Fukushima Daiichi has four units – one, two, three, four — and they're all Mark 1 designs. In addition, there's another 35 in the world, including 23 here in America, that are the same design. A group of three engineers quit General Electric in 1976 because they realized the design was not safe. Two of the

> three are still alive and living here in California, and they are my personal heroes. They understood before any of us did how seriously we really didn't understand what it was that the engineers were doing."

What is not widely known by the public is that after a nuclear reactor like a General Electric Mark 1 has been scrammed (emergency shutdown), this is not like turning off the engine in your car. The cores must continue to be cooled with a reliable source of water for up to two years before the danger passes.

Then, should the power-grid fail catastrophically and the pumps stop working, the outcome will be exactly the same as Fukushima Daiichi. Deadly China syndrome meltdowns result where the nuclear fuel melts down through the containment structure floor and burrows into the earth like toxic tree roots.

What does this mean for Americans? We have 23 Fukushima Daiichi volcanoes waiting to erupt. Once the nation's power grid fails, these nuclear plants will fail also, and there will be others as well. In the event of a major EMP event, they could all begin to fail at the same time.

This threat is not the only one.

There are numerous other sources of industrial poisoning that range from toxic metals to only God knows what else. When this happens, the consequences will be severe and long-lasting for survivor health: the average lifespan will be lowered due to deaths by poisoning that will persist for a century or more.

You need to consider this when shaping your food-centered life. It's not creative happy world blog posts and colorful television shows; it's people dying from cancers, plagues, and industrial toxins.

Using patent medicines to mask problems is not your first line of defense. Rather, your first line of defense will be a diet that bolsters the body's ability to counter these environmental threats and speeds the healing process. This is not new.

Before the advent of electricity, Americans knew how to live without electricity, antibiotics, and other modern conveniences. What they grew and ate was fresh, nutritious organic food. Consequently, they had stronger constitutions, than most of us today, and certainly stronger immune systems.

Yes, some died from cancer and heart disease, but those were not the major causes of death they are today. Rather, it was a disease, like the 1918 Spanish Flu, which killed more American soldiers than German weapons.

When choosing a diet and its associated recipes, the best way for church members to start is by reciting the food wisdom of Hippocrates three times: "Let food be thy medicine and medicine be thy food." Then, trust your gut and make it happen.

Search Outside the Box

When you research nutrition on the Internet, it is difficult to know if an article or video is being shared by sincere people with good intentions, or if is it being shared by spinmeisters. Spinmeisters never identify themselves or appear on camera; they use shills and anonymous posting for that.

Here is a search tip. Search outside the box.

When composing a search string, remember that predictable behaviors produce predictable results. Consequently, like a hungry mouse chasing the scent of click-bait, you'll find yourself in a spinmeister box.

Instead of chasing click-bait, go more in-depth and search outside the box. Search diet-related topics from the inside-out, using search strings that reference specific diet-related organs in the human body.

To illustrate the concept, let's focus on the following organs: colon, heart, pancreas, joints and skin.

- **Colon:** Communicable diseases will be a huge concern for survivors. Seventy percent or more of your body's immune system is in the colon. Healthy colons have a proper balance between helpful and harmful bacteria unless you consume foods like sugar, which causes harmful bacteria to flourish. Your survival diet plan needs to include foods rich in probiotics, such as fermented pickles, kimchi, and kombucha.
- **Brain:** If you cannot think clearly, you will fail and what happens in the colon has a direct impact on the health of your brain. This is because the mysterious microbes in our gut are essential to controlling inflammation which can cause degenerative diseases such as dementia and Alzheimer's disease. You not only want to include naturally fermented foods like yogurt and kefir, but you also need healthy fats and carbohydrates such as olive oil, grass-fed meat and butter, avocados, and whole eggs. Also beverages and foods with polyphenols such as coffee, tea, chocolate and wine.
- **Heart:** During a catastrophe, survivors will experience extremely high levels of stress, and heart attacks and strokes will be an elevated concern. Likewise, hypertension and other cardiovascular concerns will also diminish the ability of survivors to reason and function. Therefore, your survival diet plan should exclude processed foods, refined carbs, high amounts of table salt, sugar, saturated fat and excess alcohol.
- **Pancreas:** Afflictions such as diabetes and cancer have become the health plagues of the 21st century. Should the nation's power grid fail, doctors will know almost to the day when their diabetic patients will die after they run out of insulin. When you buy inexpensive 5-gallon buckets of emergency food in a box store, please read the ingredients. To keep the price competitive, they go light on the protein and heavy on sug-

ars and refined carbs. This so-called "emergency food" will spike your insulin levels into the danger zone and dull your wits.

- **Joints:** Arthritis is a debilitating inflammatory condition. Survivors will need to be able to move freely. If you're caught out in the open with a walker when things go sideways, most likely, so will you. Food that causes inflammation include sugar, high-fructose corn syrup, artificial trans fats, refined carbs, excessive alcohol, processed meat, and sodium chloride (salt). It is better to use limited amounts of sea salt or Himalayan salt.
- **Skin:** During a global cataclysm with adverse solar weather, UV levels will be higher than the present all-time high levels. Your skin is the largest organ of your body; so protecting it from these threats is helped by adding plants like avocados, walnuts, sunflower seeds and sweet potatoes to your diet. Also, the skin may be subject to painful boils from volcanic ash. Hygiene is the best defense here. When ash falls on your skin, wash it off with water as soon as possible. If water is not available, dig down into the ground for fresh soil or clay and use that instead.

All competent doctors are valuable, but alternative healers are more likely to think outside the box. For optimal results, invite a naturopathic or holistic doctor to be part of your diet plan team. They treat patients with natural therapies restoring and supporting the bodies' self-healing processes with good results.

Whether you think this is good or bad or somewhere in between is not the point. It is a simple and practical choice, to support optimum survival wellness.

Do you want fresh foods that celebrate and support life? Or would you prefer a scientific laboratory diet that is ladled out in dollops of mucus-like concoctions?

Practical Choices

Be practical when creating your diet. The pioneer recipes from the 18th and 19th centuries are quintessential survival food. On the other hand, traveling through space is not the same as spending a year staring at the east-end of a west-bound team of oxen.

Aside from occasional moments of sheer terror, space travel will be monotonous and pleasant because the spacecraft's environmental setpoints will simulate Mediterranean weather. With space travel, the Mediterranean diet is also one of the healthiest choices and it opens a range of possibilities.

On a spaceship, indoor farming will be conducted in environmentally isolated compartments where multiple growing climates can be replicated.

With this in mind, we will now create an EcoTech supersystem with multiple growing climates to demonstrate how these concepts work, using the following guidelines:

- **Farm Superfoods:** Think of all the wonderful superfood options that are available with tropical and subtropical species. Moringa, a plant native to India, also known as the "drumstick tree," "miracle tree," and "tree of life," is rich in antioxidants and nutrients.

- **Look for Smart Substitutes:** Cane sugar and sugar beets rot your teeth and gut, so ban them from your species manifest. Wise substitutes are stevia leaf and Monk Fruit. These natural sweeteners grow well in hydroponics and are easy to prepare.

- **All Things in Moderation:** A home brewed beer and a plate piled high with fried catfish and greens will be a welcome sight for one hungry person who has spent all day, standing knee-deep in some kind of gosh-awful muck to fix something important. If you were that person, would the reward of a tofu and greens banquet really float your boat after a hard day like that? This is why you want to include foods that help make life worth living. Just use them wisely and in moderation.

Your all-hazards, below-ground, grow-to-diet aquaponics facility will employ a micro-climate cropping strategy to promote a robust and inspiring food-centered life.

The mindset to achieve this goal was explained in “Chapter 15 – EcoTech Farming and Ranching,” where we defined the difference between farmers and ranchers. It was their view of the relationship between their animals and the land:

- A rancher sees the land as a home for his animals.
- A farmer sees the animals as a part of his home.

The best mindset for EcoTech farming and ranching is to be a rancher who farms and is also committed to survival and colonization. This will motivate them to take the necessary additional measures to protect and feed their livestock, both above and below ground.

Let’s review the EcoTech terminology that will help make this possible.

EcoTech Terminology

The terms used to describe the various grow-to-diet EcoTech configurations presented in this chapter are used with the following hierarchical order:

- **Supersystem:** The technospheres, biospheres, and aquasphere within the boundary lines of a Win-Win survival community property.

- **Facility:** A complete complex of functionally-related domes that are organized into huddles. They can be below-ground or above-ground. A facility will have multiple huddles and can also have multiple clusters.

- **Huddle:** The term “huddle” describes a group of structures built close to each other. With EcoTech engineering, a huddle is a functionally related group of domes.

- **Dome:** The term dome is used generically and a dome can be raised anywhere and for any role, whether it is for growing food in a DBS dome or raising an EcoShell II to provide shelter cover for livestock during extreme events.
- **Compartment:** A dome that is fully isolated by interior walls and airlocks.
- **Airlock:** An airlock is an environmentally secure passageway between clusters, domes, compartments, and corridors. It may include conduits for service lines.
- **Open Interior Cluster:** An open cluster with two or more domes that share the same ambient temperature. The compartments are not isolated with airlocks.
- **Micro-climate Cluster:** A cluster with two or more domes isolated by interior walls and airlocks and which share the same ambient temperature.
- **Multi-climate Cluster:** A functionally related group of compartmentalized domes with different ambient temperatures. These clusters can share resources with other huddles in the facility and can be configured for any role.
- **Stand-alone Cluster:** A single-climate, small-scale, and functionally related group of domes that operates as a self-contained miniature facility. It is self-sustaining and can be organized with a mix of dome types.
- **Corridor:** A corridor is a passageway used to link huddles and clusters together as part of an interconnected facility. They also are used to route facility service lines.
- **Footprint:** When building a cluster of 60' domes with shared walls, the effective footprint of the cluster will vary depending on the configuration. The term "footprint" as used here is a reference to the ring beam footing in the foundation.

Here is a special note regarding corridors: facilities will need environmental protections against the spread of airborne particulates, molds, spores, and disease. Therefore, corridor air pressures should be slightly less than in the structures it connects to. It will also need a high level of air filtration.

As you can see, "huddles" play a central role in supersystem facility designs. There are similarities which illustrate the concept.

Whether you cruise the world or ride a ferry across a bay, the vessel you sail on is organized vertically, by deck or levels. Similarly, massive deep-space colony ships could be organized using a spiral of modules or rings.

The point is that huddles are nothing more than the horizontal equivalent of decks and spirals. An advantage of building huddles while on earth is that they are less expensive to build. However, the lessons learned in an Earth-bound huddle must translate to colony-class space vessels and habitats.

From Cannabis to Space

The basic concepts for grow-to-market and grow-to-diet cropping were presented in "Chapter 19 – EcoTech Cropping."

Conceptually, growing premium cannabis in a micro-climate environment is like learning to fly a grow-to-market, single-engine Piper Cub. We've been there and done that; you have a license to fly; so now, you'll do what every pilot wants to do, earn a higher rating.

In this analogy, you're going to take what you learned to do in a single-engine grow-to-market Piper Cub and apply that to learning to fly a multiple engine grow-to-diet 747, which employs a multiple-species, multi-climate EcoTech farming strategy.

To illustrate the concept, we'll integrate three different growing environments into a single facility. At the core of this facility are environmentally paired-domes with tropical, subtropical, and temperate micro-climate suites. With such a facility, you can simulate every typical food growing environment on the planet.

The ability to grow in multiple climate zones makes it easy to add amazing superfoods to your daily diet. When big pharma disappears, the first rule of survival health will be:

"Let food be thy medicine, and let medicine be thy food." – Hippocrates

For example, one such superfood is Moringa oleifera. Also known as the drumstick tree, the miracle tree, etc. Moringa has been used in the healing arts of many cultures such as Ayurvedic medicine.

Moringa is a very rich source of antioxidants and nutrition. It is also antifungal, antiviral, antitumor and antidepressant. It is loaded with nutrition, and it helps to naturally lower the blood sugar and blood pressure. Also, when administered under professional care, it can help a failing heart, but great care must be given to finding the right dose.

For reproduction it has amazing attributes. In men, it increases testosterone and sperm count, but on the other hand, it is used in India to prevent pregnancy in women of childbearing age. For women at high-risk of a failed pregnancy, Moringa offers a natural way to help at-risk women to continue enjoying normal relations with their spouses.

Multi-Climate Cluster

The grow-to-market PCR (Premium Cannabis Ready) model in the previous chapter used a monocrop strategy in a micro-climate facility. Its isolated compartments help to prevent the spread of plant stressors.

In terms of strength and isolation, DBS domes in a multi-climate six-pack aquaponics cluster offer the following advantages:

- **Sub-Environmental Control:** In a multi-climate cluster, the ambient temperature will vary within the cluster along with other control factors such as humidity, seasonal lighting, and so forth.
- **Interior Access:** The use of airlocks on the interior walls of a micro-climate cluster allows for secure access to compartments within the cluster. Workers are able to do most of their work within the same cluster and gives them multiple exit points.
- **Multiple Hydroponic Methods:** With a multi-climate cluster, you can use a mix of hydroponic methods to make the best use of opportunities and growing space. This includes any combination of deep water culture (DWC), nutrient film technique (NFT), flood-and-drain, and media-bed solutions provided they all operate at the same ambient room temperature.

What is the same in the grow-to-market and grow-to-diet configurations is that domes and clusters are connected via a corridor or a series of corridors within the facility footprint, with the addition of service domes.

In this chapter, we're building a testbed facility for survival and off-world colonization. We will call it the "Mars Beta Facility."

Mars Beta Facility

Various scientific disciplines use testbeds to achieve design goals. The primary goal of Mars Beta Facility is a safe place to learn what hurts and what works, before what hurts harms you.

A Mars Beta facility is where your community members will plan and execute rigorous testing of ideas, tools, and technologies in anticipation of surviving here on earth and the potential colonization of other worlds. Granted, this may sound like fantasy now, but that will all change after a major global cataclysm.

For example, during the 2004 Indian Ocean earthquake and tsunami, 227,898 died and over fifteen billion dollars in damage was sustained.

Then there was Katrina in 2005 and the death and devastation it wrought upon America's Gulf Coast states. After this double whammy, many began looking outside conventional explanations for a deeper meaning.

The entertainment world observed this double-whammy with keen interest because it created a new wave of awareness, and like surfers waiting for that perfect wave, they rode it all the way to December 21, 2012.

The entertainment industry perverted the Mayan prophecy and this resulted in a false-publicity non-event. Consequently, in January 2013, public awareness dissipated in pools of shame as cable networks harvested their profits.

To those who smugly hold onto the notion that the Mayan prophecy was a non-event hoax, their arrogance blinds them to future double-whammy threats. This is why smart people can die so badly when these events occur.

During the 2004 Indian Ocean earthquake and tsunami, who did most of the dying? It was not indigenous peoples and wild animals. They knew instinctively to race to high ground and did. When the Earth shakes, you need to run to hills praying, "Feet don't fail me now."

Regrettably, the ones who did most of the dying had a more cultured view of life. They had the money, cars, homes, and such, and because of their modern consumer lifestyle, they failed to recognize the danger. Consequently, they had little time to flee to higher ground.

This brings us to the big question at hand. If we have another round of Sumatra and Katrina events, what happens after the next catastrophic double whammy?

When the first event happens, people will actively debate and discuss survival and other topics with a somber, wait-and-see attitude. After the second event of this double whammy occurs, this is when alarm, dismay, and fright will set in among the public.

Then there will be an awakening and it will fuel intense concerns. In this environment, governments and industry will look for a new Plan B for humanity. Building something like a Mars Beta Facility at this point, will be justified.

Mars Beta Dream Team

One could think of a Mars Beta facility like an underground submarine or a vessel that functions like a completely self-sufficient floating city.

Facilities here on earth and in future colony spaceships all share similar technical concerns and requirements with ocean-going vessels. Ergo, one can imagine domes as landlocked, terrestrial submarines.

In the ocean, the waves are in the water, but in a terrestrial Win-Win, they can be the horizontal seismic waves of a catastrophic 9.0+ earthquake or the tempest of hurricane winds.

To handle diverse environments, you want naval architects and marine engineers to design and build planetary facilities that serve as a testbed for future space stations and colony ships.

- **Naval Architects:** They design naval vessels for the most difficult environment in the world, storm forces at sea. Using science, advanced engineering tools, art, and a fine eye for detail, they design them to stand up to the storm forces at sea.
- **Marine Engineers:** Once a naval architect designs a vessel, a marine engineer will design and organize the systems within it to bring it to life. No detail is too small or too large, and they determine exactly how to support the vessel's mission role within the space available.

This attention to survivability in adverse conditions is essential for Win-Win all-hazards concrete domes with overcover. Like putting a puzzle together, nothing can be left out when the vessel is finished, and there can be no missing pieces. However, there is a caveat.

One might not expect to see wheelchairs in a colony ship. However, with a Mars Beta facility; disability access is a non-negotiable requirement for creating a realistic design model.

Mars Beta Facility Design Model

The concept of a space station with city-sized permanent settlements is based on the L4 and L5 Lagrangian points. These are two points in space that are located in advance of and behind the moon in its orbit around the earth.

It started in 1974 with a paper titled "The Colonization of Space" by Gerard K. O'Neill. The following year Carolyn Meinel and Keith Henson, founded the L5 Society. It would behoove your technical team to immerse itself in L5 society literature and media.

Hence, a Mars Beta facility design uses four interconnected, all-hazards below-ground farming huddles: aquaponics, farmyards, hydroponics orchards, and aquaponics orchards. These huddles are interconnected with a central corridor and employ 2' high raised floors.

A special note on the use of raised floors and walkways. The ideal material is recycled plastic decking. It is as easy to work with as wood, and you can use woodworking tools with it. How do they compare? The survival benefits of recycled plastic decking are:

- Not as slippery as wood.
- No mold or mildew like wood.
- No warping or twisting like wood.
- It can be made to look like anything
- Easy to clean and remains attractive
- Can last for a thousand years

Raised floors will allow for easy access to the water, drainage, waste, and aquasphere service lines in the facility. Not only does this help with maintenance; it also allows the ability to reconfigure the facility as needs arise.

To illustrate the concept, we'll us a Mars Beta testbed facility, beginning with the core huddle of the facility, the aquaponics huddle.

Aquaponics Huddle

The Mars Beta aquaponics huddle is multi-climate, multi-species huddle organized into three compartmentalized climate pairs, each with its own primary goal:

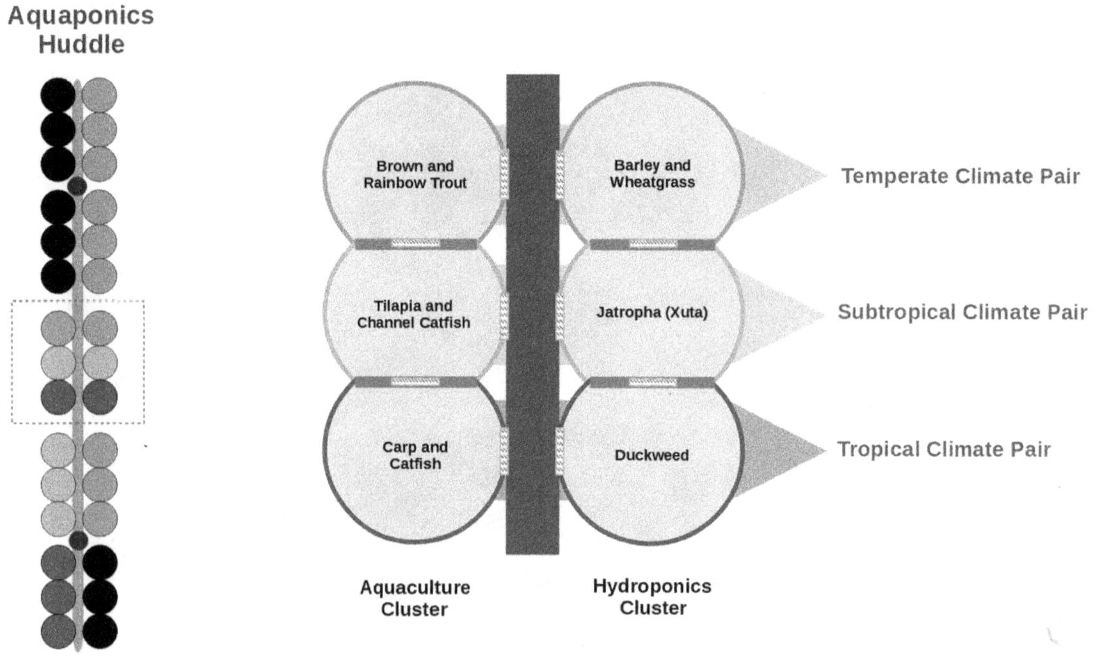

- **Temperate Climate Pair:** Fodder, fish feed, and food.
- **Subtropical Climate Pair:** Food and biofuel and biodiesel for machinery and power.
- **Tropical Climate Pair:** High-protein fodder, fish feed, and food.

The air temperature setpoint in the hydroponic sub-system dome determines the choice of plant and animal species in each multi-climate pair.

Temperate Climate Pair

The aquaculture dome supports the paired hydroponics dome and the temperate orchard huddle.

- **Aquaculture Dome:** Two species of trout, Brown and Rainbow, will be raised in the associated aquaculture dome, using the environmental setpoints of the hydroponics dome.
- **Hydroponics Dome:** Fast-growing cool weather fodder species such as barley and wheatgrass will be grown in DWC tanks.

Growing wheatgrass is highly advisable. It is ideal for juicing as an excellent food source of vitamins and minerals for survivors.

Subtropical Climate Pair

The aquaculture dome supports the paired hydroponics dome and the subtropical orchard huddle.

The ability to produce biofuel for community machinery and power is essential. While the fish will serve as good food sources, the fuel derived from plants grown in the hydroponics domes will have a direct impact on your natural energy choices.

- **Aquaculture Dome:** Tilapia and channel catfish are raised in the aquaculture dome using the environmental setpoints of the hydroponics dome.
- **Hydroponics Dome:** Jatropha biofuel and food. These trees will require a large media-bed system to stand.

Jatropha is recommended because it is considered by many experts as the leading species for biodiesel, plus it is popular with the aviation industry for use as a renewable jet fuel.

Airlines are actively seeking ways to power their jets with renewable biofuels, and several plant species are being tested. Algae and jatropha are two of them. Airlines are testing these biofuels with a blended mix of conventional jet fuel and biofuel.

A key point to remember with jatropha is that while it can be used for biofuel, most species are toxic to humans and animals. Therefore, a good choice is non-toxic jatropha.

A non-toxic jatropha known as "Xuta," grows naturally in Mexico, and locals enjoy it as a traditional part of their diet. Also known as piñón manso (mild peanut) for their flavor, locals enjoy them roasted and cooked. Xuta is also used for fish and animal feed.

Tropical Climate Pair

The aquaculture dome supports the paired hydroponics dome and the tropical orchard huddle.

- **Aquaculture Dome:** Carp and flathead catfish are raised in the aquaculture dome using the environmental setpoints of the hydroponics dome.
- **Hydroponics Dome:** Duckweed for biofuel and animal feed, primarily for the chickens and rabbits raised in the farmyard huddle.

Carp is an oily freshwater fish also known as a fatty fish. When raised in clean water, they are a tasty food fish, and this is important because oily fish like salmon and carp are excellent sources for the important Omega-3s (EPA and DHA).

However, carp is also a very bony fish. Gefilte fish or "stuffed fish" is a popular Yiddish dish made from a poached mixture of ground and deboned carp. You can use a prepared mixture of horseradish and beets to give your Gefilte fish a nice splash of flavor.

Another excellent fish species for tropical climate aquaculture is catfish, and when it comes to good eating varieties, the two top contenders are channel and flathead. Depending on the environmental setpoints, channel catfish can be raised in both subtropical and tropical clusters. Flathead catfish are better suited to a tropical climate and are tasty as well.

In the hydroponics dome, fast-growing duckweed is grown for fish and animal feed and can also be a possible food source for people. This will be the primary use, but is can also be utilized to produce biobutanol as a substitute for ethanol. Plus, it can be processed into a solvent for a wide variety of chemical and textile processes.

Duckweed is a small plant and one of the fastest-growing there is. It floats on the water's surface; so it'll grow in tanks similar to the DWC tanks in your temperate cluster but without the Styrofoam rafts. Once you find the right environmental setpoints, it can double its weight in as little as 16 hours; so this is a high-maintenance crop.

We've covered the multi-climate aquaculture and hydroponics domes in our aquaponics huddle. Now let's turn our attention to the Mars Beta farmyard huddle.

Farmyard Huddle

The farmyard huddle is comprised of 4, 3-dome multi-climate clusters with optimized environmental controls. It uses multi-climate clusters for three principal reasons:

- **Isolation:** A major concern with farming in a facility is the transmission of disease and pests. To contain these risks, the clusters are compartmentalized, with shared interior walls and airlocks.
- **Optimization:** In a Mars Beta facility, individual compartments can be optimized for additional environmental issues, such as humidity and lighting.

- **Mineralization:** In "Chapter 14 - Feeding 1,000 Martians," we learned why mineralization is the command input for all EcoTech systems and here is where the farmyard huddle plays a critical role.

The huddle has four compartmentalized clusters, separated by a common corridor.

- The two clusters to the right of the corridor are for mineralization and husbandry.
- The two to the left are for processing the output of the this and the aquaponics huddle.

In a similar manner to the Aquaponics Huddle, functional pairing is used as follows:

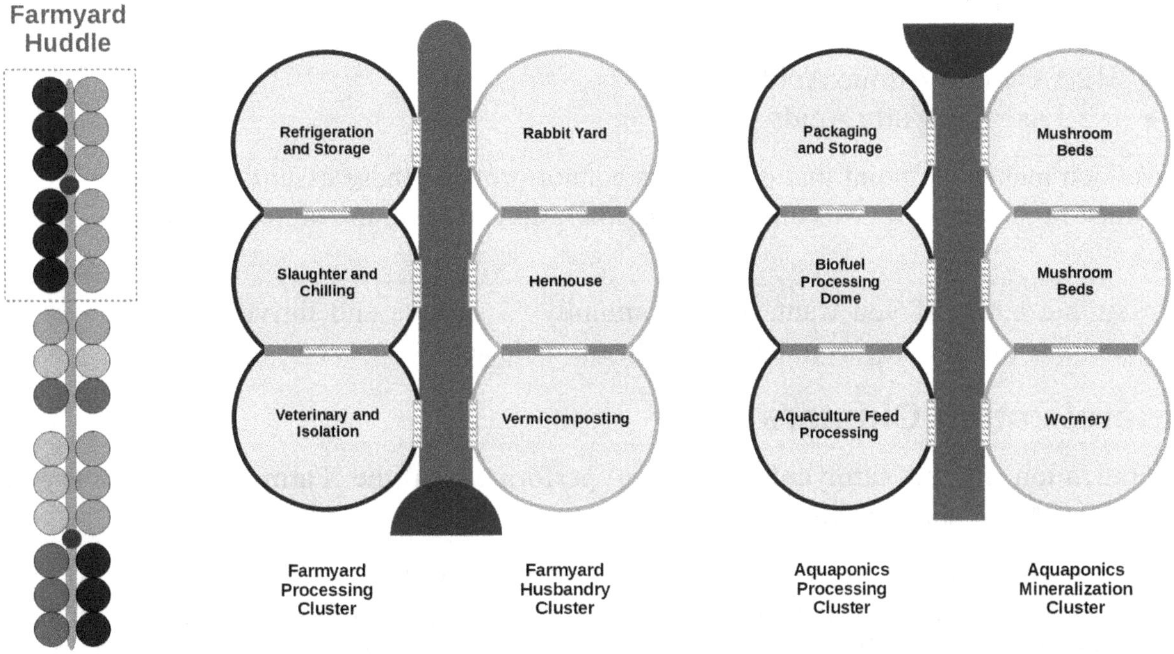

- **Farmyard Husbandry and Aquaponics Mineralization Clusters:** This cluster pair begins with the rabbit yard, henhouse, and vermicomposting compartments. Manure and plant waste from the processing domes and worm wee and castings from the wormery is utilized in the vermicomposting compartment.
- **Farmyard Processing and Aquaponics Processing Clusters:** This cluster pair is used to process finished foods, fuels, and animal feed.

It is a given that mineralization is essential, but which one are essential?

Essential Minerals

If you go online and use the search term "essential minerals," you'll need to sort through a rats nest of spinmeister advertising, special interest sites, and so forth. What will they all have in common? Nothing, because their numbers and claims will span the horizon.

A simple way to cut through the fog of product differentiation is to find a serviceable model suited to survival and colonization nutrition. Such a model was presented by Dr. Joel Wallach, in his famous lecture "Dead Doctors Don't Lie." Based on research and autopsies on humans and animals, Wallach identified the following essential nutrients:

- 60 Essential Minerals
- 16 Essential Vitamins
- 12 Essential Amino Acids
- 3 Essential Fatty Acids

Wallach makes the point that our bodies cannot produce these essential nutrients. Rather, they must be in the foods we consume, and when they are not, the deficiencies can cause disease.

In simple terms, if you want your community to survive and thrive, you rocks in your head, and this process begins in the mineralization clusters.

Mineralization Clusters

Mineralization in the farmyard huddle is performed in the Farmyard Husbandry and Aquaponics Mineralization clusters as follows:

- **Farm Animals:** The rabid yard is used to raise domestic rabbits for food, dog food, and fertilizer. It is next to the henhouse which is primarily used for eggs, meat, and fertilizer. Eggshells, plant matter, and rabbit and chicken manure are used in the vermicomposting compartment.

- **Mineralization Uptake:** In the vermicomposting compartment, rock dust, food scraps, compost from and worm castings, and worm tea are combined in the mushroom beds. As there are two compartments, a variety of mushrooms can be grown. Used for uptake, they work like above-ground pioneer plants such as dandelions.

- **Biological Mineralization:** To infuse essential minerals into the plants you're growing in your hydroponics domes, you must first get them into the fish you'll use to fertilize them organically. In the wormery, mineral-rich mushrooms are harvested and blended into worm compost for the wormery along with other nutrients. Excess worm castings, and worm tea output can be marketed for additional community revenues.

Chicken breeds can be grown with stacked yards, where different breeds are situated one above. All are slaughtered in the same humane manner.

Not all rabbit breeds are suitable for human consumption, such as the Standard Rex, which is prized for its fur and which can also be used for dog foot.

For human consumption, a rabbit in high-demand is the New Zealand breed, which can weigh up to 12 lbs. As with the henhouse, you can also grow different rabbit breeds using stacked vertical yards.

Keep in mind that this is not a free-range situation since the animals never have access to open ground. Cages and pens are only used for necessary care.

Your animals will never see the light of day, and therefore a clean kill is their only best end. Also, consider this. You will spend a great deal of time in whatever technosphere you create; it will be in a church community.

Sometimes, it's better to feed the soul than the stomach, and so you may wish to adorn your facility with these insightful words of compassion:

"The greatness of a nation and its moral progress can be judged by the way its animals are treated." —Mahatma Gandhi

For this reason, your rabbitry and henhouse domes need to employ an indoor yard design; so the animals can have natural freedom of movement within their compartments. Productive technospheres are humane and as natural as possible.

Also, a technosphere is not limited to one dome or compartment. A good example is why the henhouse compartment is adjacent to the compartment's vermicomposting compartment in the farmyard huddle.

Chickens are very fond of compost piles and their plentiful bounties of bugs, seeds, etc., to peck upon all day.

Use such characteristics to your advantage.

Instead of bringing feed to the chickens, build a chicken gateway between the henhouse and vermicomposting compartments.

At the beginning of the day cycle, open the gateway and let your chickens run into the vermicomposting dome to feed on the compost piles.

At the beginning of the night cycle, darken the lighting in the compartments, to signal the chickens that it is time to return to the henhouse for the night.

This same level of humane care and attention is used in the processing clusters in this huddle as well.

Processing Clusters

Grow-to-diet manufacturing in the farmyard huddle is where harvested plants and animals are processed into intermediary or finished products and is performed in the barnyard processing and aquaponics processing clusters as follows:

The aquaponics processing cluster is where fish feed, fuels, and chemicals are processed and stored as follows:

- **Aquaculture Feed Processing:** This compartment is where fish feed is prepared for each species of fish raised in the aquaponics huddle. Fish harvests are used for food and the processing by-products are used for making fish feed for small fry. These, plus worms from the wormery, become mineralized high-protein fish feed.
- **Biofuel and Chemical Processing:** Harvests of jatropha and duckweed from the aquaponics huddle are processed into biofuels, solvents and other essential chemicals need for community operations. Then, packaged and stored for use as required.

The farmyard processing cluster supports the processing of fresh meat, fish, and fowl and features chilling and refrigeration equipment as follows:

- **Veterinary and Isolation:** Animals get sick. In many cases, a diligent intervention can stop the illness's spread so the animals can recover in isolation. Then returned to production instead of being preemptively slaughtered.
- **Slaughter:** On a scheduled based, fish from the aquaponics huddle and rabbits and hens from the farmyard huddle are humanely processed and chilled. This also includes fresh eggs from the henhouse which are also processed into products.
- **Chilling and Refrigeration:** This cluster utilizes industrial-grade chilling and refrigeration equipment for health safety. Properly chilled animal carcasses, eggs, and fish fillets can be transferred to the refrigeration dome aging and long term storage.

Death must be instantaneous with all culled animals, and the bodies drained of blood. Air chilling is the preferred method for Ecotech farming. A killing cone is used for chickens, and a hopper popper is used for rabbits. Now let's move on to the orchards huddle.

Orchards Huddle

The multi-climate aquaponics huddle raises naturally adapted fish species for temperate, subtropical, and tropical environments.

The nitrate-rich output from each aquaculture dome is used in an environmentally paired hydroponic dome in the aquaponics huddle. It is also used in one of the three-dome, compartmentalized hydroponics clusters in the orchard huddles.

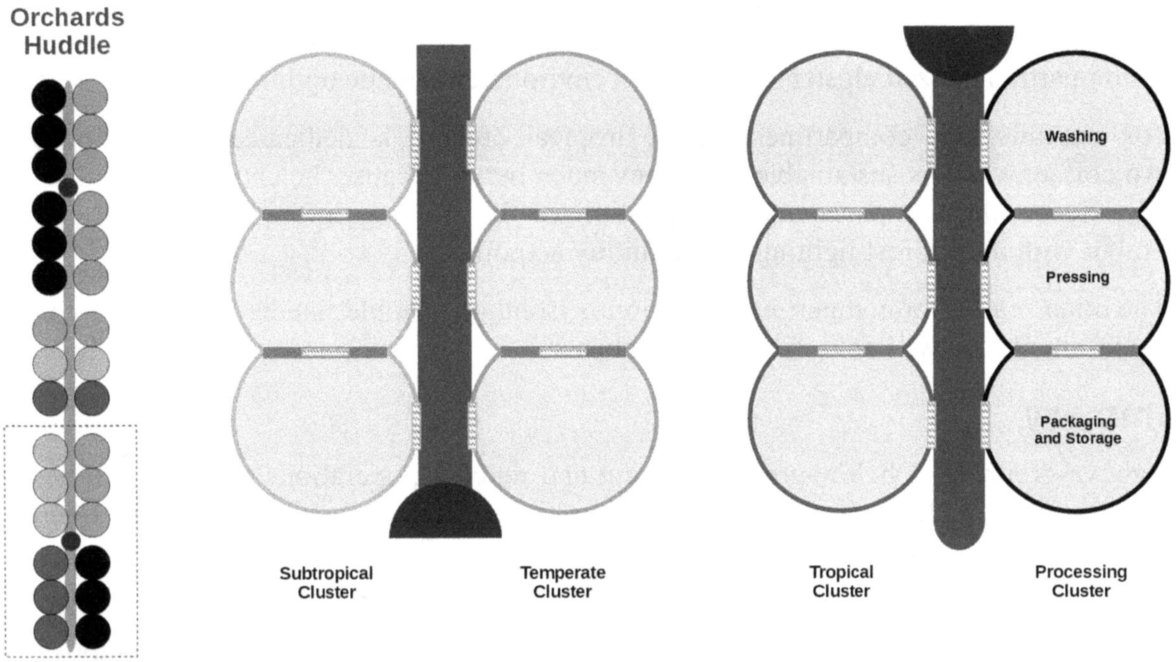

In the orchards huddle, there are four compartmentalized, micro-climate clusters. Three are for hydroponics and one is for processing. Each cluster is fully compartmentalized with interior walls and airlocks as follows:

- **Temperate Orchard:** Fruit trees such as apples and pears in deep media beds and leafy greens in nutrient film technique (NFT) channels.
- **Subtropical Orchard:** Fruit trees are mango, avocado, and superfood trees like moringa. Also, this is a great climate for growing spices and sweeteners like stevia and monk fruit in NFT or flood-and-drain systems.
- **Tropical Orchard:** Fruit trees like bananas, cacao, coffee, and papaya are in deep media beds. After that, the choices are awesome. There are aloe vera, brahmi, and comfrey for health, and basil, chilies, cilantro, mint, parsley, pepper, stevia, thyme, tumeric, and vanilla for spices.
- **Orchard Processing:** Wash stations, prep areas, packaging, and refrigeration as required.

Given that each dome in the three orchard clusters is designed for the same temperature zone, why not use an open-interior design, as opposed to the extra expense of compartmentalizing them? The answer is twofold.

Although it costs less to build an open-interior micro-climate cluster, this strategy does not allow for species optimization within the same climate zone. Conversely, with a micro-climate compartmentalized cluster, each dome's environment can be optimized.

For example, one compartment in the tropical orchard is dedicated to growing shade grown coffee, which is sustainable and tastes much better because the cherries can ripen more slowly. Hence, this compartment can be optimized for growing coffee in a tropical environment, but with deep forest lighting and humidity setpoints.

The other reason for compartmentalization is isolation. Should fate be unkind and you lose a compartment, you will not lose the entire cluster.

Summary

The above-ground and below-ground farming and ranching operations and the facilities discussed, so far, provide a complete EcoTech supersystem design capable of feeding 1,000 survivors or future space colonists with a nutritious balanced diet.

More importantly, no matter what man or nature throws at us, this Mars Beta facility will feed pioneers and survivors with a healthy diet of fresh foods when they need them most.

Now, let's give our community some cultural panache and a lot more flavor with a very unique stand-alone. The very one that will become the community's inner sanctum.

21

Inner Sanctum

In "Chapter 20 – EcoTech Supersystem," we introduced the Mars Beta facility concept. The goal is to prove it works here so we can take it there with confidence – wherever there is.

To be successful, it must produce a completely organic diet that is varied, nutritious, satisfying, and delicious. In short, three squares a day and treats.

The example facility shown in that chapter demonstrates the scope of design required to feed 1,000 people a day and addresses the following technical requirements:

- **Toolkit for Colonization:** The Mars Beta design uses three things known to exist on Mars: soil, water, and basalt rock. Hence, one can think of the Mars Beta concept as a colonization toolkit. Use what you need given the circumstances.
- **Infinitely Scalable Supersystem:** The Mars Beta facility described in the previous chapter is part of a Win-Win property supersystem, with ranching and farming above-ground and intensive below-ground farming.
- **Designed for Adaptation:** Dietary, environmental, and production needs will change over time. Therefore, the main goal is to build a proven concept design that can be quickly expanded and reconfigured.

This brings us what we'll be building in this chapter, and the axiom, "sometimes it is better to feed the soul than the stomach."

Mars Beta is about feeding the stomach. Now, we're going to feed the soul.

Inner Sanctum

Return on investment (ROI) drives corporations and organizations to seek and applaud revenue, and the Mars Beta facility discussed in the previous chapter answers that need. However, a Win-Win survival church also feed the soul in a way that celebrates and honors human dignity and self-worth.

What does that entail? An inspiring and sacred place where members can gather to celebrate new life, console sorrows, formulate plans, and to learn new skills. To this end, the orchard huddle discussed in this chapter shall serve as a springboard to the final EcoTech dome configuration discussed in this book.

In practical terms, imagine how boring life would be after years of staring at spartan, battleship-gray, and condo-white interior color schemes. Where is the ambiance?

Ambiance describes the mood, character, quality, tone, and atmosphere of restaurants. It is also the perfect term to describe EcoTech designs with high livability values that support a spiritual, food-centered lifestyle.

A multi-generational solution is a design I call the "Inner Sanctum." A stand-alone huddle with permanent orchards. An unchanging legacy gift from the founders to future generations, for the celebration of life.

Designed for contemplation and inspiration, it is where sleepless leaders can find insight and clarity in the still of the night and where a young man can propose marriage to the love of his life.

In this way, it can connect future generations with the love and wisdom of their forebearers. Hence, a design team with a balanced view of technology and inspiration is needed.

Design Team

In "Chapter 10 – Design Team and Infrastructure," we identified the members of your engineering team, beginning with the leader, a woman in her forties, a gifted custom jewelry designer, with a family and a supportive husband.

Perhaps you've wanted to ask, "Hey Marshall, whatever happened to that nice lady?"

The thought of entrusting the interior design of the inner sanctum to a right angle guy haunts me with disturbing visions of dreary, uninspiring man caves. Rather, this needs a loving eye and a woman's touch and now is the time for that nice lady to shine.

Her first step will be to choose a theme for the inner sanctum that is truly inspiring.

Design Theme

Theme-based configurations are often based on books and movies, like *Around the World in 80 Days* (1956). While the film is a bit dated, it nonetheless offers an ideal movie theme for our inner sanctum. It was set in 1872, and the plot follows Phileas Fogg on his journey to circumnavigate the world in eighty days.

Therefore, the theme for our vineyard and orchard cluster will be, "Around The World in 80 Inches," which is the approximate length of the airlocks used in this stand-alone cluster.

Here we have a delightful opportunity to create two vineyard and orchard clusters with variants of the same theme.

There is also a practical aspect for this. How can a Mediterranean diet be authentic without olive oil, grapes, juice, wine, and red vinegar? Unthinkable!

Therefore, the first variant is California's Napa Valley. A region blessed with a wonderful Mediterranean climate, and there you will often see two venerable companion species together, grapes and olive trees.

The second variant can be from another region with a Mediterranean climate, such as France, Italy, or Spain, where grapes and olives also flourish together in a Mediterranean climate.

Therefore, let's assume the two growing regions selected for the inner sanctum are Napa Valley and France. Now that we have the settings for our theme, we need to pick a time.

Although the first commercial winery in Napa Valley was established in 1861, the design theme is set in 1956, the year the movie *Around the World in 80 Days* (1956) was released.

Be assured, there is a very scientific and well-pondered rationale for selecting this period. Yours truly has always dreamed of the day when I could settle down somewhere nice in the wine country with two large rescue dogs and an old 1950's pickup truck. That's the beautiful thing about domes. They are ideal for making dreams come true, so let's get' er done.

That was fun. Now back to work.

Growing Regions

Our two "Around The World in 80 Inches" Mediterranean growing regions have been chosen. The fun of this configuration is that you can stand in France and admire the olives. Then, turn around and walk through an eighty-inch long airlock into California, just in time for a bountiful fiesta, complete with mariachi music and lots of dancing. What's not to like?

The next step in the design process is selecting suitable grape and olive varieties from each region.

It can take seven to ten years for an olive tree to begin fruiting and about three years for grapevines. Therefore, you will need potted mature plants of fruiting age of each species to be grown in both orchards for media-bed transplantation.

Also, since our inner sanctum theme is set in the year 1956, church members interested in food history, will need to recreate what everyday life was like in orchards and vineyards in those times. Why is this year useful? In 1956 our waters were still relatively pure; our skies were clear; and our nation believed in itself, and what it could do. It was a time worth remembering.

Let's review.

We have our theme, a date, and two regional settings. It is now time for the right-angle types to get up to speed because this is where science and art require a Vulcan mind-meld.

Innovation Opportunity

For you creative types, the secret of tapping the hidden potential of your right-angle team members is easy to miss. So, here it is.

Right angle types are always working the angles because that's what they do. Use it!

Let's assume that our team leader has gathered her engineering team together and briefed them on the goals for the inner sanctum with its "Around The World in 80 Inches" theme.

She says, "That's the mission folks, and now I'm looking for ideas. Anyone?"

The first to speak says, "With the compartmentalized orchards in the Mars Beta facility, they had to design for a variable cropping environment. However, the Inner Sanctum is a whole new thing. It is a permanent cropping environment, which means we can build the hydroponic media beds for a ground-level height. Folks can literally walk out of an airlock and onto the orchard media bed without navigating steps or platforms."

"I like that," she answers, "Tell me what it would look like as I'm walking through a compartment airlock?"

"I got this one," comes a snappy response from another engineer. "Walking out of the airlock, you enter the outer pathway around the dome. The vineyards and orchards are located in the center and level with the pathway. The top layer of their media beds and the pathways will merge seamlessly as a single and continuous level surface."

"I like that image," she answers cautiously, "But what does this give us in practical terms?"

Another engineer speaks up. "I do a lot of design work on harvesting and processing, and with this floor-level design, there are real advantages besides pathway access. You obviously have more height for the trees to grow, but what I like most is what we're not going to need."

With the other orchards in the facility, scissor lifts are necessary. With this floor-level design, no scissor lifts are required. Instead, electric shaker rakes and tall harvest ladders are all that's needed. No need to clutter up the view."

"I like that," she exclaims. "And no flak from our beloved bean counters. Anyone else?"

Another engineer chimes in. "We can use various colors of landscape rock for the top cover of the media beds." This sparks ideas and connections for a wonderful discussion.

The team's senior engineer, who has been quiet until now, speaks up. "One concern I have is that we have high-nutrition demand plants which means we'll have to run the aquaculture at a high rate."

"So you're talking about a plan B?"

"Precisely," replies the engineer, "There needs to be backup, and this ground-level orchard configuration is ideal for adding koi ponds, because the cluster has universal setpoints for air temperature. Consequently, linking koi ponds with the main system is possible and we can run both of them independently until needed."

"Sounds like we have a plan," she says with a beaming smile.

A short pause ensues as the ideas come together in everyone's minds, and then the room is suddenly filled with happy faces and applause. The positive vibes bring a big smile to the team leader's face, "Brilliant. Simply brilliant. I want it all. Where do we start?"

The room explodes with laughter as a voice from the back of the room rings out, "We dig!"

"That's an interesting first step," she chuckles. "I'll take it. OK folks, let's work the plan."

Inner Sanctum Configuration

The Mars Beta inner sanctum stand-alone cluster will be a single-climate, miniature facility, with a mix of open-interior and compartmentalized domes.

Arranged in a similar manner as a six-pack. There are two open-interior three-dome clusters for the orchards, which are anchored at one end by two specialized compartments and a service dome:

- **Aquaculture:** This aquaculture dome houses all of the environmental control systems and aquaculture fish farming. Two fish species will be raised in support of two, theme-based hydroponic sub-system vineyard and orchard clusters.
- **Orchard Processing:** This compartment is dedicated to harvest processing and cold storage. It also houses the related processing areas for oil presses, canning, and fermentation.

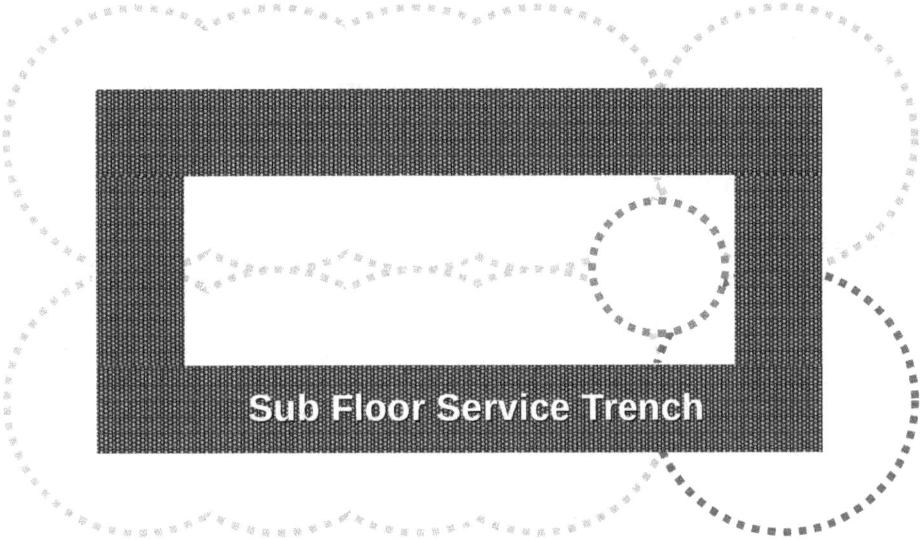
Sub Floor Service Trench

Sub Floor Service Trench

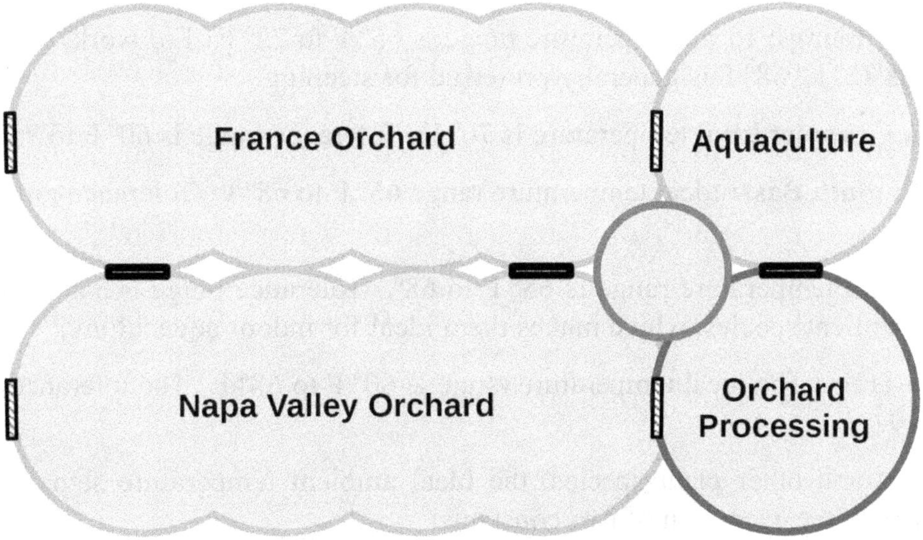
France Orchard
Aquaculture
Napa Valley Orchard
Orchard Processing

Construction begins with a deep service trench in the sub-foundation with a sump. All water and waste service lines are run here. We'll discuss this more later.

Above the trench are the aquaculture, processing, service domes, and two 3-dome open-interior vineyards and orchards.

The two theme-based variants are:

- **Napa Valley Orchard:** A 3-dome open-interior orchard cluster. There are a shared wall and airlock between the service and aquaculture compartments and the France orchard.
- **France Orchard:** A 3-dome open-interior orchard cluster. Similarly, there are a shared wall and airlock between the Napa Valley orchard and the orchard processing compartments.

A single environmental air temperature setpoint is used for the entire stand-alone cluster. However, all of the other environmental controls for each compartment and orchard cluster can be fine-tuned for the particular plant species being grown.

Environmental Control

In "Chapter 19 – EcoTech Cropping," we stated that the command input is the fish species in your aquaculture dome. With this permanent stand-alone cluster, the command input remains the same, the fish. However, with a special purpose cluster such as this, humans need to be added to the criteria.

Here are five species to use for determining the ambient temperature setpoints for the cluster and the optimized setpoints for each orchard. They are:

- **Human Beings:** Ideal temperature range is 65° F to 72° F. For work, optimal temperature is 72° F. 68° F is generally preferred for sleeping.
- **Black Crappie:** Ideal temperature is 70° F. Tolerance range is 60° F to 75° F.
- **Smallmouth Bass:** Ideal temperature range 65° F to 68° F. Tolerance range is 60° F to 73° F.
- **Koi:** Ideal temperature range is 65° F to 68°. Tolerance range is 34° F to 90° F. Koi are a resilient species, which makes them ideal for indoor aquaculture.
- **Olive Trees:** The ideal temperature range is 60° F to 68° F. The tolerance range is 20° F to 104° F.

With grapes and other plant species, the ideal ambient temperature setpoints vary with each cultivar with the exception of two constants:

- Frost-free setpoints
- Seasonal environmental cues

By combining this level of control with pest and competition free environment, below-ground farmers can produce the very best quality produce with higher yields per square yard than conventional crops. The time to harvest is also less, and all of this with just ten percent of the water needed for a conventional crop of the same size.

What makes this work? Both orchards use the same temperature setpoints, but each has the ability to signal plants when to advance through their various growth and resting stages with great precision. It's called a seasonal environment.

Seasonal Environment

Environmental setpoints in the orchards need seasonal adjustments along with corresponding changes in day and night lighting cycles.

Winter for an example, is a gradual cycle process where the average temperature is 65° F with shorter days; whereas, summer has an average temperature of 72° F with longer days.

Cluster Foundation

In the previous chapter, we created a facility with corridors and dome interiors designed to be rapidly reconfigurable, as circumstances dictate. Like the Marines say, "Improvise, Adapt, Overcome."

The inner sanctum represents an entirely different design goal with permanent interiors and cropping. It is also the only dome configuration in this book with a service trench.

Given this new trench twist, what exactly are we looking at? In a word, footprint.

Each dome or compartment in this stand-alone 8-dome cluster configuration will be connected with shared walls and airlocks above the foundation. This entire cluster is raised using a single multi-dome airform.

In other configurations, raised floors are used to run service lines throughout the cluster.

With this configuration, the service trench remains out of sight throughout the entire cluster. It is used for services lines and access, sumps, tanks, and backup manual controls.

The service trench extends under all eight domes in the cluster. Here is where the media bed tanks for the trees and vines are located. Also, the Koi ponds are mounted above the service trench with the necessary service lines and controls.

For these reasons, a service trench needs to be as wide as possible, especially in the orchards. In the service, aquaculture, and orchard processing compartments, they can be smaller. This is the case for a service trench because it does not have a load-bearing role for the dome cluster's shell. That is provided by the ring beam footer.

Therefore, a service trench affords the advantages of a basement, without the need to provide load-bearing support for the structure. However, it will need to support the weight of extremely large hydroponics tanks and Koi ponds.

Furthermore, while the service trenches are square-shaped, the media beds for the orchards and the Koi ponds are not. They are designed with curves to make them look more natural.

Like fiberglass swimming pools, media beds and Koi ponds can be built to almost any shape. The rest is mounting and plumbing. So the service trench requires ample room for service lines and a floor capable of supporting heavy farming systems.

Trench Construction

In "Chapter 11 – EcoShells I & II," we introduced the all-hazards dome foundation, which incorporates a unique sub-floor design that David B. South and I worked on back in 2016.

There are two basic earthwork excavation levels with this method.

- **Top Level:** The top level is used for the ring beam footing. The ring beam footing is the load-bearing part of the structure and defines its footprint. Eventually, the service trench will be constructed inside the footprint.
- **Bottom Level:** Inside the top level footprint, the bottom level is also excavated to a sufficient depth for a slotted-drain system and a notched-footing floor slab.

This configuration requires a special variation of the all-hazards design, and the seven principal differences are:

1. **Top Level Excavation:** The earthwork for the orchard's ring beam footing represents the highest excavation level in the foundation and defines the cluster's footprint.
2. **Bottom Level Excavation:** It is essential that the bottom level be well inside the footprint. The service trench must not compromise the cluster's load-bearing support. The depth of this level must accommodate the slotted-storm drain system at the very bottom of the foundation and the sub-floor concrete service trench above it.
3. **Wood Framing:** The service trench is built using the same methods as a poured basement. Wood forms are used to create pour areas for the entire trench system under the cluster. The walls for an all-hazards service trench should be 12" thick and the floor 18" thick. The entire trench structure is strengthened with basalt reinforcement.
4. **Concrete Pour:** The entire trench system must be poured in a single effort for maximum strength, durability, and water resistance. Your engineering team has to choose the best mix for your area and use a concrete waterproofing admixture.
5. **Sand Fill:** After the service trench has cured, the wood forms are removed and the remaining air space between the trench system and earthwork is filled with wet sand and

compacted. This is essential. The outside of the service trench must be in direct contact with the earth around it; so it can handle horizontal earthquake waves. Everything in the foundation needs to be flush level when finished.

6. **Polypropylene Dome Pad Water Barrier:** With the standard all-hazards design, the water barrier is a single sheet of polypropylene that covers the top layer of the sub-foundation. The same approach is used with this stand-alone cluster, with one exception. This polypropylene barrier must have openings for the service trench.
7. **Pour the Pad:** Pour the dome pads as you would with the standard all-hazards design. When it is cured, you are ready to place the media-bed tanks and the Koi ponds and run all the necessary service lines and control systems.

At this point, you are ready to raise the dome cluster and finish the build with a lot of special attention to the interior details.

Now Dear Reader, you've got the technical basics for building domes and growing food for survival and colonization. Are there more sub-systems and details to consider?

If this were a football game, this is when you see the ball coming at you. Do you step aside, or do you catch it and run to victory, and if so, what does victory look like?

For that we must travel far into the future.

Paradise 2315

We find ourselves on Planet Paradise, and the Terran year is 2315. When the first colonists began to settle it a century earlier, Paradise was not such a paradise. Now, it is a vibrant planet, and in the capital, the city museum has opened a massive new exhibit featuring a complete recreation of the original Mars Beta Inner Sanctum stand-alone cluster.

A group of school children is forming inside the museum's main hall. Near the entrance to the new Mars Beta exhibit, their guide, a young history major from the local university, steps onto a small pedestal to address the group. Her name is Akira, and she is a fourth-generation colonist in her early twenties.

Because the gravity of Paradise is 82% of Earth's, Akira's generation has less muscle mass, and she is slightly taller and more flexible than her Terran ancestors. Also, sunlight on Paradise is different and over time, this triggered a mutation which decreased the production of melanin. This, plus a healthy diet, has made Akira's generation easy to recognize, thanks to their large, blue-green eyes.

She smiles warmly and begins, "Good morning, children. I'm Akira and I'll be your guide today. We're going to begin our tour of the Napa Valley orchard; so please follow me as we walk to the center of the exhibit."

"Keep in mind children; it is now dawn in in the Napa Valley orchard; so please walk inside the lighted path." She leans forward toward the children grouped about her, "Who wants to go to Earth?"

With a gleeful shout, the children exclaim, "We do! We do!" With that Akira leads the group to a small circular garden area in the cluster that has a small fountain in the center and lowers a pedestal from the side of the fountain. The teacher for the class rounds up the stragglers and gives Akira a nod to let her know that she can begin the presentation.

"Children, we are standing in the middle of the Napa Valley orchard. When the first Inner Sanctum was built, the lighting cycles programmed into the environmental control system mimicked the natural cycle, both in terms of luminescence and movement. This was quite a feat when you think about the technology of the day."

"The original inner sanctum cluster was constructed with an east-west orientation," she explains while turning her body slightly to her left and then points toward the eastern side of the orchard."

"In a moment, we'll begin to see the first light of morning and the magnificent designs of a talented woman by the name of Betsy Fine. She was chosen to design the inner sanctum around a movie theme, and her mandate was a simple one, to create a special place for survivors. A place where they could feed their souls as well as their stomachs."

Akira gracefully lifts and extends her hand, "And behold children; the day comes."

As the lighting simulates the early glow of dawn, she continues, "During the Days of Darkness and Sorrow, when humanity struggled to survive on our distant home world, there were times when many feared that humankind was at the brink. It was a terribly stressful time for all, and troubled souls would wander into this orchard, as others slept, to watch the artificial sunrise together."

"But, but… it is not a real sun," one young boy blurts out.

"You're very right, and the Founders knew this. However, they found that their bodies, like those of the plants and animals they raised, could not clearly distinguish LED lighting from the real thing. Consequently, this artificial illumination could satisfy their biological need to make life work and it did."

Lowering her hand as the early glow of morning casts a warm light upon her light brown shoulder-length hair, she turns to face the children. "And now, I am going to advance the environmental clock to midday, so you can see the vineyards and orchards in all their splendor."

Akira cues the exhibit system by gracefully raising her hands palm up. The lighting slowly keeps pace, and advances to midday levels.

"Children, every nook and cranny of this cluster had a sacred meaning to the Founders, and this very place where we now stand is called the wedding ring. It was here that young couples took their vows before the entire community. During weddings, the only light in the orchard aside from safety lighting was from the sea of light that was created by everyone at the ceremony who held a candle in their hands."

"Can I get married that way?" a young girl asks enthusiastically.

"You know that's one of our most popular questions," Akira explains. "It is why our curators are now working to develop a special program to do just that." With a wink, she adds, "And yes, I want the same thing too."

"Now, children please turn around and face the shared wall." She waves her hand across the view of the shared wall behind them.

"Betsy Fine decided to use this side of the cluster with the shared wall as a backdrop for a sleepy little Napa Valley town from 1956. This was the year the movie, *Around the World In Eighty Days*, was first released. This is also the theme for the Inner Sanctum."

Akira points to an area of the shared wall between the first and second airlocks to her left.

"Betsy named the entire shared wall Calistoga, after a small Napa Valley town. And here we see her first false front structure, the Calistoga Cafe."

The interior lights in the false front cafe sparkle to life. "Each of Betsy's false-fronts has enough space for something useful, such as a snack bar or a small library, but it was the areas directly in front of the false fronts where everyone gathered.

"In everyday life, the Calistoga Cafe served as a snack bar and rest area, and people would often come here during the day to enjoy sack lunches. Designed like a bistro with a patio, there were plenty of tables and chairs, and the founders would often come here to discuss important matters over cups of hot herbal tea."

Then Akira points to her right at an area of the shared wall between the second and third airlock, "Over there is Oak Barrel School." The lighting inside the false front brightens and reveals children's books and playthings stacked on wooden shelves. In front is a play area with small tables, and tiny handmade barrel chairs made for the children.

"During those difficult times of the Days of Darkness and Sorrow, families lived and worked together, and children were never far from their parents. As they studied and played at the Oak Barrel School, their parents would be working elsewhere, but they could hear them from anywhere in the orchard.

"Between the Cafe and the School," she now points towards a separate area that extends from the center of the orchard to the pathway around the false fronts. "This area was for the nursery and the Koi ponds. It was the most complex and difficult part of the orchard to build. Nowhere on the floor of this orchard will you find any sharp angles. Everything is curved in a natural manner and the Koi swim in tanks situated between the media beds in the nursery."

One child asks in a curious voice, "Is that where the fish babies were made?" The whole class breaks out in laughter. Akira says in a firm loud voice, "Don't laugh children, it's a good question. And speaking of babies, during those difficult times, a lot of babies were born, and this was a good thing."

"A special role for the inner sanctum was to encourage young couples to get married, be happy and make babies. You see children, during the Days of Darkness and Sorrow, radiation and diseases shortened the average lifespan on Earth to fifty years of age for much of the last half of the 21st century."

The children collectively gasp.

"When you consider that our average lifespan here on Paradise is more than twice that, the courage of our Founders was simply amazing. Yet, they knew, that for humanity to survive, they needed to start making babies, even during the worst of times. Now, if you'll follow me, we'll continue."

Akira steps down from the pedestal and leads the group to a wide area in the nursery surrounded by Koi ponds. She waits patiently as the children rush to kneel beside the ponds to admire the fish.

After a few moments, the teacher claps her hands to get their attention, and the children dutifully turn their attention back to Akira.

"When the Mars Beta Inner Sanctum was first built," she continues, "The nursery was an area set aside for raising new trees and vines from cuttings. It was designed to serve a functional role while being somewhat eye-pleasing, but that was about it. However, not long after the beginning of the Days of Darkness and Sorrow, the many destructive social experiments of the time did more to drive families apart than to bring them together. Realizing this, the Founders saw an opportunity to create a culture of compassion that would bring families together."

Gingerly stepping around the seedlings in the nursery, she knelt next to one. "My family line, as did many of yours, started in the inner sanctum where young couples took their vows before the community." Cupping her hands around the tiny transplant, she continues, "and when they had children, they celebrated what we now call the sprouting."

"On our home world, Earth, this family tradition of the sprouting continues to this very day. A fresh sprout is planted in the nursery in their name every time a child is born. Both parents were also awarded small tree-shaped gold pins that were designed by Betsy Fine, one for each child."

Extending her arms straight out, Akira slowly pivots on her heels.

"Look about you, children. This nursery is the highest spot in the orchard, and this is by design. From here you can see all of the olive groves and grapevines in the orchard. While the rest of the orchard floor is flat and continuous, this spot is about two feet higher."

The children look around as she adds, "This unique rise was not necessary for any technical reason. Rather, it was a year or so after the orchard became operational that they reconfigured it this way to send a message to their communities. Their highest purpose was to bring life to the lifelessness of tragedy. Each time parents stood here with their newborns, it was an affirmation of hope and purpose for all. It was a compassionate and inspiring call to carry on, and they did."

Now the teacher speaks up, "The children keep asking about the Sound of Music."

"Well then," Akira acknowledges with a wink and a nod, "It's showtime. Children, please follow me. We're going to the Calistoga Cafe to enjoy a fruit snack and watch a brief presentation of scenes from the movies our founding families enjoyed most during the Days of Darkness and Sorrow. And as we all know, what they loved most were musicals with happy endings."

Excited about enjoying treats and movie scenes, the children run to the Calistoga Cafe with Akira and the teacher strolling behind.

"Attention children," Akira says, pointing to the opposite wall of the orchard, "Betsy Fine had a sheer stroke of genius here. As you can see, the outer wall on the opposite side of the orchard is painted with a scenic panorama. The horizon is painted at about eye level. It wraps around the circumference of the orchard to each end of the cluster and blends in with the false fronts on the shared wall. Therefore, no matter where you are in the orchard, you can see this panorama."

Moving their attention from left to right, Akira begins to describe the various scenes depicted in the panorama. There were field workers harvesting grapes and old couples walking hand-in-hand together. "What Betsy did, that was so brilliant and yet so simple, was to leave plenty of room in the panorama for later generations to add their own embellishments."

"What you see now is a depiction of the original hand-painted panorama. Over the years, the pigment faded, and in 2067 the panorama was visually mapped and the walls were coated with digipaint. This brings me to an interesting bit of trivia. When planning this exhibit, our curators debated whether to use a hand-painted panorama or programmable digipaint. They decided on digipaint for one reason. So that we could show you this."

Pointing straight ahead with both hands, she says, "What you see now is a recreation of how the panorama looked the day the Orchard began operations." With a snap of her fingers, new elements begin to appear in the panorama and she points to a depiction of a kilometer-long colony spaceship in low earth orbit.

"This depiction shows the low-Earth orbit launch of the Proton Four Colony ship in 2059. It was the first to be equipped with a faster-than-light drive. The ship was massive, and this representation is actually to scale. If we were alive then, this is what that Proton Four launch would have looked like."

With another snap of her fingers, another new element appears. "And here we see the signing of the Colony Initiative of 2173. The heads of all colony families gathered in the original Mars Beta Inner Sanctum on Earth to define the Universal Rights of all communities to govern themselves in peace."

Before Akira can move on to the next depiction, the children begin chanting, "Sound of Music." The teach shakes her head and shrugs as the chanting grows repetitiously louder.

Akira smiles warmly. "Your wish is my command children, and in a moment we'll enjoy treats and the movie, but first I have a question for all of you. Here is the question. What does it mean that we are here today?"

Most of the children are silent, though a few try unsuccessfully to answer the question. Finally, the group goes silent.

Looking into their bright young faces, Akira says with a solemn voice, "The fact that we are here today is important, and here is why: The Founders, who built this orchard and who struggled to survive during the darkest time in human history, never once stopped believing in us. They never stopped believing that those who would come after them would continue to carry on far into the future to this world. We are the living proof of their belief, their faith, and their love."

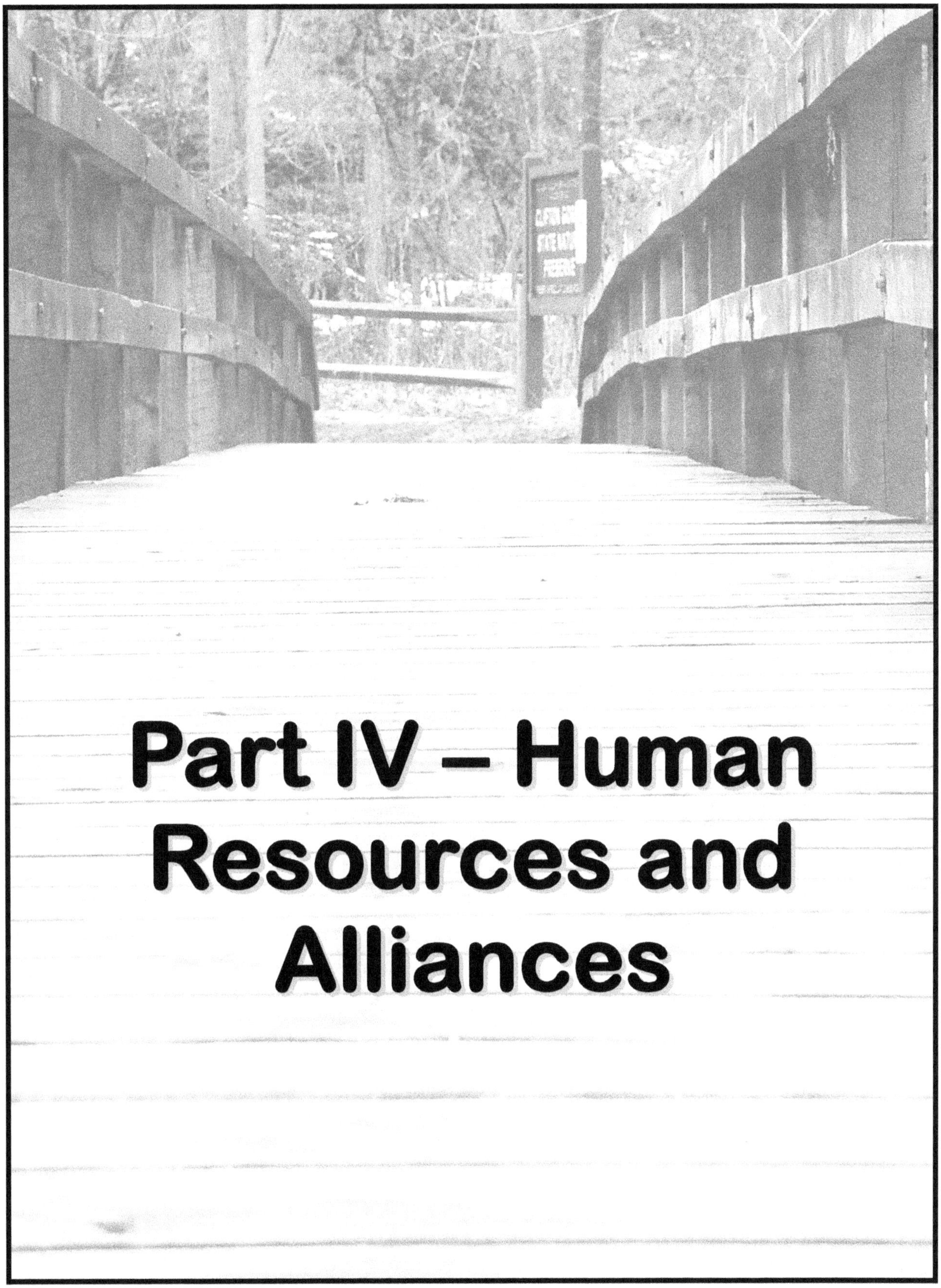

Part IV – Human Resources and Alliances

22

Life Umami

Umami is a funny-sounding Japanese word for a savory taste with an indescribable deliciousness: there's a uniquely rich and satisfying yumminess to it.

What your senses tell you about *umami* is more direct. "Oh yeah, now that's what I'm talking about. Whatever it is, it's the good stuff – more good stuff!"

When recruiting the membership of a Win-Win church, retreats are the ideal place to vet prospective residential members for a church ranch.

What you're looking for in prospective members is a life *umami* craving that is strong enough to power their commitment to survive with like-minded others and ensure the survival of our species by colonizing space.

To put it simply, the lifestyle of living and working on a ranch as a survivor and future colonist must satisfy a deep inner craving. When it is satisfied, they will experience a sense of life *umami* that resonates with their mind, body and soul. Not only during or after a cataclysm but long before it.

Granted, this is not an easy task. So, is waiting for things to go sideways before actively recruiting for your church ranch possible? Yes, but you will not be able to easily distinguish the genuine people from the pathological liars.

Candidate Screening

When things go sideways and people are faced with the end of life as we know it, many among the unprepared will become pathological liars.

What makes them pathological?

When confronted with death, desperate people will act out to get the assistance they seek. They are completely sincere when they offer their assurances because they believe they are speaking the honest truth.

Hollywood has come up with a movie line that hits this nail right on the head.

"A person is smart. People are dumb, panicky, dangerous animals." – Men in Black (1997)

The upshot is this: your church is not a government. While you will be as generous as possible, nowhere is it written that you must give aid to all who apply. Rather, you must prioritize your resources so that stouthearted survivors are always at the top of the list.

Stouthearted Survivors

Previously, we learned that government experts tell us that, should the nation's power grid collapse catastrophically, the vast majority of Americans will die. The grid failure itself is not what will kill most. Nor will it be a fatalistic death wish.

The eventual killer of most will be social programming.

We live in a consumer driven society where many, if not most, Americans have been programmed to think; if life as they know it should cease, their best course of action is to end it.

This is why you hear many say, "If it's that bad, I want to be at ground zero," and other such posturing. With this in mind, the following observation has context.

Everyone wants to live, but there are few who have the will to survive long periods of extreme hardship.

Who are those few? They are the stouthearted. By definition they are courageous, stubborn, and possess a stout spirit. It does not matter how difficult the path; they suck it up, stay frosty, and soldier on.

"When God destroys
a world, he always
keeps a few good
seeds for the next."
Robert Reiland, (1924-2016)
JESUS
THIRD
TEMPLE
Reiland

The stouthearted have a special role and to quote a dear old friend, Robert Reiland, author of *Jesus and the Third Temple*, he once told me, "When God destroys a world, he always keeps a few good seeds for the next."

The stouthearted are among the good seeds that God wants to save for the next civilization. Why is this so? Because they must shoulder a special burden.

Should humanity ever find itself teetering at the brink of oblivion, the stouthearted will be the first to answer the call, and through a fusion of sacrifice and providence, they shall prevail.

To those who hear the call, they can know this; in a survival community, they can be trained for any job. What truly matters is that they are stouthearted, or they sincerely desire the inspiration and help of those who already are.

Now Dear Reader, let's go looking for some good seeds, and the first step in this journey of the gathering is about self-honesty.

Self-Honesty

As Polonius says in *Hamlet,* "To thine own self be true." Let this be your guiding motto when evaluating potential church ranch residents and here is why. In order to survive, you must be able to execute quickly the following three action steps:

- Assess your current situation
- Develop a plan
- Take action on that plan, even if it is not the best.

People, who are good at lying to themselves, can blind themselves to things others clearly see. In other words, their assessment is flawed, and this causes them to freeze up due to a lack of confidence. Or, they are likely to make an uninformed decision. This flaw can be a matter of character, but the usual suspect is social programming.

When building your church membership, be mindful that we live in a consumer society that programs us each day with a subliminal barrage that envelopes us in comfort bubbles. Therefore, when we feel that we've made a savvy buy, we experience a transitory moment of consumer nirvana. Problem solved.

The prospect of survival planning is so dark, that folks tend to shop for savvy deals that offer them a peace of mind. This is the whole point of the commercial shelter industry. Once the sale is transacted, folks experience consumer nirvana, and the problem is solved.

Or is it really?

Who Can You Trust?

There are many differences between a Win-Win survival church and commercial shelters. The main difference that transcends them all is, who can you trust?

Let's assume a major event has occurred for example, and the clients of a shared commercial shelter facility are scrambling to make it to the shelter before it is sealed. Even though you paid extra for a nicer room, whoever is sleeping in the next compartment could be a drug dealer with a bag full of guns, and he snores like a pig. Of course, this was not supposed to happen.

Initially, there will be calls to pull together, and all will shout hurrah. That is until the food supplies dwindle to a precarious level. That's when the consumer bar tab comes due, and all realize that they are in a crowded lifeboat with a raucous cast of characters and not nearly enough supplies. Once the power struggles begin, the discord will bail more water into the lifeboat than out of it.

It all comes down to one question. Will your commercial shelter neighbor have your back, or will it come down to one less mouth to feed?

Remember, the problem with peace of mind solutions is that like bad insurance policies, they work well, until needed. The lesson here is survival is not about a person, place, or thing. It is a state of mind.

Those who possess it can project ideas and concepts far into the future; and without self-delusion about how a possible choice could play out.

When you see this ability in candidates, it could be a sign that they have the right stuff.

The Right Stuff

When building a Win-Win ranch community, you will have a mix of permanent and temporary residents. After a security check, what you want to see is a:

- Life umami connection. A hunger for being there.
- Desire for Comradery. This is essential because all residents will live and work together as brothers and sisters committed to survival and space colonization.
- Reliable member of the community.

The next thing you want to see is whether the candidate is stouthearted. In other words, are they, at the very least, capable and willing, to get back in the saddle after being bucked off?

The survival criteria for this determination and the relevant questions are:

- **Character:** Can I trust you to have my back?
- **Courage:** Will you come to my aide?
- **Commitment:** Will you come to my aide at the risk of your own life?

Comradery is not about being friends, being loved, or being allowed to love. It is a simple understanding. You're my brother. You're my sister. No matter what it takes; I've got your back. Where we go one, we go all, and no man is left behind. This is the right stuff and finding it requires an ability to see that which is hidden.

Hidden Files

What you look for in a resident church member cannot be measured with a computer exam. Rather, this is about creating a living culture of survival. To illustrate the concept, let's use something familiar like our laptop and desktop computers.

When we operate a new computer for the first time, the default setting for the file explorer disables the Show hidden system files option. This is best for the average user. Hidden files are just cryptic clutter for them.

However, power users or system administrators, trying to isolate a problem or a weakness in the system, often enable the Show hidden files option. Now, let's apply this to evaluating candidates for permanent ranch residency.

What you need is someone who knows how to read those cryptic files. Namely, a combat experienced Sergeant who has been there and done that.

Your Cadre

After founding your church and acquiring property, one of the first people you want to invite into the church is a recent war veteran with ground combat experience.

Thanks to our endless wars, there is a vast pool of talent out there. You want a non-commissioned officer specifically with the rank of E-7 or higher.

The E-7 ranks by service branch are:

- **Air Force:** Master Sergeant
- **Army:** Sergeant First Class
- **Marine Corp:** Gunnery Sergeant
- **Navy:** Chief Petty Officer

The ideal candidate will have completed one or more tours of duty in a front line arena and have the mental and physical fitness to work all tasks on a church retreat or ranch. It is essential that the candidate is happily married, and the spouse shares the same life *umami* connection.

Regardless of his or her military rank designation, in a Win-Win community, the rank is designated the Top Sergeant. Your Top leads the home guard and is directly supported by a small cadre.

Empathy

Our founding fathers wisely advised us, that if we do not hang together, we'll all hang separately. In a future disaster, most of those who survive will have done so by helping each other.

This is where an existential human connection is crucial to survival. Empathy is the ability to identify with others about a situation and their feelings. This is what survival with like-minded people means. You accomplish this through the building of unshakable bonds of comradery.

Therefore, empathy becomes your command input for survival comradery. Everyone in your Win-Win survival community's membership must share empathy with each other, as co-equal brothers and sisters. This is the necessary foundation upon which a common bond of survival comradery is established.

The members of your community will come from all walks of life, and regardless of their station, achievements, and education, the rules are the same for all. Everyone battles. Everyone works. And everyone participates.

It is the same for the community's goals: to manage resources, to raise children, and to be a light of hope for all. Therefore, in a post-catastrophic world, there is no time for failed social experiments.

It is back to basics time, where survival is building a successful community, one family at a time. This is a given for your Top Sergeant and cadre.

Building the Cadre

Your Top Sergeant and cadre are your first permanent residents and the core of your home guard. They and church founders live on church properties rent-free for life.

When you interview prospective candidates, you need to explain, that if chosen, they must form a cadre consisting of other combat veterans with the same health and family criteria.

Members of your home guard are other veterans, first responders, law enforcement, and fire and rescue. They report to the cadre.

Note, scheduling flexibility is necessary for first responders because they typically work heavy schedules and often through the holidays. Therefore, tasking them for a ranch or retreat activity will be a challenge. However, they may have time to organize training events for church members living in their areas.

When time comes for your first responders to bug out to the ranch, they will serve multiple roles; emergency volunteers being one of them. During crisis events, available church members are encouraged to volunteer their time for local emergency efforts.

A Win-Win is a church that farms and your cadre will be your initial farm labor. Therefore, you provide accommodations for them.

After the Top Sergeant has assembled the cadre, their first mission is to build a small RV park on church property for travel trailers and fifth wheels. The church provides the tools, equipment and materials. The cadre provides the labor, which may require some combat engineer skills; so plan accordingly. This initial objective, building the RV farm labor park, will provide a good opportunity for them to get to know each other.

The second objective is to formulate a plan to execute the cadre mission.

Cadre Mission

The aim of the church is to build a property with 150 members. One third or more this number is your home guard. The rest of the community will consist of the church's leadership and other members who are organized around functional lines, such as ranching and farming.

Some may find their first assignment to be unappealing, but then again, if you want to eat, KP is a necessary task for everyone at some point or another.

The home guard is comprised of the cadre, veterans and first responders, including law enforcement, fire and rescue, and paramedics. The controlling authority for the home guard is the veteran cadre.

The cadre will reside on the property and serve as the community's security team. During project planning, they advise the church leadership how to plan and build various structures and defensive positions around the property.

The mention of defensive positions may seem odd in light of this book's subtitle which states that the church's role is to prepare for cooperation, not confrontation.

However, this does not mean that you blithely ignore the need to defend the church from attack.

Rather, through preparedness, those on the prowl for "spoils" will see the church as a very hard target. One that would cost them dearly and with little guarantee of success. A price this costly will encourage predators to move on in search of softer targets.

When we say hard target, what exactly do we mean?

Defensive Preparation

When it comes to defensive preparation, you either get it or you do not. Those, with exaggerated sensibilities against guns, and who are afraid of them, or who have a political desire to end 2nd Amendment rights, are not suitable for any Win-Win survival group.

You must have people who will protect each other without hesitation. This is essential to survival comradery. Remember the rules.

Everyone fights.
Everyone works.
Everyone participates.

The bottom line is this. Beware of those who demand special exceptions, because their mission is often about self-service, and they're only happy when they get their way.

So, prepare thyself. Because if there is one thing that will mark a dividing line among the interested candidates for your church, it will be the church's concealed carry rules.

A way to address this is to require that new members of the church undergo a security background check. Or, they can present a valid and current concealed carry permit from any state.

Remember, your church is not a government agency. You do not need to take all who apply. You accept the ones you know will stay frosty, get the job done, and cover your back without complaints.

By stating this policy upfront when discussing your church, you'll spare yourself the grief of dealing with overly sensitive and impractical personalities. More to the point, you'll probably save a life, if not your own. When worse-comes-to-worse, expect unprepared civilians to choke under fire.

For those who feel a more evolved sensibility is required, politely thank them for their time and tell them it's not a good fit. This may sound harsh but do not allow them to reapply. Why? Because you will never know if they are acting out to get what they want.

Meanwhile, training is the responsibility of the home guard, and this is not a guy thing.

Women, Youth and Guns

Let's assume that your cadre chooses the Smith and Wesson M&P 9mm Shield as the standard conceal carry firearm for the church. Designed as a working man's conceal carry, it is also easy for men, women, and youths of appropriate age to operate. It is light and comfortable to carry in a holster or purse.

Why the emphasis on women and youths?

The reason is your worst nightmare.

Under a Mad Max scenario, maniacs have overrun your community. They'll likely dispatch the men first, and then take their time raping, enslaving, and killing the women and children.

This is an ugly thing to consider, but one that you must and here is the relevant question for parents and church members alike.

Do you leave the young ones defenseless and hiding under floorboards with a blind hope of rescue? Or do you let them fight for their lives?

Consider this. A camouflaged twelve-year-old boy or girl, with a .22 caliber bolt-action sniper rifle a good scope and a silencer can inflict a lot of pain from out of nowhere. However, there is a caveat.

Their marksmanship skills need to be such that they can knee-cap a charging rapist at 100 yards, so he is an easy target for the adults.

The point here is that the children in a Win-Win survival community are only asked to maim the attackers, not to kill. In earlier times, children did both, and they do have their own minds. This is why continual marksmanship training is essential, and there are a lot of excellent resources.

One well-tuned to the needs of women and youth is Project Appleseed. Their programs are standardized for .22 rifles with scopes and offer a superb range of skilled marksmanship training programs and events. You can find them on the Internet at www.appleseedinfo.org.

Also, some of the Veterans organizations such as The American Legion offer Marksmanship programs and classes for students.

There are other weapons used exclusively by your home guard, like the .50 caliber Barrett M82 sniper rifle. A standard issue for the military, it's not used for stopping people, though it certainly can. Rather, it's used to stop vehicles and to punch through walls.

If a gaggle of maniacs in a one-ton 4X4, plows through your zigzag fence, a .50 caliber bullet will stop their vehicle dead. If they are smart, they'll retreat. If not, they'll run into another ambush, and this time, they will be the intended targets.

The point is that when your design team begins planning work on church property, the input of the cadre is essential. They will need a clear line of sight into designated kill zones and areas where invaders can be isolated, turned away, or terminated.

These are the strategic and tactical mission goals. However, the cadre also has a sacred role as well. They create and nurture a bond of survival comradery; one that draws all of the members of the church together for the purpose of survival.

Survival Comradery

In order for a Win-Win community to survive and thrive, it must be cohesive, and what makes this work is comradery. We also know it as the sense of brotherhood and of being a band of brothers. It is unique, and there is no other feeling in the world like it. It is why one-third of your community, at a minimum, should be your home guard.

The others are civilians, and they can be grouped in different ways. Nonetheless and regardless of position, they are civilians and what was said earlier bears repeating.

We live in a consumer society where Americans have been programmed into thinking that if life as they know it ceases, their best course of action is to end with it.

Those who know and who have been trained to succeed in life or death situations, are not affected because they know how to turn it off. This is why your cadre is the core of your church community. Their sacred mission is to turn civilians with the right stuff, or the promise of it, into a unified band of pioneers with an unbreakable bond of comradery.

Another way to see this is to imagine a Win-Win survival church as a brick wall.

The civilians are the bricks. They give this wall its dimensions and strength. The cadre and home guard are the mortar that binds it together into one strong structure. Together they stand, and together they say, "Brother, sister, no matter what it takes, I've got your back."

Founders, I caution you to always remember this one thing when you make your decisions.

Comradery is a desire that can transcend time, distance, and adversity, but it flounders in doubt. Let there be no doubts about your resolve or your wisdom.

23

Food Club and Folk School

Dear Reader, you know how to form and fund a church, raise domes, and how to grow a complete diet during a cataclysm and beyond when humankind goes to the stars. All of this is necessary, but you need good people to make it work. They need the will to survive and to thrive through a long period of hardship.

In the previous chapter, you learned that in order for a Win-Win community to survive and thrive, it must be cohesive. In this chapter you will learn how to create a food club and a folk school to grow your community and to generate revenue streams for church operations.

After your first property has been acquired and is fully operational, you start a food club, which is similar to other current community supported agriculture schemes. Your cadre will play a central role in your Win-Win food club.

Win-Win Food Club

A retreat is likely to be the first property your church acquires. With either the turnkey or incremental funding models, the need is the same. You will need a nearby safe haven with a base for a convoy of vehicles to get to another church property.

Retreats are ideal for building food clubs. You go to a retreat to learn, to grow, and to make a few mistakes along the way. A farm or a ranch is where you take what you've learned from those mistakes. So the journey is making things work and being able to laugh while you're picking up the pieces.

This takes us back to basics. A church is a gathering; whereas a religion is an explanation. A survival church is not a religion because one's religion is a sacred right of personal heritage. Therefore, there is no proselytizing within the church, but outside of the church, what are you going to share and promote?

A Food-Centered Life

A Win-Win food club offers online participation and local events to join in the creation of a food-centered life for survival and colonization.

Food club members will play a role in the learning process and their purchases will help fund the church.

Imagine you work a nine-to-five job and it's lunch time. You sit down in the lunchroom with a heated organic survival lunch, and it smells wonderful. Next thing you know, you're sharing it with co-workers and telling them about community.

In addition to interesting meals, club members can visit your church retreat and purchase foods produced by the church. They are also invited to vote on recipes for your survival and space diets and to place orders.

The strategy is not to find one or two main recipes and produce large quantities. Rather, you want to do a lot of small taste testing runs. There are real advantages to this strategy.

If you purchase a property large enough to build grow-to-diet kitchens, the strategy is simple. Grow what you can and for the rest, network with local organic farmers and organic cooperatives; they'll surely appreciate the sales.

A Win-Win church food club is a rising tide that lifts all boats; so how do you spread the word? Through the first contact.

First Contact

Two founders with a banjo and a snappy tune on YouTube is one way to make first contact with people, but there is also a more practical approach. Like running for office, you pick a forum, press the flesh and mingle with people.

Church members who reside in a large metropolis can be highly effective. Find trade shows and events where you can rent a booth and set up a display. A 10'x10' booth is plenty. No flashy demos or gimmicks; these only buy back the sale.

You want to draw folks to your booth and establish rapport to advocate a food-centered life. All you need is a back wall with a banner, lots of eye-catching photos, and a few small tables and chairs.

In the corner of the booth, you may have a few boxes of packaged church survival food single meal servings. Depending on the event, you may want to stockpile additional supplies nearby.

The back wall of the booth is critical. It is your draw, and you want to mount a few rows of colorfully rich and engaging framed photos. You use these as focus points.

No need to worry about running out of ideas. Once you start doing this, mission creep sets in, and then you're the one trying to keep up. Here are three examples:

- **International Space Station:** Use a photo of astronauts working onboard to describe the Mediterranean setpoints and how they are the basis for the space diet.
- **Modern-Day Pioneer Reenactors:** Use a photo of reenactors with their wagons and teams to explain the survival diet and how food club members will help to select survival recipes using 18th and 19th century pioneer cookbooks.
- **Mother and Daughter Marksmanship:** Here people see a close-up of a mother showing her daughter how to shoot a .22 rifle. The message is that self-defense is a family affair.

The ISS and reenactor pictures above will engage passersby. Then use the marksmanship photo to help qualify prospective church members. If they like the food concept but hate guns, then graciously thank them for visiting the booth; and to enjoy the rest of the show.

Remember, you're not a government. You pick and choose who you want to serve. When you see genuine interest and feel it in your gut, explain the program and offer a show special.

If they purchase a membership to the food club at the show, they receive a signing bonus of two different survival meals. Point to the boxes and tell them to take their bonus meals with them that day. Be sure to let them know that they can cancel for any reason within thirty days, and their membership fee will be fully refunded within 3-5 working days. Also, they can keep the bonus food.

Here is a tip. What makes top sales producers successful is that they always ask for the business, and not just once, but continuously. A friendly question or nudge is all that is necessary. "If you want to give our program a try, let's see what we have for bonus meal choices and get you signed up."

If you get a yes, make it so. If there is hesitancy, move on to discussing your church internet sites where they can follow how recipes are chosen, grown, processed, and shipped.

Then ask for the order again. For example, "Some people call us webcam farmers because we video everything. That way you experience the food you eat, literally from seed to salad bar. If this is something you want to be a part of, pick your bonus meals and let's get you signed up today."

If you get a yes, make it so. If there is still hesitancy, move on to how club members can share their taste testing videos with other food club members. All who purchase meals are invited to prepare and taste in a video that becomes part of the research archive.

Then ask for the order again by saying something like, "Imagine how much fun it will be seeing their reactions and sharing your own for a very important mission. If this is something you want to be a part of, let's find you a bonus meal and get you signed up today?"

If you do not close them on the third attempt, stop. Full stop.

Tell them, "I've enjoyed meeting you today, and I thank you for your kind interest. Please enjoy the rest of the show."

Given that top sales producers never stop at three closes, why the limit? Because you have a church, and you could eventually wind up living with this person.

As they say in Texas, "Good deals come together quickly, and bad ones seldom do." You'll fare better in the long run by screening a large pool of candidates to find the ones who get it, and who want to get with the program.

For those who do sign up, you may want to keep a special treat in reserve for them.

Remember that part about two founders with a banjo and a snappy tune on YouTube? Here is where you do it in style. Be yourself, be corny, have fun, laugh, cry, but above all else, inspire. Give them a heartwarming welcome to the club and a DVD to take home and enjoy.

Folk School

A Win-Win survival church is a church that farms and ranches, and to ensure your own success, you need a robust arts and crafts program.

Therefore, all properties need to hold special events where people are informed and entertained. You want this to evolve eventually into a Danish-style folkehojskole (folk school).

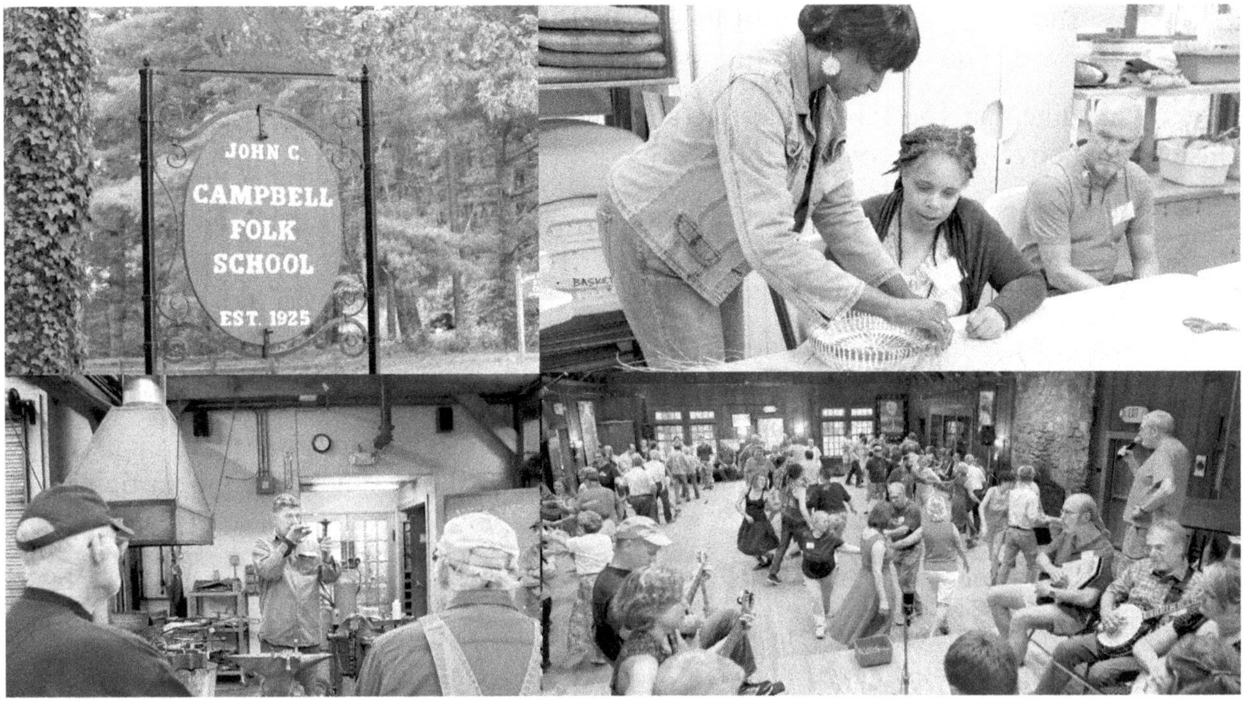

Folk Schools were started by the Danes to stem the loss of young rural generations to the appeal of the cities. Or as an old Andrew Bird lyric so aptly puts it:

How ya gonna keep 'em down on the farm,
After they've seen Paree'

Prior to a cataclysm, life on a Win-Win ranch will be about solving problems, raising children, and making life work. For those born to the saddle or to the tractor so to speak, this is life.

But for city dwellers adjusting to country life, they're going to have that go-go drive, and actually, that's great. Use it. Have them do something special, that they can sink their teeth into, a folk school.

A magnificent model for this is the John C. Campbell Folk School in Brasstown, NC. Their website is at www.folkschool.org.

When you examine their catalog, you will know why people from all around the world come to take their courses. They've been doing this for a very long time, and they are very good at it.

Also, be sure to read their history page. The founders Olive Dame Campbell and Marguerite Butler were amazing women, and their school offers an inspiring model for Win-Win ranch communities.

Creating something similar to what these remarkable women achieved takes time and patience. So how do you try? A good first step is something practical that can serve a dual role.

Let's imagine that you can devote five acres to a huddle for an arts and crafts DBS dome cluster with above-ground cover as follows:

- 40' residence
- 40' workshop and storage
- 20' service dome and playroom

The four clusters in this huddle are arranged in a half-circle around a community area for public events that feature a central stage area for plays, dances, exhibitions, and such.

Each cluster will be built for a specific purpose such as carpentry and plumbing. When making those choices, make sure that these members are willing, if not eager, to participate in building a folk school.

However, why does your Win-Win community need to start a folk school in the first place?

People need to be taught how to survive and how to colonize space, which is why every Win-Win community must manage and pass its knowledge along to future generations.

Founders need to foster an ethic of working, learning, and teaching. The goal is to build an all-hazards folk school complex with dormitories.

Arts and Crafts Groups

Using the John C. Campbell Folk School catalog as a reference, the various arts and crafts groups a Win-Win ranch will likely consider can be grouped in a folk school catalog.

Therefore, let's organize different Win-Win requirements into catalog groups with their related job functions on a ranch, the largest property type:

- **Aquasphere Group:** This group works on all things water, which would include rainwater harvesting, plumbing, recycling, and waste management. The workshop dome is used as a testing laboratory and a work area for environmental fabrication and storage.

- **Light and Power Group:** This group works on all things electrical. Their key term is load, which describes the power demand; every device in your community adds to the overall load. No hypothetical discussions or exotic custom designs required. It's all off the shelf now, so all your power group needs to know is how much, where, and when? The workshop dome requires storage areas and several workbenches.

- **Woodworking Group:** You need carpenters, woodworkers, and cabinet makers. Dome interior build-outs will use mortise and tenon construction. This style of woodworking, common in Amish communities, uses dovetail joints and dowels instead of bolts and screws. This eliminates as much metal from inside the domes as possible, which also helps to prevent emotional aggravation due to radiation. This workshop needs a table saw, band saw, drills, sanders, routers, and shelves for racks and storage.
- **Metal working Group:** You will need a machinist, a fabricator, and a blacksmith. The machinist also should be a tool and die maker so he can make his own tools. The fabricator makes whatever you need from sheet and structural metal and has an essential role in building your aquaponics system. He should also be a welder. Your blacksmiths make hinges, cutlery, and so forth and build the custom biofuel and wood-fired welded steel stoves with firebricks for your survival kitchen.
- **Fabric and Household Group:** Nowhere is it written that one must wear drab attire. This is especially important for the morale of your families. You need a designer and seamstress, a spinner and weaver, a leather/canvas worker, and a shoe cobbler. Sewing rooms, looms, and a large workbench area are required.
- **Health and Hygiene Group:** In addition to holistic medical practitioners, you need a candle and soap maker, an essential oil distiller, and a compounding pharmacist who can produce prescription grade pain medications with the medicinal plants and herbs, such as poppies, cannabis, and natural aspirin made from willow tree bark that you grow. The community also needs surgical anesthesia like ether or chloroform, as well as penicillin and other medications.
- **Equestrian Group:** This group resides in a special horse boarding area on the ranch and is directed by a horse whisperer and barn manager. Support roles include a saddlery and leather maker, a farrier with some blacksmith's skills to care for horses' hooves, a wainwright to make and repair wagons, and a wheelwright to make or repair wooden wheels.
- **Home Guard Group:** Your Top Sergeant will assemble a cadre of veterans. They have been trained at taxpayer expense and can play essential roles in a Win-Win survival community. This is a windfall of talent. In addition to security, fire and rescue, other roles include gunsmith, armorer, communications, construction engineering, logistics, and planning.

Building a folk school will take time, and in the interim, you organize public Win-Win fairs.

Win-Win Fairs

A Win-Win survival fair provides an excellent opportunity to meet and entertain the public and to demonstrate how a food-centered community functions. In terms of revenue, if your ranch is in a rural area where city dwellers like to visit and vacation, your Win-Win fairs could be very profitable.

Let's start with the five-acre area we previously discussed for an arts and crafts huddle with a central stage area for plays, dances, exhibitions, and so forth. To use that for a Win-Win fairground, double the acreage around the arts and crafts huddle.

This will give you room for picnic areas, restrooms, parking, a small food court, and most importantly, living culture ranch-life exhibits. Here are a few examples:

- **Equestrian Round Pen:** These circular pens are used to work intensively with horses. They are used to train and exercise animals. They are also used for breaking horses. There is one near your stables, and you'll build a second one in the fairground area. It features scheduled living-culture performances where animals are exercised and trained. Between performances, pony rides for the little ones are popular.
- **Petting Zoo:** A fully operational ranch will have rabbits, goats, sheep, and fish. The zoo will have an area for children to pet the animals, plus a small pond stocked with Koi fish that they can feed. A petting zoo is easy to build and popular with little ones.

- **HAM Shack:** The communications center for the community should be located in a below-ground all-hazards DBS dome. In the fairground area, an EcoShell II can serve as a HAM shack. The radios are remotely linked to the main antenna system for the ranch, and attendees can work with community HAMs to make international short-wave contacts.
- **Family Theater:** Remember our two founders with a banjo and a snappy tune on YouTube? They're the ones introducing the family entertainment acts performed by your church members. Performances of fables and popular stories will be popular with children and parents alike. A 30' EcoShell II would be ideal as a small theater with a stage and benches.
- **Hay Rides:** Hayrides are great get-together special events at fairs. Your ranch will already have draft animals and wagons, and this will be a profitable way to use them. Have a nice picnic on the trail, where everyone can enjoy tasty ranch food and a scenic view.

Yes, this list of ideas is on the verge of going totally out of control, which is the whole point. Make your communities and fairs fun with lots of interesting things to see and do and oodles of tasty, organic foods and treats. Look to be inventive about routine tasks about the property such as the wonderful world of goat grazing.

Say what?

Goat Grazing

Cows, horses and sheep are grazers. They like grass. Goats are browsers with an appetite for weeds and a digestive system designed to break down pioneer plants. They're commonly used today to as four-legged weed whackers and contracted out by commercial herders.

Using portable fences, they move the goats through an area to be reclaimed, cleared or weeded. Herders tell us that they are always fun to watch so buy some comfy lawn chairs and coolers and offer guided tours.

Also keep in mind that goats are raised as work or meat animals. The meat animals can be troublesome and are not suitable as work animals. But they are tasty!

Working goats are nature's gift to soil amendment, because land that has been damaged in a severe event can be naturally restored with the help of goat grazing. This is because goats love to eat weeds and are blessed with digestive systems that can fully digest the seeds, rendering them lifeless. Consequently, their droppings and urine are powerful fertilizers.

Goats poop where they eat, so they need to keep on the move. This is a good thing because they trample the overcover with light compression, and work in the fertilizer to create a nice overcover. This will amend the soil and its ability to retain moisture from the rains as you retain some additional revenues as well.

24

Strategic Alliances

A Win-Win community ranch is a sizable project, and regardless of where you locate; it is imperative that you integrate with the local culture as a net-positive gain for the greater community. This is the basis of your good neighbor strategy.

It is essential that you explain your Win-Win survival church in a consistent and respectful way. When integrating into a new community, some may be wary of a church without a formal religion. The concept will be unfamiliar to them, and you should respect this.

Respect really is the correct word, because each church needs to find its own way, and there is no one size to fit all solution. To illustrate the concept, here is how we explain our church to others. Feel free to use it as a reference for presenting your organization.

A Constitutional Church

This book is published by the Knowledge Mountain Church of Perpetual Genesis, which is a constitutional church. Our mission is to serve the will of God by forming small communities to survive extreme disasters and later to colonize space and ensure the survival of our species.

Our church was founded on the Perpetual Genesis philosophy of the founder, Marshall Masters. It is his heritage and it maintains that God's mission is the perpetual creation of life from the lifelessness of the void. Therefore, serving God's will in this philosophy is about making an eternal commitment. Members are not required to adopt this philosophy personally, but rather, to respect it as a matter of personal heritage and to honor its goals.

Those who decide to become a Perpetual, need only offer up their commitment with this simple prayer: "God, I'm with you in your mission of Perpetual Genesis. I'm presently incarnated in this world and in this species. When my job is done here, send me where you need me and I will faithfully continue to serve your mission."

That's all there is to it because everything else is a matter of personal heritage, and this right must be respected by all church members regardless of their original faiths and beliefs. Knowledge Mountain is a constitutional church. In a manner of speaking, our dogma and doctrine are based on the Constitution of the United States as originally written in 1776.

When our founding fathers created the Constitution of the United States, no "official" faith was designated as the state-approved religion for the country.

What is protected in the Constitution is the freedom of assembly, freedom of association, and freedom of religion. It does not tell us how to pray to God, but rather, it designates faith as a personal right.

Why do we call it a church instead of a temple, fellowship, or other such names? The IRS calls it a "church." If the IRS decides to use "cockamamie" instead of "church," then cockamamie it would be.

The point is that religion is founded on dogma and doctrine, whereas a constitutional church derives its organizational authority from the Constitution of the United States and pledges its "allegiance to the Flag of the United States of America, and to the Republic for which it stands, one Nation under God."

The upshot is this. A Constitutional survival church is also based on American exceptionalism and for one reason, tolerance.

There is no perfect form of governance and America has a mixed history, but on balance no other form of governance, in the history of humankind, has so successfully embodied the inalienable rights of personal freedom and religious tolerance as America.

When future space colonists found new worlds, they will be well-served to base their governance model on the US Constitution, whether in whole or in part. Therefore, when this church goes to the stars, the Constitution will go with it.

What Your Church Offers

It is vital to the success of your Win-Win church ranch that you integrate into the local community as a reliable team player. You have a lot to offer; so before we discuss community concerns, it is important to understand why a Win-Win church is desirable in any country:

- **Not a Religious Belief System:** A Win-Win ranch is a constitutional church that farms and teaches farming. It promotes a food-centered lifestyle that celebrates and honors human dignity and self-worth.
- **No Competition:** You never compete with local businesses and churches. However, your church will engage in local interfaith efforts.
- **New Community Revenues:** A Win-Win church will help support the local economy.
- **New Farm Revenues:** Your grow-to-diet food club will create new commercial revenue opportunities for local organic farmers and collectives.
- **Local Traditions:** When diversity does not divide us, it makes us stronger together. A Win-Win church honors local traditions and heritages.
- **Tourism Magnet:** Tourism is a rising tide that lifts all boats in rural communities within driving distance of a metropolis. Your food club, fairs, and folk school operations will also attract customers to established businesses in the area.
- **Disaster Relief:** During a disaster, your church will donate fresh food to local food banks, and members will serve as trained volunteers with local law enforcement and fire and rescue operations during a crisis.

Your church can offer other benefits as well. However, there may still be concerns since your community is organized for survival.

Prepper shows on cable television, like Doomsday Preppers, turned prepping into clown car entertainment, so people may see you through an entertainment prism. They'll wonder if you are just another bunch of "gun rack preppers," as I call them.

A real-life example reveals the truth of it.

Local Concerns Matter

A few years ago, during reconnaissance to the Kalispell/Whitefish area in Northwest, Montana, our team observed that the locals had a disdain, if not borderline fear of preppers. The area is a natural magnet for them and the problem is to know how many of them are already there.

I got a rough answer to that question while visiting a large army surplus store in the area with a volunteer.

Army surplus stores are high-priced museums these days with gear that used to sell for peanuts, and now are priced like collectibles. However, they do carry a wide selection of camping and extreme weather gear. That was the reason we were there. My researcher was looking for winter boots, and while he was trying on boots for size, I found myself in a revealing conversation with the store owner.

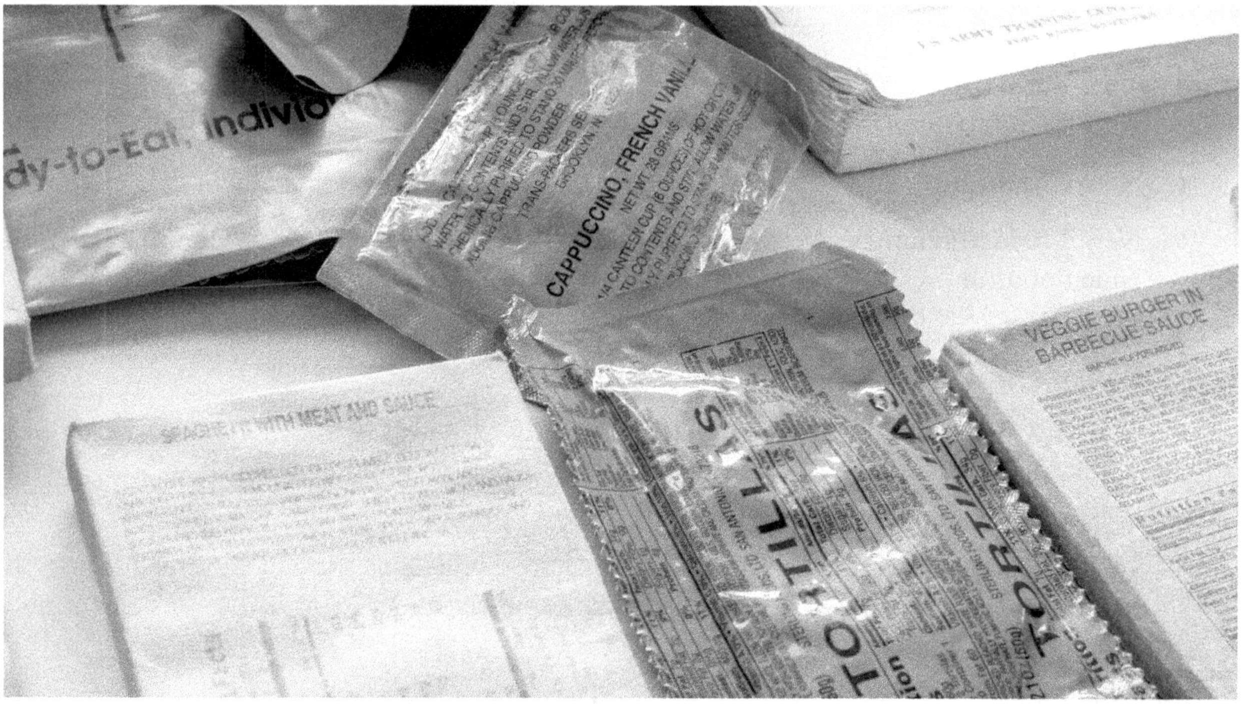

I noticed there were only a few Meals Ready to Eat (MRE) packages on the shelf, and they were not the tasty ones.

They reminded me of being in the army during the '70s and eating C-rations canned in WWII. If you got something like ham and Lima Beans, you couldn't give it away.

The store owner told me it was all that remained from a big MRE sale. These meals are a huge demand item for preppers. After a long search, the owner found a supplier and bought enough to fill a 40' trailer. We're talking about thousands of meals.

After they were delivered, the store owner ran a small advertisement in the local paper and sold out in less than two weeks, except for the few I saw.

A lot of folks bought them for outdoor recreation. But on this scale, the bulk of the purchases were likely made by gun rack preppers with lots of cash. This made me take notice of another indicator.

I began to notice the number of old 4x4 pickup trucks that were painted in camouflage with gun racks that were on the road and parked around town. Once I did, they stood out like road reflectors in the headlights.

During that reconnaissance, we met a few of these preppers. Some were good-hearted kindly people and most engaging

But then we learned why the locals are worried about the more militant types and for good reason. There were those who would joke, "If I see you in my rifle's scope, I own you." This is not good. All of this brought the local animus into focus.

Elusive gun rack preppers racing about the countryside playing survival games scare people. This behavior begs a serious question.

When things go sideways, how will local governments and law enforcement deal with gun rack preppers? God forbid that it devolves into a worst-case scenario where people on both sides take up arms.

Worst Case Scenario

During the 1980s, a cult leader, by the name of Bhagwan Shree Rajneesh, acquired the 64,000 acres, Big Muddy Ranch, that straddled Wasco and Jefferson Counties in Central Oregon. He developed the city of Rajneeshpuram.

The population of Rajneeshpuram, by some estimates, was 2,000 in 1983 and grew to 3,000 the following year. As it grew, local residents became alarmed by the sight of followers throwing flowers on the cult leader's Rolls Royce.

The nation was still deeply disturbed at this time by the 1978 mass suicide at Jonestown, Guyana. Cult leader, Jim Jones, and his inner circle conspired and directed a mass murder of his followers and a visiting congressional delegation in his jungle commune. Over 900 died, including 300 underage minors.

Religious intolerance of the Rajneesh was a minor concern, but what really exploded local resentment was the Rajneeshpuram residents registered to vote. Locals could see that their numbers would effectively disenfranchise their votes. This pressed them to fight for their sense of identity and political freedom. As a result, a bitter struggle developed between the residents and Rajneesh and his followers.

Both sides took up arms. As the tensions built, the international press got involved. This triggered the Federal Government to step in and end the conflict and Rajneeshpuram met its end as well.

The Netflix documentary series *Wild Wild Country* (2018) is well worth watching. You'll see what happens when people with the best of intentions fall out of a stupid tree and hit every branch coming down.

What was their single greatest mistake? Naive, political miscalculations.

When county-level leaders are looking at your church for the first time, they may have one question in mind. Are you part of the solution, a part of the problem, or a victim?

County-Level Alliances

When you are creating new alliances with county officials and offices, you want to hear the stock welcome speech, "Get along and follow the rules, and we'll do just fine."

Here are a few tips to help you get that response:

- **Respect Local Government:** Regardless of how others view your church, as spokesperson, you want to be thought of as an honest, pleasant, and intelligent person. As such, you must be discreet and always seeking a pathway to success through honest cooperation. No matter where you are in the world, genuine respect and a pleasant demeanor are usually welcomed and appreciated.
- **Build Alliances with Elected Officials:** Sheriffs are the highest law enforcement officers in counties and since they are elected, they answer to the voters. Police chiefs serve at the pleasure of a mayor and can be removed at any time. Invite both to dinner, but build your alliance with the sheriff.
- **Come Bearing Support:** As a church, be happy to participate in their community outreach, neighborhood watch, and other programs. In general, pay for your obligations and avoid politics.

In terms of the overall cost to build a fully operational Win-Win ranch, land cost is a speed bump. If you hit it the wrong way though, you're calling for a tow truck. Of course, whoever is funding or financing your project will not take that news too kindly either.

Escrow Due Diligence

Win-Win farms and ranches will often be located in unincorporated areas and we'll use that as an assumption. Here is where an established and well-respected local realtor is your ace in the hole first contact.

After you put earnest money on a property and go into escrow, your realtor will need to assist you with your due diligence. Print this on a sticky and place it on your realtor's file folder:

Job No. 1. Protect my investors, funders, and members.

That means, your first due diligence speed bump is the plan.

Step 1 – County Planning

Typically, a community has a comprehensive plan for its development that projects for 20 years. Expect it to be periodically updated.

The plan explains what the goals are for that period of time for the community, and how it executes that plan. Your Win-Win ranch property must be consistent with and complement that comprehensive plan.

For this to work, you should retain a planning professional to represent you. Someone who understands the planning process, how things work, and who speaks their language.

You want an American Institute of Certified Planners (AICP) credentialed planner to represent your church. Their website is at www.planning.org.

If you're lucky, the county's comprehensive plan will be online. If not, your planner will need to visit the local office to review the necessary documents and make the following determinations:

- **Development Regulations:** The development regulations will determine your eventual Win-Win community plan.
- **Red Flag Concerns:** What if you are buying a ranch in the middle of an area designated as a future industrial area? That's a red flag.

Remember, there are no perfect properties, but you can get pretty close. However, in the end, you'll get what you get. If your planner sees a red flag issue at this stage, go no further until it is resolved. Always be prepared to pull back from prospective land purchases.

However, if your planner sees no reason to delay, take a closer look at the property.

Step 2 – Property Analysis

Before investing in further planning and permitting efforts, conduct a detailed evaluation of the property. There will be existing reports, but they are often dated. What you want is an escrow due diligence snapshot of the property in terms of:

- **Geology:** The single greatest cost factor in building a Win-Win ranch will be the geology of the land itself. If blasting is needed, the less there is the better because if you are building on an igneous rock bed, you'll need enough dynamite to start a quarry. Likewise, you do not want to build on sandstone or near a fault line.
- **Aquasphere:** You need to conduct laboratory tests of all water sources on the property. Beware of pesticides and industrial waste either on the property or that can come from adjacent properties. Also, rural areas often rely on the practice of water dowsing with a forked stick or another device to identify underground water sources. A good dowser can not only tell you where water is to be found, but it's quality, depth, and likely production volume as well.
- **Off-Grid Power:** A property with an all-year creek or stream sufficient for hydroelectric power offers huge advantages. Be sure to evaluate seasonal volume flows and heights. Also, check for possible areas to position solar panels and geothermal heating, ventilation, and air conditioning (HVAC) wells.
- **Soil:** You want to work with a local agronomist to analyze the soil in likely farming areas on the property and to advise you on the best local source for overcover soil and what to use.

From the very beginning, you must be clear with your realtor and everyone, that you want your farm or ranch to be a certified organic operation by the U.S. Department of Agriculture (USDA).

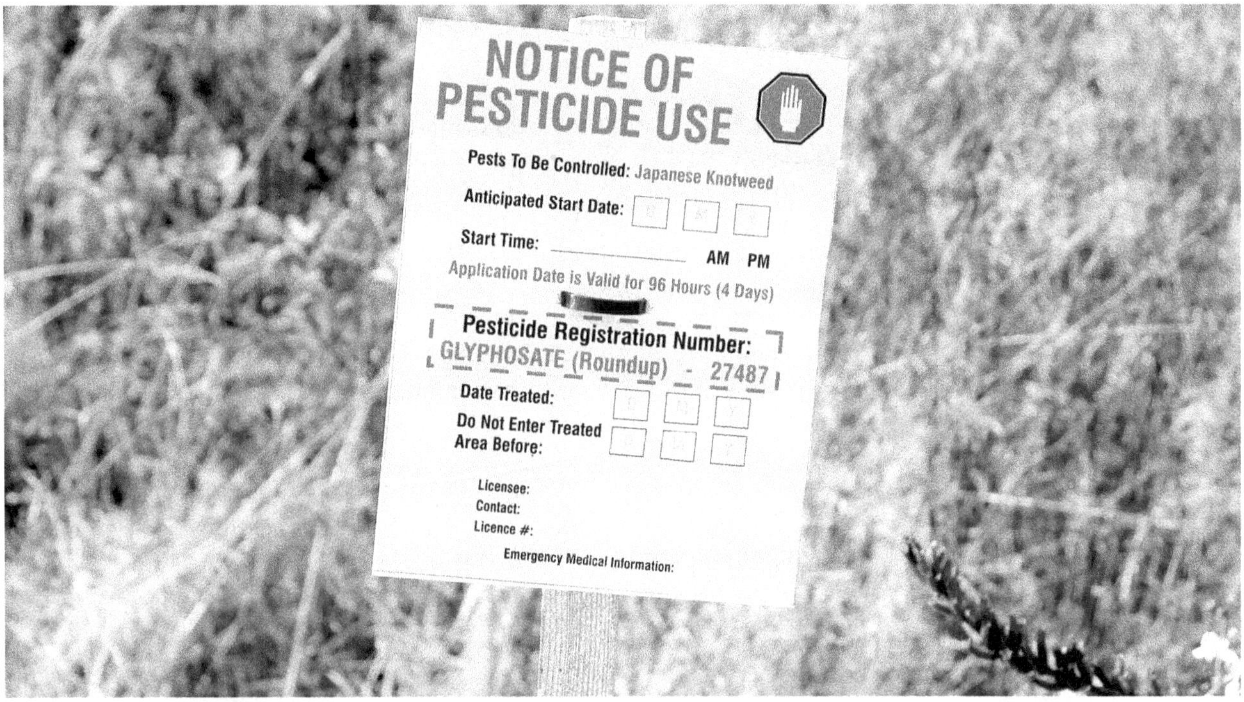

The point here is that you use the USDA organic requirements and the biggest regulation of them all is:

> *"Any land used to produce raw organic commodities must not have had prohibited substances applied to it for the past three years." – USDA*

In other words, if someone is selling you land that was treated with the herbicide Roundup in the last growing season; it is essentially poisoned for three years. Full stop. Any such treatment within the last three years is cause for rejection.

However, the kind of land you'll be looking for is what realtors call "vertical land." Lots of hills and valleys with a few acres of farmable land. The odds are that the present owners were ranching and not farming which means the land should be in good shape.

After you've completed the planning and property analysis and if there are no red flags, you're over the biggest hurdles. Next step, the county supervisor.

Step 3 – County Supervisor

A Win-Win ranch is a multi-million dollar project. If a county supervisor does not have the time to meet with you, you're likely in the wrong county.

Ask your realtor to invite the county supervisor and guests to lunch with you at their choice of restaurant. Your treat. This will help to create a relaxed ambience when you introduce yourself and your church.

If during the conversation, if you get a question about your church being different here is a way to deal with it:

> You've asked a serious question that needs asking, and I salute you for it. We're a small, peaceful family-oriented church that farms and teaches farming. With that in mind, I am compelled to ask a question most difficult to voice. Yet, I am responsible to my investors, funders and members and so I must. What is the current situation in this county and are there concerns for our community?

At this point, someone will probably refer you to the sheriff, if he or she is not already at the table. When a supervisor meeting ends with handshakes and smiles, schedule an appointment with the county sheriff.

Step 4 – County Sheriff

A county sheriff, will be your most important county alliance and as such will be aware of two federal emergency and survival programs: Community Emergency Response Team (CERT) and Amateur Radio Emergency Service (ARES).

Very few rural sheriffs have these programs. Not because they do not want them. They truly do want them but they lack the funding and herein is an alliance building opportunity. Help them launch a county-level emergency volunteer citizen program.

As a certified volunteer in the Washoe County Community Emergency Response Team (CERT) program, I was issued a Sheriff's photo ID. As a certified Amateur Radio Emergency Service (ARES) HAM operator, I regularly trained with other volunteers in a very sophisticated Emergency Operations Center in Reno, Nevada (REOC).

What kind of people did I train with? The kind you want to have as neighbors.

If the sheriff wants the programs and can find locals to volunteer, do what you can to help. As for the costs, that goes under community relations.

Assuming that all goes well, your next due diligence step brings you back to your certified planner.

Step 5 – Compliance Analysis

By this time, you will have completed your land and community due diligence. The final step in due diligence is to have your certified planner complete the following steps:

- **Codes and Regulations:** What are the governing codes and regulations your engineering team will need to comply with at the county, state, and federal levels?
- **Permit Duration:** Permits are typically issued for a limited number of years. With a turnkey funding model, this is not an issue. However, with the incremental funding model, the permit expiration date is a hard deadline.
- **Pre-Application Conference:** Meet with the local planning department to assess permitting requirements. If permitting is burdensome, full stop.

After reviewing the codes and regulations with your engineering team, you'll know if there are open matters requiring clarification and their importance. However, it should be clear sailing by this stage.

The next step would be to work with your certified planner and realtor to find a permitting manager who is local. You're looking for someone local with solid experience with large, engineered projects in that county.

From conception to implementation, your permitting manager will be your primary contact for the county permitting department.

At this point, if your contract allows for a contingency clause, as it should pending successful permitting, you have a choice to make:

- **Refund:** Analysis shows that permitting costs and time are too burdensome.
- **Close Escrow:** Based on your pre-application conference, you have the confidence to close.

You are now ready to engineer and permit your project.

Step 6 – Permitting

Your permitting manager will work with your certified planner and a state-licensed engineer to prepare your permit application.

After the engineer signs off on it, the permitting manager will present it to the county permitting department.

Once the permit is issued, as long as construction is completed before it expires, you are grandfathered from further changes to the development code or regulation.

Even if you are using incremental funding, you should permit your entire project in advance, instead of as you go. If you stage your permitting in steps, you'll expose yourself to future permitting complications.

Now Dear Reader, this is where you pick up a shovel and get 'er done.

25

Spread the Word

Assuming you do everything described and build a Win-Win property, what is the one thing that can make it a pointless waste of time, money, and life? The failure to communicate.

People have been socially programmed to see their smartphones as the end-all and be-all of communications. Unless they have an interest in radio technology, they cannot project forward into a future, where it is possible that the nation's power grid has collapsed. After that happens, smartphones will be sought out by future archaeologists as electronic grave markers.

The members of your home guard will fully understand this and the paramount need for a robust communications system, because during the worst of times, the worst will have the best radios.

For this reason, your Top Sergeant will task a trained veteran to build, operate, and maintain a fully equipped communications system that has local line-of-sight and shortwave HAM radio equipment. Then, every member will be issued a classroom copy of our book *Radio Free Earth*, which will be used to train them in survival two-way communications.

Your cadre can begin instilling comradery in the membership, by teaching them an essential survival skill. Members will also learn in the process another valuable survival skill. The ability to run to the roar.

Run to the Roar

The first step in gaining the courage to deal with long periods of survival hardship is learning to run to the roar. This is a phrase that has been around decades and refers to a manner in which African lions hunt.

Hunting is not just for male lions. They let the lionesses do all the work, and as they age, lions slow down just like we do.

When young they can easily bring down a healthy gazelle. However, once they age, it will only end in fruitless chases. Being instinctive hunters, they found a way to turn this lemon into lemonade ages ago. When the pride observes a herd of gazelle or any other target herbivores, they split up.

Downwind of the game, the young lionesses crawl slowly on their bellies through the tall grasses of the Savannah until they find the perfect ambush position. They are not seen, smelled, or heard this way.

After they are in position, the old lionesses then circle to an optimal point upwind of the game, where they are easily heard and smelled.

Once the trap is set, the old lions begin roaring as loud as they can.

Hearing both the roars and the smell of lions, the game bolt away from the perceived threat, straight into the jaws of the young lionesses laying in ambush downwind of them in the tall grass. The rest of the story is about who is coming to dinner.

Here is the point. If you are going to survive a global cataclysm, you must have the courage and self-awareness to run to the roar and not run naively straight into a hidden trap, like some panicky animal.

How do you instill this courage in your civilian survival community members?

Not by lecturing them, this much is certain. Rather, you need to work with them to build a living pioneer culture of survival and colonization in your community.

For veterans this kind of mission role is right up their alley because their life umami was forged in a cauldron of battle and survival. For them it's about trusting your brothers and sisters to cover your back, and if there is unique experience to be emulated for survival and colonization, this is it. This is the good stuff.

This is how your home guard gives your community the wisdom and strength to endure hardship through comradery, and what your community gives them in return is love and appreciation for who they are and their noble sense of mission.

What is the first future destination beyond hard times?

A time I call "the backside."

The Backside

Previously, I referred to a time I called, "The Days of Darkness and Sorrow," which serves as a generic, worst case event label. Let's leave the rest to the imagination. Between now and the day such a dreaded outcome happens, Win-Win survival churches will organize radio communications networks for sharing valuable intelligence and knowledge.

During such a time, there will be terrible hardship, and magnificent inventiveness to deal with it shall spring forth. People will find new cures, new solutions, and new hopes. They will share them with others and without the suppression by moneyed special interests and those in government that collude with them.

As odd as this may sound, in the midst of destruction, there will be a renaissance of invention to meet it. At first it will be with HAM radios over vast distances, but other new ways will be found also to the future, a Star Trek future that we can hope for and believe in.

Where will you find me in the meantime, Dear Readers, during The Days of Darkness and Sorrow?

If things have gone sideways and you are huddled in a bunker tweaking an old CB radio because you heard through the grapevine that a church has started broadcasting each night at 8 PM on channel 8, you may hit pay dirt when you hear me say:

"You're listening to Radio Free Earth, and I'm your host Marshall Masters, welcoming you to the Win-Win Family Hour."

Appendix

Alphabetical Index

www.ingramcontent.com/pod-product-compliance
Lightning Source LLC
Chambersburg PA
CBHW080224270326
41926CB00020B/4139
* 9 7 8 1 5 9 7 7 2 1 7 2 1 *